COMPUTER APPLICATIONS

Textbook for Class X
(As per CBSE Syllabus Code 165)

Illegal for sale
or distribution outside
Indian Sub-continent.
Books found outside this
market may be treated as
illegal/ pirated books.

Pinky Gupta

www.bpbonline.com

FIRST EDITION 2022

Copyright © BPB Publications, India

ISBN: 978-93-91030-77-3

All Rights Reserved. No part of this publication may be reproduced, distributed or transmitted in any form or by any means or stored in a database or retrieval system, without the prior written permission of the publisher with the exception to the program listings which may be entered, stored and executed in a computer system, but they can not be reproduced by the means of publication, photocopy, recording, or by any electronic and mechanical means.

LIMITS OF LIABILITY AND DISCLAIMER OF WARRANTY

The information contained in this book is true to correct and the best of author's and publisher's knowledge. The author has made every effort to ensure the accuracy of these publications, but publisher cannot be held responsible for any loss or damage arising from any information in this book.

All trademarks referred to in the book are acknowledged as properties of their respective owners but BPB Publications cannot guarantee the accuracy of this information.

CBSE is in no way connected with this book. This Book is written solely for the benefit and guidance of students appearing of CBSE Examination.

Distributors:

BPB PUBLICATIONS
20, Ansari Road, Darya Ganj
New Delhi-110002
Ph: 23254990/23254991

DECCAN AGENCIES
4-3-329, Bank Street,
Hyderabad-500195
Ph: 24756967/24756400

MICRO MEDIA
Shop No. 5, Mahendra Chambers,
150 DN Rd. Next to Capital Cinema,
V.T. (C.S.T.) Station, MUMBAI-400 001
Ph: 22078296/22078297

BPB BOOK CENTRE
376 Old Lajpat Rai Market,
Delhi-110006
Ph: 23861747

To View Complete
BPB Publications Catalogue
Scan the QR Code:

Published by Manish Jain for BPB Publications, 20 Ansari Road, Darya Ganj, New Delhi-110002 and Printed by him at Repro India Ltd, Mumbai

www.bpbonline.com

Dedicated to

NAVEEN GUPTA

About the Author(s)

Pinky Gupta is M.Sc (IT), MCA and B.Ed from Maharshi Dayanand University, Rohtak, Haryana. She is graduated from Delhi University in B.Com (Hons.). She has also completed 'A' Level course from Department of Electronics and Accreditation of Computer Courses (DOEACC, under Ministry of Communications & Information Technology, Government of India) and also, a 3 year certified course in Diploma in Advanced Software Technology (DAST) from CMC Ltd.(then , a Govt. Enterprise)

She has 14 years of rich professional experience in the field of education. Currently, working as the HOD, Computer Science in a reputed school in Delhi, She is also handling the entire CBSE related work, various Olympiad examinations and competitions organised by CBSE and by different schools. For her outstanding performance in Class-XII as a teacher, she has received an "Appreciation Letter" from the "Hon'ble HRD Minister Smt. Smriti Zubani Irani" in the year 2015.

Acknowledgements

Acknowledgement is the way of giving thanks to those who all put their efforts and give their valuable constructive suggestions in bringing the book. The experience is both internally challenging and rewarding. Therefore, first of all, I thank to my Almighty, Guru Ji, who always showers his blessings on me and without whom I couldn't even imagine to complete this task.

I wish to express my sincere gratitude to all those who have helped me make this work possible giving their constructive feedbacks and suggestions.

Special thanks to Mr. Manish Jain, CEO, BPB Publication who supported me in many ways and made it possible for me to work on this exciting project.

I am also grateful to my friends and peer group for their valuable suggestions and for their efforts in the bringing this book.

I am thankful to my son Yashvardhan Goel and daughter Agrima Goel for giving me their creative ideas and technical support. I am also grateful to my family members who are the real force behind me writing this book.

Last but not the least, I am also thankful to the entire publishing unit, coordination unit and DTP team for producing this book presentable and error-free.

— Pinky Gupta

Preface

Computers has a great role and impact in our daily life. Considering this aspect CBSE has introduced the subject, Computer Applications. Here in, students learn how to create web pages by using HTML and CSS, know about Networking concepts and cyber netiquettes. The book adheres to revised curriculum of class X issued by CBSE.

The book is divided into 3 units. Each unit is subdivided to simplify the concept and content.

Unit 1: Basics of Internet covers complete understanding about internet, service provided by internet, functions of networking and how it works.

Unit 2: Covers the concept of HTML and CSS that helps students to create web pages. CSS make web site look more attractive by using various properties and style sheets. Form designing in HTML helps students to create various types of registration forms, employee profile etc. it helps students to collect some data from the site visitor.

Unit 3: Covers the concept of Cyber ethics. It emphasises on network netiquettes, software licensing, open source software, freeware, shareware, plagiarism, intellectual rights, digital divide and much more.

Students will be able to differentiate between open source software and proprietary software, freeware and shareware.

The key feature of the book is that each chapter has been written in a simple English language that begins with the basics of all concepts and steadily builds the pace so that students will find it easy to understand and can handle complex topics towards the end of the book.

Term Wise Syllabus

Learning Outcomes

1. Ability to create a simple website
2. Ability to embed images, audio and video in an HTML page
3. Ability to use style sheets to beautify the web pages.
4. Ability to Interface a web site with a web server and record the details of a user's request.
5. Ability to follow basic cyber ethics
6. Ability to familiarize with network concepts.

Distribution of Marks and Periods TERM I + TERM II

Unit No.	Unit Name	Marks	Periods	
			Theory	Practical
1.	Networking	15	17	05
2.	HTML	25	30	50
3.	Cyber ethics	10	08	10
4.	Practicals	50	-	-
	Total	**100**	**55**	**65**

TERM I

Sr No.	Unit Name	Marks
1.	Cyber ethics	10
2	HTML	15

Unit 3: Cyber ethics

- Netiquettes.
- Software licenses and the open source software movement.
- Intellectual property rights, plagiarism and digital property rights.
- Freedom of information and the digital divide.
- E-commerce: Privacy, fraud, secure data transmission.

Unit 2: HTML – I

- Introduction to web page designing using HTML: create and save an HTML document, access a web page using a web browser.

- HTML tags: html, head, title, body, (attributes: text, background, bgcolor, link, vlink, alink), br (break), hr(horizontal rule), inserting comments, h1..h6 (heading), p (paragraph), b (bold), i (italics), u (underline), ul (unordered list), ol (ordered list), and li (list item). Description lists: dl, dt and dd. Attributes of ol (start, type), ul (type).
- Font tags (attributes: face, size, color).
- Insert images: img (attributes: src, width, height, alt), sup (super script), sub (subscript).
- HTML Forms: Textbox, radio buttons, checkbox, password, list, combobox.

TERM II

Unit No.	Unit Name	Marks
1.	Networking	15
2	HTML	10

Unit 1: Networking

- Internet: World Wide Web, web servers, web clients, web sites, web pages, web browsers, blogs, news groups, HTML, web address, e-mail address, downloading and uploading files from a remote site. Internet protocols: TCP/IP, SMTP, POP3, HTTP, HTTPS. Remote login and file transfer protocols: SSH, SFTP, FTP, SCP, TELNET, SMTP, TCP/IP.
- Services available on the internet: information retrieval, locating sites using search engines and finding people on the net;
- Web services: chat, email, video conferencing, e-Learning, e-Banking, eShopping, e- Reservation, e-Governance, e-Groups, social networking.
- Mobile technologies: SMS, MMS, 3G, 4G.

Unit 2: HTML – II

- Embed audio and video in a HTML page.
- Create a table using the tags: table, tr, th, td, rowspan, colspan
- Links: significance of linking, anchor element (attributes: href, mailto), targets.
- Cascading style sheets: colour, background-colour, border-style, margin, height, width, outline, font (family, style, size), align, float

Suggested Lab Exercises

- Create static web pages.
- Use style sheets to enforce a format in an HTML page (CSS).
- Embed pictures, audio and videos in an HTML page.
- Add tables and frames in an HTML page.
- Decorate web pages using graphical elements.
- Create a website using several webpages. Students may use any open source or proprietary tool.
- Work with HTML forms: text box, radio buttons, checkbox, password, list, combo box.

- Write a blog using HTML pages discussing viruses, malware, spam and antiviruses
- Create a web page discussing plagiarism. List some reported cases of plagiarism and the consequent punishment meted out. Explain the nature of the punishment in different countries as per their IP laws.

Breakup of marks for the practicals:

S.No.	Unit Name	Total Marks	Term-1 Marks	Term-2 Marks
1	**Lab Test (20 marks)**			
	HTML (design one web page based on a diagram)	20	10	10
2	**Report File + viva (20 marks)**			
	Report file: At least 10 HTML pages. (Term-1: At Least 5 HTML Pages, Term-2: At least 5 HTML Pages)	14	7	7
	Viva voce (based on the report file)	6	3	3
3	Project (that uses most of the concepts that have been learnt)	10	5	5
	Total Marks	50	25	25

Downloading the code bundle and coloured images:

Please follow the link to download the
Code Bundle and the *Coloured Images* of the book:

https://rebrand.ly/48f87b

Errata

We take immense pride in our work at BPB Publications and follow best practices to ensure the accuracy of our content to provide with an indulging reading experience to our subscribers. Our readers are our mirrors, and we use their inputs to reflect and improve upon human errors, if any, that may have occurred during the publishing processes involved. To let us maintain the quality and help us reach out to any readers who might be having difficulties due to any unforeseen errors, please write to us at:

errata@bpbonline.com

Your support, suggestions and feedbacks are highly appreciated by the BPB Publications' Family.

Did you know that BPB offers eBook versions of every book published, with PDF and ePub files available? You can upgrade to the eBook version at www.bpbonline.com and as a print book customer, you are entitled to a discount on the eBook copy. Get in touch with us at **business@bpbonline.com** for more details.

At **www.bpbonline.com**, you can also read a collection of free technical articles, sign up for a range of free newsletters, and receive exclusive discounts and offers on BPB books and eBooks.

BPB is searching for authors like you

If you're interested in becoming an author for BPB, please visit **www.bpbonline.com** and apply today. We have worked with thousands of developers and tech professionals, just like you, to help them share their insight with the global tech community. You can make a general application, apply for a specific hot topic that we are recruiting an author for, or submit your own idea.

The code bundle for the book is also hosted on GitHub at **https://github.com/bpbpublications/Computer-Applications-Textbook-for-Class-X-**. In case there's an update to the code, it will be updated on the existing GitHub repository.
We also have other code bundles from our rich catalog of books and videos available at **https://github.com/bpbpublications**. Check them out!

PIRACY

If you come across any illegal copies of our works in any form on the internet, we would be grateful if you would provide us with the location address or website name. Please contact us at **business@bpbonline.com** with a link to the material.

If you are interested in becoming an author

If there is a topic that you have expertise in, and you are interested in either writing or contributing to a book, please visit **www.bpbonline.com**.

REVIEWS

Please leave a review. Once you have read and used this book, why not leave a review on the site that you purchased it from? Potential readers can then see and use your unbiased opinion to make purchase decisions, we at BPB can understand what you think about our products, and our authors can see your feedback on their book. Thank you!

For more information about BPB, please visit **www.bpbonline.com**.

Table of Contents

Chapter 1 Basics of Internet 1-37

Introduction 1
1.1 What is Network? 1
1.2 What is Internet? 2
1.3 Evolution of Internet 3
1.4 Managing Bodies of Internet 4
1.5 Working of Internet 4
1.8 Uses of Internet 5
1.6 Components of Network 7
1.7 Concept of Protocol 9
1.9 Internet Terminologies 17
1.10 Web Addressing System 24
1.11 Blogs 26
1.12 Newsgroup 26
Let's Revise 27
Learning Zone 28
Activity Zone 37

Chapter 2 Internet and Web Services 38-88

Introduction 38
2.1 Information Retrieval 38
2.2 Search Engine 39
2.3 Working of Search Engine 42
2.4 Finding People on the Internet 45
2.5 Web Services 46
2.6 Mobile technologies 74
Let's Revise 76
Learning Zone 77
Activity Zone 88

Chapter 3 Basic HTML Elements 89-138

Introduction 89
3.1 What is HTML? 89
3.2 Advantages/Features of HTML 90
3.3 Characteristics of HTML 90
3.4 Tags and Attributes 90

3.5 Writing and Saving HTML Documents 92
3.6 Structure of HTML document 92
3.7 Categories of HTML Tags: Container and Empty 92
3.8 Working with tags 93
3.8 Special Characters in HTML 109
3.9 Logical and Physical Text Styles 110
3.10 LISTS IN HTML 113
Let's Revise 123
Learning Zone 124
Activity Zone 138

Chapter 4 Images, Links, Tables 139-208

Introduction 139
4.1 Inserting Images 139
4.2 Inserting Links in HTML 145
4.3 Inserting Tables in HTML 154
4.5 The <CAPTION> tag 179
Let's Revise 180
Learning Zone 181
Activity Zone 207

Chapter 5 Creating Forms, inserting Audio and Video in HTML 209-247

Introduction 209
5.1 What is form? 209
5.2 Working of HTML Form 210
5.3 Creating from using Form Element 210
5.4 Attributes of FORM tag 211
5.5 The Input element 213
5.6 Attributes of Input element or Form Controls 213
5.7 Explaining different types of form elements 215
5.7 Embedding audio and video in html web page 226
Let's Revise 228
Learning Zone 229
Activity Zone 247

Chapter 6 Cascading Style Sheet (CSS) 248-302

Introduction 248
6.1 What is CSS? 248
6.2 Advantages of CSS 249
6.3 Limitations of CSS 249

6.4 Methods of Using CSS 250
6.5 Cascading Order 254
6.6 CSS Comments 255
6.7 CSS PROPERTIES 256
Let's Revise 285
Learning Zone 285
Activity Zone 302

Chapter 7 Cyber Ethics 303-326
Introduction 303
7.1 What is Cyber Netiquette? 303
7.2 Meaning of License 304
7.3 Software License and Open Source Software Philosophy 304
7.4 Open Source Software 305
7.5 Terminologies related to Open Source Software 306
7.6 Open Source License 306
7.7 Intellectual Property Rights 307
7.8 Plagiarism 309
7.9 Digital Property Rights 311
7.10 Freedom of Information 313
7.11 Digital Divide 313
7.12 E-commerce and Cyber Ethics 314
7.13 Cyber Fraud during E-Commerce 315
7.14 Secure Data Transmission 315
Let's Revise 317
Learning Zone 318
Activity Zone 326

Sample Question Paper (Term 1) 327-333

Marking Scheme (Term 1) 334-335

Sample Question Paper (Term 2) 336-340

Marking Scheme (Term 2) 341-342

APPENDIX – A 343-344

APPENDIX – B 345-347

1 Basics of Internet

Outline of the Chapter

- Introduction
- What is computer network?
- Components of data communication
- Terminologies used in networking
- What is network?
- Need or advantages of networking
- Protocol of internet

Learning Objectives

- To know about network and computer network
- To know about the various advantages of networking
- To know about the various components of network
- To learn about modem, types of modem, ISP, internet browser, access software
- To learn about various protocols
- To learn about web site, web server, home page, URL, blogs and newsgroup
- To learn about Web Addressing system like DNS, IP Addressing System

INTRODUCTION

In modern scenario, there is a need of sharing data and information among the users. To facilitate this process, **Internet** has brought the world closer, through many aspects of collaborative communication. **Electronic mail system** which has replaced the traditional method of communication such as telegraph, radio, and other communication methods, this prodigious technology has now engulfed almost all the industries. The internet has filled the geographical gaps which earlier hindered fast communication and other human interactions.

This chapter is completely dedicated to the **Internet**, its working, why is it required, components used and other related concepts.

★ **So, let's know about network and internet.**

1.1 WHAT IS NETWORK?

A network is a collection of several devices which are connected with each other either wirelessly or with wires. The main objective of the network is to share the data or information among several users.

Definition

A network is an interconnected collection of autonomous computers that can share and exchange information.

Consider the given examples:

a. Think of the devices such as mobile phone, fax machine, computer system, and printer at your home. You have connected all these devices with each other either through Wi-Fi connection or with wires. *(Figure 1.1(a))*

b. Similarly, think of the network of five friends viz. Bob, Eliza, Ken, Mary, Christina who all are communicating with each other, sharing their thoughts, views, and so on. *(Figure 1.1(b))*

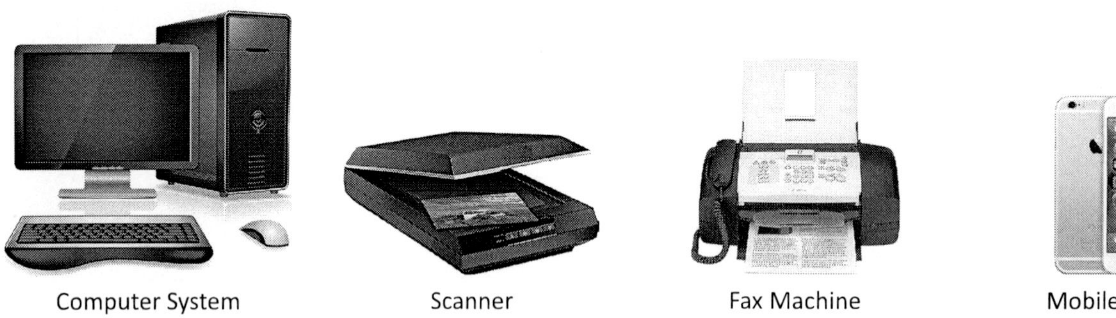

Figure 1.1 (a): Network between home devices

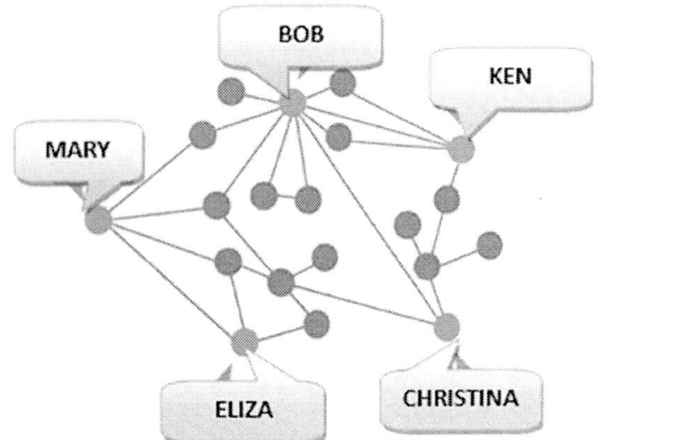

Figure 1.1 (b): Network of five friends

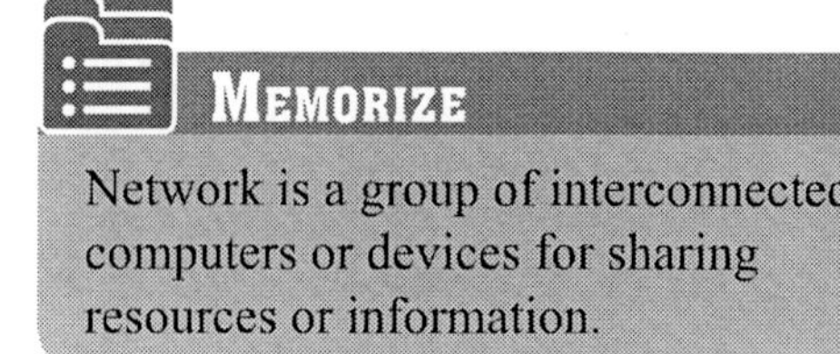

Network is a group of interconnected computers or devices for sharing resources or information.

✱ **Now, after network, let's know the meaning of internet.**

1.2 WHAT IS INTERNET?

Internet is a network of networks which consist of various inter-connected networks. All those networks may belong to same or different types of organizations.

Consider an example, a network of a business, government network, domestic network, academic network, and so on; each of these networks might connect hundreds or thousands of computers.

The initial idea of the internet is credited to **Leonard Kleinrock** in 1961.

Definition

Internet is a network of the computers connected with one another all over the world.

Figure 1.2 shows various organizations are connected with each other.

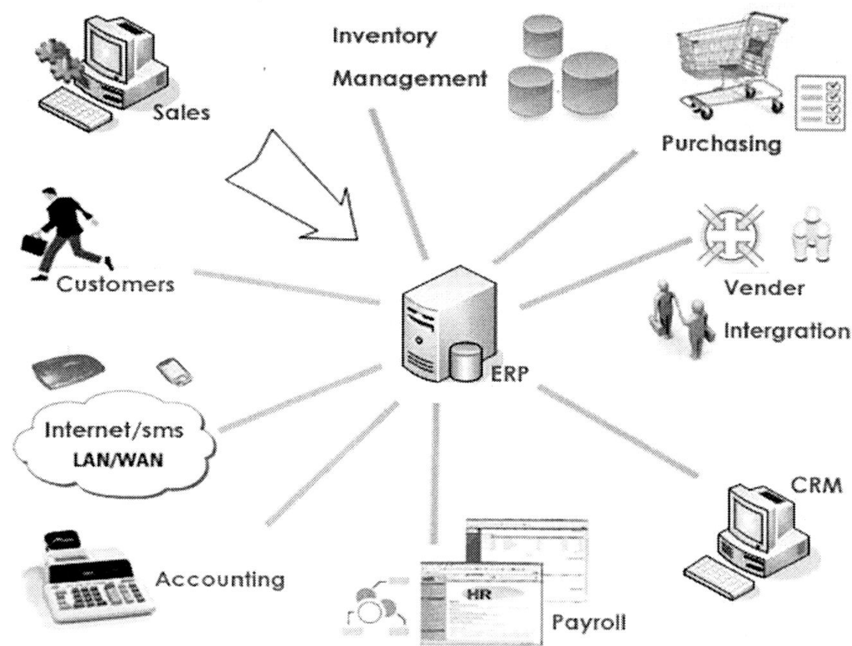

Figure 1.2: Internet between several organizations

✱ **Let's know how internet has emerged.**

1.3 EVOLUTION OF INTERNET

The internet is not evolved in one day, rather it took decades to become a more powerful, efficient, and reliable network. The various stages on which the internet is evolved are:

Stage-1: Advanced Research Agency Network (ARPANET): ARPANET is the first network that came into existence in 1969 named by U.S Department of Defense. It is the project where handful of computers were connected at different universities and US Defense for sharing of data, messages; playing long distance games and socialize with people to share their views.

Extra Byte

The first ARPANET message was sent on **October 29, 1969**.

Stage-2: National Science Federation Network (NSFNET): In mid-80's another federal agency National Science Federation Network created a new network which was more capable than ARPANET. This network is used only for academic research and not for any kind of private business activity. Later on, many private companies with their own private network combined with ARPANET and NSFNET to make more capable and broader network. So, NSFNET was the internetworking that links two or more networks to make a large network for sharing of data and messages.

Stage-3: Private Network: Several private organizations and people started working to build their own networks, named private networks, which were later (in 1990's) connected with ARPANET and NSFNET to form the Internet.

Stage-4: Internet: In 1990's, Internet came into existence which is a network of networks. The internet has evolved from ARPANET. The computers are connected through worldwide that comprise a large network known as internet. Millions of domestic, business, and government networks are connected with each other with the purpose of sharing files, data, e-mailing, files, and so on. In internet, most of the computers are not connected directly to the internet. Instead they are connected to smaller networks which are then connected to a backbone network through gateways. (*Figure 1.3*)

Figure 1.3: Evolution of Network

✱ Now, it's the time to know about the various entities who manages internet.

1.4 MANAGING BODIES OF INTERNET

Now, the question arises as who manages the internet? The answer is that the internet is not governed or manages by any single entity or organization. Instead, there are several well-known volunteer groups or organizations that help in managing internet.

The following is the list of main organizations that play an important role in the managing of the internet:

No one person, company, organization, or government runs the Internet. It is a globally distributed computer network comprised of several interconnected autonomous networks.

- **Internet architecture board (IAB):** IAB is a technical advisory group of the Internet Society. It is responsible for administration of Internet assigned numbers and liaison of the Internet Society in liaison relationships with other organizations concerned with standards.
- **Internet Engineering Task Force (IETF):** It is responsible for resolving technical and operational problems on the Internet and to develop Internet standards and protocols. Members of IETF consist of network designers, operators, vendors, researchers, and other interested individuals.
- **Internet Assigned Numbers Authority (IANA):** IANA oversees all **unique parameters** on the Internet, including **Internet Protocol (IP)** addresses and manages the **Root Domain Name Service.**
- **InterNIC:** It provides various registration services to the internet community.

✱ Do you know how internet works? So, let's know working of internet.

1.5 WORKING OF INTERNET

By the time, you have cleared about the meaning of network, internet, and how it has been emerged. But the question arises as how these computers are connected with each other?

To understand this, you should know about some important terms, which are:

- **Gateway:** It helps in connecting dissimilar networks over the internet.
- **Backbone:** It is a central hub where all the devices or networks are connected through it. It is a part of computer network which interconnects various similar or dissimilar networks providing a path for the exchange of information.
- **Internet service provider (ISP):** Organization such as **Airtel**, **BSNL** that provide internet connection to users.

Definition

- A gateway is a hardware device that connects networks using different protocol by passing data packets through a common point after translation.
- A packet contains data which is to be sent to the sender computer. It consists of four parts viz. protocol, sender's IP address, Receiver's IP address and the message/data.

To understand how the internet works, consider the given steps:

1. The data from the source computer is divided into number of small equal sized fragments known as **packets**.
2. Each packet has a **unique identification number** plus the **IP address** of destination computer.
3. Each packet is sent randomly from source computer to destination computer.

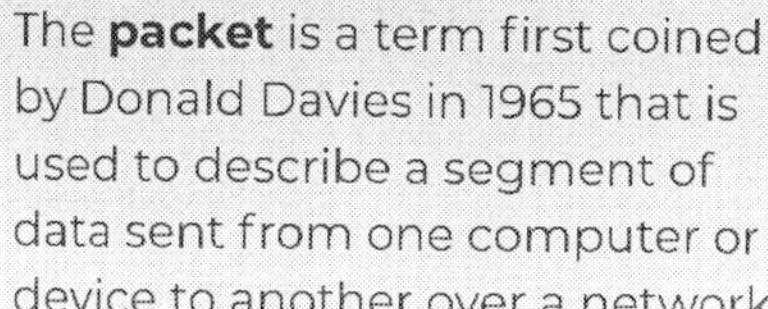

Extra Byte

The **packet** is a term first coined by Donald Davies in 1965 that is used to describe a segment of data sent from one computer or device to another over a network.

4. At destination computer, all the packets are re-assembled in a proper sequence number and form the original data. (*Figure 1.4*)

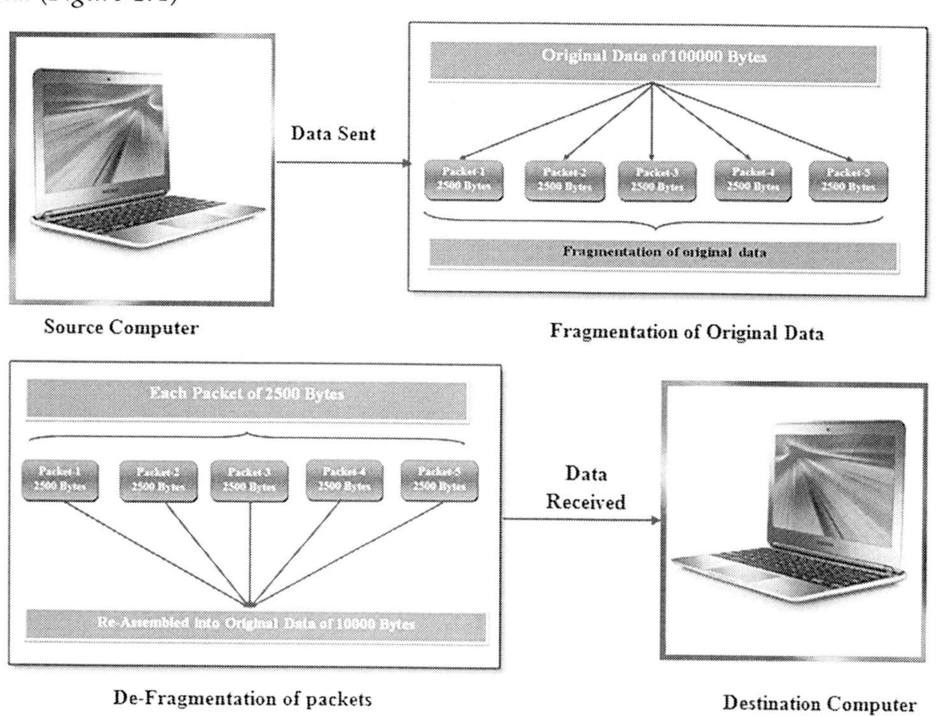

Figure 1.4: Fragmentation & De-fragmentation of packets

MEMORIZE

When data is divided into number of small packets/ fragments then the process is known as **fragmentation** and when all packets/fragments are reassembling into an original message then this process is known as **defragmentation**.

Check Your Progress

Answer the following questions.

1. Define fragmentation and defragmentation.
2. What do you mean by gateway?
3. What is backbone in terms of network?

* Let's know about various uses of internet.

1.8 USES OF INTERNET

Today, it is becoming very difficult to live without internet. Internet is a feast for all of us and without it you cannot even imagine to live. From searching of information to communicate with people, you all depend on internet.

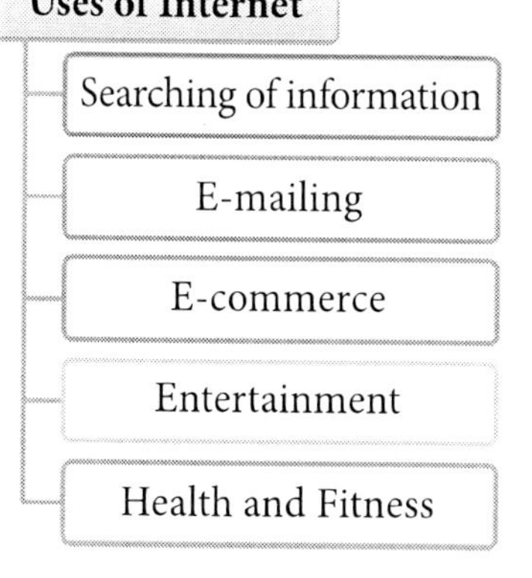

Figure 1.5: Uses of Internet

Some of the common uses of internet are:

- **Searching of Information:** Internet helps in searching for any kind of information. Various search engines help in doing so. While searching you are exploring various websites and web pages. Some commonly used search engines are **Google**, **Yahoo**, **AltaVista**, **Netscape**, and so on.
- **E-mail:** The expanded form of e-mail is **electronic mail**. It is the fastest means of sending and receiving messages. You can send textual messages or attach documents or other types of files which can be downloaded and save on your desktop. E-mail has become the most popular and important service provided by internet.

- **E-commerce:** E-commerce means **business through online** where selling and purchasing of goods is online. E-commerce provides the facility to sell goods or products online by displaying the money, quality, and the features of the product. In a same way, customer can buy the products online without physically going to the market. It saves time and money both which may be incurred during travelling.
- **Entertainment:** Internet provides various online games. You can also watch online movies or listen to music and so on.
- **Health and fitness:** Health is wealth. In today's world, everybody wants to be fit and healthy. Keeping this in view, they see various websites that provide streaming on yoga, exercises, and other health related videos. People have now become more aware about various diseases and can book online appointment with the doctor in case of emergency. Internet plays vital role in providing extensive information related to health and fitness.

Apart from all these, internet plays a big role in communicating with people through various social networking sites, person can create their own blogs for posting their updates or can do discussions and share their thoughts on newsgroups and online discussion forums.

✱ Let's know the various advantages and disadvantages of internet.

Advantages of Internet

The advantages of internet are as follows:

1. You can send and receive information through e-mail service. Your messages are delivered instantly to people anywhere in the world.
2. You can gather information for new job openings. You can also apply online for jobs.
3. Any kind of information on any topic is available on the internet. The search engine on the internet can help you to find data on any subject that you need.
4. You can also shop online. There are many online stores and sites that can be used to look for products as well as buy them using your credit card.
5. This is one of the most happening and fun things to do via the Internet. You can download innumerable, games, music, videos, movies and a host of other entertainment software from the internet.

Disadvantages of Internet

The disadvantages of Internet are as follows:

1. There are hundreds of vendors selling products of various brands. You get confused with too many choices.
2. You feel helpless when the internet connection is down.
3. You always remain engaged with many online activities such as checking e-mails, socializing, chatting, online shopping, business-deals, etc.

4. If you use the Internet, you may be facing grave danger as your personal information, such as name, address, credit and card number, etc. can be accessed by other culprits to make your problem worse.
5. Virus is nothing but a program which disrupts the normal functioning of your computer systems. Computer attached to the Internet are more prone to virus attacks and they can end up into crashing your whole hard disk.

✱ Now, let's discuss various components of network for communication.

1.6 COMPONENTS OF NETWORK

For establishing a computer network, one must have to fulfill the given requirements:

1. Computer system
2. Modem
3. Telephone or cable connection
4. Internet service provider
5. Internet browser software
6. Internet Access software

1. **Computer System:** In a network, computer system is the main component through which the data is transferred.
2. **Modem:** The expanded form of modem is modulator-demodulator. It is a device which is connected with the computer system that converts digital signal into analog signal and analog signal into digital signal. It facilitates the efficient communication between several devices across telephone cables.

   Types of Modem

   Modem is of two types:

   a. Internal Modem b. External Modem

Definition

Modem is a modulator-demodulator that converts digital signal into analog signal and analog signal into digital signal.

✱ Let's know about these types of Modems.

a. **Internal Modem**
   - This is the modem which is pre-installed inside the main computer in the form of card.
   - It is comparatively cheaper and slower than external modem.
   - Since, it is a part of circuit board; it remains fixed and hence non-portable.
   - Once installed, it requires little or no upkeep to maintain its appearance. (*Figure 1.6*)

Figure 1.6: Internal Modem

b. **External Modem**
   - An external modem is a small box-shaped device and externally connected with the main computer system with a cable.
   - External modem is comparatively expensive and faster than internal modem. (*Figure 1.7*)
   - External modems are portable as these are not fixed inside the system.
   - Upkeep of external modem is required as they are installed externally.

Figure 1.7: External Modem

3. **Internet Service Provider**

ISP is an **Internet Service Provider,** a company that provides internet access to its users in addition of other related services such as website creation and virtual hosting. These companies charge money on a monthly or yearly basis for internet access and provide them the username and password. All internet connected devices executes your request (searched information) through ISPs in order to access servers to download web pages and files, and those servers themselves provides you the requested through their own ISP.

Some of the famous Internet Service Providers are: **America online (AOL)**, **Spectra net**, **Videsh Sanchar Nigam Limited (VSNL)** and **Satyam Online**.

4. **Internet Access Software**

Internet access is the ability to connect to the Internet by using computer system, mobile devices etc. Internet access software is software that provides controlling, blocking, accessing or restricting internet and network access.

Extra Byte

The first web browser was called **World Wide Web** and later changed its name to **Nexus**. It was created by Sir Tim Berners-Lee and was released in 1990.

5. **Internet Browser Software**

An internet browser, also known as a **web browser** or simply a **browser**, is a software program that enables you to access internet and helps in viewing or downloading web pages on your computer.

For example, Mozilla Firefox, Google Chrome, Opera, Apple Safari, Internet Explorer (now known as **Microsoft Edge**), AOL etc.

6. **Internet Access Software**

It is used to set up and control the internet connection with your computer system. Two main components of internet access software are: **Dialer software** and **TCP/IP network software.**

a. **Dialer software:** This software directs the modem to dial a telephone number and to get your computer identified at the ISP's by providing you the username and password to get it authenticated.

b. **TCP/IP software:** It allows your programs to communicate over the internet once you get connected with the internet.

Check Your Progress

Fill in the blanks.

1. ____________ type of modem is in the form of card.
2. ____________ allows your programs to communicate over the internet once you get connected with the internet.
3. The full form of ISP is ____________.

Communication over internet is possible through several internet protocols that helps in transferring data from sender to receiver. But, in order to transmit and receive that data, there must be some rules that govern the internet. Those rules are known as **protocols**.

✱ **Let's know the meaning of protocol and various internet protocols.**

1.7 CONCEPT OF PROTOCOL

A protocol is a set of rules which helps in communicating between different computers. Different networks have different computers that are working on different configuration, operating system, and so on. Now, to enable successful internet connectivity between all those computers and networks, it is important that there must be some rule to understand the language of each computer. It is a **protocol** that governs internet.

In other words, protocol ensures the successful communication with another computer located on the next desk or half-way around the world.

1.7.1 Types of Protocols

Definition

Protocol is a set of rules that helps in communicating different computers.

The various types of protocols used over internet are:

1. Transmission control Protocol/Internet Protocol (TCP/IP)
2. Hypertext Transfer Protocol (HTTP)
3. Hypertext Transfer Protocol Secure (HTTPs)
4. Simple Mail Transfer Protocol (SMTP)
5. File Transfer Protocol (FTP)
6. Post Office Protocol (POP3)
7. Remote Login (TELNET)
8. Secure Shell (SSH)
9. Secure File Transfer Protocol (SFTP)
10. Secure Copy Protocol (SCP)

Extra Byte

TCP/IP protocol suite, was designed in 1970s by DARPA scientists—Vint Cerf and Bob Kahn, persons most often called the fathers of the Internet.

✱ **Let's discuss the functioning of these protocols.**

1. Transmission Control Protocol/Internet Protocol (TCP/IP)

Data is divided into number of small packets at the source computer, which is send over the network and at the destination computer all those packets are rearranged sequentially into original data. This process has been taken place by two networking protocols named as **TCP** and **IP**.

TCP is the **Transmission Control Protocol** which is responsible for fragmentation of the message/data into number of small chunks which are known as **packets**. It is also responsible for re-arranging all packets into original data/message at the destination computer.

IP is the **Internet Protocol** and is responsible for sending these packets/chunks on the destination computer.

Both TCP and IP reside on the source and destination computers.

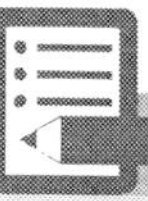

Definition

TCP/IP stands for **Transmission Control Protocol/Internet Protocol.** It is a set of networking protocols that allows communication between two or more computers helps transmitting data in the form of packets.

Functions of Transmission Control Protocol

The functions of Transmission Control Protocol are:

1. At source computer, TCP breaks the original message into number of small packets.
2. At destination computer, TCP re-assembles all packets into original message.

Function of Internet Protocol

The function of Internet Protocol are:

1. It helps in routing packets from source computer to destination computer in random order.
2. It helps in receiving all packets at destination computer.

Data is divided into number of small packets at the source computer, which is send over the network and at the destination computer all those packets are rearranged sequentially into original data. This process has been taken place by two networking protocols named as TCP and IP.

Advantages of TCP/IP Protocol

The advantages of TCP/IP Protocol are as follows:

1. It is an open source so everyone can use for communication.
2. It provides scalability feature.
3. TCP/IP is an **interoperable** i.e. it allows two different systems to communicate over heterogeneous network.
4. It provides better through throughput when used on **MODEM** or **LAN**.

MEMORIZE

TCP is responsible for fragmentation of the message/data into number of small chunks which are known as **packets** whereas IP is responsible for sending these packets/chunks on the destination computer.

Check Your Progress

State whether the following statements are True or False.

1. TCP is an open source so everyone can use for communication. __________
2. Protocol is a set of rules that helps in communicating different computers. __________
3. TCP is responsible for sending these packets/chunks on the destination computer. __________

2. Hyper Text Transfer Protocol (HTTP)

HTTP is used to transfer all files and other data (resources) from one computer to another on the World Wide Web. This protocol is used to transfer hypertext documents over the internet. HTTP defines how the data is formatted and transmitted over the network.

Extra Byte

The term HTTP was coined by **Ted Nelson**.

Functions of Hyper Text Transfer Protocol

The functions of Hyper Text Transfer Protocol are:

1. It helps in transmitting web pages over the internet from one computer to another.
2. It helps in communicating web server and web browser to display web pages over the internet.

Definition

The Hypertext Transfer Protocol (HTTP) is a set of rules for exchanging files (text, graphics, images, sound, video and other multimedia files) on the WWW.

Working of HTTP protocol

When an HTTP client (browser) sends a request to an HTTP server (web server), the server accepts the request, process it and sends responses back to the client. After the request is serviced by a server, the connection between client and server across the Internet is disconnected. Every time a new connection is made for a new request sent by the client to the server.

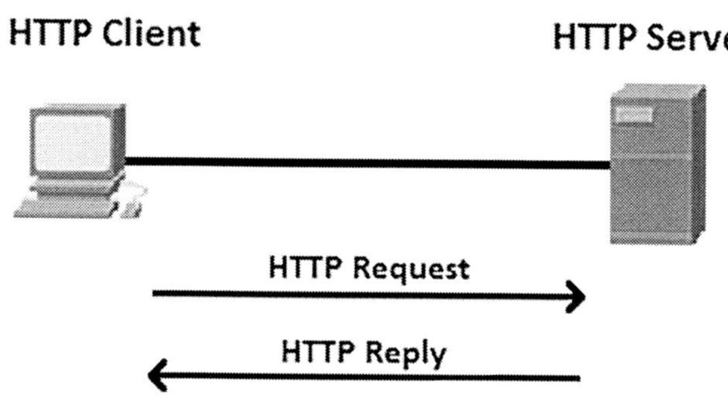

Figure 1.8: Working of HTTP protocol

MEMORIZE

HTTP stands for Hypertext Transfer Protocol. HTTP (Hyper Text Transfer Protocol), is used for transferring information like document, file, image, video between computers over internet.

Note: The standard port for HTTP connection is 80.

2. Hyper Text Transfer Protocol Secure (HTTPs)

Hyper Text Transfer Protocol Secure (HTTPs) is the **secure version of HTTP**, the protocol over which data is sent between your browser and the website you are connected to. The **S** at the end of **HTTPs** stands for **Secure**. It means all communications between your browser and the website are encrypted and protected so that no other unauthenticated user can see the communication between you and the web server. HTTPs is used to protect highly confidential online transactions like online banking and online shopping order forms.

For example, https://www.axisbank.com/

Definition

Hyper Text Transfer Protocol Secure (HTTPs) is the secure version of HTTP. It sends data between the client (browser and the server over the network through secure connection. The 'S' in https ensures that the link or a website is secure.

Note: HTTPs uses port 443 to transfer its information.

MEMORIZE

The client uses this HTTPs protocol to send secret information such as online transaction, credit card details etc. to the server across the internet connection. The purpose of HTTPs is to ensure the protection, integrity, and privacy of the data exchanged between a server and a client (usually a browser).

3. Simple Mail Transfer Protocol (SMTP)

Simple Mail Transfer Protocol (SMTP) is the standard protocol for e-mail services on a TCP/IP network. This protocol works at the application layer. It is a **connection-oriented protocol**.

SMTP is created and maintained by the **Internet Engineering Task Force (IETF)**.

Functions of Simple Mail Transfer Protocol

The functions of Simple Mail Transfer Protocol are:

1. It is used for sending e-mail messages between client and server.
2. It uses TCP to send messages to another host.
3. Apart from transferring e-mail, SMTP also provides notification regarding incoming mail.
4. In case, message cannot be delivered, an error report is sent to the sender which makes SMTP a reliable protocol.

Definition

Simple Mail Transfer Protocol (SMTP) is a program used for sending electronic messages to other computer users based on e-mail addresses over the internet.

Note: By default, SMTP works on three ports i.e. Port 25, Port 2525 and Port 465.

For receiving messages another protocol **POP** or **POP3** (post office protocol) is used. Thus, e-mail clients require addresses of both an SMTP server and another server that processes incoming messages (usually, POP or IMAP). (*Figure 1.9*)

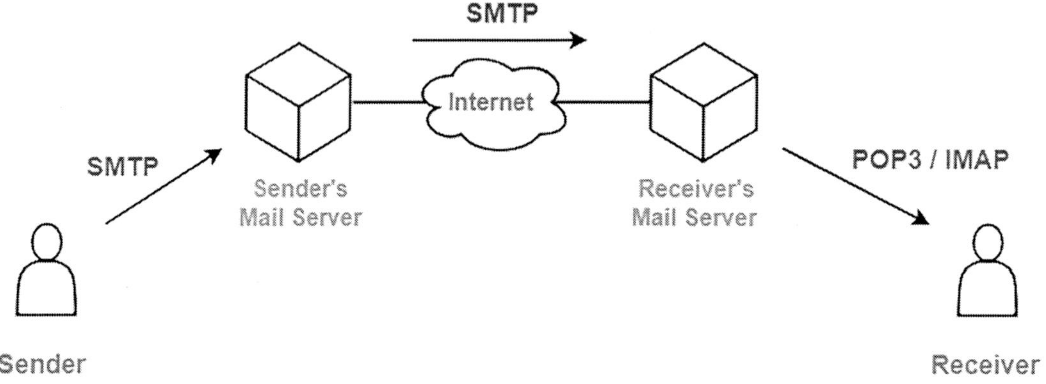

Figure 1.9: Working of SMTP protocol

MEMORIZE

Simple Mail Transfer Protocol is a protocol for sending e-mail messages between the users over an internet.

4. Post Office Protocol 3(POP3)

The Post Office Protocol 3 protocol is a simple and a standard method to receive e-mail messages. The advantage of POP3 is that once the messages are downloaded, an internet connection is no longer needed to read the mail. A user can read all e-mails offline as these are saved on the computer's hard disk.

In POP3, 3 signifies version 3. This protocol allows you to download e-mail messages on your computer.

The major **advantage** of POP3 is that the user can read all e-mails offline as these are saved on the computer's hard disk.

The major **disadvantage** of POP3 is that you will run shortage of space because all e-mail messages are downloaded and saved on your computer system.

Note: POP3, by default works on two ports i.e. Port 110 and Port 995.

Definition

Post Office Protocol 3 (POP3) is used for receiving e-mail messages and keep the mail located on the local device (computer or mobile) for future use.

Functions of POP3

The functions of POP3 are:

1. This protocol is used for receiving e-mail messages.
2. It is used to download and save messages on local computer.
3. User cannot modify the messages on server.
4. Disk space may be full due to saving of messages locally.

MEMORIZE

When you use POP3 to connect to your e-mail account, messages are downloaded locally and removed from the e-mail server.

5. Internet Message Access Protocol (IMAP)

IMAP stands for Internet Message Access Protocol. It was first proposed in 1986. It is used for receiving e-mail messages without downloading them on the local computer/device.

There are five different versions of IMAP as given below:

- Original IMAP
- IMAP2
- IMAP3
- IMAP2BI
- IMAP4

Extra Byte

IMAP was first designed as a remote mailbox protocol in 1986 by **Mark Crispin**.

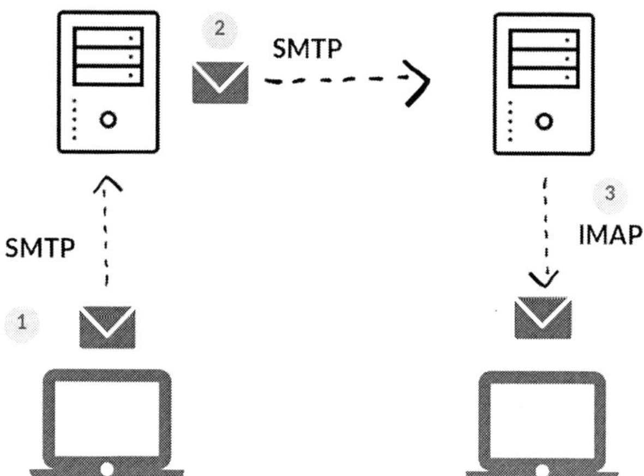

Figure 1.10: IMAP

Definition

The Internet Message Access Protocol (IMAP) is a mail protocol used for accessing e-mail on a remote web server from a local client.

Extra Byte

It was developed in the early 1970s by **Abhay Bhushan** while he was a student at MIT.

Functions of IMAP

The functions of IMAP are:

1. A user can manipulate the e-mail message without downloading them on the local computer.
2. The e-mail is kept and maintained by the remote server.
3. It enables us to create, manipulate and delete remote message folders called mail boxes.
4. IMAP enables the users to search the e-mails.
5. It allows concurrent access to multiple mailboxes on multiple mail servers.

MEMORIZE

IMAP and POP3 are the two most commonly used Internet mail protocols for retrieving e-mails.

6. File Transfer Protocol (FTP)

FTP is the simplest and most secure way of exchanging files over the Internet. It helps in sharing of files from one system to another having different directory structure or different file naming conventions.

Functions of File Transfer Protocol

The functions of File Transfer Protocol are:

1. Transmitting and sharing of files (computer programs and/or data).
2. Indirect or implicit use of remote computers.
3. To shield a user from variations in file storage systems among different hosts.
4. To transfer data reliably and efficiently.
5. FTP uses the Internet's TCP/IP protocols to enable data transfer.

Definition

FTP is a means of transferring files from computer to another over the internet. Transferring files from your computer over the internet is called **uploading** and transferring files from internet to your computer is called **downloading**.

Note: FTP is an interactive system. The FTP client that comes with Windows NT or 2000 is a character-based client

Working of FTP

To understand how FTP works, one should keep in mind that FTP works in combination with TCP/IP protocols as it is a protocol the Internet requires to carry out commands.

During FTP communication there are two computers. One computer called **local host** machine is connected to the internet and other machine known as **remote machine** or remote host is also connected to the internet. The client's machine connects to the remote host's IP address. The user enters the username and password as credentials.

FTP software runs series of FTP commands in the remote host machine and allows transferring files between the machine. *Figure 1.11* shows how FTP works.

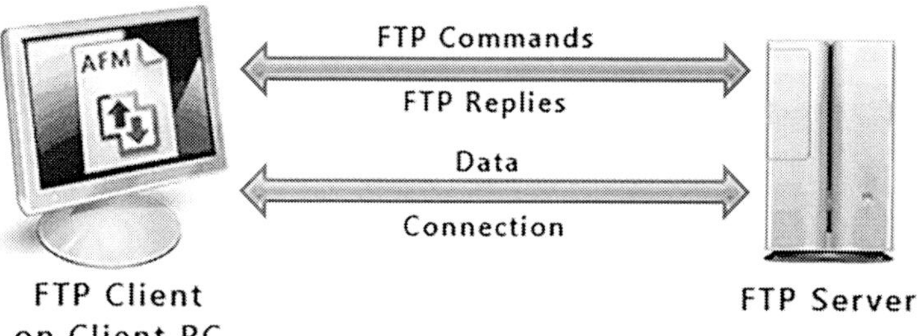

Figure 1.11: Working of FTP

MEMORIZE

FTP can allow you to transfer files over any two computers, as long as they both have an Internet connection. You can share folders that contain data like music, Word documents and more.

Problem: One problem with downloading files over the Internet is that some files are so large that it can take a tremendous amount of time to download them. As a way to speed up file transfers and save space on the FTP server, files are commonly compressed. Many different methods are used to compress files. After the files have been downloaded, you will need to run the decompression software such as PKUNZIP to decompress the files to use them.

Note: The standard Port number for FTP is 21.

5. Secure Shell (SSH)

Secure Shell protocol is used for logging in to and executing commands on a remote machine. It is a method for secure remote login from one computer to another. It is a secure way to access a computer over an unsecured network. It is a remote administration protocol that allows users to control and modify their remote servers over the Internet.

Definition

SSH is a protocol by which communication can takes place safely through an ensured network.

The syntax of using SSH command is:

SSH{user}@ {host}		
SSH	**{user}**	**{host}**
Secure Shell command	Represents the account you want to access	**{host}** refers to the computer you want to access. This can be an IP Address or a domain name

Functions of Secure Shell

The functions of Secure Shell are:

1. It provides various methods for securing data while transferring/communicating between devices over the network.
2. It protects communication with full encryption of data and follow various security mechanism.

Note: SSH uses a well-known TCP port 22.

MEMORIZE

Secure Shell provides strong authentication and encrypted data for communications between two computers connecting over the internet.

6. Secure File Transfer Protocol (SFTP)

Secure File Transfer Protocol provides file transfer and manipulation functionality over any reliable data stream. It runs over the SSH protocol. It supports the full security and authentication functionality of SSH. SFTP is designed to be more platform-independent and is available on most platforms. It supports the full security and authentication functionality of SSH.

Note: SFTP port number is the SSH port 22.

SFTP was originally designed by **Tatu Ylonen** for SSH 2.0 in 1997-1998. It runs over the SSH protocol. SFTP protect against password sniffing and man-in-the-middle attack.

Definition

SFTP is a Secure File Transfer Protocol that allows sharing of data with full authentication, facilitates data access and data transfer using encryption functions. It is part of the SSH Protocol.

Functions of Secure File Transfer Protocol

The functions of Secure File Transfer Protocol are:

1. It transmits files over the network in a most reliable way.
2. It provides security of data while transmitting from one system to another system.
3. It supports multiple concurrent operations at one time.

Telnet was developed in 1969 with a purpose to remote login the system. It is not a secure protocol, as when you log in into a remote host using Telnet, your username and password is sent.

MEMORIZE

SFTP (SSH File Transfer Protocol) is a secure file transfer protocol. It runs over the SSH protocol. All data is encrypted before being sent across the network.

7. TELNET (Remote Login)

Telnet is a remote login protocol that helps a user to login another user's terminal without being a user of that terminal. A user who is logging in his own system get an access to login another user system and can perform various functions such as accessing or sharing files to/from the remote system. With Telnet, a user logs on as a regular user with whatever permissions he may have been granted to the specific application and data on that computer.

Definition

Telnet is a network protocol used on the Internet or local area networks to provide a interactive text-oriented communications facility using a virtual terminal connection.

The syntax of using telnet protocol is:

telnet hostname port		
telnet	**hostname**	**port**
telnet protocol	It is the account name or user name	{host} refers to the computer you want to access. This can be an IP Address or a domain name

Functions of Telnet

The functions of Telnet are:

1. It helps in remote login to the system.
2. It helps in trouble shooting the remote web or mail servers.
3. It is not a one-way protocol; it can be used to send and receive information.

Note: The default port number for Telnet client connections is 23. However, if you want to change this number between 1024 and 32,767.

Working of Telnet

The user connects to the server by using the Telnet protocol, which means entering Telnet into a command prompt. The user then executes commands on the server by using specific Telnet commands into the Telnet prompt. To end a session and log off, the user ends a Telnet command with Telnet.

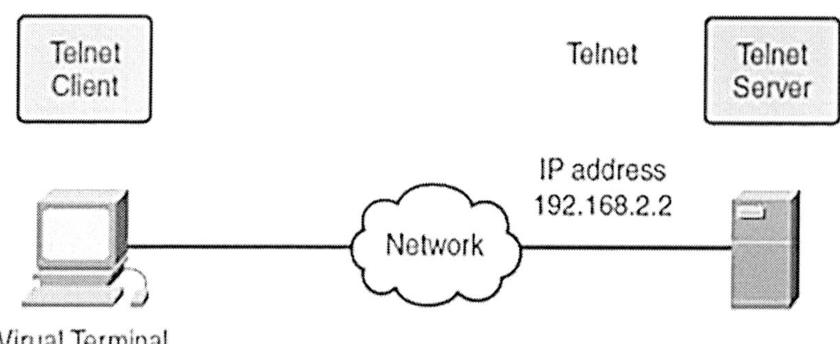

Figure 1.12: Working of Telnet

Difference between Telnet and FTP

S.No.	Telnet	FTP
1.	It uses port no. 23 for the connection.	It uses port no. 21 and 20 for control and data connection.
2.	Telnet is less secure than FTP.	FTP is more secure than Telnet.
3.	The user needs to log in first in remote machine.	The user needs not to log in to the remote machine.

8. Secure Copy Protocol (SCP)

Secure Copy protocol allows you to transmit files in an encrypted mode from one system to another. Most SSH clients include SCP capability. SCP uses Secure Shell (SSH) for data transfer and uses the same mechanisms for authentication, thereby ensuring the authenticity and confidentiality of the data in transit.

Definition

SCP is a means of securely transferring computer files between a local host and a remote host or between two remote hosts. It is based on the Secure Shell (SSH) protocol. SCP commonly refers to both the Secure Copy Protocol and the program itself.

Functions of Secure Copy Protocol

The functions of Secure Copy Protocol are:

1. It helps in transmitting data over the network.
2. The data being sent is encrypted and therefore it is protected against any unauthenticated use.

MEMORIZE

The Secure Copy Protocol or SCP is a secure transmission protocol and helps to transfer computer files securely from a local to a remote host.

Check Your Progress

Answer the following questions.

1. Which protocol is responsible for breaking the data into packets?
2. Which protocol is responsible for routing packets from sender to receiver?
3. Which protocol is responsible for remote login to the computer?

* **Let's move on to know various terms related to internet.**

1.9 INTERNET TERMINOLOGIES

1. World Wide Web (WWW)

World Wide Web is an information service that is used for sending and receiving information over the internet through various web pages. These web pages are interlinked with each other through **hyperlinks**. Web pages may contain text, images, videos, and other multimedia components, as well as web navigation features consisting of hyperlinks. All these web pages are designed by using a special markup language known as **hypertext markup language (HTML)**.

Definition

The WWW is an internet based global information system. It makes available multimedia information from over 4 million computers around the world.

Web pages are accessed by using any web browser such as Internet Explorer, Mozilla Firefox, and Google chrome. The World Wide Web is based upon clients and servers where client is sending request and the server process that request and sends responses. A **WWW client** is called a **web browser** and a **WWW server** is called a **web server**.

MEMORIZE

WWW is a set of programs and protocols that allows the user to create and display multimedia web pages and linked on the internet.

Features of WWW

The features of WWW are as follows:

1. It is interactive and dynamic in nature.
2. It is cross platform dependent i.e. you can access web information from any computer hardware running any OS using any type of display.
3. It is graphical and easy to navigate.
4. It provides a single interface to many services.

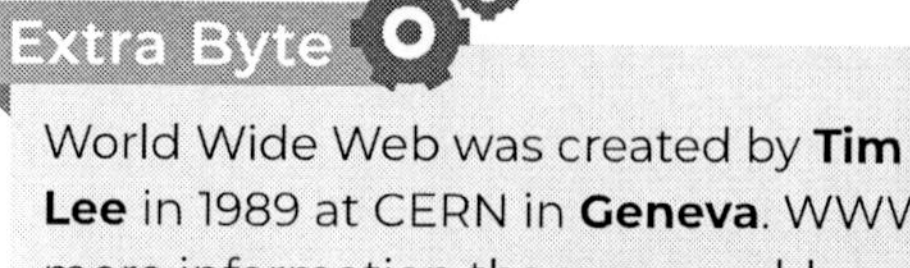

World Wide Web was created by **Tim Berners Lee** in 1989 at CERN in **Geneva**. WWW provides more information than you could ever digest in a lifetime, linked together in various ways, available for you to browse whenever you want.

Difference between WWW and Internet

S.No.	WWW	Internet
1.	WWW is a way of accessing information over the internet.	It is a massive network of networks, a networking infrastructure.
2.	The web uses HTTP protocol, to transmit data.	Information that travels over the internet does so via a variety of languages known as Protocol.
3.	Created by Tim Berners Lee	No such creator.
4.	It provides the dynamic network via a variety of different protocols and methodologies.	Internet provides the structure to access the network.

Check Your Progress

Fill in the blanks.

1. ____________ is an information service that is used for sending and receiving information over the internet through various web pages.
2. A WWW client is called a ____________ and a WWW server is called a web server.
3. ____________ provides a single interface to many services.

2. Web Server and Web Client

Web Server: A web server is a collection of several web pages which are interlinked with each other. A web client is an application (web browser) that communicates with a web server, using **Hypertext Transfer Protocol (HTTP)**. In general, you can say that the machines that provide services (Web servers or FTP servers) to other machines are known as servers and the machines that are used to connect to those services are **clients**.

Web Client: Web client is a web browser that sends request to the server. It communicates with the web server using hypertext transfer protocol.

Difference between Web server and Web client

A web server is a software that stores web pages or websites. Its main function is to process web client's request and send response to web client.

Web client is an application that sends request to web server and communicates it by using Hypertext Transfer Protocol (HTTP).

Definition

A web server is a program that runs on a website and is responsible for replying to web browser requests for files. The basic objective of the web server is to store, process and deliver web pages to the users.

A web server is a program that runs on a computer connected to the internet. Web Server waits for a request to finds the documents and generates the information if required and sends back to the browser that requested it. A single web server may support multiple websites, or a single website may be hosted on several linked or mirrored web servers. (*Figure 1.13*)

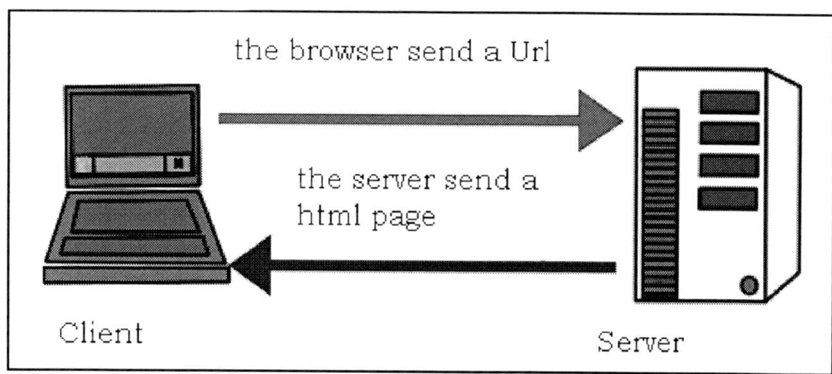

Figure 1.13: Web Server and Web Client

Some most popular web servers are: Apache web server, Netscape enterprise web server, Microsoft internet information server, and so on.

Types of web server

There are mainly four types of web servers: Apache, IIS, Nginx and LiteSpeed.

WWW	Internet
Apache Web Server Apache HTTP SERVER	Apache web server is one of the most popular web servers developed by the Apache Software Foundation. Open source software, Apache supports almost all operating systems such as Linux, Windows, Unix FreeBSD, Mac OS X and more.
IIS Web Server Microsoft IIS	A Microsoft product, IIS is a server that offers all the features such as Apache. It supports all the platforms that run Windows operating system.
Nginx Web Server NGINX	Nginx is the next open source web server after Apache. It comprises of IMAP/POP3 proxy server. The significant features offered by Nginx are high performance, stability, simple configuration and low resource usage.

LightSpeed Web Server 	A high-performance Apache drop-in replacement, LiteSpeed (LSWS) is the 4th popular web server on the internet and is a commercial web server.

MEMORIZE

Web client is a web browser that send request to web server. A web server stores web documents and responds to the requests made by web browsers.

3. Web page

Whenever you search for any information over the internet, it displays several websites and when you click on any website, it opens a required page. That page is known as **web page** which may consist of textual or graphical information in the form of images, audio, video, and hyperlinks. Those hyperlinks help you to navigate to another section of the same web page or a different web page. All web pages are written by using a markup language known as **hypertext markup language** (HTML).

For example:

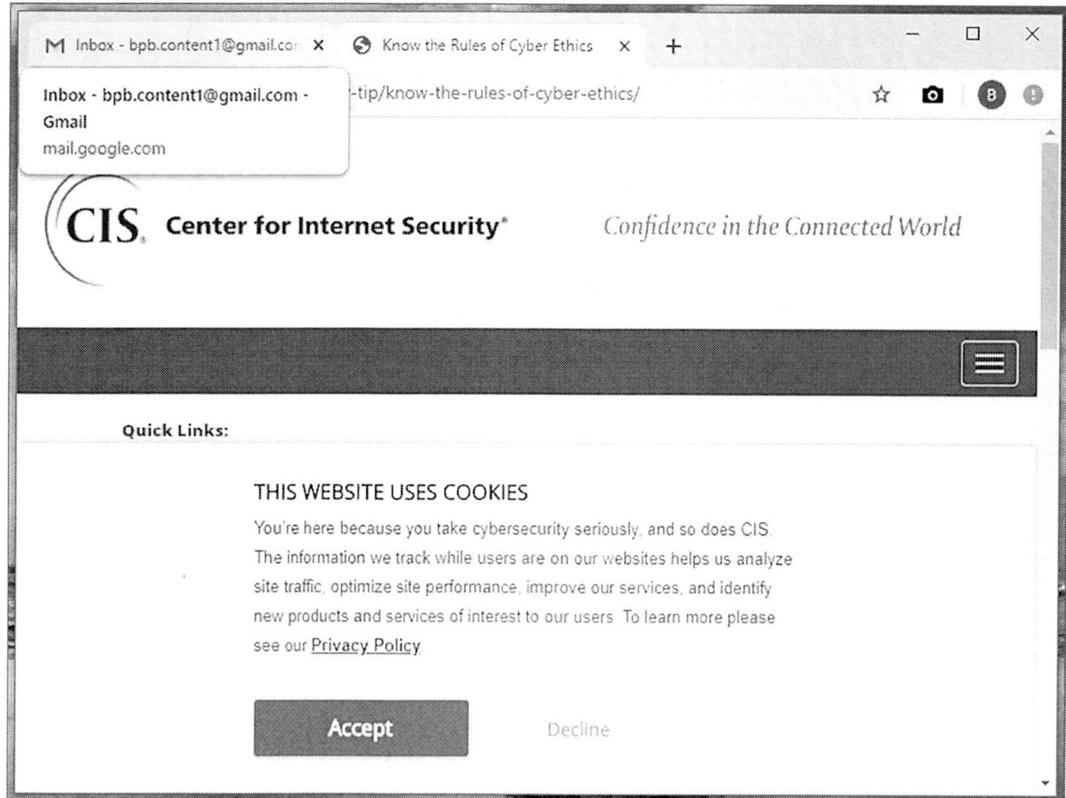

Figure 1.14: Example of a Web Page

Difference between Website and Web page

S.No.	Website	Web page
1.	A website is a collection of Web pages belonging to a particular person or organization.	A web page is a document commonly written in Hyper Text Markup Language (HTML) that is accessible through the Internet or another network using an Internet browser.

S.No.	Website	Web page
2.	A website is a combination of text, image and multimedia.	A web page can be considered as a single entity.
3.	There is no extension used in the URL of a website.	The web page URL has an extension.
4.	The content in the website changes according to the web page.	The web page contains more specific information.

Static and Dynamic Web pages

Static Web pages

Static Web pages are very simple. These pages are written in languages such as HTML, JavaScript, CSS, etc. For static web pages when a server receives a request for a web page, then the server sends the response to the client without doing any modification. These pages are fixed and display the same content for every user. The only way that a user can interact with a static page is by clicking hyperlinks and filling in forms

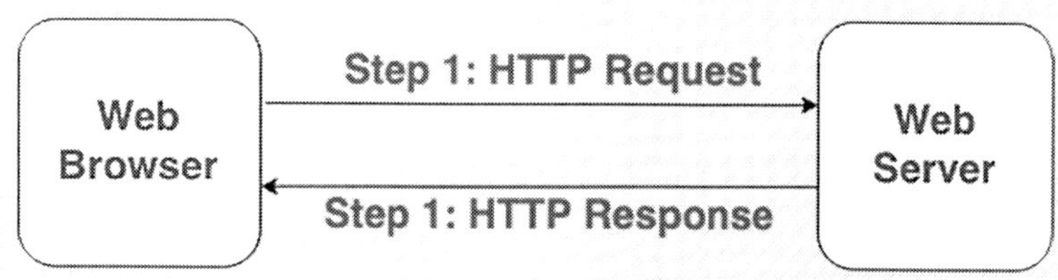

Static Web Page

Dynamic Web Pages

Dynamic Web Pages are written in languages such as CGI, ASP, ASP.NET, etc. In dynamic web pages, the Content of pages is different for different visitors. It takes more time to load than the static web page. Dynamic web pages are used where the information is changed frequently, for example, stock prices, weather information, admission criteria in schools, examination dates etc. Dynamic websites are ultimately based on HTML and CSS as well, but server-side scripting is required to make it functional.

4. Home page

The first page of any website is known as a home page. It is the page that shows several links to the other sections of the same page or to the other documents which are inter-related with each other.

Advantages of home page

The advantages of home page are:

1. It helps viewers to find out what they can find on that site.
2. It makes the visitors more comfortable with the website.
3. It helps the users to click on links and get on to the required page.

5. Website

A website is a collection of various web pages, images, videos, audios, or other kind of digital assets that are hosted on one or several web servers. The first page of a website is known as **home page** where all the links related to other documents are displayed. You can access a website by typing its name on the address bar or by typing its complete URL.

Example of various websites are **cbse.nic.in, Google.com, amazon.in, bpbonline.com, edudel.nic.in.**

Extra Byte

The first Indian website is **rediff.com**. Rediff.com was the first website domain name registered in India in **1996**.

Types of Website

Following are the types of Website:

1. **Brochure:** Brochure websites are used by small businesses that need a simple online presence.
2. **e-Commerce:** An e-commerce website is a website through which users are able to pay for a product or service online. Well known examples are **e-Bay** and **Flipkart**.
3. **Portal:** A portal website brings together information from lots of different sources on the web.
4. **Wiki:** A wiki website is one which allows people to collaborate online and write content together. The most popular example is **Wikipedia** itself.
5. **Social media:** Social media is also one of the types of website platform that allows you to share the images or ideas. They encourage online interaction and sharing. The most popular social media website is **Facebook**.

MEMORIZE

A website is a collection of several web pages which are related with each other through hyperlink.

First page of a website is known as home page.

A web browser is a www client that navigates through the www and display web pages.

Check Your Progress

State whether the following statements are True or False.

1. First page of a website is known as home page. __________
2. The most popular social media website is Google. __________
3. Brochure websites are used by small businesses that need a simple online presence. __________

Web Browser

Web Browser is a software that helps in accessing web pages and thus it is also called **Web client**. It helps the user to navigate through the **World Wide Web** and display web pages. Some of the most popular web browsers are **Mozilla Firefox**, **opera**, **AOL**, **Webkit**, **Iceweasel**, **Google Chrome**, **Safari**, and **Internet Explorer**.

Definition

A Web browser is a program you use to view pages on Net and navigate the WWW. Browsers are sometimes referred to as Web Clients.

MEMORIZE

A web browser is a www client that navigates through the www and display web pages

Types of Web Browser

There are following types of Web Browser are as follows:

1. **ncSA Mosaic:** Mosaic was the first full-color graphical browser and was the instrumental in making the web as popular as it is today.
2. **Lynx:** It is only connection you have to the Internet is through a dial-up text only UNIX account, you are limited to text browsers, such as Lynx.
3. **Netscape Navigator:** It is supported and provides up-to-the minute features including an integrated news and mail reader, support for Java applets, and ability to handles plug-ins or more new features yet to be developed.
4. **Microsoft Internet Explorer:** New on the scene but expected to make a significant impact in the coming months is Microsoft's new browser Internet Explorer, usually called Explorer.
5. **Mozilla Firefox 2.0:** It is fast, full-featured web browser that makes browsing very efficient. Firefox includes pop-up blocking, tab-browsing, integrated Google searching and simplified privacy controls that let you cover your tracks more efficiently.

6. Hyper Text Markup Language (HTML)

HTML is a language which is used to create web pages which are then displayed by web browsers. This language tells the browser how to display text, pictures, and links on the screen. HTML is a language that supports multimedia documents which consists of audio, video, graphics, pictures, and so on. It also helps in creating hyperlinks so that various documents can be linked together. When a person clicks on a specified link, then the document related to that link displays. HTML is a document layout and hyperlink specification language i.e. a language that uses various coded elements known as **tags** for formatting the document and to specify the hyperlinks.

Features of HTML

The features of HTML are as follows:

1. HTML can be used to display any type of document on the host computer, which can be on any computer.
2. It is a platform independent language.
3. HTML is used to make text look attractive as it provides various formatting features.
4. It has the additional feature of linking one document with another using the feature of hyperlink.

7. Uniform Resource Locator (URL)

Uniform Resource Locator is the complete address or path of a website which you have to type on the address bar to locate the website on a web server. A URL is also referred to as **Web address**.

A URL contains the following information:

a. The protocol which used to an access the resource and then colon and two slashes.
b. The location of the server (whether by IP address or domain name).
c. The port number on the server (optional).
d. The location of the resource in the directory structure of the server.
e. A fragment identifier (optional). (*Figure 1.15*)

The syntax of typing the URL is: type//address/path

Here:

- **type** specifies the type of server
- **address** is the address of the server
- **path** tells the location of file on the server

For example,

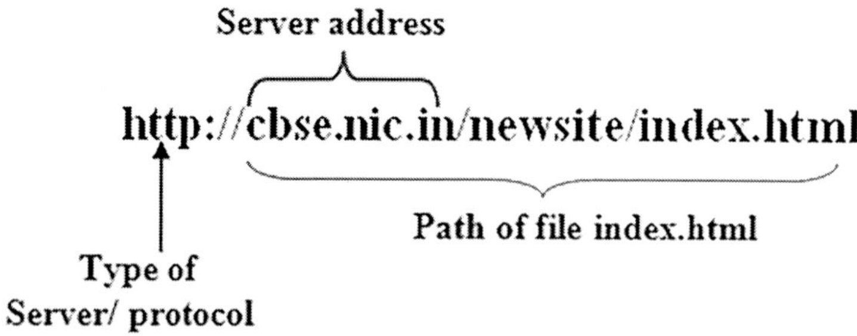

Figure 1.15: Parts of URL

1.10 WEB ADDRESSING SYSTEM

By now, you have become aware that the internet is a **network of networks** and on each network several computers are interconnected. Each computer has a **unique address** that may be in the form of numbers or in characters.

Types of Web Addressing System:

Internet Engineering Task Force (IETF) has provided two types of web addressing system:

a. **IP addressing system:** IP address is the **Internet Protocol address** which is a unique address of any website or a network. It is a **logical address** of **32 bit** containing a set of 4 numbers vary from 0-255 and is separated by dots called periods. In other words, the length of IP address is 4 bytes.

Characteristics of IP address

The characteristics of IP address are:

1. IP address is unique for every machine and therefore no two machines can have the same IP address.
2. It is in the form of numbers such as 162.192.30.90.
3. Its length is 4 bytes where each byte is separated by dots.
4. IP addresses are global and standardized.
5. IP address can directly be types to access a webpage instead of typing the name of a website.

✱ **Let's know how to find IP address of your system.**

To know the IP address of your system, follow the given steps:

1. Do one of the following:
   a. In Windows 8.1, select the **Start** button, start typing **View network connections**, and then select it in the list.
   b. In Windows 7, open Network Connections by selecting the Start button and then selecting **Control Panel**. In the search box, type **adapter**, and then, under **Network and Sharing Center**, select **View network connections**.

2. Select an active network connection, and then, in the toolbar, select **View status of this connection.** (You might need to select the chevron icon to find this command).
3. Select **Details.** Your PC's IP address appears in the **Value** column, next to **IPv4 Address.**

b. Domain Name System/ letter Addressing System: Domain name is a unique name given to each website. The **Domain Name System (DNS)** is a system that converts IP addresses into letter addressing system. As it is difficult to remember IP addresses of all websites, it's better to type the name of websites.

Consider an ***example,*** instead of remembering IP address as 168.23.198.1 for any website, it would be easier if you type the name as www.abc.com (assumption).

Domain name consists of two parts:

a. Name of the domain

b. Extension of the domain

The name of the domain comes before the web extension.

For example, in the URL

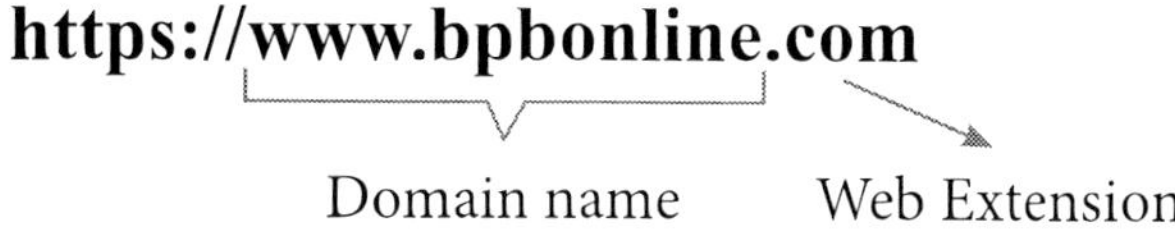

Some other examples of valid URL are:

http://www.edudel.nic.in/

https://udaan.com/

https://kheloindia.gov.in/

https://www.incometaxindia.gov.in

The popular domain name extensions are shown in *Table 1.1*:

Table 1.1: Domain Name Extensions

Entity	Extension
Commercial	.com
Organization	.org
Government	.gov
International organization	.int
Military	.mil
Educational	.edu
Information	.info
Network	.net
Business	.biz
Mobile devices	.mobi
Asia-pacific regions	.asia

The DNS uses country codes to specify the country to which a specific website belongs. It consists of two letters in its extension.

For example,

https://www.cbse.nic.in/index.html

Country Code

Here, **cbse.nic.in** is a complete **domain name** in which **.in** represents the **country code** for India.

Some country codes are:

- .in for India
- .au for Australia
- .fr for France
- .us for United States

1.11 BLOGS

Blog is an **online journal** or a **personal diary** where an individual writes his/her thoughts about a specific topic, posts some write-up, and share his/her views. Blogs are personal web pages which are used by technical or non-technical users. Blog is the shortened form of **Weblog**.

In blog, websites entries are called **posts** and the person who post entries are called **Bloggers**. Blogs allow user to edit, update, or delete the post as per the requirement. There are many sites like blogger.com and wordpress.com that let you to create a blog for free. You don't need any web design experience.

Advantages of Blogs

The advantages of blogs are as follows:

1. It helps in interacting with different bloggers across the world.
2. It helps in improving your writing skills.
3. Blogs make easy to connect with social media.
4. Blogs are also the valuable source of information.
5. Blog is a good helping tool for carrying out certain day-to-day activities.

Extra Byte

The word **Weblog** was invented on December 17, 1997 by **Jorn Barger** who also invented his own blog labeled Robot Wisdom.

Disadvantages of blogs

The disadvantages of blogs are as follows:

1. Blogger is isolation from society.
2. Bloggers don't have fixed source of income.

Definition

The term blog is also known as weblog which refers to an online journal. People use blog to post their opinions, stories and other writings as well as photos and videos.

MEMORIZE

Blogger is a person who post his opinions on a specific event, pictures, poems, stories and share his views. Blogging is the process of creating and updating blog.

1.12 NEWSGROUP

Newsgroup is an **online forum** or a **bulletin board** where an individual's posts their views or discuss on a specific topic by posting messages on a news server.

A good ***example*** of a newsgroup is a **Computer help** group where individuals discuss about various computer related problems.

Examples of newsgroup are:

- alt.politics
- talk.religion
- sci.physics
- comp.software.testing

Advantages of Newsgroup

The advantages of Newsgroup are:

1. The main advantage of newsgroup is that it is free to subscribe and post.
2. There is a FAQ, (**Frequently Asked Question**) section on a newsgroup, which is always helpful for those who are not sure of certain things.

Definition

A newsgroup is defined as an online discussion forum that is accessible via Usenet. It is comprised of several thousands of electronic discussions where people can share their views and opinions with like-minded people.

Disadvantages of Newsgroup

The disadvantages of Newsgroup are:

1. A newsgroup is not as quick as an e-mail or even a mailing list.
2. The information on newsgroup submitted may be fake or not relevant as the people who are posting may have no real idea of what they are talking about.
3. It is not user friendly and the risk of viruses is high.

Check Your Progress

Answer the following questions.

1. Name any two ISPs.
2. How is a Web page different from a home page?
3. What is URL? Give one example of valid URL.

Let's Revise

- Network is a group of computers or devices which are interlinked with each other.
- Internet is a network of networks.
- For communication between several computers, various web protocols are required.
- TCP/IP protocol helps in communicating over the network.
- TCP fragments the original message into several packets at source side and defragments them at destination side.
- Packets are of equal size, having unique number and contain destination's IP address.
- Web server is the normal system where all web sites are stored.
- Web browser is an application software that enables to access web pages.
- Web page contains textual information, images, audio, video, and hyperlinks.
- Hyperlinks are the links of various web pages which when clicked let you jump to other web pages.
- All web pages are formatted by using a markup language known as hypertext markup language.
- HTTP helps in browsing various web pages and communicate web server with web browser.
- SMTP protocol is used to send e-mail messages whereas POP3 protocol is used for receiving e-mail messages on the receiver's side.
- FTP is used for downloading and uploading files over internet.
- Blog refers to an online journal where people share their views and posts messages.
- Newsgroup is an online bulletin board where people interact with each other and share their opinions on specific topic.

Learning Zone

SECTION A: OBJECTIVE TYPE QUESTIONS

A. MULTIPLE CHOICE QUESTIONS.

1. Full form of HTTP is:
   a. Hypertext transmission control protocol   b. Hypertext transfer protocol
   c. Hyper textual transmission protocol   d. Hyper transmission textual protocol
2. Which protocol is used for uploading and downloading files over network?
   a. SMTP   b. TELNET   c. FTP   d. HTTP
3. First page of a website is called:
   a. Web page   b. Home page   c. First page   d. Web server
4. It is a collection of several web pages.
   a. Web site   b. URL   c. Web server   d. Both a. and b.
5. ____________ part of http://www.webaddress.edu represents domain name.
   a. http   b. www   c. webaddress.edu   d. .edu
6. ____________ is a client software that helps the user to navigate WWW.
   a. Web site   b. Browser   c. Web page   d. Web server
7. Every computer on a network exchange information according to certain rules called as ____________.
   a. Protocols   b. Networking   c. Surfing   d. Browsing
8. Which protocol is responsible for breaking up data into small pieces at all source computer?
   a. IP   b. TCP   c. SMTP   d. HTTP
9. The domain extension .mil refers to a type of website.
   a. Commercial   b. Government   c. Military   d. Educational
10. Which of the following is are popular web browsers? (Delhi 2019)
    a. FireFox   b. Safari   c. Navigator   d. All of the above
11. ISP stands for:
    a. Intranet Service Provider   b. Internet Service Provider
    c. Inter Service Provider   d. International Special Products
12. Which of the following internet protocol provides secure data transmission between services and browser with the help of encryption.
    a. HTTP   b. HTTPs   c. TELNET   d. ARPANET
13. Hypertext is:
    a. Text with a picture   b. Normal text
    c. Text that contains a link to another web page   d. Web pages
14. The IP address consist of how many bytes?
    a. 4 bytes   b. 3 bytes   c. 32 bytes   d. 16 bytes

15. The internet is governed by:

a. ARPANET b. NSFNET c. IETF d. None of the above

16. Who described the transmission control protocol in 1974?

a. Tim Berners Lee b. Vinton Gray Cerf c. ARPANET d. NSF

17. The 's' at the end of HTTPs stands for:

a. Social b. Secure c. Strong d. Smart

18. This protocol is also called PUSH protocol:

a. POP3 b. HTTP c. SMTP d. FTP

19. This is an internet browswer.

a. Apple Safari b. Satyam Online
c. TCP/IP d. APL

20. This governs the internet:

a. W3C b. US Government c. IGF d. None of these

Ans.	1. b	2. c	3. b	4. a	5. c
	6. b	7. a	8. b	9. c	10. d
	11. b	12. b	13. c	14. a	15. d
	16. ?	17. b	18. a	19. a	20. d

B. FILL IN THE BLANKS.

1. ____________ is the expanded form of SSH.
2. A gateway is a device that helps to connect ____________ networks.
3. Full form of ISP is ____________.
4. ____________ is a version of FTP.
5. ____________ is a website where an individual can post their pictures, videos and share their opinions.
6. The domain extension for government is ____________.
7. ____________ is a numeric addressing system.
8. ____________ is a system that converts IP address into domain name.
9. The country code of France is ____________.
10. IETF stands for ____________.
11. The first network that pioneered the internet was ____________.
12. The device used to connect dissimilar networks is called a ____________.
13. The person who is known as the father of computers ____________.
14. ____________ is the person who has created e-mail.
15. A unique address that computer uses to identify itself and communicate with other devices on the network ____________.

16. An electronic document written by using HTML language ____________.

17. SMTP is created and maintained by ____________.

18. ____________ is a remote login protocol.

19. ____________ is the secure version of HTTP.

20. A ____________ can consist of text, photos, images, hyperlinks, advertisement and more.

Ans. 1. Secure Shell 2. Dissimilar 3. Internet Service Provider 4. SFTP
5. Blog 6. .gov 7. IP address
8. Domain Name System 9. .fr 10. Internet Engineerin
11. APRANET 12. Gateway 13. Charles babbage 14. Ray Tomlinson
15. IP address 16. Web Page 17. IETF 18. Telnet 19. HTTPs 20. Blog

C. STATE WHETHER THE FOLLOWING STATEMENTS ARE TRUE OR FALSE.

1. Internet is a network of networks.
2. The full form of FTP is File Transmission Protocol.
3. TCP is used for routing packet over the internet
4. S in HTTPs specifies that it is a secure site.
5. Website is a collection of several web pages.
6. A web page can consist of only textual information.
7. First page of a website is known as home page.
8. Jump are the links that enables you to jump from one web page to another web page.
9. Domain extension is always a three-letter name.
10. IP stands for Interconnect Protocol.
11. Web browser is an online diary or journal displayed in a reverse chronological order.
12. A packet is a block of data of definite size.
13. Downloading means data is sent from your computer to the internet.
14. The protocol in URL is always followed by //.
15. SCP encrypts files and verifies user authentication.
16. .au is the country code for Africa.
17. HTML code consist of tags and attributes.
18. Airtel and BSNL are the examples of ISPs.
19. Opera web browser was first released in 1995.
20. Safari is not a graphical browser and therefore cannot support pictures, images, audio or video on a web page.

Ans. 1. True 2. True 3. False 4. True 5. True
6. False 7. True 8. False 9. True 10. False
11. False 12. True 13. False 14. True 15. True
16. False 17. True 18. True 19. True 20. False

SECTION B: SOLVED THEORY QUESTIONS

1. **What is Internet?** *[Sample Question Paper 2020-21]*

Ans: Internet is a network of networks. It is a collection of several networks which are interconnected with each other either through cables or without cables.

2. **What are the various components required to have internet?**

Ans: The various components for internet are:

a. An Internet connection.
b. A Modem.
c. Internet access software
d. Protocol
e. A program which controls the communication of data over the hardware component

3. **What is the difference between website and webpage?**

Ans: Website is a collection of several web pages whereas a web page is a single page that is formatted by using HTML language. Each web page has a unique address, called URL that identifies its location on the network.

4. **Define web browser. Name two popular browsers.**

Ans: Web browser is a client machine or a communication program that reads and interprets HTML documents on the WWW (World Wide Web).

Some popular Web browsers are:

a. Microsoft Internet Explorer
b. Netscape Navigator
c. Mozilla Firefox
d. Safari
e. Opera

5. **Define WWW.** *[Delhi 2018, 2019]*

Ans: WWW can be expanded as World Wide Web. It is an information system of interlinked hypertext documents that are accessed via Internet and built on the top of the Domain Name System. It has also commonly become known as the Web.

6. **Which two protocols are used for communication between computers?**

Ans: The TCP and IP protocols are used for communication among computers.

7. **Define protocol.**

Ans: A protocol is a set of rules required to carry out communication over a network.

8. **Discuss the functioning of TCP and IP protocols.**

Ans: TCP is the transmission control protocol and is responsible for dividing the message into number of small fragments called packets and then reassembles all packets into original message whereas IP is the Internet protocol and is responsible for sending and receiving packets over the network.

9. **What is the main difference between IMAP and POP3?**

Ans: The POP3 protocol assumes that there is only one client connected to the mailbox. In contrast, the IMAP protocol allows simultaneous access by multiple clients. IMAP is suitable for us if our mailbox is about to be managed by multiple users.

10. **What are the two web addressing methods?**

Ans: The two web addressing methods are:

a. Domain Name system or Letter Addressing System.
b. IP addressing system or Number Addressing System.

11. What is the number addressing system?

Ans: The number addressing system is also known as IP addressing system. It is in the form of numbers. Each IP address comprises of 32 bits or 4 bytes where each byte is separated by dots/periods.

12. Explain the letter addressing system.

Ans: The web address of any computer or network can be given using alphabets. This is called the letter addressing system and it is popularly known as the Domain Name System (DNS).

13. Explain any three methods of Internet access.

Ans: The methods of Internet access are:

a. Dial-up connection: It is a connection between the computer and the ISP with the help of a modem. Dial-up connection is a limited time-duration connection that uses a telephone line to connect to the ISP server.

b. ISDN: ISDN lines are used to transmit data over digital telephone lines.

c. Broadband Service: Broadband Internet access, often shortened to broadband, is a high-data-transmission rate Internet connection.

14. What is a modem? Explain how it works? What are its two types?

Ans: The full form of Modem is Modulator and Demodulator. It is a computer peripheral device that allows us to connect and communicate with other computer via telephone lines. It converts the digital data into analog data and vice-versa. The process of converting digital data into analog data is called Modulation and the process of converting analog data into digital data is called Demodulation.

There are two type of Modem:

a. Internal Modem: Internal Modem is a Modem which is placed inside the CPU. It is in the form of card.

b. External Modem: External Modem is a Modem which is placed outside the CPU. It is a box shaped device.

15. List various advantages of e-mail.

Ans: Advantages of e-mail are as follows:

a. It is the fastest means of communication over network.

b. It saves money, paper and time.

c. It allows users to send and receive messages according to their comfort and convenience level.

d. Provides the space to store incoming and outgoing e-mail messages for future reference.

e. User can delete and edit message as per their requirement.

f. For sending e-mail, it is not necessary that the receiver must be online as the sent mail is stored in the inbox of receiver's account.

16. Define ISP. Name some popular ISP companies of India.

Ans: ISP stands for Internet Service Provider; it provides the internet connection to the user along with username and password, which is needed to configure the Internet connection on the computer. Some popular ISP companies of India are: MTNL, Airtel, Reliance, BSNL.

17. What is the purpose of a web browser? Give the name of any two popular web browsers.

Ans: A web browser is an application program used for exploring the information resources available on the World Wide Web to retrieve the required information. Two popular web browsers are Google Chrome and Mozilla Firefox.

18. What is the difference between the Internet, Intranet, and Extranet?

Ans: The terminologies Internet, Intranet, and Extranet are used to define how the applications in the

network can be accessed. They use similar TCP/IP technology but differ in terms of access levels for each user inside the network and outside the network.
Internet: Applications are accessed by anyone from any location using the web.
Intranet: It allows limited access to users in the same organization.
Extranet: External users are allowed or provided with access to use the network application of the organization.

SECTION C: APPLICATION ORIENTED QUESTIONS

1. **In the URL, http://www.wikipedia.org/, identify the domain name and domain extension.**

Ans: The domain name is Wikipedia.org and domain extension is .org.

2. **Internet is a series of interconnected computers throughout the world. Name any one of the services that is offered on internet and any one of the internet service providers.**

Ans: e-Commerce, e-Business, E-mail, Web Browsing, e-Learning, e-Governance are the services offered on internet and BSNL, MTNL, Airtel, Vodafone, Idea Cellular, Reliance Communications, Aircel, Tata Teleservices, Telenor India, Videocon, Atria Convergence Technologies etc., are the internet service provider.

3. **Komal works in an MNC and works online from home also. She needs a fast internet connection. Which type of internet connection is best suited for her? Also, she needs to upload and download the files from remote sites. Which protocol will help her to perform this activity?**

Ans: DSL OR Broadband OR Wi-Fi connection will be best suited for her. File transfer protocol (FTP) will help her to perform this activity.

4. **Arvind Mohanthy has a leather business. Very often he requires information from internet about latest developments in leather technology around the world. So, he wants an internet connection for his desktop computer.**
   a. Suggest any two popular internet service providers in India.
   b. Suggest two websites that could help him search for required information.

Ans: Two popular internet service providers in India are: Airtel, BSNL, MTNL.
Two websites that could help him search for required information are: google.com, yahoo.com.

5. **Identify web addresses and e-mail addresses from the following:**
   a. www.scrapbook.com   b. aba@crapbook.com
   c. www.countrywide.co.in   d. 123@hotshot.co.in

Ans: Web addresses are: www.scrapbook.com www.countrywide.co.in
E-mail addresses are: aba@crapbook.com 123@hotshot.co.in

6. **Write the web extensions for the following type of organization.**
   a. Education   b. Government

Ans: a. .edu for Education   b. .gov for Government

7. **Palvi is desperately interested in joining a weight loss program. But she has many questions in mind that she wants to discuss with people across the world. Name the tool that provide such social discussions.**

Ans: Blog or weblog.

8. **Nishi wants to open the website of her school. In the web browser Window, where should she type the URL of the school web site?**

Ans: She should type the URL in the address bar of the browser Window.

SECTION D: SELF - ASSESSMENT

A. FILL IN THE BLANKS.

1. ____________ protocol is used for fragmentation and defragmentation of packets.
2. ____________ is the system where a number or IP addresses are used instead of typing the URL.
3. Chrome remote desktop software needs ____________ web browser at both ends.
4. The full form of FTP is ____________. *[Delhi 2018]*
5. ____________ is the correct term when the two devices on the network send messages to each other.
6. ____________ internet service connects you to a news server on the internet.
7. ____________ prefix is used in the beginning of the web address.
8. Easy news is an example of popular ____________.
9. ____________ is a collection of newsgroups where the users can post messages on different topics.
10. A ____________ protocol used to connect Usenet servers and transfer newsgroup articles between systems over the network.

B. STATE WHETHER THE FOLLOWING STATEMENTS ARE TRUE OR FALSE.

1. ARPANET was the first network that pioneered the internet.
2. In the URL ftp://abc.com, ftp stands for domain name.
3. Modem is a device that converts only digital signal into analog signal.
4. External mode is in the form of the card.
5. Google chrome is a popular web browser.
6. Protocol is a set of rules that governs internet.
7. HTML is a type of protocol.
8. Web pages on a website are linked to each other through hyperlinks.
9. The process of storing websites on a web server is called hosting.
10. In packet transmission of data, data is transmitted in a chronological order and therefore there is no sequence number of the packet.

C. TICK THE CORRECT ANSWER.

1. Who was the predecessor of the internet?
   a. ASAFENET　b. ARPANET　c. TELNET　d. FTP
2. It is the valid e-mail address:
   a. yoga@yoga.com　b. agrima@hotmail.com
   c. abc$gmail.com　d. myaccount%gmail.com
3. The protocol used for internet is:
   a. TCP　b. HTTP　c. TCP/IP　d. none of these

4. When the name of the website is used instead of using IP address, it is called:
   a. Number naming system
   b. Domain naming system
   c. Both a. and b.
   d. None of these
5. The first page of every website is known as:
   a. House page
   b. Home page
   c. Front page
   d. Rear page
6. Internet address is a:
   a. 8-bit number
   b. 16-bit number
   c. 32-bit number
   d. 64-bit number
7. Protocols are set of rules to govern:
   a. Communication
   b. Standards
   c. Metropolitan communication
   d. None of Above
8. What do you mean by broadcasting in Networking?
   a. Means addressing a packet to all machine
   b. It means addressing a packet to some machine
   c. It means addressing a packet to a particular machine
   d. It means addressing a packet to except a particular machine
9. Which of the following is reliable communication protocol?
   a. TCP
   b. IP
   c. UDP
   d. All of the above
10. This is the telecommunication protocol that all computers must use to be part of the Internet.
    a. Internet Protocol
    b. FTP
    c. Border Gateway Protocol
    d. DHCP
11. To join the internet, the computer has to be connected to a:
    a. Internet architecture board
    b. Internet society
    c. Internet service provider
    d. None of the mentioned
12. Which one of the following protocol is not used in internet?
    a. HTTP
    b. DHCP
    c. DNS
    d. None of the mentioned
13. POP protocal is *[Sample Question Paper 2020-21]*
    a. used for composing an email message
    b. used in ricising incoming dmails by pulling the message from server to client.
    c. used in sending outgoing emails
    d. None of the above
14. HTML is used to create:
    a. Machine language program
    b. High level program
    c. Web page
    d. Web server
15. Verification of a login name and password is known as:
    a. Configuration
    b. Accessibility
    c. Authentication
    d. Logging in

D. ANSWER THE FOLLOWING QUESTIONS.

Type A: Very Short Answer Questions.

1. What do you mean by network and internet?
2. Define the following terms:

a. Web Server b. Web Browser c. Website (Delhi 2009)
d. Web Page e. Home Page

3. What do you mean by Protocol?
4. What is the significance of URL? *[Sample Question Paper 2020-21]*
5. What do you mean by blogger and Posts?
6. What is the purpose of newsgroup?
7. What would the following domain extension indicate?
   a. .org b. .uk
8. What all characters are not included in an e-mail address?
9. Briefly discuss the role of web browser in Internet Surfing. *[Sample Question Paper 2020-21]*
10. Name any two popular web sites.
11. What is homepage? *[Sample Question Paper 2020-21]*
12. Name any two popular web browsers. *[Delhi 2018]*
13. How can you differentiate between web client and web server? *[Sample Question Paper 2020-21]*
14. Explain the term HTTP. Why is it required? *[Delhi 2005]*
15. What is the full form of URL? *[Sample Question Paper 2020-21]*

Type B: Short Answer Questions.

1. Explain the functioning of the following protocols:
   a. TCP and IP b. FTP and SFTP c. SMTP and POP3
2. Differentiate between hypertext and hyperlink. *[Delhi 2018]*
3. How domain name system is the easier method of web addressing system as compared to IP addressing system?
4. Mention some uses of internet. *[Delhi 2006]*
5. Identify the domain names and URLs from the following list: *[Delhi 2015, 2016]*
   a. abc@abc.com b. doyogaeveryday.com
   c. www.doyogaeveryday.com/index.html d. 192.168.0.1
   e. http://cbse.nic.in
6. What is blogging? Discuss its advantages and disadvantages.
7. What happens when you click on the hyperlink?
8. Name the web service that allows users to post their messages on different topics.
9. How is uploading different from downloading?
10. Explain SSH and it's working.
11. Define client server concept in terms of networking.
12. What is the purpose of using blog?
13. Describe the concept of Domain name extension.
14. Which group from the rules that define how internet works?
15. State one similarity and dissimilarity between HTTP, FTP and HTTPs.

Type C: Long Answer Questions.

1. Discuss fragmentation and defragmentation of packets.
2. Give the minimum requirements for connecting to the internet.
3. What do you mean by hosting? Explain.
4. Discuss the evolution of internet.
5. As life gets busier, it becomes difficult for everyone to keep track with school- college friends, old colleagues, old neighbors and favorites teachers. It is important to keep in touch with all your near and dear ones. At times people sitting miles away doing similar kind of activity or solving similar kind of problems can help you to achieve goals faster by sharing their experiences. Similarly, people belonging to different socio-economic background can change your perspective and can enhance your understanding of various cultures.
   a. Suggest the real time tools that are suitable for the above-mentioned activities.
   b. What is the generic name used for such tools?
6. A school has two separate computer networks. One is used for keeping pupil and staff records. The other is for pupils to use in lessons to help with their learning and to store their work.
7. Pupil use the Internet quite frequently in their lessons to help them with their work. Discuss the advantages and disadvantages of this as far as a pupil is concerned.
8. Sampoorna international school is planning to create a website showing various objectives, facilities and features of the school. Suggest some basic requirements they must acknowledge while developing the website. (CBSE 2011)
9. Palvi wants to establish an internet connection in her cybercafé. Mention the things she requires to set up the connection.
10. Do you think you should follow forum etiquettes when using any online forum? Find out and list all those etiquettes.
11. How various components such as web browser, web server, internet protocol or remote login help in networking?
12. What is HTTP and what port does it use?
13. Define IEEE in the networking world?

SECTION E: LAB EXERCISE

1. **Open the Google chrome.**
   a. Create a blog of your favorite topic.
   b. Write two to three blogs.
   c. Show the blogs to your teacher.

Activity Zone

1. Discuss in detail with the students about the various protocols and their functions.
2. Tell students to search for some sites for creating blog.
3. Teach students to create a blog for themselves and note down the various features of blog.
4. List the various advantages and disadvantages of internet, blog and newsgroup.

2 Internet and Web Services

Outline of the Chapter

- Introduction
- Information retrieval
- Locating sites using search engines and finding people on the net
- Web services
- Mobile technologies

Learning Objectives

- To know about how the information is retrieved from the internet
- To know about search engines and it's Working
- To know how to find people on the Internet
- To know various web services such as: chat, email, video conferencing, e-Learning, e-Banking, e-Shopping, e-Reservation, e-Governance, e-Groups, social networking
- To know mobile technologies such as SMS, MMS, 3G, 4G

INTRODUCTION

The internet has emerged as a fastest technology of communication. It is impossible to imagine a world without the internet. All activities from communication to entertainment are heavily rely on internet. Today, the internet does more than just connecting computers. It is a source of information, a social platform, and a business network. The internet has diverse uses depending on the needs of an individual or and therefore, the importance of the internet in our daily lives is unquestionable.

Internet has made our lives so easier that you can purchase anything while sitting at home. You need not to waste time and money which may incurred during travelling. Instant messaging takes place. You can do online reservation of airways or railways. If you want to watch movies, then you can do online booking as per your convenience. So, everything has become easier and instant through internet.

This chapter will let you know the various service provided by World Wide Web that has made our lives easier and vibrant.

2.1 INFORMATION RETRIEVAL

Information retrieval means searching information from the internet. once, you are connected with internet, you are ready to retrieve information. For finding information, a web browser is required which

Extra Byte

Web browser is an application software that helps in accessing information from the internet.

helps you to access the web sites to search the required information. A browser is an application program that sends request to the web server and web server gives reply to the request.

To visit a specific site, you need to type a URL of that specific web site. URL is a web address that helps you to open a particular web page. ***For example***, to access the information related to Elections 2020, the URL of a website is typed on an address bar of a web browser window is shown in *figure 2.1*:

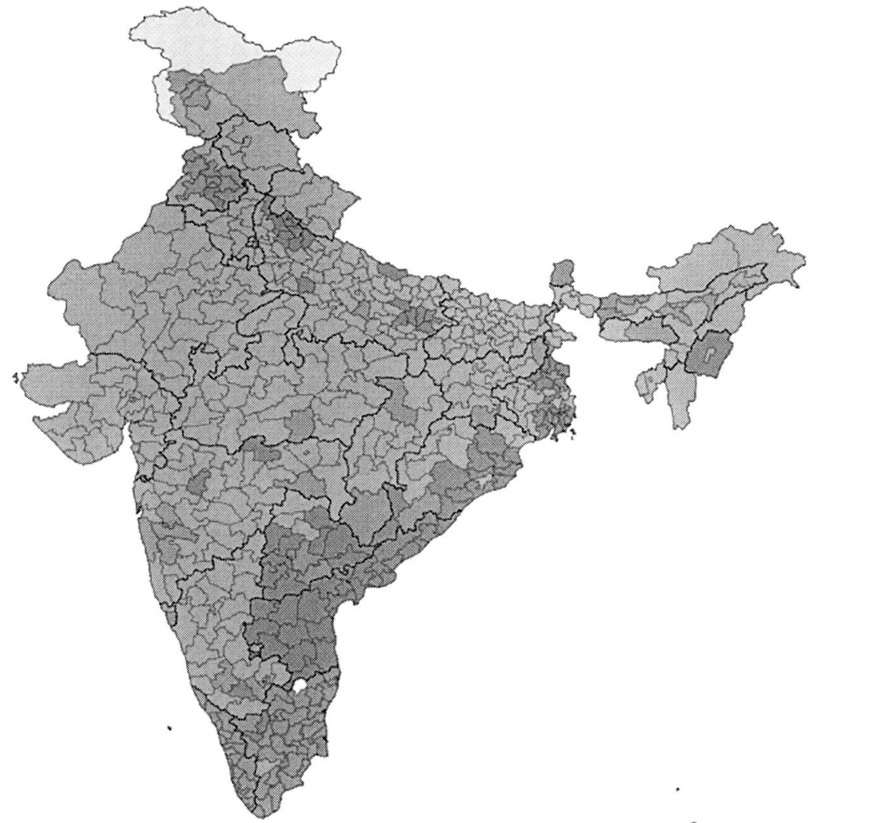

Figure 2.1: Searching information about elections from internet

Once you open a web page, you can store the information on your system. This process of retrieving the information from the net and storing on your system is known as **downloading**.

Some popular websites on the internet are:

- Google.com
- Yahoo.com
- eBay.com
- Twitter.com
- Linkedln.com
- Facebook.com

2.2 SEARCH ENGINE

Search engine is an application that helps user to search for a specific information from the internet when the user does not know the name of the site or the URL of the site. ***For example***, if you want to know about **what is network topology**, and you don't know what website should be opened for this then, you simply use a search engine, type your question in the search bar and it will provide you the links of several websites that contain answer of your questions.

Definition

Search Engine is a program that searches for a specific information, locates that information stored in the database which matches the corresponding keywords or characters entered by the user.

For example, Google which is a search engine, you just type your question and it will show you the URLs of several websites.

Different Search Engines

Search engine provides a high-quality search result that meets the user's requirement. Some popular search engines are:

Google Search Engine: Google was invented by **Larry Page** and **Sergey Brin** in January 1996 when they were both Ph.D. students at Stanford University in Stanford, California. Google is the most popular search engine that shows various linked pages and thus increases the ranking of the linked pages. It also examines the relevance of the content being searched with respect to latest updates. Additionally, Google captures almost 85% of mobile traffic.

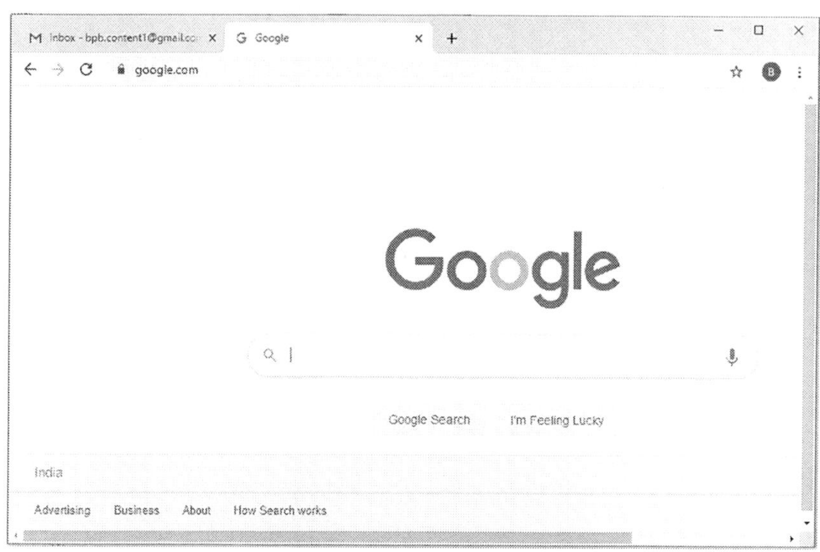

Figure 2.2: Google Search Engine

Bing Search Engine: Bing search engine was launched by Microsoft CEO **Steve Ballmer** in **May 2009**. It is another popular search engine. The pages on Bing look similar to Google's web pages in terms of category and a similar white background, with same link color as blue and green URLs. However, Bing additionally offers Rewards, a program that gives you points when you search or shop on the engine, and then allows you to redeem those points for gift cards, non-profit donations, and more.

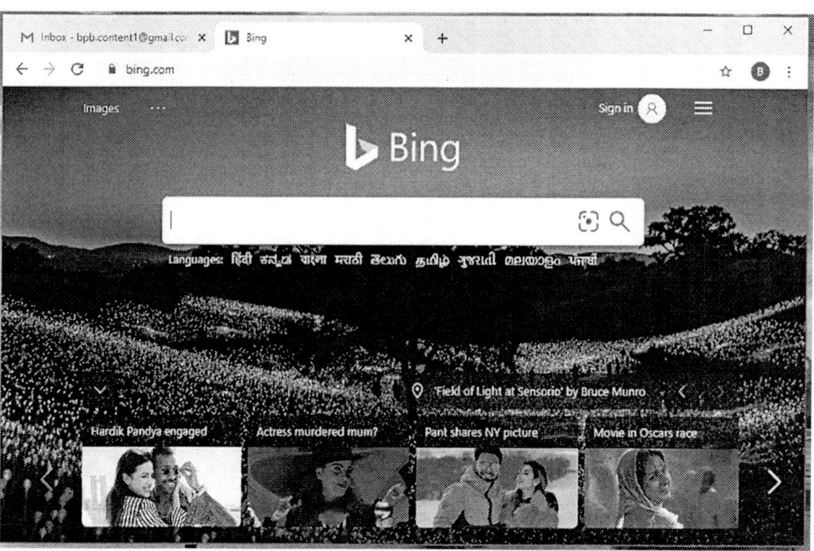

Figure 2.3: Bing Search Engine

Yahoo Search Engine: The new Yahoo! Search offers various services and tools to help you find whatever you're looking for, faster and easier than ever. Yahoo uses a powerful search algorithm powered by its crawler to list webpages related to keywords entered by the user. Yahoo also helps in searching for news stories, pictures, and audio/video.

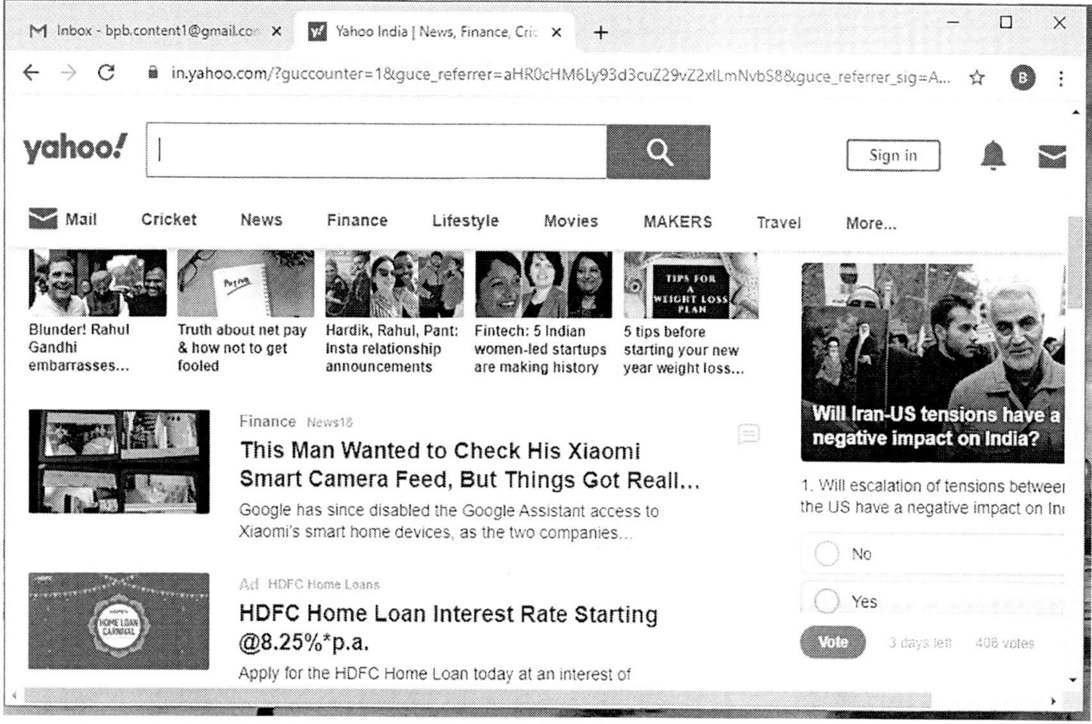

Figure 2.4: Yahoo Search Engine

Baidu Search Engine: Baidu is China's largest search engine capturing over 75% of China's search market. The search engine looks similar to Google with a white background, blue links, and green URLs. Baidu offers about 57 search and community services, such as Baidu Baike and a keyword-based discussion forum.

Figure 2.5: Baidu Search Engine

Internet and Web Services

2.2.1 Finding Information Using Search Engines

There are several search engines that fulfills your purpose.

For example: Google.com, Yahoo.com, Bing.com, Ask.com, Wow.com. All these search engines are used for finding information from the internet.

Consider an example of the most popular search engine and find the information by following the given steps:

1. To visit the site, type **http://www.google.com** on the address bar of a browser window.
2. Type the text in a text box for which you want to search the information.
3. Now, press **enter** key or click on the **search button**. The search engine will search for the information and display the links to the web pages which contain information related to your text. (*Figure 2.6*)

For example,

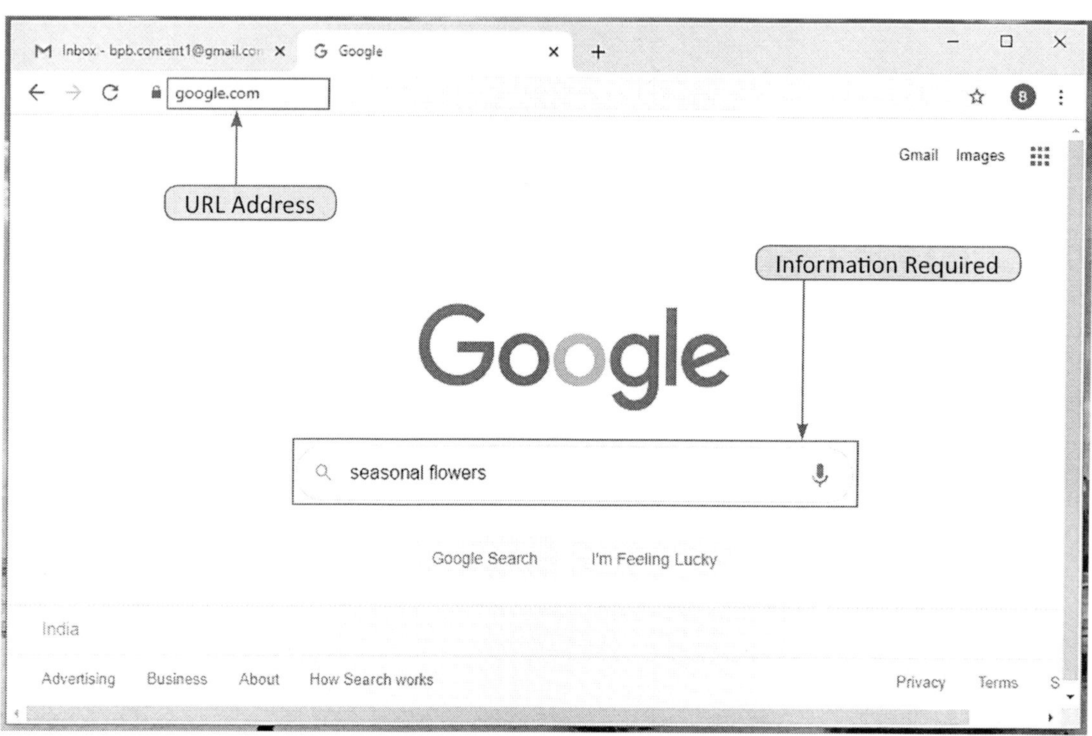

Figure 2.6: Google Search Engine

2.3 WORKING OF SEARCH ENGINE

Search engines are used to retrieve required information an any specific topic. It displays the relevant links of several web pages that contain the required information. But, do you know that how search engine works? How does a search engine display such matching results as per your query?

Archie was the first tool which was developed in 1990 and is used for searching an information on the internet.

✱ **So, let's know the elements of search engine.**

2.3.1 Elements of Search Engine

1. Web Crawling

Web crawling is the process of crawling or searching for the websites that contains the links of web pages for the required information. This job is done by spiders or crawlers which is a software program that browses the internet in a systematic manner. Whenever any request is sent by a user to a search engine in the form of keywords, it sends out a team of robots (crawlers or spiders) to locate the websites that contain the new and updated information. As soon as the web crawler finds the links of those web pages, it creates an index of those web pages in its huge database for later search. This makes the search quick and easy. (*Figure 2.7*)

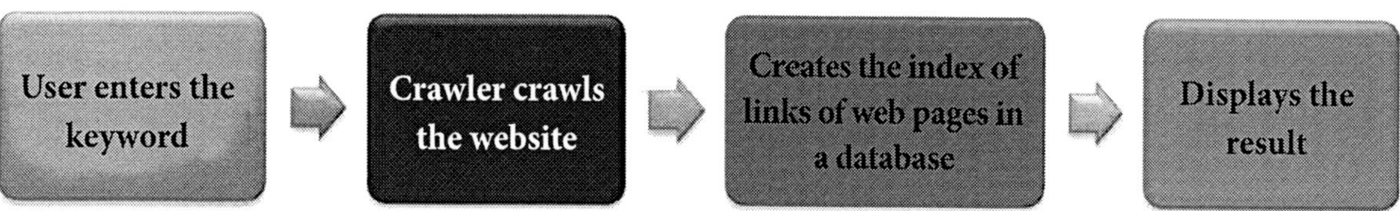

Figure 2.7: Steps for Searching Information

Consider the example given in *figure 2.8*, where the user enters some keyword in a search engine, then the web crawler locates a website for the required information, stores its link in a google database and display the result to the user.

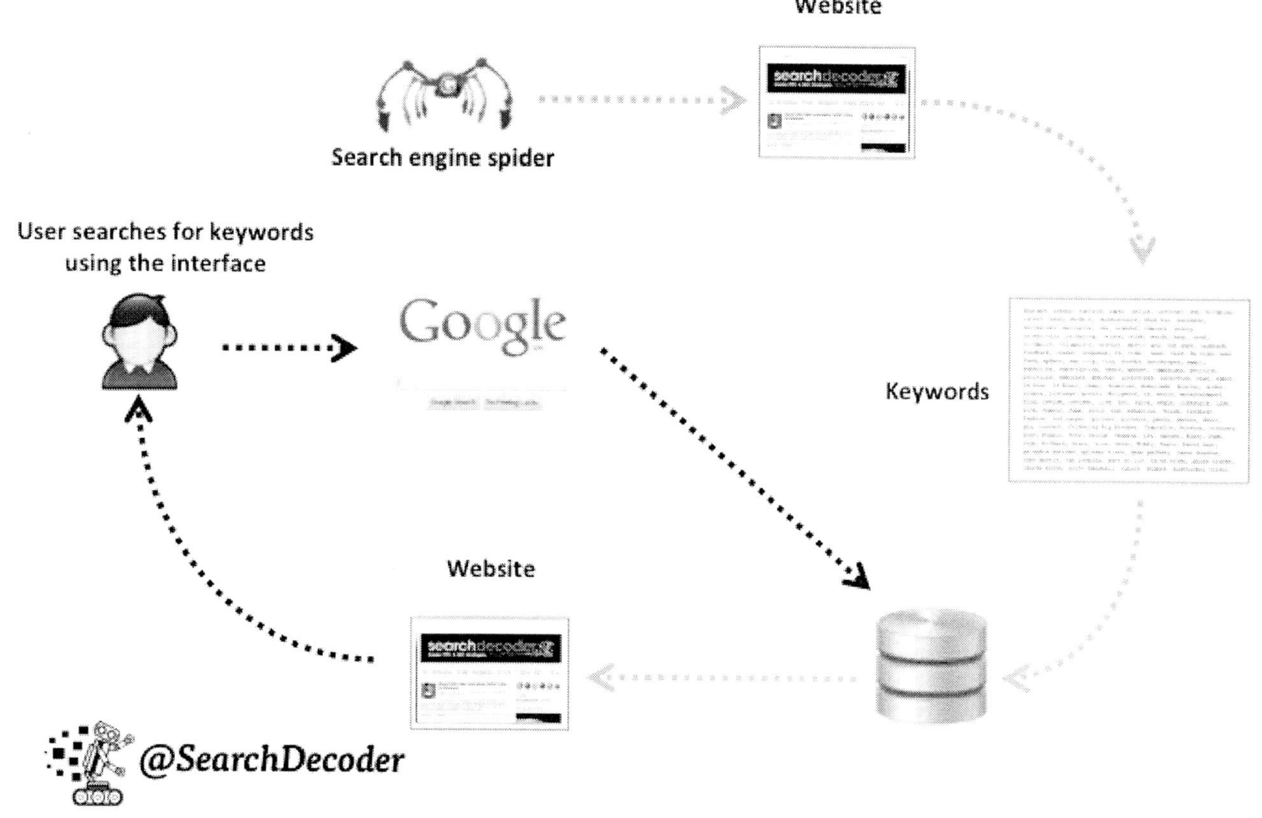

Figure 2.8: Web Crawling

Definition

Web crawling is the process of crawling or searching for the websites that contains the links of web pages for the required information.

2. Indexing Software

Indexing software is a software where the web crawler stores the list of all websites or the links of those websites that contain the required information. This software fetches the information from the websites and then prepares the index of the available information. The data is then stored in a large database of a search engine.

Definition

The indexing software extracts information from the documents and web addresses, prepares an index for it and store in the database.

3. Search Algorithm

Search algorithm is the algorithm or a mechanism that finds the searched keywords in the database. If the searched keywords are found, then the corresponding websites and web pages are displayed.

Consider an example, suppose you want to find out about the election commission of India, and you type these keywords in a Google search engine it will display several links of those websites that contains this information. (*Figure 2.9*)

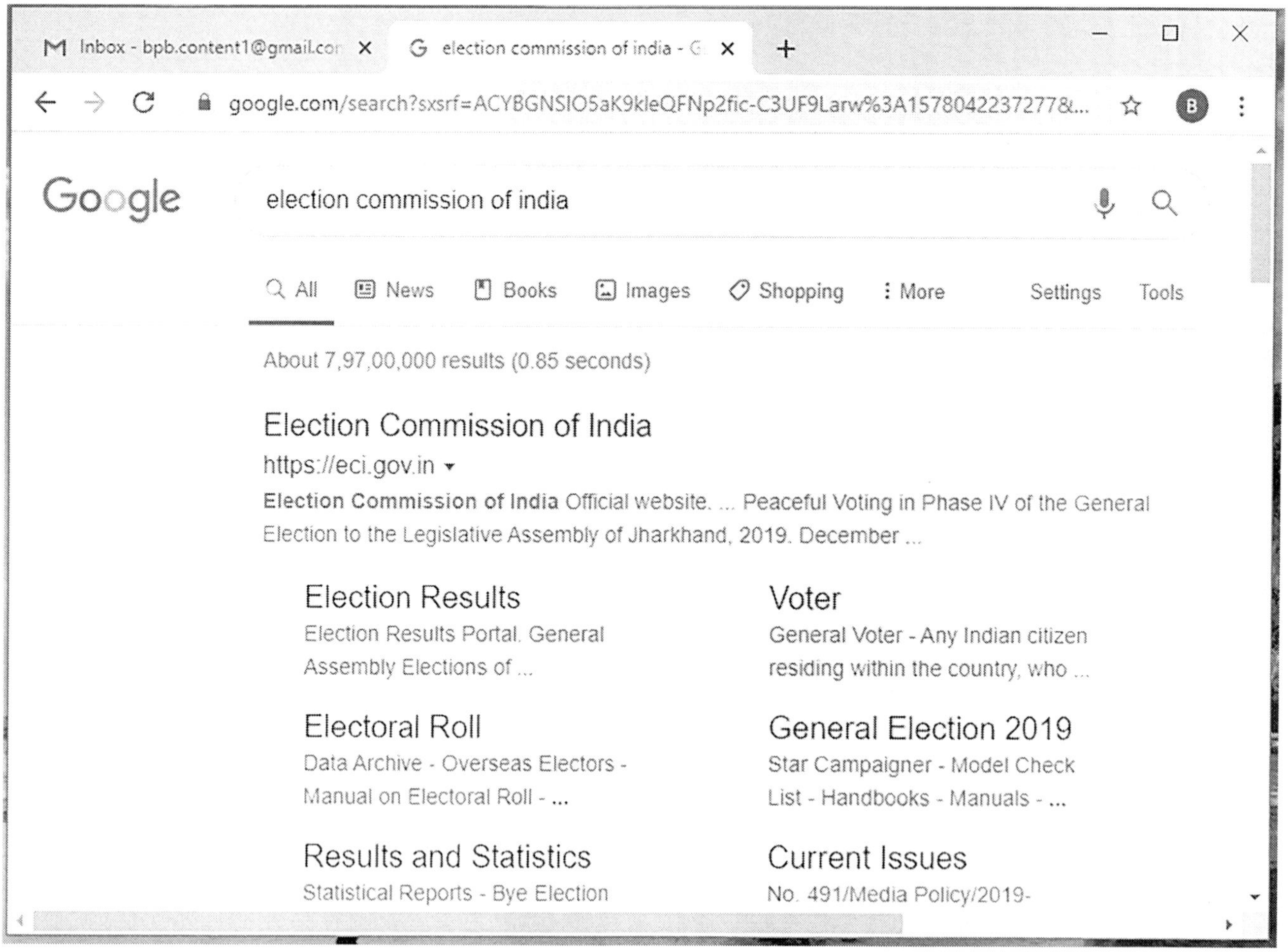

Figure 2.9: The Google Search Engine Result for Election Commission of India

Definition

Search Algorithm is the algorithm or a mechanism that finds the searched keywords in the database. If the searched keywords are found, then the corresponding websites and web pages are displayed.

Tips for searching information on the web

Following are the tips to search information:

Search for a specific phrase: If you want to search for a specific phrase, then enclose the phrase in double quotes. For example, instead of typing weather, type **weather in Delhi**.

Use of hyphen (-): if you want that a searched page should not include some words the use hyphen (-). For example, to search for books but not for spiritual books then type books –spiritual. In this way, search engine will display the list of all books except spiritual books.

Translating speech into text: you can convert your speech into text for finding information. For this, go to the Google home page, click the microphone icon and start talking. Whatever you say will be converted into text and gives you the searched information.

Try an advanced search: Google's advanced search page lets you fill out a form with options for a detailed, specific page.

Calculation: You can also use some basic calculation operators such as +, -, /, *. For example, 45 * 90 will give you 4050 (calculated result by Google).

2.4 FINDING PEOPLE ON THE INTERNET

Search engines are not only used for searching any information. Instead you can use it to know about any person, locate his contact number, e-mail address, and so on.

For example,

Figure 2.10 displays the page from people.yahoo.com where you can search a person either by his first name, last name, city/town or state.

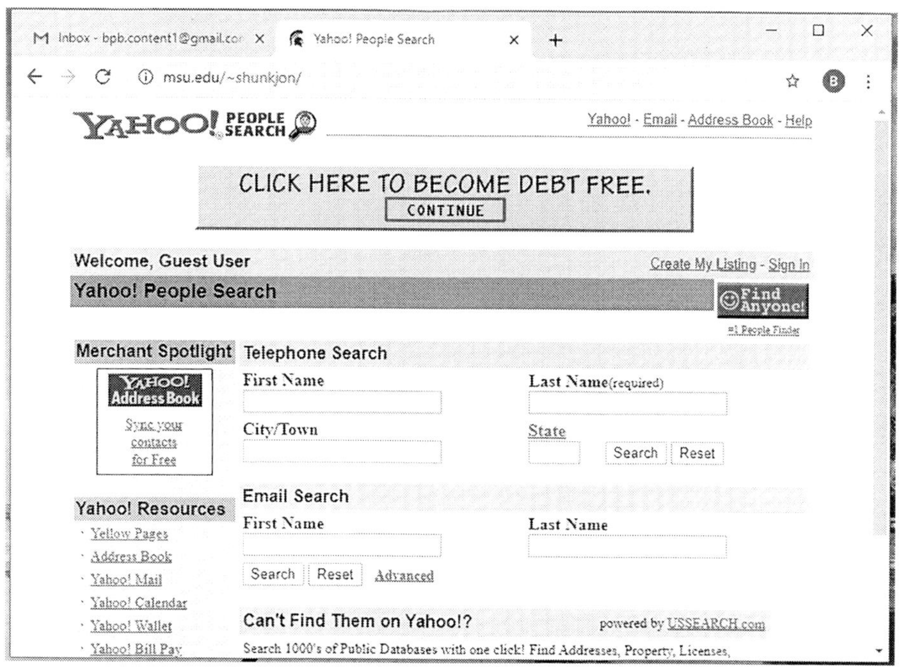

Figure 2.10: Finding people on www.people.yahoo.com

Sites which help you to find people on the internet are:

- http://www.people.yahoo.com
- http://www.whowhere.com
- http://www.truePeopleSearch.com
- http://www.classmates.com
- http://www.peekyou.com

Through internet, two computers talk with each other in the same way as two persons are talking with each other. When there is a digital talk, you say two computers are chatting for exchange of information. They communicate with each other with the help of technology and programming standards used on Internet. World Wide Web provides these kinds of services that make the communication between people easier and quicker.

* **Let us discuss the various services provided by World Wide Web.**

2.5 WEB SERVICES

The various services or facilities provided by world Wide Web are:

1. Electronic Mail or E-Mail

You all are aware about the traditional method of sending and receiving the messages to each other. ***For example***, in earlier days, pigeons, were used for sending and receiving letters, then letters are sent via Post office which were delivered by postman was used, and after that communication are done over landline telephone and so on. But all these methods were time consuming. Now, in modern era, **e-mail**, a short form of **electronic mail**, method is used for sending and receiving messages. It is an electronic method where the user is sending a message electronically i.e. through computer and the receiver receives the message electronically. It allows people to interact quickly all around the world at any time.

It also facilitates the user to send the same message to multiple recipients at the same time. You can also send files through attachments, which can be textual files, pdf, video, or audio files. The speed is also much higher than the speed of the traditional postal or the courier service.

Definition

E-mail is a method of exchanging messages between people using internet enabled digital computing devices.

Protocols used in E-mail Service are:

- **SMTP:** SMTP is expanded as **Simple Mail Transfer Protocol**. It is the protocol whose function is to send e-mail messages to the recipient of messages.
- **POP3 and IMAP: POP3** is expanded as **Post Office Protocol** and **IMAP** is expanded as **Internet Message Access Protocol**. Both these protocols are responsible for retrieving messages from a mail server over a TCP/IP connection.

Parts of E-mail address

For sending and receiving e-mail, one should have an e-mail address. This address works similar as that of your postal address. While sending an e-mail, you enter your e-mail address and recipients e-mail address to whom you want to send message.

The various parts of email address are:

1. **Username:** It is the name of a person's account.

2. **@ symbol:** It separates the username with the domain name.
3. **Domain name / Host name:** It is the name of mail server whose representation appears in the client computer when he/she opens his/her inbox.
4. **Domain extension:** It refers to the domain extension.

For example,

palvigupta@gmail.com			
palvigupta	**@**	**gmail**	**.com**
user name	@symbol	Domain Name	Domain Extension

★ **Let's discuss various fields of e-mail message.**

Fields Associated with an E-mail Message

Putting everyone's email addresses in **To** or **CC** field reveals everyone's email addresses to everyone else. This way you are not just sending the intended information across, but also, you're distributing email addresses to everyone which could be misused.

1. **To:** To field is used to write the e-mail address of the person to whom the message is to be sent. It asks the user to enter recipient e-mail address.
2. **Cc:** Cc means **carbon copy**. This field is used when you want to send the same e-mail message to multiple recipients. This is also called keeping **CC recipients in the loop**. However, this field optional.
3. **Bcc:** Bcc means **blind carbon copy**. This field is used when you want to send the same e-mail message to multiple recipients but you don't want to share the list of e-mail addresses to everyone that all have received the same message. Bcc is generally used when you want to send bulk e-mail. This field is also optional.
4. **Subject:** This field is used to write the title or subject of the email message for which you are writing the message. If you skip this field, then the following message appears, when you click on a send button: **"Send this message without a subject or text in the body?"**

Note: A valid e-mail address will always have contained a special symbol @ after the username.

For example, smith@hotmail.com, agrima@rediffmail.com, yashvardhan@yahoo.co.in are all valid e-mail addresses.

Check Your Progress

State whether the following statements are True or False.

1. E-mail is a method for sending and receiving messages electronically.
2. Is palvigupta86@gmail.com is a valid e-mail address.
3. Indexing software is the process of crawling or searching for the websites that contains the links of web pages for the required information.

★ **Let's understand the various components of a message Window.**

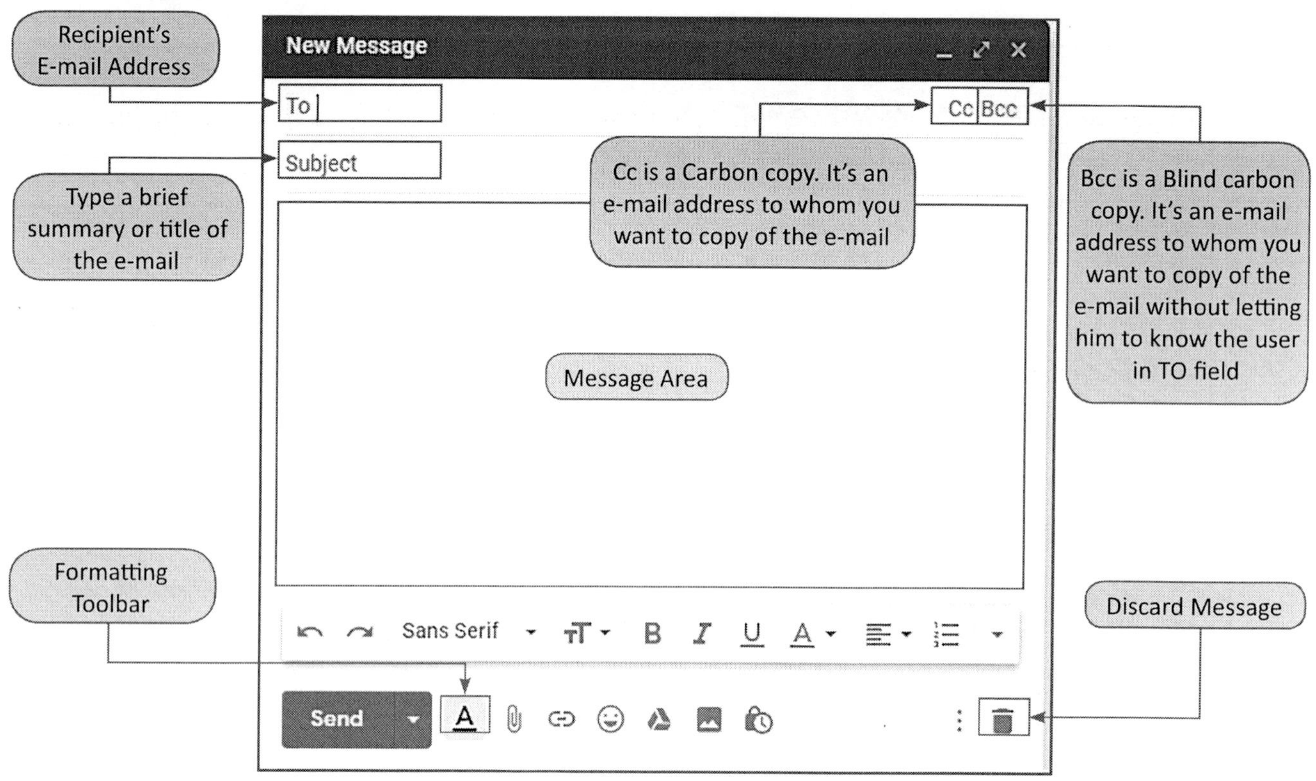

Figure 2.11: Components of E-mail

✱ Let's know the difference between Cc and Bcc fields.

Difference between Cc and Bcc

S.No.	Cc	Bcc
1.	It stands for Carbon Copy.	It stands for Blind Carbon Copy.
2.	E-mail addresses in Cc field are displayed to all the recipients.	E-mail addresses in Bcc field are not displayed to any of the recipients.
3.	It is used to keep other people in the loop.	It is used to secretively send e-mail copy to other people.
4.	When Reply to All option is used, all Cc recipients would receive the reply.	On Reply to All, Bcc recipients do not receive a reply.
5.	Cc is often used when a group of people are engaged in teamwork.	Bcc is often used to send bulk e-mail. Recipients are generally not part of a team.

MEMORIZE

Cc is the carbon copy and is a way to send copy of e-mail messages to multiple recipients at the same time.

Bcc is a blind carbon copy and is a way to send an e-mail messages to multiple recipients without letting them to know each other.

✱ Let's know how to create an E-mail account.

Creating an e-mail account

By this time, you should know how to create an e-mail account for sending and receiving messages electronically. This can be done from any website such as Google.com, yahoo.com, rediffmail.com, and so on.

Here we are using google.com for creating an account:

Steps to create an E-mail account:

1. Connect your computer with internet and open any web browser.
2. Type in the address bar of a browser Window. It will open the google page and show you two icons on the right-hand side of the Window. (*Figure 2.12*)

Figure 2.12: Opening search engine Google.com

3. Click on Gmail at the top right corner of the page.
4. You will now be in the **Sign in** section. As you don't have a Google account yet, you need to create one. Click **Create an account**. (*Figure 2.13*)

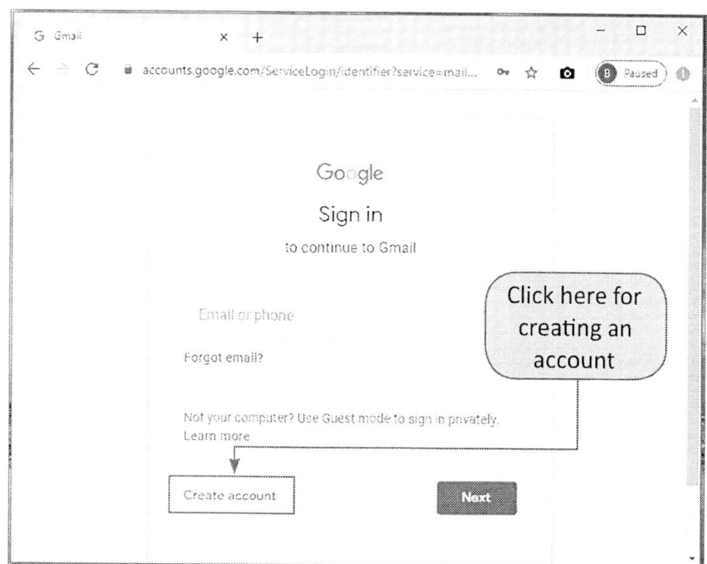

Figure 2.13: Create an account

5. Doing so takes you to the first page in the account creation section. Type the **First name** and the **Last name**. Then create a Gmail **Username**. Type your preferred **Password**. Then click on **Next** button. (*Figure 2.14*)

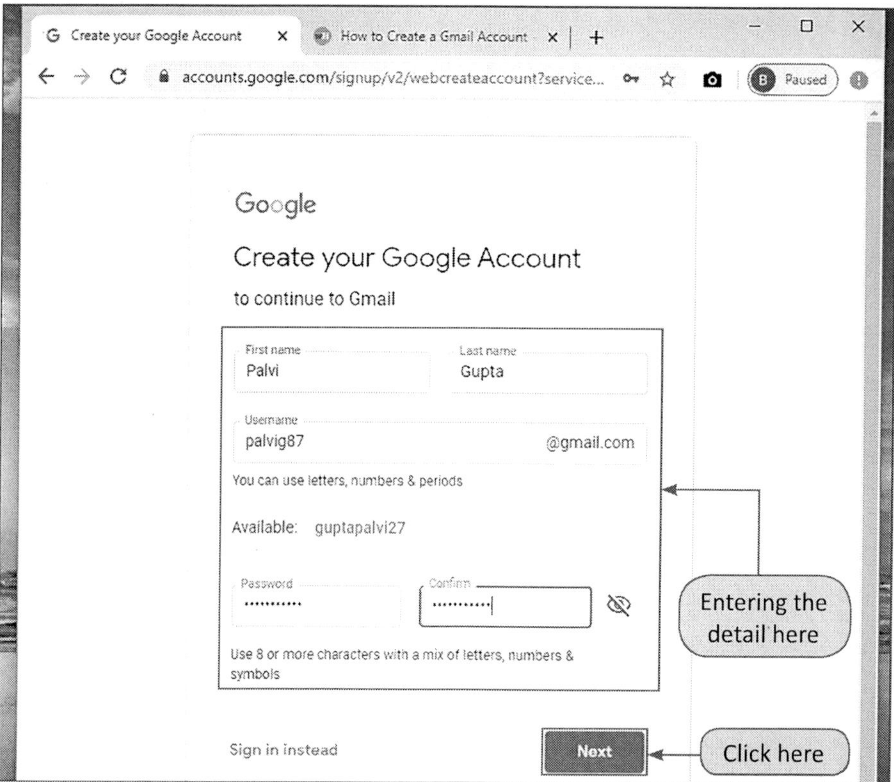

Figure 2.14: Filling the form

6. Type your phone number. A verification code will be sent on your mobile number. Enter the code. Click on **Next** Button.

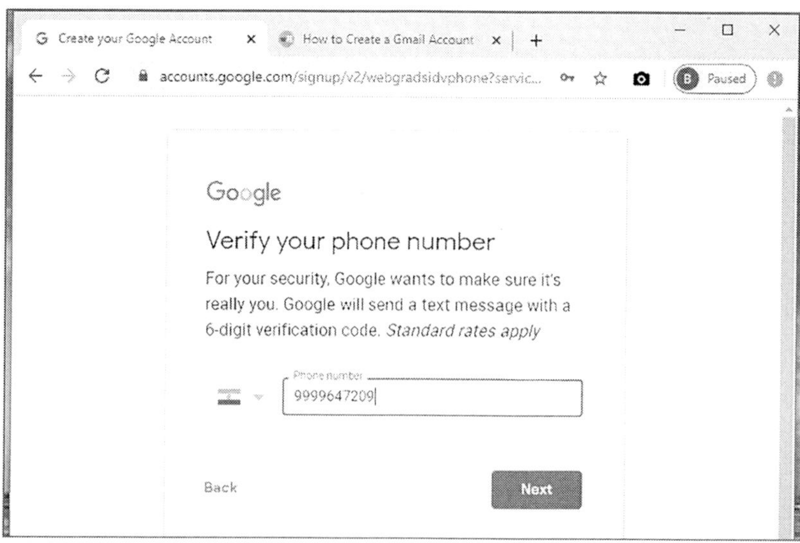

Figure 2.15: Verification of Phone Number

7. Type the **Recovery email address, Your Birthday** and **Gender**. Then click on **Next** Button. Click on **I agree** button.

   Your Gmail Account is opened.

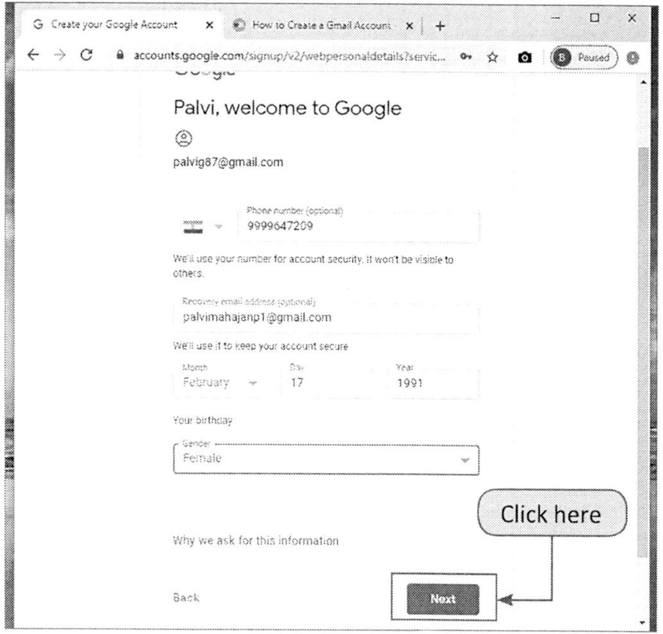

Figure 2.16: Enter user Details

* **Next step is to log in your account and to see the mails.**

Sign into your e-mail account and viewing your messages

After creating an e-mail account, you will be able to open it and view the mails stored in your inbox. To view all these mails, follow the given steps:

1. Type **http://www.gmail.com** in your browser Window.
2. The screen will appear asking for entering **Username.**
3. Click on **Next** button to enter the **Password.**
4. Click on **Sign in** button. The e-mail account Window of the Gmail will appear.
5. Click on the **Inbox** button on the left pane of the Window to view all the received messages.
6. Various messages will appear in the right pane. Click on any e-mail to read it. The message will be displayed.

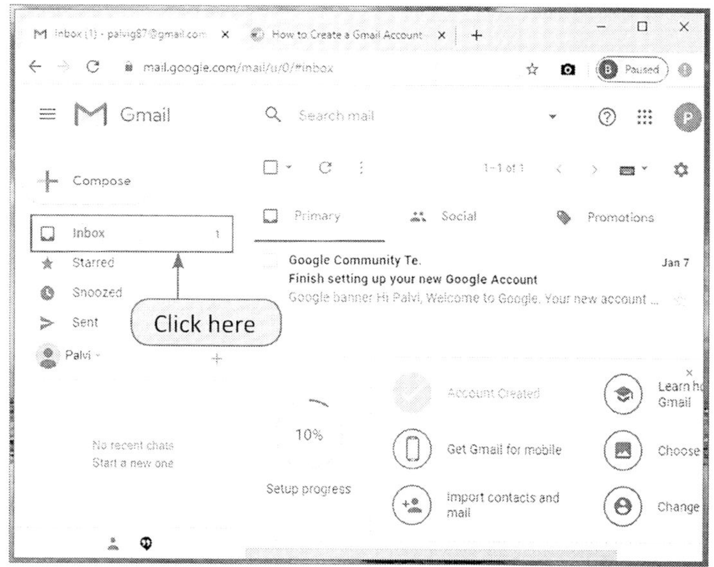

Figure 2.16: Gmail Window

Deleting E-mail Messages

It is a good practice to delete e-mail messages which are of no use to avoid clogging up your inbox with junk mails. So, this section will let you know how to delete the messages from your inbox.

Delete e-mail messages

To delete e-mail messages, do this:

1: Log into your e-mail account and make sure you are on the dashboard (main page) of your account.

2: Go to your inbox and view all messages.

3: Check your messages which are no longer to be needed. When you have identified these, click the select box to the far left of each e-mail so that a tick appears in the box.

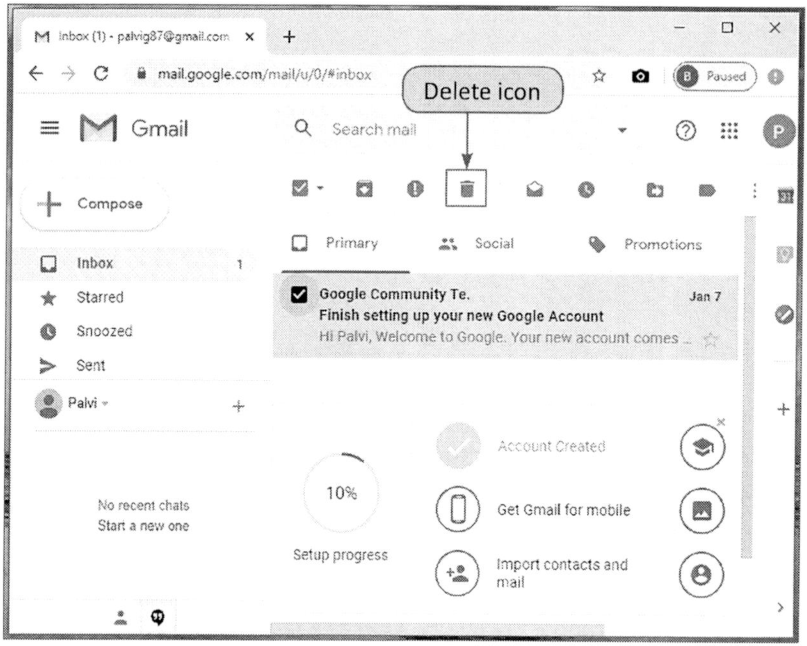

Figure 2.17: Selecting mail to be deleted

4: Once you have selected an e-mail that you wish to delete, click the delete icon. You can also delete an e-mail by opening it and then clicking the delete icon.

5: Your selected e-mail will be deleted.

6: If you wish to delete more than one e-mail, click the select box of each e-mail that you wish to delete, as mentioned in Step 3.

7: Click Delete once again.

Sending E-mails to multiple recipients

One of the most important features of an e-mail account is that you can send the same message to multiple recipients at the same time. This can happen by using the fields CC or Bcc. Cc means **carbon copy** and Bcc means **blind carbon copy**.

✱ **Let's know how you can use these fields for the same.**

Sending e-mails to multiple recipients

Steps for sending e-mails to multiple recipients, do this:

1. Sign into your e-mail account by entering Username and Password.

2. A dashboard appears for your account. In the top left, click on **Compose** button.
3. A new e-mail Window will open. In the "To" field, add **recipients**. If you want, you can also add **recipients** in the «Cc» and «Bcc» fields.
4. Type the subject for which you are sending mail.
5. Write your complete message.
6. At the bottom of the page, click on **Send** button. (*Figure 2.18*)

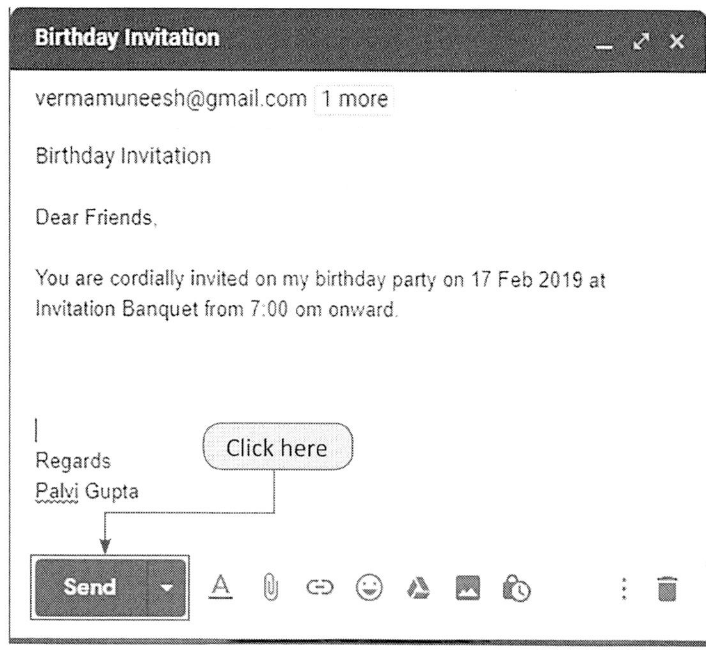

Figure 2.18: Sending mail to multiple recipients

★ Let's know the various advantages and limitations of E-mail.

Advantages of E-mail

The advantages of E-mail are:

1. **Eliminate the use of stationery:** This technical method has eliminated the use of pen and paper methodology for sending and receiving messages. Now, you have to type the e-mail address of those people to whom you want to send messages.
2. **Economical:** Sending and receiving messages through e-mail is an economic method as it cut down the cost of purchasing stationery and spending money on posting through couriers especially, if it is an overseas mail.
3. **Fastest media:** It is the fastest way to communicate with people as the sending and receiving of messages is done in seconds. If you want to send an urgent message to your friend who is sitting abroad, then he can receive an e-mail in a very short span of time.
4. **Records of messages maintained:** You can maintain the records of the messages which have sent and received along with the e-mail addresses of senders and receivers which can be used further reference.
5. **Attachments:** Through e-mail, you can not only send textual messages but also send files by an attachment feature which enables you to attach any type of file (.docx, .xlsx, .pdf, .wav, .jpg, .gif) etc.
6. **Multiple recipients:** The same e-mail can be sent to multiple recipients at the same time by using the feature Cc or Bcc.

Limitations of e-mail

The limitations of e-mail are:

1. **Technical knowledge:** A person who is sending mail must have some technical knowledge and should know the meaning of its various features. For e-mails, the e-mail account must also be created.
2. **Hardware and software requirement:** As it is an electronic mail, the foremost necessity is the computer system and internet connection. Software that supports sending and receiving e-mail is also required.
3. **Impersonal:** It is an impersonal method as it does not involve handwriting and signature of a person.
4. **Virus attack:** Most viruses come through e-mail which contains attachment of files. When you download those files and open them, they contain the virus that can disrupt the normal functioning of your system or might crash your system also.
5. **Spam mail:** Sometimes you receive unwanted mails from various agency whose main purpose is to get your personal information such as to know your bank account number or credit/debit card number by tempting you to avail different offers. These kinds of mails are spam mails or unsolicited mails that may create the problem for the e-mail account holder.

2. Chatting

Chatting is another service which is provided by web

When two or more people are communicating with each other digitally or electronically then it is known as **Chatting** or **Web Chatting**. For chatting through computers or mobile phones, it is mandatory that both persons should be online. In other words, both persons should be active on internet at that point of time. Chatting cannot be done offline.

Extra Byte

UNIX "talk" was a first network chat software which was used for chatting in 1970s.

For example, **WhatsApp** is a most popular internet application where two or more persons are chatting through textual messages by using mobile phones. When there is a communication between several people at the same time, it is called **group chatting** and when it is done between two persons only, then it is known as **individual chatting**. But, in both cases, all participants must be online.

The protocol used for chatting is **Internet Relay Chat (IRC).**

Several browser interfaces provide the chat facility these days such as **Instant messaging**, **Windows**, **Skype** and **ICQ** (Short form of 'I Seek You'). With the invent of 3G technology not only text data but video data can also be streamlined at the same time.

Definition

Chatting is a virtual means of communication where two or more people communicate from any part of the world. It does not require face-to-face communication and physical presence.

MEMORIZE

There are two basic modes of chatting on internet.
Text based chat: It enables users to communicate through text messages.
Multimedia based chat: It enables users to communicate through audio and video transmission of data.

Check Your Progress

Multiple choice questions.

1. A web service that send and receive messages in real time is known as:
   a. Instant chat b. E-reservation c. E-learning d. E-mail
2. Another name of chatting is:
   a. Web chatting b. Online chatting c. Both a. and b. d. None of these

Precaution: Chatting can be dangerous. So, for safe chatting, never give your personal information to anybody. Be sure that chat id would not reveal your e-mail address if you are chatting with unknown person.

3. Video Conferencing

The video conferencing is a virtual face-to-face online communication between two or more people who are sitting at different locations around the world. While communicating, it is necessary that the participants of video conferencing must be online.

Through this web service, they are able to transmit both the audio and video data. (*Figure 2.19*)

The first video call was made in **1964**. A caller could not only hear the voice on the other side of the line, but also could see his/her picture.

In video conferencing, all users must have a web camera known as **webcam** for fetching the video and a microphone for transmitting voice data.

Figure 2.19: Video Conferencing

Definition

Video conferencing is a technology where two or more persons can communicate with each other face-to-face through audio and video. This usually refers to communication between two or three or more users who are located at different locations.

Components of Video Conferencing:

1. Computer System with at least 1 GB of RAM and a dual-core processor.
2. High-resolution webcam capable of producing high-quality video.
3. Microphone and Speaker.
4. A fast network connection.
5. Video conferencing software. (*Figure 2.20*)

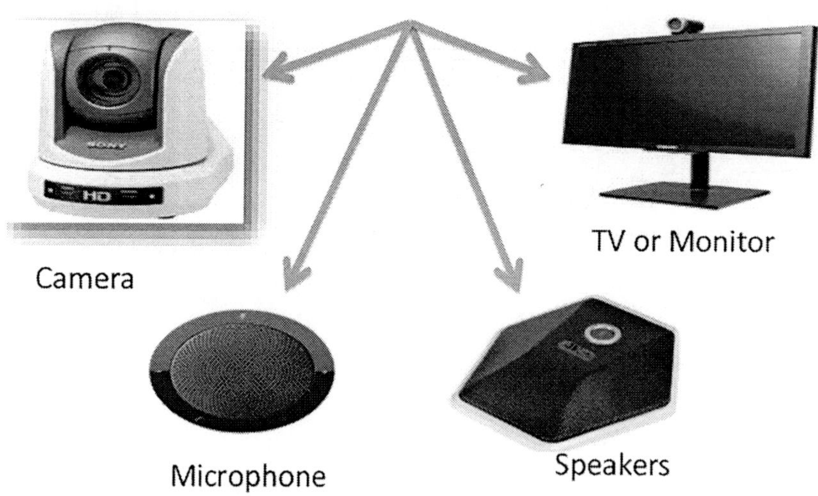

Figure 2.20: Components of Video Conferencing

Video Conferencing Software

Video conferencing software are freely available on the internet. Some of them are briefly explained below:

Zoom Meetings offers a video conferencing and messaging solution for desktop and mobile devices. It is very easy to set up, and offer a wide range of scalable features.

GoToMeeting is the standalone web conferencing service provided by LogMeIn. It provides an integration of audio and video conferencing, as well as screen sharing.

TrueConf is the best free video conferencing tools for remote teams, which provides various facilities such as video conference recording, chat, screen sharing, slideshow, reactions and much more.

Skype is a VoIP software application that enables users to share text, voice, and video messages between computers, tablets, mobile devices and smart watches through internet.

* **Let's know various advantages and disadvantages of video conferencing.**

Advantages of Video Conferencing

The advantages of Video Conferencing are:

1. **Reduced traveling cost:** As video conferencing does not require physical presence, there is no travelling cost which would incur during the meeting.
2. **Increased productivity:** The people meet in the virtual world where the discussions takes place instantly without meeting each other and the decisions about a problem are thus made faster. This leads to increased productivity.
3. **Eco-friendly:** Since conferencing between people is possible even without travelling from one place to another through video conferencing, a lot of petrol or fuel is saved.
4. **No time constraint:** Video conferencing can be done at any time wherever you stay. There is no time boundation to do it. Even if the members are at different parts of the world, all they have to do is login from their machines.
5. **Better Communication:** You can interact with people through images, videos, audio, and text by this web service. Screen sharing is also possible for more clarity and explanation of ideas.

MEMORIZE

Main advantage of video conferencing over teleconferencing is that users can see each other. When a video conference is held for informal purposes, it is called a **video call** or **video chat**.

Disadvantages of video conferencing:

The disadvantages of Video Conferencing are:

1. **Technical issues:** Video conferencing is highly dependent on high speed internet connectivity. If internet connection would not be fat enough, then there will not be a successful video conferencing as it will create interruption. These types of technical issues can delay the discussions among the participants sitting in remote areas.
2. **Expensive:** As it requires a high-quality web camera, speaker, microphone and other hardware devices, it is an expensive mode of communication.
3. **Lack of technical knowledge:** Participants of video conferencing must have a prior technical knowledge as to what all devices are required, creating the account, how to login the system, how they can share the screen and many more.
4. **Lack of personal contact:** A handshake and an eye contact are essential aspects of many business meetings. Some meetings require face-to-face interaction. But, video conferencing is a virtual meeting and you cannot judge people without talking them personally.
5. **Delay in communication:** There is a short time lag between speaking and receiving a response that can interrupt the flow of a conversation.

Do: Be sure that your camera is properly positioned on the main monitor you will be using for the video conference. Also, turn off all notifications, closing or minimizing running applications and muting cell phones, streaming radio, etc., to avoid distraction during video conference.

Check Your Progress

Answer the following questions.

1. Give two examples of video conferencing from daily life.
2. State one advantage of video conferencing over face-to-face business meeting.
3. Write down the components of video conferencing.

4. E-Learning

E-learning is an online method of learning and delivering information to students of universities or the employees of companies. E-learning can also be termed as a network enabled where the skills and knowledge are transferred digitally. A large group of people can participate for e-learning without travelling to remote places. E-learning does not require classroom teaching and therefore no physical presence is required.

Most universities design the courses in such a way that the students can register themselves online and get its content and

CBT is a Computer-based Training Services that refers to the use of computers as a main component in education.

WBT is a Web-based Training is similar to CBT and is delivered over the internet using a web browser.

CSCL is a Computer Supported Collaborative Learning latest method used for teaching and learning online.

free lectures. These courses also help an individual to assess their knowledge online. Various online quizzes help in evaluation of the knowledge of an individual.

E-learning is an online method of learning and delivering information to students of university/school/colleges or the employees of companies. It is an online method for delivering information digitally.

Extra Byte

The first testing machine was invented in year 1924 that allowed students to test themselves. In 1954, "BF Skinner", a Harvard Professor, invented the "teaching machine", which enabled schools to administer programmed instruction to their students

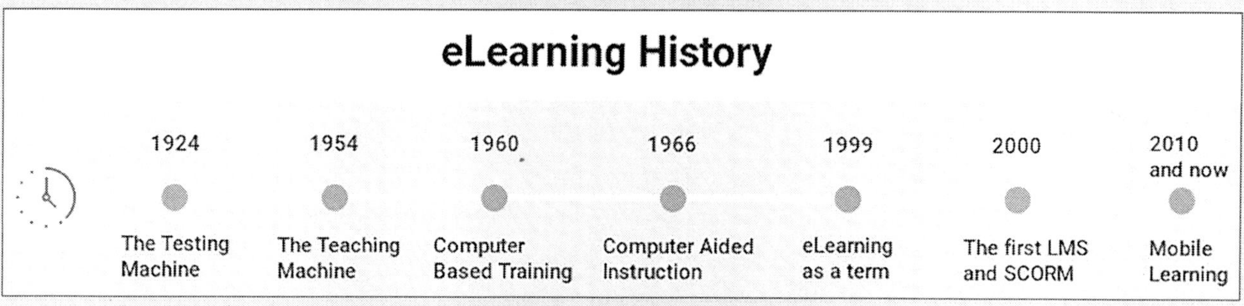

✱ **Let's know various advantages and disadvantages of E-learning.**

Advantages of e-learning

The advantages of e-learning are:

1. E-learning is helpful for handicapped students who cannot go from one place to another for classroom teaching.
2. No need to attend institution to get information.
3. It is a virtual teaching method and therefore no classroom teaching is required.
4. It is an inexpensive method to get knowledge as it does not involve high fee to be paid.
5. The E- Learning provides an opportunity to the student to complete the course at their own pace.
6. The universities from across the globe keep offering the on-line courses. This is possible through E-learning. Online courses also provide certification to their students.
7. It is a platform where the students can share their knowledge through online discussion forums.
8. E-learning promotes active and independent learning.
9. Students may have the option to select learning materials that meets their level of knowledge and interest.

Disadvantages of e-learning

The disadvantages of e-learning are:

1. The first and foremost important thing is that a person should have proper hardware and software for online learning.
2. Fast internet connection should be there.
3. Students waste a lot of time in searching sites for good online learning material.

4. There is no group study and therefore decreases their motivation for learning concept.
5. Sometimes it becomes boring for them to view long video lectures.
6. Learners with low motivation or bad study habits may fall behind.
7. Instructor may not always be available when students are studying or need help.
8. Lab work is difficult to simulate in a virtual classroom.

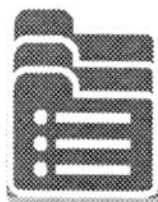

MEMORIZE

Some popular E-learning sites are: **Khan Academy, Coursera, W3 Schools, Ted-Ed, Codecademy, Open Culture, Open Yale Courses, Academic Earth, Unacademy, Bijus, etc.**

Check Your Progress

Fill in the blanks.

1. _______________ is a Computer-based Training Services that refers to the use of computers as a main component in education.
2. _______________ is an online method of learning and delivering information to students of university or the employees of companies.
3. _______________ is a Computer Supported Collaborative Learning latest method used for teaching and learning online.

5. E-Reservation

E-Reservation System is an online reservation system where you can book your tickets for hotels, railways, airways, online. It is the system that enables the customer to book a ticket without travelling to the booking system that may consume a lot of time and money. Since, such systems are internally integrated with the database of the companies, the booking system helps to monitor access to the client as long as there is availability of the seats or rooms.

Figure 2.21 shows checking the availability and booking seats for railways.

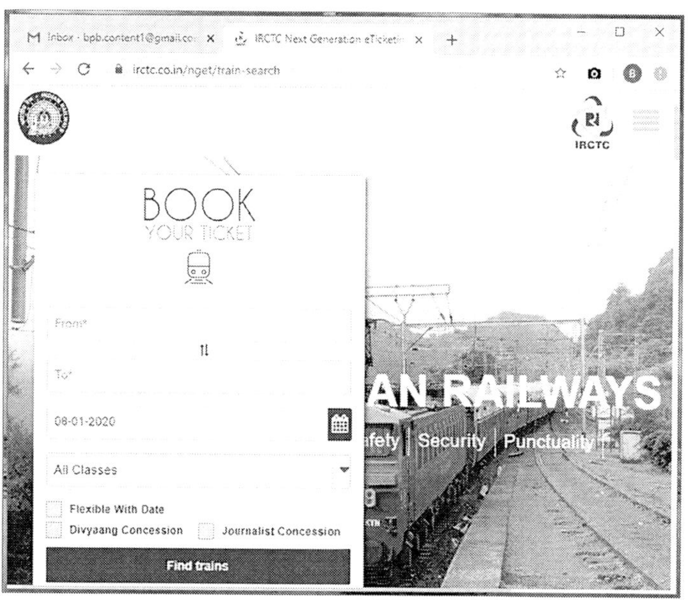

Figure 2.21: Booking ticket online

Definition

E-reservation is a method of booking online tickets for railways, flight journey, movies through internet.

★ **Let's know various advantages and disadvantages of E-reservation.**

Advantages of E-reservation

The advantages of E-reservation are:

1. You can check the availability of the seats by sitting at home.
2. As this service is available 24x7, you can avail this facility as per your own convenience.
3. It saves time as there is no need to go to the booking office.
4. You can also cancel your booking without going to the concerned office.
5. It provides global access to the customers for booking from anywhere at any time.
6. It reduces administrative costs for businesses as fewer human agents are required

Disadvantages of E-reservation

The disadvantages of E-reservation are:

1. In order to book through an online booking system, one must have an access to internet.
2. It is required to be updated every time with customer's requirement.

MEMORIZE

Some of the websites for e-reservation are:

www.irctc.co.in
www.makemytrip.com
www.booking.com
www.bookmyshow.com

★ **Let's know the various steps for booking Railway Tickets on TRCTC website from a browser enabled mobile phone**

Step 1: type the URL https://www.irctc.co.in in address bar of the browser Window.

You will see the home page of the website as shown below:

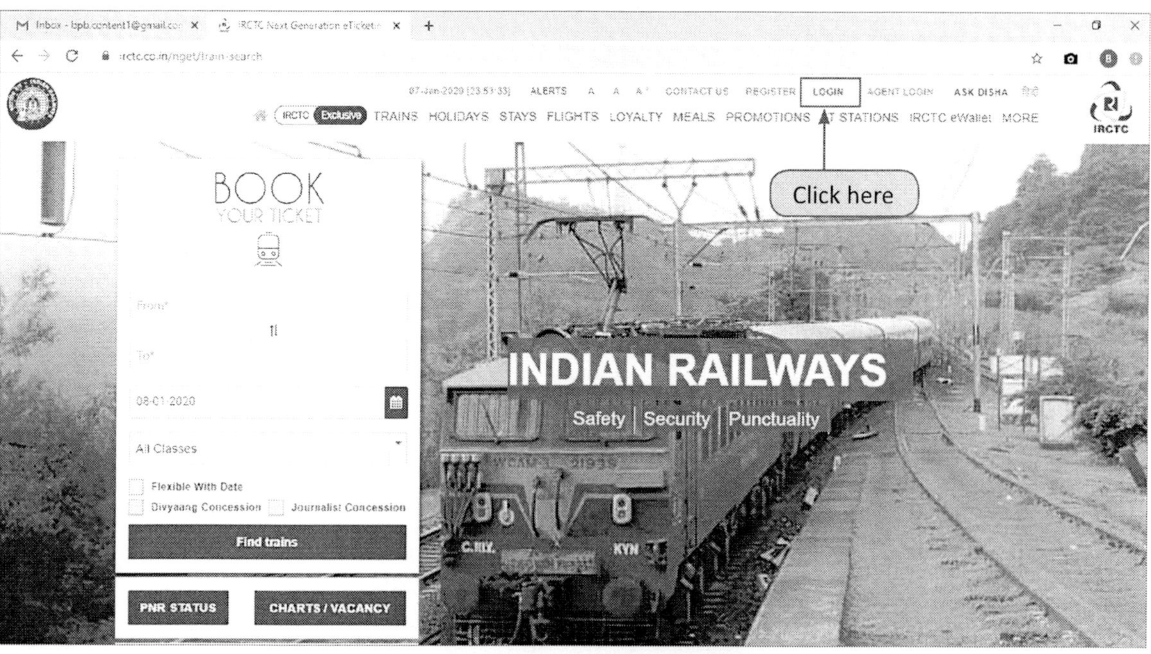

Fig 2.22: The IRCTC home page

Step 2: Click on the **Login** button. The login page appears as shown in *figure 2.23*.

Step 3: Enter your existing IRCTC **User ID** and **Password**.

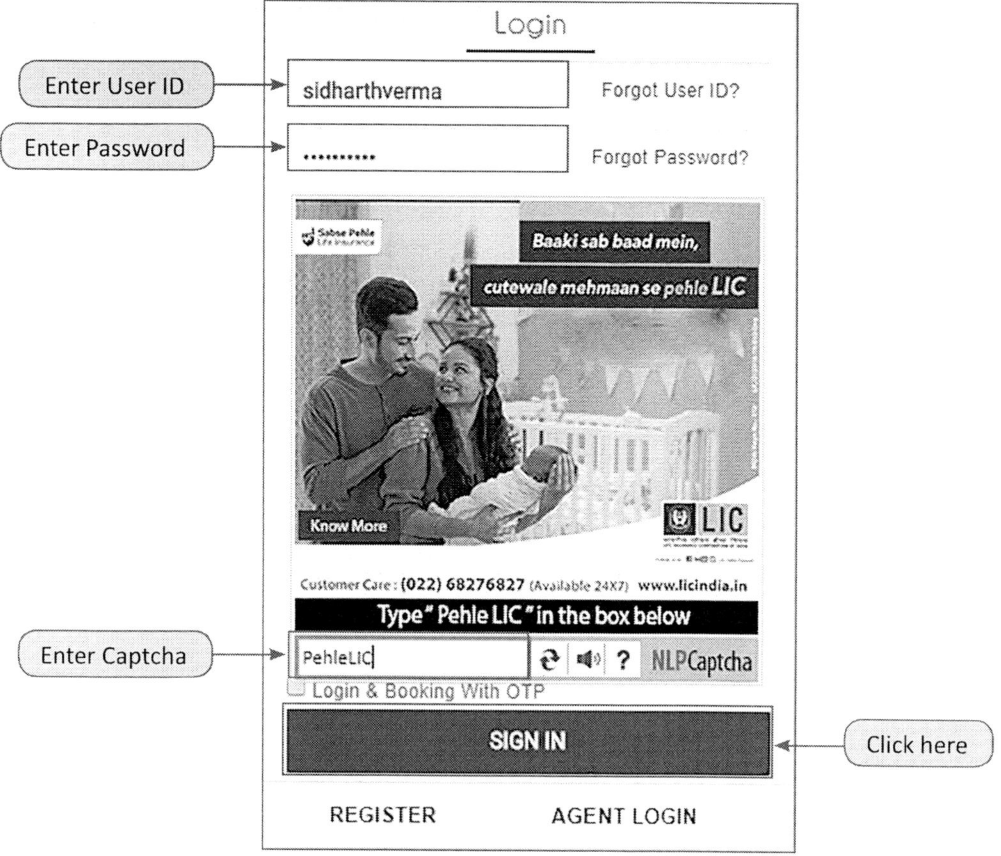

Figure 2.23: Login Page of IRCTC

Step 4: Enter the source and destination address of your journey. You have to also enter the date of journey. You may add the class of the seat in this screen or in a later screen. Finally, click on the **Find** trains button.

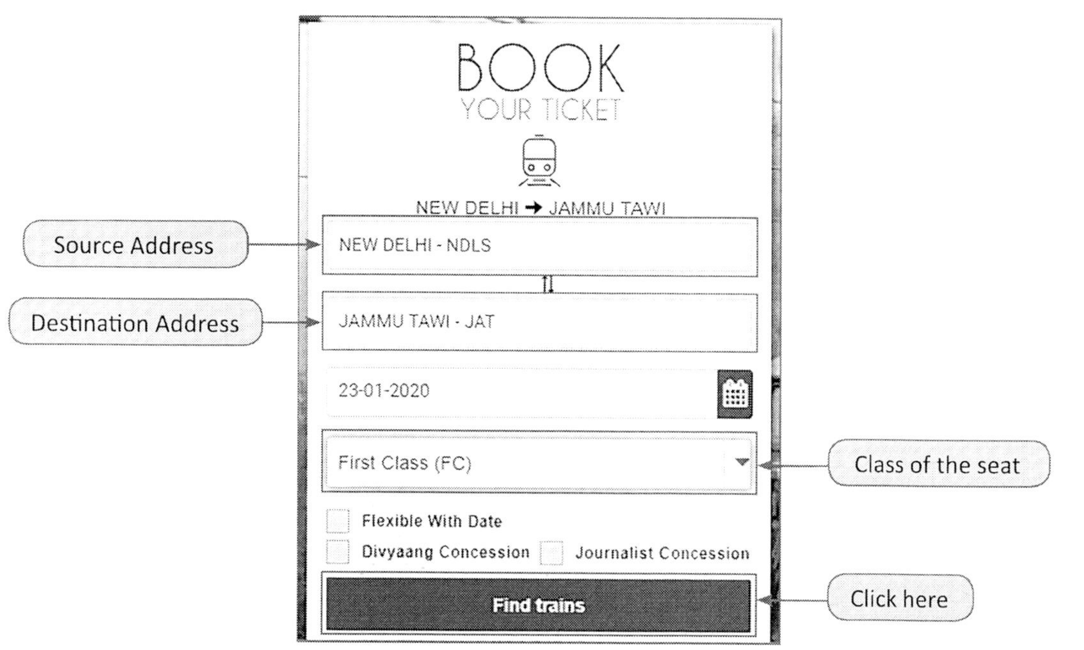

Figure 2.24: Source and destination address added

Step 5: A list of trains comes up that take you from the source to the destination. At this stage, you may choose your class of seat as well as check the availability of the ticket, click on the **Check availability & fare** button for the seat.

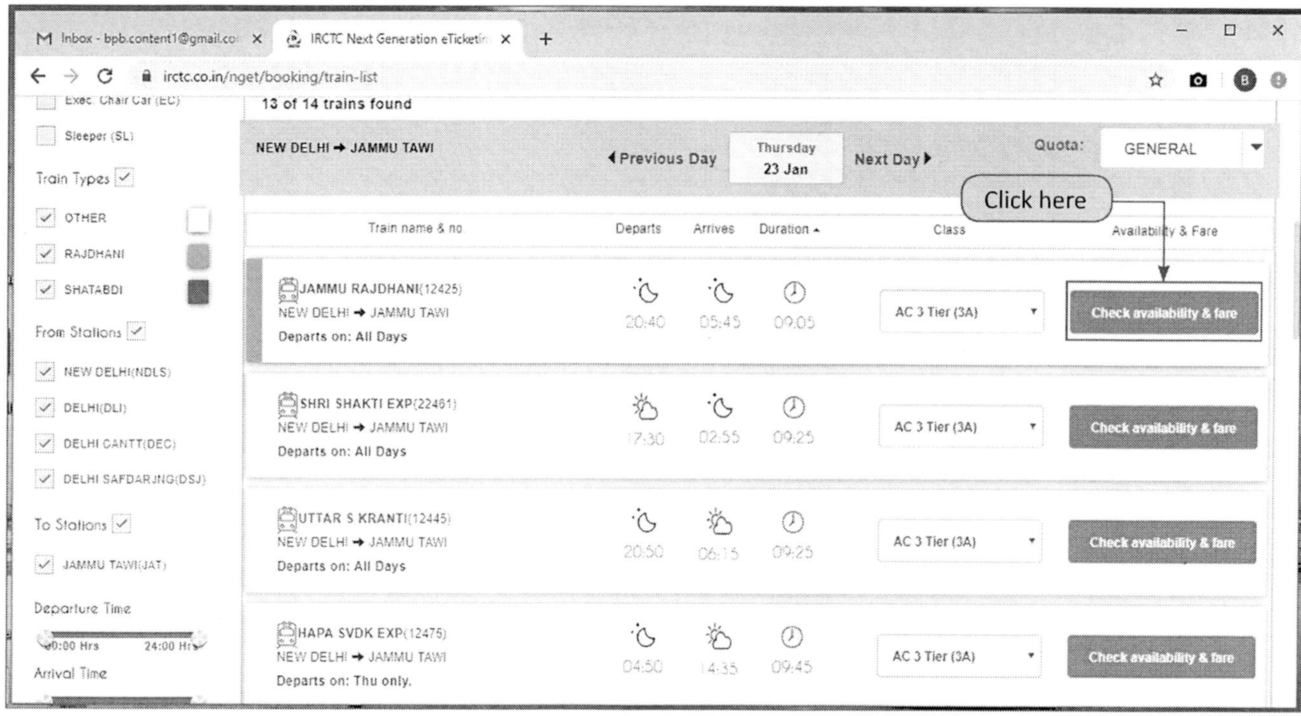

Figure 2.25: List of trains shows up on page

Step 6: The screen shows up with the kind of availability that is there for the ticket. If the ticket is available for booking, **AVAILABLE** shows up. For **RAC** seats, RAC shows up and **WL** for Waiting List, the following kind of links show up.

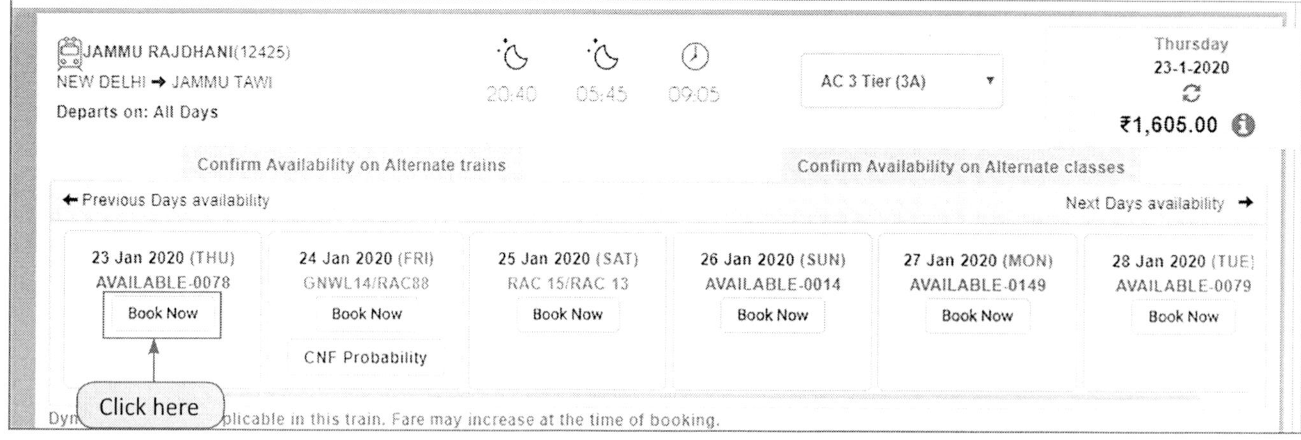

Figure 2.26: Seat availability status on various dates around the booking date

Step 7: Click on the **Book Now** button. You will be greeted by the screen for making available the people who wish to occupy the seat(s).

Step 8: Enter Name, age and gender of the person with the preference of the seat (lower, middle or upper) and Food choices (Veg, Non-veg or No food).

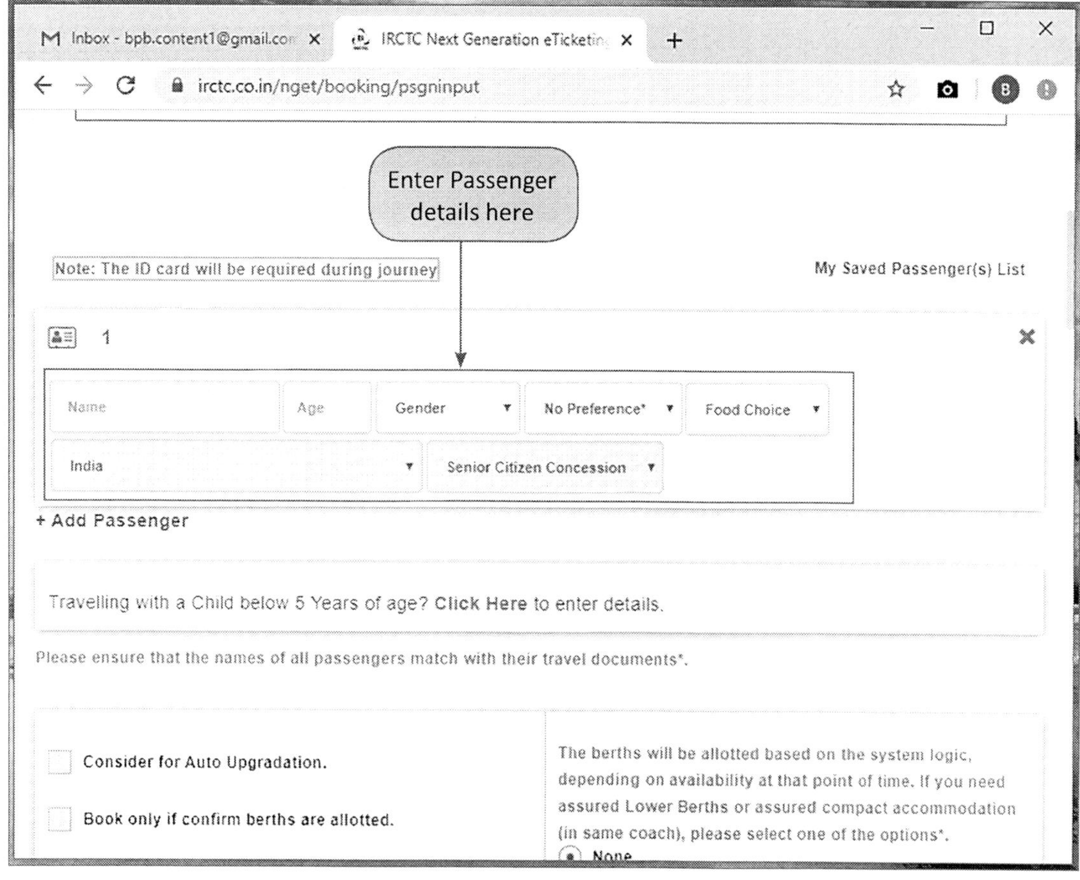

Figure 2.27: Enter Passenger details

Step 9: After entering passenger details, respond to the **Captcha** query. Select the payment mode to proceed and click on **Continue Booking** button to go the next steps.

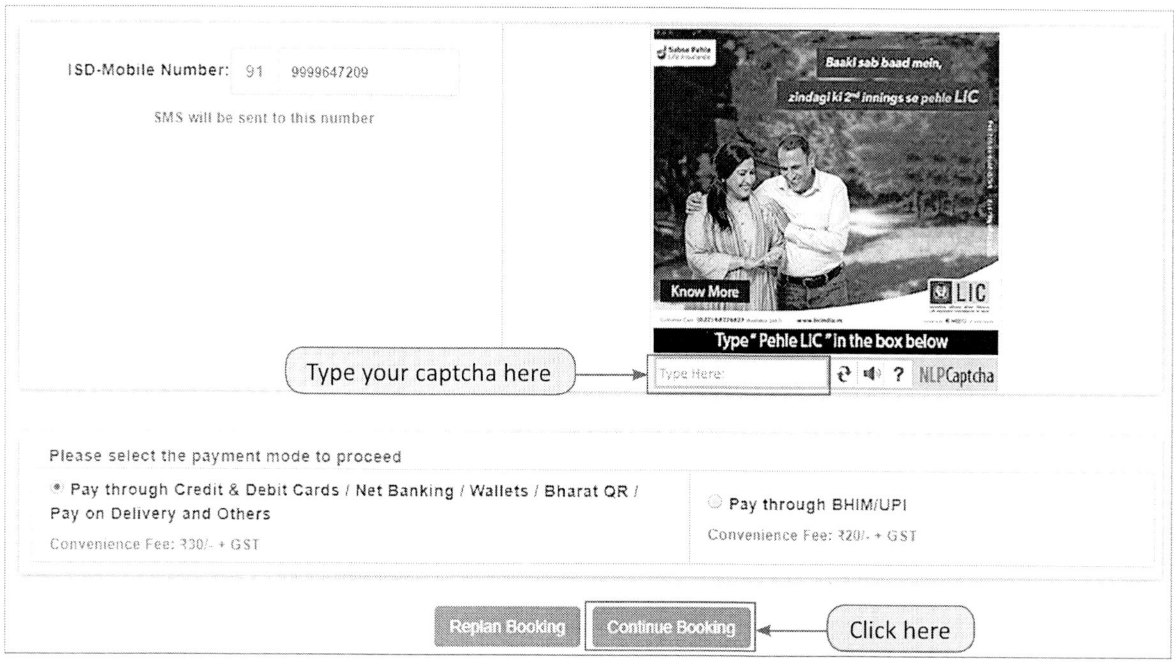

Figure 2.28: Payment Mode selected

Step 10: Seat availability details and passenger details are displayed. Click on the **Continue Booking** option.

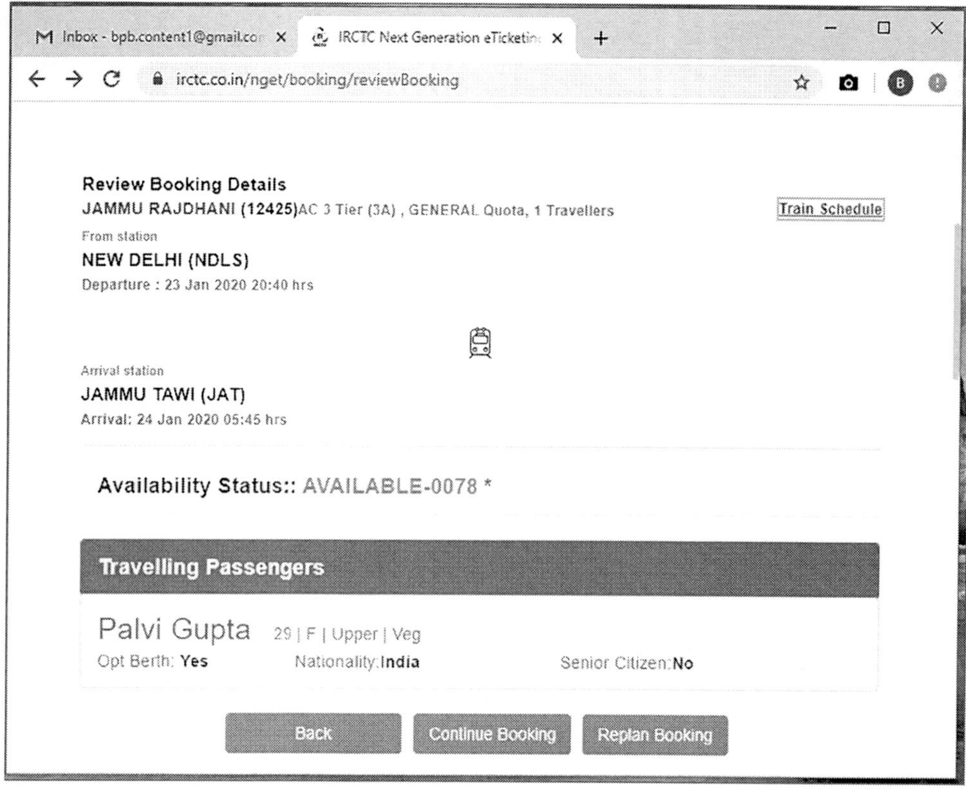

Figure 2.29: Ticket booking details

Step 11: Click on the **Credit Card/ Debit Card/UPI (Powered by IRCTC)**. The user will be directed to the **Safe and Secure Payment page.**

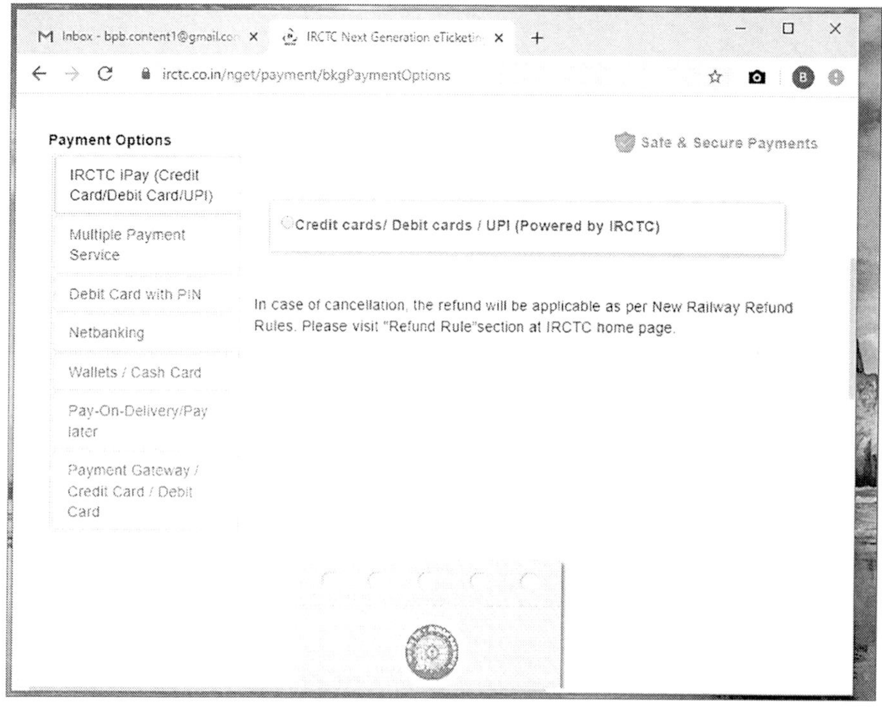

Figure 2.30: Payment options to pay for ticket fare

Step 12: Select any one of your choice method of pay. Click on the **Make Payment** from the link on Webpage.

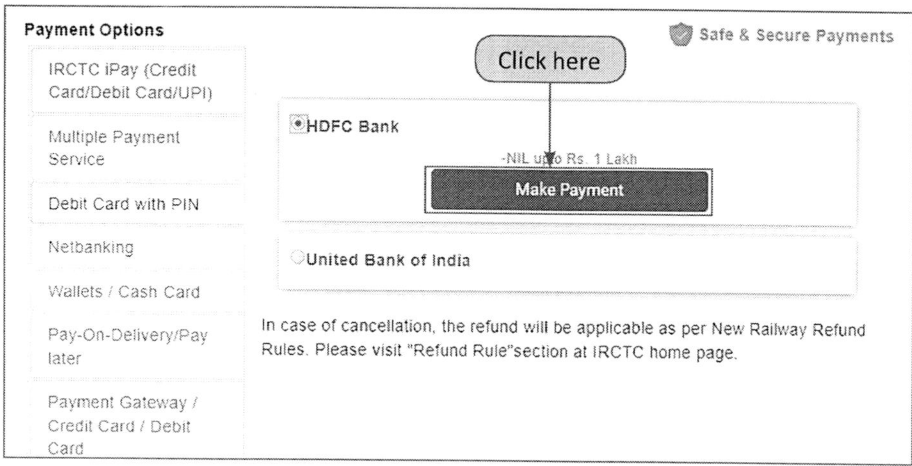

Figure 2.31: Options to make the payment process

Step 13: Enter the details of your debit/Credit card, expiry date, CVV number, ATM Pin and enter the characters box. Click on the **Pay** button finally.

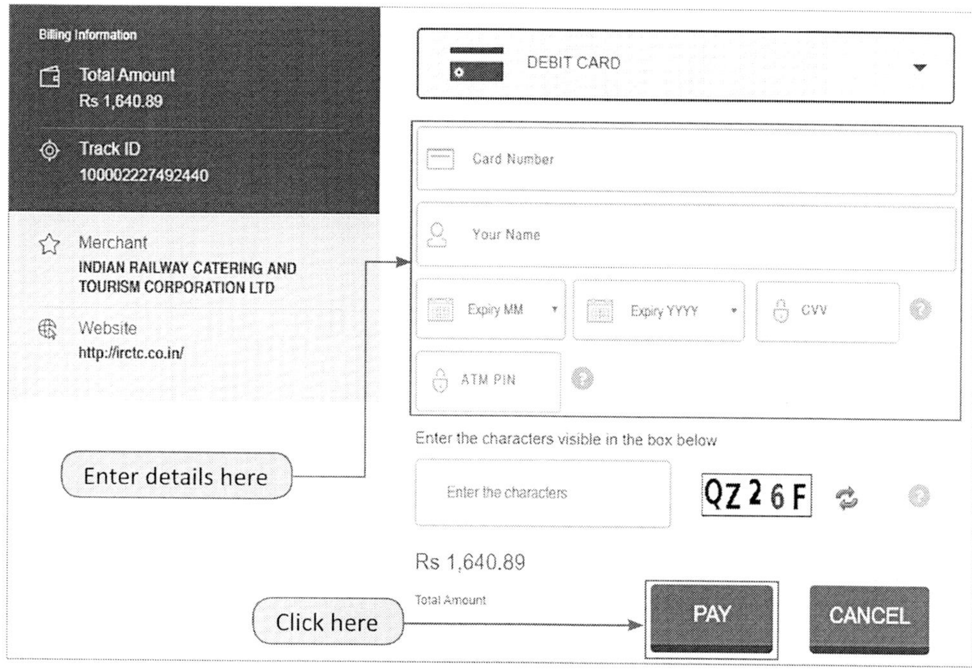

Figure 2.32: Payment process in progress

Step 14: After the above steps the tickets get booked in that particular train and shown to you. You may take a printout of the same.

Do's and Dont's:

- A senior citizen can avail senior citizen concession by clicking on senior citizen option.
- While doing e-reservation, make sure that the process is completed successfully and e-ticket is generated.
- Don't press back or refresh button while making online payment for e-ticket.

Check Your Progress

Answer the following questions.

1. What is the full form of IRCTC?
2. Give examples of e-reservation sites.
3. Write one word for making reservations of flight or movie through internet.

6. E-Shopping

One of the greatest advantages of internet is online shopping which is known as **e-shopping**. Now, you can sell and buy products online without going to the market. E-Shopping has not only changed the way consumers are shopping for the products but has also changed how the product moves from manufacturers to the end user. Now, customers can purchase various products and avail different facilities which are offered through online shopping. Payment has to be made through secure transaction. (*Figure 2.33*)

Figure 2.33: Online shopping

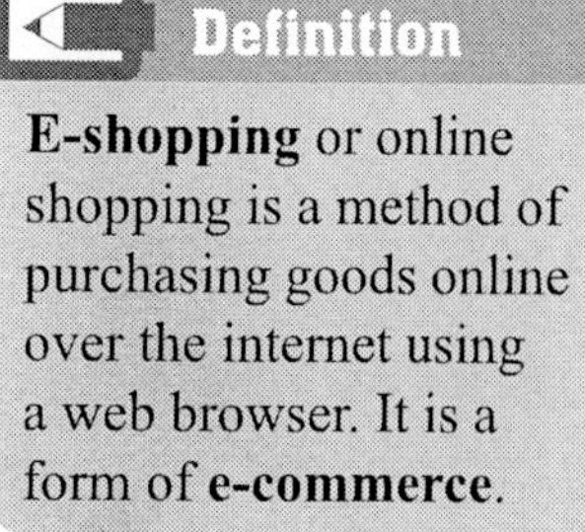

Definition

E-shopping or online shopping is a method of purchasing goods online over the internet using a web browser. It is a form of **e-commerce**.

✱ Let's know various advantages and disadvantages of E-shopping.

Advantages of E-Shopping

The advantages of e-shopping are:

1. It reduces time for customers as they can do search from their home and compare prices.
2. They can also avail discount or other kind of offers which are provided by different sites for a specific product.
3. The payment can be done either through debit or credit card; so, no cash is required during the receiving of a product.
4. It helps in delivering the products from manufacturer to the customer without storing large number of products.
5. Businesses benefit from immediate funds availability and mostly customers pay for the product through e-payment online.

Extra Byte

Some popular e-shopping sites are: Amazon.com, Ebay.com, Craigslist.com, Etsy.com, Walmart.com, Wish.com, HomeDepot.com, Flipcart.com, Target.com

Disadvantages of E shopping

The disadvantages of e-shopping are:

1. Customers are not able to know the exact quality of the product as they are not able to touch and feel the products.
2. Different sites show different prices for the same product that may lead confusion to the customers.

3. People who are sitting in remote areas may not have a technical knowledge to access and order products online.
4. Businesses have to manage the logistics of delivering products just-in-time.
5. Businesses have to continually protect against fraud and returning of the products sold.
6. It may cause delay in shipping. Moreover shipping charges make product expensive specially in low cost items.

Do's and Dont's:

- Always place orders from a secure connection.
- Before entering any personal or credit card info onto a shopping site look to see if the web address on the page begins with "https:", not "http:"
- If you are buying a Gift Card, read the Terms and Conditions.
- Don't use an e-store that requires more information than necessary to make the sale.
- Do not use a debit card or check as these do not have the same security protections in place for you should a problem arise.
- Avoid offers that seem "too good to be true".

Check Your Progress

Multiple choice questions.

1. It is the service that helps in purchasing goods online:
   a. E-purchasing b. E-shopping c. E-learning
2. ____________ is a form of e-commerce.
   a. E-shopping b. E-learning c. E-group

7. Social Networking

Internet has brought people together through social networking. It is a platform where people communicate with each other, share their thoughts and opinions without being close geographically. People of common interest can interact with each other from anywhere in the world through internet. With the popularity of social networking sites, more and more people can become part of an online community. They will be able to make new friends as well as share their lives online from wherever they are located. Business organization can showcase their products online in which the people are interested, they follow and review those products. Various sites such as Twitter, Facebook has enabled people to talk about recent updates in country, share their views, commenting on them etc. A company may use social networking to demonstrate its customer service level and enrich its relationships with consumers. (*Figure 2.34*)

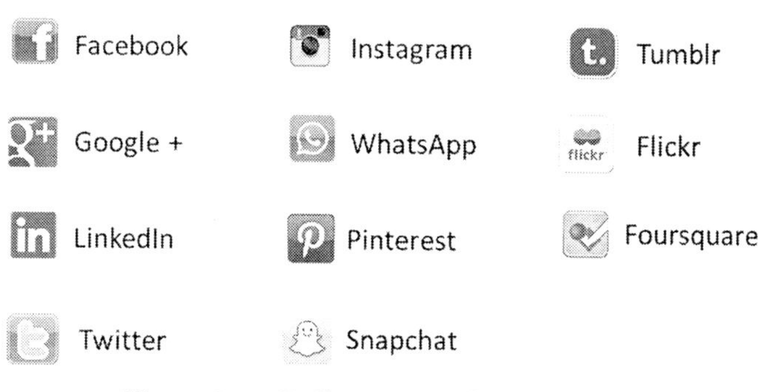

Figure 2.34: Different social networking sites

* Let's know various advantages and disadvantages of social networking.

Advantages of Social Networking

The advantages of Social Networking are:

1. Social networking sites help us to find your relatives, friends etc.
2. For social networking there is no need to install any special software or to make necessary changes/ settings in your PC.
3. It is an easy way to find more customers and people and engage them in your network.
4. It is very cost-effective technology to connect with your customers on a personal and professional level.

Disadvantages of Social Networking

The disadvantages of Social Networking are:

1. Social networking usually requires you to enter your personal details.
2. A person can have to bear harassment or cyber bullying.
3. Being online you are at risk of facing cases of cyber stalking and theft identity.
4. It is a time-consuming method to find people on net.
5. It can create eyes related problem for continuous work on a computer.

Extra Byte

1. In **Twitter**, the original limit of tweets was 140 characters but on November 7, 2017 it was extended to 280.
2. **Facebook** was founded by "Mark Zukerberg" along with fellow Harvard College students namely, "Eduardo Saverin", "Andrew McCollum", "Dustin Moskovitz" and "Chris Hughes".
3. **Instagram** was created by "Kevin Systrom" and "Mike Krieger" and launched in October 2010.
4. **YouTube** was created by "Chad Hurley", "Steve Chen" and "Jawed Karim" in February 2005.
5. **WhatsApp** was founded by "Jan Koum" and "Brian Acton" and was launched in 2009.

MEMORIZE

Some popular social networking sites are:

Facebook, WhatsApp, WeChat, QZone, Tumblr, Instagram, Twitter, Google+, LinkedIn.

Check Your Progress

Fill in the blanks.

1. ______________ was founded by Jan Koum and Brian Acton and was launched in 2009.
2. ______________ sites help us to find your relatives, friends etc.
3. ______________ is the most popular networking site.

8. E-Groups

E-group is an online group of people who can exchange their ideas, e-mails, file attachments to each other. E-Group (groups, community and clubs) is a feature provided by many social network services which helps you create, post, comment to and read from their **own interest**. Through e-groups users can share information among each other. The group is created by a single person who is known as **administrator** of the group. This is the person who can add or delete a person from the group. ***For example***, **WhatsApp** group is created by a single person where more than 200 people can be there as participants and are able to share messages, files. They can communicate with each other just by sending a single message which can be seen by all other members of that group. Administrator can maintain that group and hence provide the entire set of users to communicate with each other. The important fact is that only the users within the group have the access and any user who is not in the group will not get the permission to access. Similarly, by using Google group, you can organize meetings, conferences and other events where people of same interest or backgrounds can participate.

Definition

E-group is an online group of people who can exchange their ideas, e-mails, file attachments to each other. The group is created by a single person who is known as **administrator** of the group.

MEMORIZE

MSN group is a group of websites created by Microsoft that hosts several personalized online groups.

The various e-groups are:

- www.groups.google.com
- www.groups.yahoo.com
- www.grupbox.com

9. E-banking

E-banking is an online banking services where people can access their bank account from anywhere around the world. Online banking allows user to conduct financial transactions through the Internet. Online banking is also known as **internet banking** or **web banking**. Now, the people can deposit, withdraw or transfer their money online either by using their credit or debit cards. It also allows the user to pay various bills such as telephone bills, electricity bills, water bills etc. through online payment. (*Figure 2.35*)

In order to access the service, clients have to register themselves for their bank's online banking service by creating a password. Once it is done, they can use the service to do all their banking.

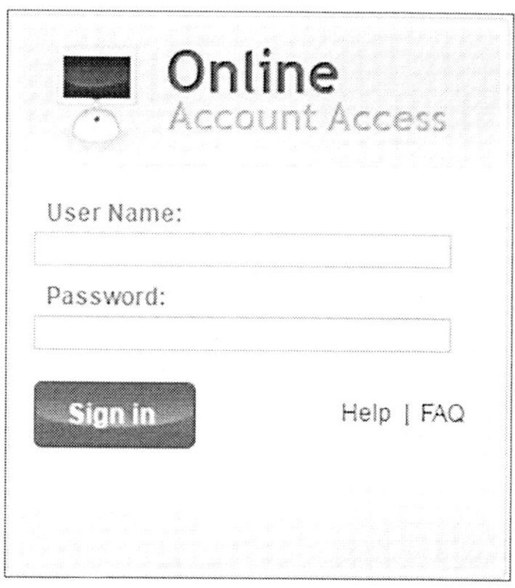

Figure 2.35: Online Banking

Some Popular services under e-banking in India

- ATMs (*Automated Teller Machines*)
- Telephone Banking
- Electronic Clearing Cards
- Smart Cards
- EFT (*Electronic Funds Transfer*) System
- ECS (*Electronic Clearing Services*)
- Mobile Banking
- Internet Banking
- Telebanking
- Door-step Banking

Definition

E-banking is also known as internet banking. It is a facility that provides users to make online payment, transfer funds, or to conduct a wide range of financial transactions through the bank's website.

✱ Let's know various advantages and disadvantages of E-Banking.

Advantages of E-banking

The advantages of e-banking are:

1. Consumers are not required to visit different bank branch to complete their basic financial transaction.
2. It saves time and human effort.
3. Now, the various bills and checks can be deposited online.
4. Customers can sell and buy their products online by transferring amount through debit/credit cards.
5. Consumers can also monitor their accounts regularly, allowing them to keep their accounts safe.
6. Customers can earn cash back points with purchase rewards provided by different sites.
7. Online banking helps in managing more than one saving account at the same bank.

Disadvantages of online banking

The disadvantages of e-banking are:

1. Technical knowledge is required for the successfull processing of transaction.
2. Online banking does not help if a customer needs access to large amounts of cash as most ATM cards have certain limits.
3. Consumer accounts can be hacked if they are not accessing safely with a secured user credentials.
4. Online banking is dependent on a reliable internet connection.

Extra Byte

- **NEFT: National Electronic Funds Transfer (NEFT)** is a payment system that help people to electronically transfer money from one bank to another bank branch. Fund transfers through the NEFT system do not occur in real-time basis and the fund transfer settles in 23 half-hourly batches.
- **RTGS: Real Time Gross Settlement (RTGS)** is another payment system that occurs in real time. The RTGS system is primarily meant for large value transactions that require and receive immediate clearing.
- **IMPS: Immediate Mobile Payment Services (IMPS)** is a real time instant inter-bank funds transfer system managed by National payment corporation of India.

MEMORIZE

While doing E-banking, it should be remember not to disclose your username and password to any other person. Create a strong password so that it cannot be hacked by any unauthenticated person.

Do's and Dont's:

- Ensure Secure Access by creating strong password and change your passwords frequently.
- Please ensure safe banking through Internet.
- Always type the address of the bank's website in the address bar of your browser. The URL (address) would be secured beginning with 'https://'
- Always clear your browser cache after each session.
- Installing effective anti-virus / anti-spyware software on your computer / mobile devices and update it regularly.
- Always Register Application for "Two Factor Authentication" and protect your Internet Banking by using One Time Password (OTP).
- Never share your credentials to anyone.
- Do not store passwords in a file on any device (including mobile or similar devices) without encryption.
- Never save your password on any computer.
- Never open/download any attachments if the mail is not from a trusted source.
- Always logout completely when finishing your work online.
- Never access internet banking from Cyber cafés and other public computer.

10. E-governance

"A transparent smart e-governance with seamless access, secure, and authentic flow of information crossing the interdepartmental barrier and providing a fair and unbiased service to the citizen."

By: Dr. APJ Abdul Kalam

E-governance provides the citizens to access information about their rights and the required services at their doorstep. Accordingly, the government recognize the need to deliver faster and efficient services to ordinary citizens through e-governance which is an effective instrument of administration. With the advancement of technology, it helps to improve access to information and services because these have provided economic and social development opportunities, facilitated participation and communication in policy and decision-making processes and empowered the weakest groups. In this way, there is a direct interaction between government and citizens. It also helps in improving transparency between government and citizens. Various sites offer services in local languages that make a difference in the lives of the rural people. ICTs also play a critical role in speeding up the flow of information and knowledge between government and citizens and transforming the way in which governments and citizens interact.

Definition

E-governance is an application that provides the citizens to access information about their rights and delivering government services in a quick and efficient manner.

MEMORIZE

E-governance is carrying out the functions and services through the utilization of **ICT (Information and Communication Technology)** and helps saving a huge amount of money.

* **Let's know various advantages and disadvantages of E-governance.**

Advantages of e-governance

The advantages of e-governance are:

1. It is the fastest method to transmit high volume of data by cutting down stationery cost for official purposes.
2. There is a transparency between government and citizen for accessing important information.
3. Once the functions of the government are available, you can hold them accountable for their actions.
4. It helps in the growth of **GDP (Gross Domestics Product)**.

Disadvantages of e-governance

The disadvantages of e-governance are:

1. The major disadvantage of e-governance is the loss of interpersonal communication that many people consider it vital.
2. It requires computer literacy to access information by people.
3. As Cybercrime can be there for steeling important information, it may result into breach of data that can make people lose confidence on the Government to govern people.

E-Governance/ICT initiatives has immense role in the enhancement of improving accessibility, cutting down costs, lessening corruption, extending help and increased access to un-served groups in India. Various apps launched by Government of India are:

- **Swachh Bharat Abhiyaan:** It is app where you can post the picture of a garbage piled in your locality. It will automatically be forwarded to the nearest municipality office to do the needful.
- **Umang:** UMANG stands for 'Unified Mobile App for New-Age Governance'. It is developed by the Ministry of Electronics and Information Technology to promote Digital India initiative. It is a one-in-all app which provides over 100 services such as e-payment of bills, filing income tax, booking a gas cylinder, checking provident fund account and many more.
- **Digi Locker:** Digi Locker is an important facility from where you can store and retrieve important certificates such as voter ID Card, PAN Card, BPL Card, driving license, vehicle registration, educational certificates, from Cloud. It also facilitates students to get their mark sheets of board examination, passing certificates, certificates of any online CBSE competitions etc.
- **Mygov.in:** It is a portal that works as a platform where Government is participating with citizens policies and share its creative suggestions by connecting people with central ministries and related government organizations.

Check Your Progress

Answer the following questions.

1. Name the web service that provides the facility of paying tax using income tax department's official site.
2. Write the URL for updating your Aadhaar card information.
3. Name any two web sites for paying your telephone bills online.

11. Blogs

A blog is also known as **web log** which is storage area of your personal opinions, pictures, hobbies, interests, commentaries etc. It is actually a modern online writer's column method where the person is sharing his/her views on any topic, upload photographs, commenting about special events, add comments to the stories etc.

The first blog was Links.net and was created by Justin Hall, in 1994. The term "weblog" was coined by **Jorn Barger** on 17 December 1997.

Initially, blogs started out as online personal diaries, but in a technology-driven world, now they have also been taken up by businesses as an informal method of communicating with customers and clients. A person who writes a blog is simply known as a **blogger** and the method is known as **blogging**.

Definition

Blog is a website that allows you to write an online diary or where you can share your opinions on a specific topic or you can post poems, write up of any event, news etc.

There are different types of blogs such as:

- Personal blogs
- News and views
- Company blogs
- Micro blogs

✱ **Let's know various advantages and disadvantages of Blogging.**

Advantages of Blogging

The advantages of blogging are:

1. Once you create your own blog, you can access it anytime and from anywhere in the world.
2. You can add your comments; put photographs, share assignments with your students etc. on a blog.
3. You can edit, modify, or delete your existing posts at any time.
4. You can also view the status in terms of how many viewers have seen your posts and can follow you. This increases your popularity on web.
5. Blogs build the profile of the blogger and showcase his/her talent and expertise.
6. The cost of blogging is very low and is the cheapest form of advertising.

Disadvantages of Blogging

The disadvantages of blogging are:

1. You should have a technical knowledge as how to create a blog.
2. As blogging is an online diary, it must be updated every time otherwise the viewers would lose interest in seeing your blog.
3. Blogging is time-consuming and therefore, you must be active in posting.
4. As you know that is is globally seen, you need to put a check on your language.

Memorize

A person who is writing online diary on a blog is known as blogger and the method is known as **blogging**.

2.6 MOBILE TECHNOLOGIES

Mobile technology is a form of technology that is mostly used in cellular communication and other related aspects. A mobile application also may be known as an **app, web app, online app, iPhone app** or **smartphone app**. It means portable technology that uses various IT services such as:

- Laptop, tablets and notebook computers
- Smartphones
- Global positioning system (GPS) devices
- Wireless debit/credit card payment terminals

and these portable devices uses various technologies such as Wi-Fi, Bluetooth, 3G, 4G, GPRS, Virtual private network, etc.

2.6.1 3G Technology

3G technology was introduced in year 2000 that provides much higher data rates with speed from 144kbps- 2mbps. ***For example***, CDMA2000/EV-DO, WCDMA/HSPA+, TD-SCDMA.

> **Extra Byte**
> The SMS concept was developed in 1984 by **Friedhelm Hillebrand** and **Bernard Ghillebaert** and the first text message was sent in 1992 from Neil Papworth, a former developer at Sema Group Telecoms.

Features of 3G Technology

The salient features of 3G Technology are:

1. It has introduced more efficient ways of carrying data with faster web-services.
2. Live chat, fast downloading, videoconferencing etc. are also possible over mobile phones.
3. It allows the user to do video conferencing and play 3d games.
4. A user can see live streaming on smart phones.
5. It provides broadband internet services.
6. It allows user to send and receive large e-mail messages.
7. High bandwidth is required.
8. Splits channel into time intervals enabling a single user to get all the resources at once.

2.6.2 4G Technology

Unlike previous generations of mobile technology, 4G mobile technology uses ultra-high broadband internet services with much faster higher data speed typically between 100 mbps-1gbps.

Features of 4G Technology

The features of 4G Technology are:

1. It is used for internet access on computers also, and it will be totally wireless.
2. 4G provides internet access, high quality streaming video and "anytime, anywhere" voice and data transmission at a much faster speed than 3G.
3. Delivering faster and better mobile broadband experiences.
4. Providing more data capacity for richer content and more connections.
5. The "anytime, anywhere" feature of 4G is also referred to as **MAGIC (Mobile multimedia)** anytime/anywhere.

2.6.3 Short Message Service (SMS)

Short message service is a wireless service that allows individuals to send textual messages. It is the oldest technology to send messages which was invented in 1980s. With a SMS, you can send a message of up to 160 characters to another device. If a message exceeds this limit, it is broken up into multiple segments of 160 characters each, depending on its length. For SMS to be sent, it is not necessary that the mobile phone should be connected with internet. SMS is sent from a mobile phone or a pager.

Extra Byte

The first MMS capable phones were introduced around 2002 in conjunction with the first GSM network. The Sony Ericsson T68i is the first **MMS** capable cell phone.

2.6.4 Multimedia Message Service (MMS)

MMS stands for **Multimedia Messaging Service** and is used to send multimedia messages. It is the most popularly used to send pictures, but can also be used to send audio, phone contacts, and video files. MMS messages do not have a standard limit. While their maximum size depends on the carrier and the device receiving the message, 300 KB is often mentioned as the largest size most carriers will reliably handle.

Definition

SMS is the short Messaging Service that enables you to send and receive short text messages through mobile phones, computer or other mobile devices.

★ **Let's know various advantages and disadvantages of SMS and MMS.**

Advantages and Disadvantages of using SMS

Advantages	Disadvantage
SMS goes directly to receiver's mobile phone.	The message size is limited and therefore it does not allow user to send very long text messages.
SMS can reach anywhere irrespective to the receiver's locality.	It is not possible for the sender to know that whether the recipient has read message or not.
SMS can be forwarded just by typing recipient's name.	Through SMS, you cannot attach files.
SMS can easily be tracked using the delivery repots. You are able to see whether the messages have been delivered or not.	Unwanted SMS are also broadcasted for advertising purpose that can annoy you.
You can send individual messages or group messages.	SMS can be saved for later stages also.

Advantages and Disadvantages of using MMS

Advantages	Disadvantage
MMS allows you to transfer voice messages than conveying only text messages.	Older mobile phones are not compatible for transferring MMS.
Through MMS, you can send video, emoticons, animated GIF's or audio files	MMS can be sent only when you have an internet connection.

Check Your Progress

Multiple choice questions.

1. A text message that you can send to another mobile device:
   a. Multi-media message
   b. Short message service
   c. Short messaging service
   d. Tweet
2. MMS stands for ______________.
   a. Multimedia Messaging Service
   b. Multimedia Message Service
   c. Multiple Messaging Service
   d. Multiple Message Service

Let's Revise

- The World Wide Web provides various web services like chatting, emailing, video conferencing, e-learning, e-shopping, e-reservation, e-groups and social networking.
- E-mail is an electronic mail used to send and receive messages electronically.
- Protocols used for e-mail are SMTP, POP and IMAP.
- Information can be retrieved by using any search engine such as Google, Yahoo, Bing etc.
- The electronic chat is the communication between two or more individuals using their computers
- Video conferencing is a virtual face-to-face communication among several people who are sitting on different remote areas around the world.
- Each of the end user must have camera, internet connection, computer and microphone to capture the video data and the voice data in real time.
- The E-Learning is a method of providing guidance and/or delivering information to students of schools, university or the employees of companies.
- E-Reservation System is an online reservation system that enables hotels, resorts, property owners, operators, theater operators and transport companies to maximize revenues without having to put human booking agents.
- Online shopping is the purchase of products and services over the Internet using a desktop or laptop.
- E-groups are a list of e-mails, users that can share information among each other.
- E-governance is an online service provided by government to provide information to citizens by using ICT technologies.
- Mobile technology is a wireless communication technology to send and receive information through Wi-Fi, broadband connection or virtual private networks.
- SMS is a short message service used to send textual messages
- MMS is a multimedia service used to send multimedia messages.

Learning Zone

SECTION A: OBJECTIVE TYPE QUESTIONS

A. MULTIPLE CHOICE QUESTIONS.

1. Which application is used to retrieve information from the Internet?
   a. Web browser b. Website c. URL d. Computer
2. Full form of e-mail is:
   a. Electric mail b. Electoral mail c. Electronic mail d. Elective mail
3. Identify the software that helps you in sending and receiving e-mails:
   a. MS Word b. Internet Explorer c. MS Outlook d. MS Excel
4. What do you understand by video conferencing?
   a. A word processing software b. A Web browser
   c. A mode of communication d. A Web server
5. Which of the following is not a search engine?
   a. Google b. Ask.com c. Bing d. Skype
6. Which one of the following services is not provided by the Web?
   a. Chat b. Video conferencing c. CPU d. E-mail
7. Which of the following is an example of an e-mail address?
   a. http://www.gmail.com/e-mail b. c:\Windows\e-mail
   c. sample@gmail.com d. @gmail.com
8. What does URL stand for? (Sample Question Paper 2016-17)
   a. United Route Line b. Uniform Resource Locator
   c. Unknown Redirection Link d. Upload Redirection Link
9. The following is not the name of e-shopping portal:
   a. Amazon b. E-bay c. Twitter d. Naaptol
10. It is the method of sending textual messages through mobile phones.
    a. MMS b. SSM c. SMS d. SMM
11. Self-paced learning modules allow students to work at their own speed is known as:
    a. E-shopping b. E-learning c. E-reservation d. E-tutorial
12. Which one of the following is an e-Shopping website?
    a. Flipkart b. Amazon c. Snapdeal d. All of above
13. Mozilla Firebox is a:
    a. Web Browser b. News Website c. Graphing Package d. Word Processor

14. A web service primarily for the use of information and communication technology by government sectors to improve the quality of services and provide information to the citizens on time and in a cost-efficient manner is:

    a. E-commerce   b. E-banking   c. E-reservation   d. E-governance

15. A term that defines learning done at a computer connected to network giving an opportunity to learn anytime and anywhere.

    a. E-banking   b. E-learning   c. E-shopping   d. E-reservation

16. An e-mail can be sent to:

    a. A receiver even if he is offline

    b. A person who has an e-mail account on some other search engine

    c. Many people at a time

    d. All of the above.

17. A program that searches documents for specified keywords and returns a list of documents:

    a. E-mail   b. Search engine   c. Video conferencing   d. E-shopping

18. The facility provided by the Indian Railways to book train tickets online.

    a. E-reservation   b. E-commerce   c. E-learning   d. E-rail

19. This is used to establish social relations and stay in touch with your friends or family members using internet.

    a. Social networking   b. E-groups   c. E-governance   d. None of the above

20. The essential component of video conferencing is:

    a. Printer   b. UPS   c. Mouse   d. Webcam

Ans.	1. a	2. c	3. c	4. c	5. d
	6. c	7. c	8. b	9. c	10. c
	11. b	12. d	13. a	14. d	15. b
	16. d	17. b	18. a	19. a	20. d

B. FILL IN THE BLANKS.

1. ____________ is the method of virtually connected with people face-to-face.
2. ____________ means to search the information from the search engines.
3. ____________ is the expanded form of SMS.
4. Two search engines can be ____________ and ____________.
5. ____________ is also known as online diary.
6. ____________ is the person who post on blogs.
7. Selling and purchasing of goods online is known as ____________.
8. Booking tickets online is known as ____________.
9. Protocol used for receiving e-mail is ____________.
10. ____________ are a list of e-mails, users that can share information among each other.
11. A spider is also known as ____________. (Delhi 2013)

12. ____________ is the facility to extract your inportant certificates like mark sheet, ID Card etc.

13. ____________ is also known as online banking. (Delhi 2019)

14. Transparency in e-governance is directly links to ____________.

15. ____________ is fast, reliable and economical mode of communication.

Ans. 1. Video Conferencing 2. Information retrieval 3. Short Message Service 4. Google.com, Yahoo.com 5. Blog 6. Blogger 7. E-shopping 8. E-Reservation 9. POP/IMAP 10. E-groups 11. BOT 12. DigiLocker 13. Internet Banking 14. Accountability 15. E-mail

C. STATE WHETHER THE FOLLOWING STATEMENTS ARE TRUE OR FALSE.

1. E-mail is a web service to send and receive mails.
2. Bcc is a carbon copy where the receiver can view the email address in the To box.
3. To forward an e-mail, click the reply button.
4. If you are not connected to internet, you cannot check your latest e-mails.
5. E-learning is a web service that sends and receives text messages in real time.
6. SMS is a short form of short message service.
7. The use of technology has made our life easier.
8. A website is a collection of various web pages.
9. The extension of government site is .government.
10. 4G mobile telecommunication technology is meant to provide what is known as ultra-broadband access for mobile service.
11. Mail sent to your friends is stored in the sent mail folder.
12. Drafts folder will consist of e-mail messages that are component but not yet sent.
13. In an e-mail id the username is followed by $ symbol.
14. Online shopping stores are not open on national holidays.
15. You can access bank's website even if the internet connection is not available.
16. Learning through DVD or CD-ROM or over a television channel is called an online learning.
17. Twitter is a portal for online shopping.
18. In a website, pages are linked through a system of hyperlink that enables you to go from one site to other site.
19. Payment by credit card is widely accepted method of payment for online shopping.
20. A web page is a collection of several websites.

Ans. 1. True 2. False 3. False 4. True 5. False 6. True 7. True 8. True 9. False 10. True 11. True 12. True 13. False 14. False 15. False 16. False 17. False 18. True 19. True 20. False

SECTION B: SOLVED THEORY QUESTIONS

1. **What do you understand by search engines? Name any five search engines.**

Ans: A search engine helps in searching an information according to the specified criteria. To use a search engine, the user just needs to go to its home page, type a keyword or a search criterion in the search box and click the Search button. The relevant information is displayed on the screen instantly.

Five commonly used search engines are:

a. Google: http://www.google.com
b. Yahoo!: http://www.yahoo.com
c. AOL.com: http://www.aol.com
d. Bing: http://www.bing.com
e. Ask.com: http://www.ask.com

2. **Name the parts that are separated by the @ sign in an e-mail address.** **(Delhi 2010)**

Ans: The two main parts are username and hostname.

3. **Name any five services provided on the Internet.**

Ans: The Internet provides various services that are as diverse as the Internet itself. Some of these services are as follows:

a. E-mail
b. Search engines
c. Chatting
d. Video conferencing
e. Blogs and forums

4. **Name the devices used to connect to the Internet.**

Ans: The following devices are required for connecting to the Internet:

a. Computer
b. Modem
c. Transmission medium
d. Network Interface Card
e. Internet Service Provider (ISP)

5. **List the different types of blogs.**

Ans: Some of the commonly used types of blogs are as follows:

a. Personal blogs
b. Corporate and organizational blogs
c. Genre blogs

6. **What is the difference between the Cc and Bcc fields?**

Ans: Cc: It refers to the Carbon Copy field. The recipients whose e-mail addresses are added in the Cc field would receive a copy of the mail.

Bcc: It refers to the Blind Carbon Copy field. The recipients whose e-mail addresses are added in the Bcc field would receive a copy of the mail; however, the identity of these recipients would not be disclosed.

7. **What do you understand by a blog?**

Ans: A blog is also known as web log which is storage area of your personal opinions, pictures, hobbies, interests, commentaries etc. It is actually a modern online writer's column method where the person is sharing his/her views on any topic, upload photographs, commenting about special events, add comments to the stories etc.

8. **Define video conferencing. List down the freely available video conferencing software.**

Ans: The video conferencing is a virtual face-to-face online communication between two or more people who are sitting at different locations around the world. Through this web service, they are able to transmit both the video and audio data. In video conferencing, all users must have a web camera known as webcam for fetching the video and a microphone for transmitting voice data

Some freely available video conferencing software are: TCPCam, Ekiga or GnomeMeeting, Skype for Linux, Brosix and Goober.

9. What do you understand by e-learning? Mention five advantages of e-learning.

Ans: E-learning is an online method of learning and delivering information to students of university or the employees of companies. E-learning can also be termed as a network enabled where the skills and knowledge are transferred digitally. A large group of people can participate for e-learning without travelling to remote places. E-learning does not require classroom teaching and therefore no physical presence is required.

The advantages of e-learning are:

a. E-learning is helpful for handicapped students who cannot go from one place to another for classroom teaching.
b. No need to attend institution to get information.
c. It is a virtual teaching method and therefore no classroom teaching is required.
d. It is an inexpensive method to get knowledge as it does not involve high fee to be paid.
e. The E- Learning provides an opportunity to the student to complete the course at their own pace.
f. The universities from across the globe keep offering the on-line courses. This is possible through E-learning. Online courses also provide certification to their students.

10. Write the various advantages of online shopping.

Ans: The advantages of online shopping are as follows:

a. Providing facility of shopping from any trader and at any time.
b. Providing benefits to customers from time to time, such as discounts and gifts.
c. Saving of time by shopping through virtual window.
d. Providing price comparison between different products.
e. Offering information about newly launched products to customers.
f. Providing correct and complete information regarding the products.

11. What do you mean by e-groups?

Ans: E-groups are a list of e-mails, users that can share information among each other. A single administrator can maintain that group and hence provide the entire set of users to communicate between each other.

12. What are the societal impacts of e-governance?

Ans: The various societal impacts of e-governance on a society are:

a. Improve efficiency of administration and service delivery.
b. Reduce waiting time.
c. Reduce cost of availing the services.
d. Keep a tab on corruption to some extent.
e. Increased public participation.
f. Increase transparency & increased accountability of government offices.

13. List some major e-learning sites.

Ans: Major E- Learning Sites:

a. Moodle portal (http://www.moodle.org)
b. W3Schools (http://www.w3schools.com)
c. eXe Project (http://www.exelearning.org)
d. Xerte Project (http://www.nottingham.ac.uk/xerte)

14. Write any one application each of e-Governance and e-commerce.

(Sample Question Paper 2019-20)

Ans: Application of E-Governance

a. Filing of online application forms for Aadhaar card, passport.

The application of E-Commerce

a. Able to do online transactions.

15. Give one difference between 3G and 4G. **(Sample Question Paper 2019-20)**

Ans: a. The speed of 4G is about 10 times faster than 3G.

b. We can stream audio and video content using 4G.

16. Kuhu has just learnt how to do online banking. Name any two precautions that she should take to prevent online fraud. **(Sample Question Paper 2019-20)**

Ans: a. Do not share user id and password with anyone.

b. Avoid doing transactions from cybercafé and other public places.

17. What is the purpose of a web browser? Give the name of any two popular web browsers.

Ans: A web browser is an application program used for exploring the information resources available on the World Wide Web to retrieve the required information.

Two popular web browsers are Google Chrome and Mozilla Firefox.

SECTION C: APPLICATION ORIENTED QUESTIONS

1. Anita receives an e-mail from her friend Aakash. In this e-mail, Aakash mentions what to do and what not to do to keep you healthy. Anita likes this mail and wants to share it with other friends. How can she send the same mail to her other friends but without knowing others e-mail addresses?

Ans: She can send the same mail to her other friends by performing the following steps:

a. Click the Forward link.

b. Type the e-mail addresses of the recipients in the Bcc text box.

c. Click the Send button.

2. The XYZ bank has started the facility of e-banking for its customers. Mention two benefits that the customers will get by using the service.

Ans: The two benefits that the customers will get by using the e-banking service are as follows:

a. A customer can perform banking transactions electronically without having to visit an actual bank.

b. Delivery of cash can be done instantly to customers by using Automated Teller Machine (ATM).

3. Rakesh wants to study online and for this he asked his friend for the same. How could he achieve his goal? Mention its benefits also.

Ans: He should use the concept of e-learning. It is learning with the help of electronic resources like computers, tablets, smart phone, internet.

Benefits of E-Learning are:

a. It is time saving as well as removes the distance barrier between learner & teacher.

b. It has quicker delivery cycle times than traditional classroom-based instruction.

c. It is less expensive to set-up an e-learning environment.

4. What is VTC? How does it take place?

Ans: The full form of VTC is Video conferencing or Video Tele Conference (VTC) represents a real-life meeting environment. It has brought the world much closer than it was before. With the help of VTC facility, we can see other people while talking to them.

A camera takes the video picture and also records the associated audio. The picture and the audio signal are converted into compressed digital signals. This converted audio and video signal are transmitted through a modem to the other end where they are converted back into the picture and audio, which is projected on the screen on the screen and heard through the speakers.

5. **Mr. Ram wants to send some money to her wife who is in some other city. Tell him the easiest way to transfer money through bank.**

Ans: E-Banking is the easiest way to transfer money through bank.

6. **Kavita set up the following Auto Delete options on her web-based e-mail account.**

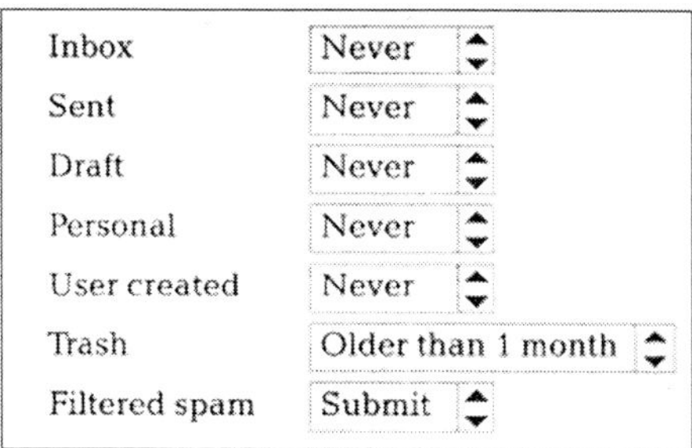

Inbox	Never
Sent	Never
Draft	Never
Personal	Never
User created	Never
Trash	Older than 1 month
Filtered spam	Submit

What is the most likely reason, she has set the trash folder to delete "older than 1 month"?
Kavita wants:

a. All e-mails to have a delete date
b. All sent e-mails to be deleted after 1 month
c. All deleted e-mails to only remain in the trash folder for 1 month
d. All e-mails in her inbox to be moved to the trash folder after 1 month

Ans: Option c. All deleted e-mails to only remain in the trash folder for 1 month.

7. **Mr. John has a prepaid internet connection where he has a data limit of 14 GB. The average size of an e-mail attachments which he can download is 1.4 MB. Approximately, how many e-mails can John download without exceeding his data limit?**

Ans: 10000 mails.

8. **As life gets busier, it becomes difficult for everyone to keep a track with school & college friends, old colleagues, old neighbors and favorite teachers. It is important to keep in touch with all your near and dear ones. At times, people sitting miles away doing similar kind of activity or solving similar kind of problems can help you to achieve goals faster by sharing their experiences. Similarly, people belonging to different socio-economic background can change your perspective and can enhance your understanding of various cultures.**

a. Suggest two real time tools that are suitable for the above-mentioned activities.
b. What is the generic name used for such tools? **(Sample Question Paper 2010-11, 2016-17)**

Ans: a. Facebook and Twitter.
b. Social Networking.

9. **Laleema Chakradhar wants a broadband connection for accessing her mails and staying informed about the latest happenings in the field of Biotechnology. Can you suggest two Internet Service Providers of India to be approached for the same? (Sample Question Paper 2010-11, 2016-17)**

Ans: VSNL, Airtel etc.

10. **Rashmi has to send an e-mail to Raees. She also wants to send the same e-mail to Vandana but does not want Raees to know about it. Which option out of 'cc' or 'bcc' should Rashmi use to enter the email address of Vandana? (Sample Question Paper 2019-20)**

Ans: Bcc (blind carbon copy).

11. **Kanika wants to buy a new pair of shoes for herself but she can't afford to go to the market due to shortage of time. Suggest her a way which internet service will help her to buy shoes without going to the market.**

Ans: She can buy shoes by using e-shopping method and can explore flipkart.com, amazon.in online sites.

12. **Yashvardhan is studying in Simla and his parents are residing in Delhi. Yashvardhan needs some money to purchase books. How can Yashvardhan's parents send money to him?**

Ans: Yashvardhan's parents can transfer money to Yashvardhan's account through online banking service.

13. **During the summer break, Agrima wants to do a certification course but due to scorching heat she does not want to attend classes. Suggest her a solution such that she utilizes her time well.**

Ans: Agrima can use an online learning web service for doing a certification course.

SECTION D: SELF - ASSESSMENT

A. FILL IN THE BLANKS.

1. When you want to send a same e-mail message to multiple recipients, then select option ____________.
2. In e-mail, the content is written ____________ place.
3. Subject in e-mail specifies ____________.
4. ____________ is a feature that allows a user to view multiple pages in the same window.
5. ____________ is a client-server protocol based on character-oriented data exchange over the network.
6. ____________ is a wireless internet-based service that allows you to do financial transaction.
7. ____________ and ____________ are two popular web browsers.
8. The ____________ is the maximum speed of data in 4G cell phone technology.
9. ____________ number of characters including spaces are allowed in text messages through SMS.
10. ____________ is a service/application that allow people to make and receive free voice and video calls between computers via internet and regular telephone lines.
11. A ____________ is a business activity on internet that is between two companies where the end user is not involved.
12. The URL of website of UDAAN is ____________.
13. Combination of keystrokes that represent some emoticons or feeling are called ____________.
14. Exploring various websites on the internet is called ____________.
15. The software that allows you to surf internet pages is called a ____________.

B. STATE WHETHER THE FOLLOWING STATEMENTS ARE TRUE OR FALSE.

1. Different people have different e-mail addresses.
2. If you want to forward the same message to different user, you should click on forward button.
3. Video conferencing is a service through which you can talk to your friend face-to-face.
4. E-learning is a site where you can pay your bills online.
5. Flipkart and amazon are two popular e-shopping sites.
6. Short forms used on the internet while sending e-mails, SMS, chat etc. are called emoticons.
7. Bcc is an abbreviated form of blind carbon copy.
8. Full form of MMS is Mix Media Service.
9. Uploading files to a distant computer is done by Telnet.

10. The IP address does not contain username.
11. Kunal$gmail.com is a valid e-mail address.
12. POP is used for receiving e-mails.
13. ISP is expanded as Internet Service Provider.
14. Spam mail is an unsolicited mail sent to numerous recipients through e-mails.
15. .org is an extension of organization.

C. TICK THE CORRECT ANSWER.

1. How ICT enables employees to communicate?
   a. E-mail   b. Video conferencing
   c. Internet chat rooms   d. All of these
2. Which of the following accepts HTTP requests from the client, processes it and delivers the response?
   a. Website   b. Web Browser   b. Web page   d. Web Server
3. Which of the following keyword is used to find web pages that do not contain the mentioned keywords?
   a. AND   b. OR   b. NOT   d. – (MINUS)
4. An e-mail address will definitely contain this special symbol:
   a. $ b. @   c. *   d. %
5. ____________ is a collection of messages normally text posted by individuals to a news server.
   a. Newsgroup   b. E-mail   b. Newsreader   d. TELNET

D. WRITE THE URL OF THE WEBSITES FOR THE FOLLOWING.

1. To reserve a train from Delhi to Mumbai.
2. To book latest movie ticket in cinema hall.
3. To book tickets for viewing theatre in Shri Ram Auditorium.
4. To search for a best, find through some social networking sites.
5. To upload you latest photographs online.
6. To book hotel room for spending summer vacations.

E. ANSWER THE FOLLOWING QUESTIONS.

Type A: Very Short Answer Questions.

1. What do you mean by information retrieval?
2. Write few names of major E-Governance project in India.
3. Define the terms e-groups, blogs, and mobile communication.
4. Who is blogger?
5. Differentiate between Cc and Bcc. (Delhi 2013)
6. Expand SMTP. (Sample Question Paper 2019-20)
7. Name any two main parts of e-mail address with the help of an example. (Delhi 2008)

8. What are the components of E-shopping?

9. What is telnet?

10. Which of the following is/are a popular Web Browser(s)? (CBSE Paper 2019)

a. Firefox b. Safari c. Navigator d. All of the above

11. Write the URL of any one e-Governance website. (CBSE Paper 2019)

12. Give example of two e-reservation sites. (Delhi 2013)

13. Give the full forms of the following: (Delhi 2006)

a. FTP b. URL

14. Write the web extension (top level domain names) given to websites of the following types of organization: (CBSE Paper 2008)

a. Educational b. Government

15. Name any two major services provided by internet for schools. (Delhi 2006, Outside Delhi 2005)

Type B: Short Answer Questions.

1. Write the various steps for creating Gmail account.
2. What is E-Learning? Write few names of E-Learning web sites.
3. Write two positive and two negative societal impact of E-Learning.
4. What is the difference between Chatting and Video conferencing?
5. What are the advantages and disadvantages of Video conferencing?
6. What are the categories in which E-banking is divided?
7. What is e-Groups? (CBSE question paper 2019)
8. How does FTP works? (Delhi 2007)
9. What is the difference between downloading and uploading a file? (Delhi 2005)
10. Why HTTP is called the backbone of World Wide Web (WWW)?
11. What is the role of TCP/IP protocols in networking?
12. When using a search engine, what does a minus sign used with keywords in the search box mean? Explain with suitable box. (Delhi 2007)
13. Differentiate between web pages and websites. (Delhi 2008)
14. What is hypertext? (Delhi 2013)
15. Expand the following acronyms:

a. W3C b. Wi-Fi c. TCP/IP d. TELNET

16. Palvi wants to buy a new dress for her coming birthday. Suggest her the best way to choose and get it at home.
17. Akhay wants to open his account in one of the popular social networking sites. Suggest him which site he should use.

Type C: Long Answer Questions.

1. Explain web browser.

2. How an e-mail address and URL are different from each other? Explain with suitable example. (Delhi 2018)

3. Sharvan Joshi is a student of Political Science and is a keen researcher of Political issues related to various countries and states. He wants to share his research and his own opinion on these issues on day-to-day basis with everyone on the World Wide Web. He is also interested in collecting views of others to enhance his research and knowledge related to his area of interest. He belongs to a middle-class family and can't afford his own website. Also being a non-technical person, he can't create a dynamic website to deal with day-to-day inputs. (Sample Question Paper 2016-17)

   a. Suggest an easy way for Shravan to achieve the same.

   b. Also name any two popular websites providing free services that can help Shravan in this regard.

4. What is mobile banking? What are the services provided by Mobile Banking?

5. Explain various elements of email with the help of an example.

6. Briefly discuss the role of a web browser in Internet surfing. (CBSE question paper 2019)

7. Briefly explain the significance of Video conferencing. (CBSE question paper 2019)

8. Mr. Gupta is a farmer who is using internet to improve his crop production. He uses a search engine to collect the information. (Delhi 2017)

   a. Explain what is search engine.

   b. Give some examples of search engines.

9. Mr. Amit's head office is in Bengaluru and he lives in New Delhi. There are other branches in Jaipur, Hyderabad and Ahmedabad. He often uses video conferencing to connect with other branch managers and take updates.

   a. List two advantages of him using video conferencing.

   b. List two problems that he faces while doing conference.

   c. Suggest him the best solution to overcome with the above problem.

   d. How would he share files and actions points of the meeting?

   e. Suggest him the new marketing and selling strategy.

SECTION E: LAB EXERCISE

1. You are a student of Class-X and your teacher has given you some worksheet to do.

   a. Send a mathematics worksheet as an e-mail attachment to your friend and ask him to solve it and then mail to you as an attachment.

   b. Download the attachment that you received.

   c. Save it on the desired folder and edit it.

   d. Send it to your friend along with some other friends by putting them in Bcc.

2. Use any search engine and find about the following:

   a. Google hangouts

   b. Skype

   c. Google drive

   d. Microsoft OneDrive

3. **Find out the apps that help you to do the following:**
   a. Learning new language
   b. Sharing learning material
   c. Creating presentations online
   d. Reading eBooks
   e. Doing chatting face-to-face
4. **Write the steps for withdrawing money from ATM machine.**

Activity Zone

1. Tell your students to make a list of different e-mail addresses of your friends and invite them on your school for annual function.
2. Tell your students to make a list of different e-shopping sites and differentiate between them in terms of discount they are offering on different types of clothing.
3. Conduct an oral quiz based on this chapter.
4. Ask students to collect information on different online services available in your school along with list of software and hardware running for them.
5. List the several benefits of our government to go paperless.
6. Tell students to figure out steps for online booking for railway tickets on IRCTC website from a browser enabled mobile phone.

3 Basic HTML Elements

Outline of the Chapter

- Introduction
- What is HTML?
- Advantages of HTML
- Features of HTML
- Tags and attributes
- Categories of tags
- Special characters in HTML
- Logical and physical text styles
- Lists in HTML

Learning Objectives

- To know about HTML, its advantages and features
- To know the meaning of tags and attributes
- To know the categories of tags i.e. empty and container tags
- To know the meaning of logical and physical text styles
- To know about various tags such as HTML, BODY, HEAD, TITLE, B, I, U, FONT, SUB, SUP, OL, UL, DL, DT, DD, STRONG, H1..H6, P, CENTER, <!—and → tags

INTRODUCTION

The internet is a sea of data and information. This data or information is accessed in the form of web pages. Each web page is created by using a special language known as **hypertext markup language (HTML)**. HTML tells the browser how to display the contents of a HTML document i.e., a document that includes text, images, audio, video, and hyperlink to other web pages.

This chapter will help you to create web pages by using various HTML tags, how to save HTML documents and how to view these web pages.

3.1 WHAT IS HTML?

HTML is a hypertext markup language which is used to create and design web pages. A web page consists of several text, images, graphics, and hyperlinks to various other web pages which is designed by using various HTML elements.

HTML tells the web browser how to display these contents and also helps in making a web page interactive through various hyperlinks which are inserted into it.

Definition

HTML is a hypertext markup language which is used to create and design web pages. It defines the structure of a web page and determines how data can be displayed online.

It is to be remembered that HTML is a language for creating web pages only and therefore it is not a word processing tool or a desktop publishing solution or even a programming language such as C, C++, and so on. It is used for formatting and to display text, images, tables, and hyperlinks in a web browser.

In other words,

What is HTML?	What it is not?
HTML is a Web Page Layout Language.	HTML is not a Word Processing Tool.
It is a Hyperlink Specification Language.	It is not a Programming Language.

Note: Hypertext is a text that contains links to other text which when clicked redirects you to another webpage/website on the internet.

* **Let's know various advantages and features of using HTML.**

3.2 ADVANTAGES/FEATURES OF HTML

HTML offers several advantages which are given below:

- HTML document is a plain text and therefore can be easily modified.
- No special software knowledge is required for writing HTML documents.
- A simple text editor such as **Notepad**, **Notepad++** or **Gedit** is required to write HTML documents.
- It is very easy to learn HTML codes as it is not a programming language such as C or C++ whose syntax is complex.
- HTML is also used for designing effective presentations with the help of its all formatting tags.
- You can display HTML documents on any platforms such as **Macintosh**, **Windows** and **Linux**.
- Besides text, you can also insert graphics, videos and sounds to the web pages to make web pages more interactive and attractive.
- It is supported by almost all web browser such as **Internet Explorer**, **Mozilla Firefox**, **Google chrome**, and so on.

3.3 CHARACTERISTICS OF HTML

- HTML is a **case insensitive language** that means the tags written in lowercase or uppercase have same meaning.
- All HTML tags must be opened by using angular brackets < >. ***For Example,*** <B>.
- HTML tags must be closed by using **forward slash** (/) before writing the name of the tag. For Example, </B>.
- HTML tags may be **container** or **empty tags**. Container tags must be closed whereas empty tags need not to be closed.
- HTML document must **begin** with <HTML> tag and **closed** with </HTML> tag.

* **Let's know about the various HTML tags and their associated attributes.**

3.4 TAGS AND ATTRIBUTES

HTML is made up of elements known as **tags** or **coded elements**. These tags or coded elements are commands that indicate how a specific part of web page should be displayed.

All HTML tags are written inside angular brackets (< >) such as <BODY> and ends by using forward slash (/) prior to the tag name such as </BODY>.

Attributes add some additional functionality to the tag. Attributes are written along with the tag name at the time of opening the tag which must be assigned to some value.

The syntax of using attribute is:

```
<Tagname AttributeName= "Value of Attribute">
```

For Example, to set the background color of a web page, the attribute is **bgcolor** and the statement can be written as:

<BODY BGCOLOR = "GREEN">		
BODY	BGCOLOR	GREEN
Tagname	Attribute	Value of attribute

i.e.: <BODY bgcolor = "GREEN">

Definition

Tags are the coded elements formed by a pair of angle brackets (< >). They instruct the web browser how to display the content in a web page. **Attributes** provide some additional information about the tag. An attribute defines a property for an element, consists of an attribute/value pair, and appears within the element's start tag.

Versions of HTML

- **HTML 1.0** was the first version of HTML and was released in 1992. It had only 22 elements.
- **HTML 2.0** was released in 1995. It also supported forms, change of page background and use of tables including all features of HTML 1.0
- **HTML 3.2** was released in 1997. It was used for creating tables and various advanced options for form elements. This version also allowed web pages to include complex mathematical equations.
- **HTML 4.0** Previously, HTML 4.0 was named as **COUGAR** and was released in 1998. It provided new elements for style sheets, scripts, frames, tables, forms, and so on.
- **HTML 5.0** was released in October 2009. It is the new web standard. It introduces several new elements and removes some elements from HTML 4.

MEMORIZE

- HTML tags are used to mark-up HTML elements.
- HTML tags are surrounded by the two characters < and >.
- The surrounding characters are called angle brackets.
- HTML tags normally come in pairs like <b> and </b>.
- The first tag in a pair is the start tag, the second tag is the end tag.
- The text between the start and end tags is the element content.HTML tags are not case sensitive, <b> means the same as <B>.
- HTML tags are used to mark-up HTML elements.
- HTML tags are surrounded by the two characters < and >.
- The surrounding characters are called angle brackets.
- HTML tags normally come in pairs like <b> and </b>.
- The first tag in a pair is the start tag, the second tag is the end tag.
- The text between the start and end tags is the element content.

* **Now, it's the time to know how to create and save HTML document.**

3.5 WRITING AND SAVING HTML DOCUMENTS

The steps for writing, saving HTML document and then displaying web page are:

1. Open any text editor such as **Notepad**.
2. Start writing HTML code.
3. Save the file with extension **.html** or **.htm**. ***For example***, first.html or first.htm.
4. Open the file by using any web browser such as **Google Chrome** or **Mozilla Firefox** or double click on the file.

3.6 STRUCTURE OF HTML DOCUMENT

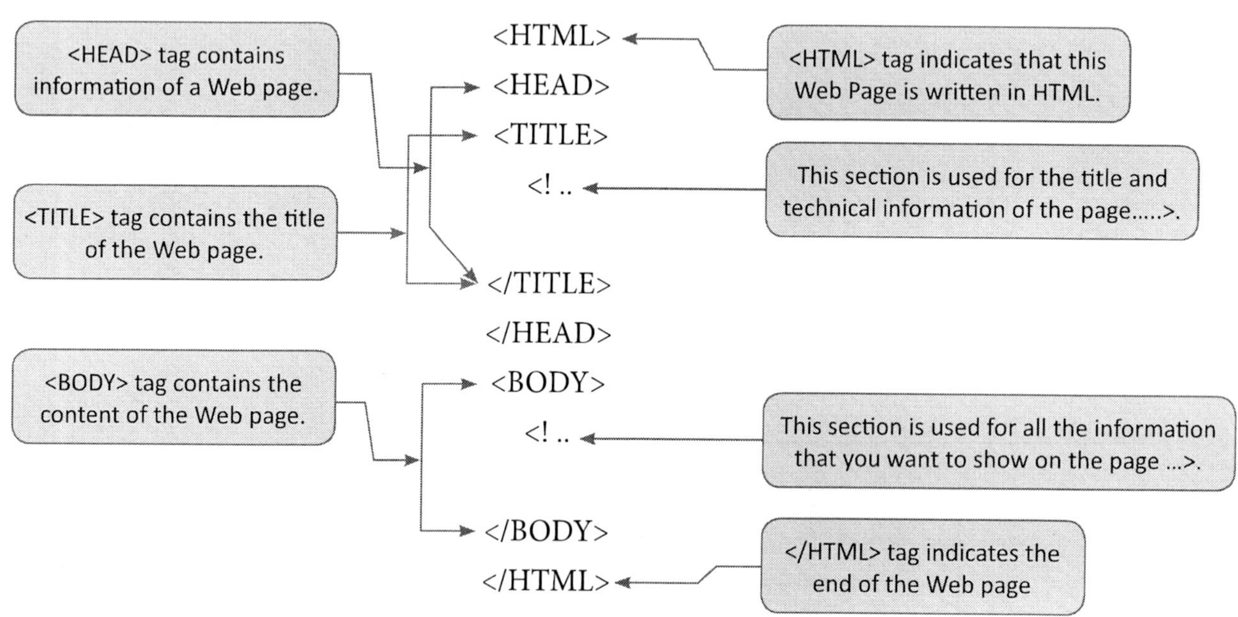

Figure 3.1: Structure of HTML document

Let's explain the various sections of the above HTML document structure.

- <HTML> : It identifies that the document is an HTML document.
- <HEAD> : It contains information about document including its TITLE, scripts used, style definition and other descriptions.
- <TITLE> : Contains TITLE which appears on browser' TITLE bar.
- <BODY> : Contains many other tags and attributes, which specifies what to be displayed on browser.

* **Let's know the categories of HTML tags.**

3.7 CATEGORIES OF HTML TAGS: CONTAINER AND EMPTY

HTML document is a collection of opening tag, closing tag and content between them. However, there are some tags which do not contain any content and therefore need not to be closed.

Based on this there are two types of tags: **Container Tags** and **Empty Tags**.

3.7.1 Container Tags

The tags which are required to be closed are known as container tags. These are also known as **Paired tags**.

For Example,

<HTML> ....</HTML>

<HEAD> ....</HEAD>

<TITLE> ....</TITLE>

<B> ....</B>

The container tags affect everything whichever is written between the starting and end tag.

Definition

Container tags are those tags which have opening and closing tags. They must be closed by using forward slash (/).

3.7.2 Empty Tags

The tags which need not to be closed are known as empty tags.
For Example, <HR>, <BR>, <IMG>, and so on.

Do's and Don'ts

- Always close container tags with forward slash (/). For example, </B>.
- Do not close empty tag. However, if closed then it will not flash any error.

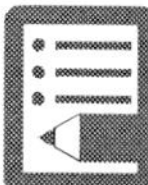

Definition

Empty tags are those tags which have only opening tag but not closing tag.

Check Your Progress

Fill in the blanks.

1. HR and BR are ________________ types of tags.
2. HTML files have extension ________________.
3. There are ________________ types of tags in HTML.

3.8 WORKING WITH TAGS

All HTML documents consist of several tags that provide various formatting features such as how to display text, graphics and links. The contents of HTML document is always written inside the BODY tag.

* **Let's explain the functionality of tags with their attributes.**

3.8.1 <HTML> ..... </HTML>

This tag marks the beginning and the end of HTML document. It may contain <HEAD> and <BODY> tag.

Table 3.1: Commonly used Attributes are:

Attribute	Value	Description
DIR	LTR	It specifies the direction of text in the document either Left-to-Right (LTR) or Right-to-Left (RTL).
Lang	En,Fr etc.	It specifies the Language used in the document.

For Example,

<HTML Lang=EN DIR = LTR>

3.8.2 <HEAD> ..... </HEAD>

This tag defines the document header. It contains information like title, script, and style, and so on.

3.8.3 <TITLE> ..... </TITLE>

This tag contains the title and identifies its content in a global context. TITLE is displayed in the title bar of the Browser.

For Example,

<TITLE> My First Page </TITLE>

Note:

- You should only have one <title> tag.
- The content of the title tag must be short or less than 64 characters.
- If there is no title tag, then your web browser will display the filename as a title of your Web page.

3.8.4 <BODY> tag

<BODY> tag is the main tag that contains the entire content of a Web page. The actual web content is written between this paired <BODY> tag. It is the **container tag** and supports number of attributes that helps in displaying the Web page.

Table 3.2: The various attributes of <BODY> tag are:

S. No	Attribute Name	Function	Example
1.	Bgcolor	It is used to set the background color of a web page.	<BODY Bgcolor="Pink">
2.	Background	It is used to set the background image of a web page.	<BODY Background="C:\My Pictures\Flowers.Gif">
3.	Text	It is used to set the color of the text of a document. The default color of the text is black if not set by this attribute.	<BODY Text="Red">
4.	Link	It is used to set the color of the text links on a web page.	<BODY Link="Green">
5.	Alink	It is used to set the active link color of a web page. These are the hyperlinks which are not clicked or visited by the user so far. By default, the active link color is blue until it is specified.	<BODY Alink="Red">
6.	Vlink	It is used to set the visited link color of a web page. Visited links are those hyperlinks which have been clicked or visited by the user. By default, the visited links appear in purple color.	<BODY Vlink="Yellow">
7.	Leftmargin	It is used to set the left margin of a web page and to specify the empty space at the left side of a web page. The value of the margin is defined in pixels.	<BODY Leftmargin="30">

8.	Rightmargin	It is used to set the right margin of a web page and to specify the empty space at the right side of a web page. The value of the margin is defined in pixels.	<BODY Rightmargin="30">
9.	Topmargin	It is used to set the top margin of a web page and to specify the empty space at the top of a web page. The value of the margin is defined in pixels.	<BODY Topmargin="30">
10.	Bottommargin	It is used to set the bottom margin of a web page and to specify the empty space at the bottom of a web page. The value of the margin is defined in pixels.	<BODY Bottommargin="30">

Program 3.1: To create a web page that will make the use of all attributes of BODY tag.

```
<HTML>
<HEAD>
<TITLE> Attributes of BODY tag</TITLE>
</HEAD>
<BODY Background= "perspective.jpg" Bgcolor="yellow" Text="Blue" Link="blue" Alink="blue"
Vlink="purple"  Leftmargin="150" Rightmargin="150" Topmargin="150" Bottommargin="150">
"If you want to be the best, you have to do things that other people aren't willing to
do."
</BODY>
</HTML>
```

After writing the above code in notepad editor, save a file as BODY.HTML. When you open this file by using web browser, the output window will be shown as below (*Figure 3.2*):

Output of the program is given below:

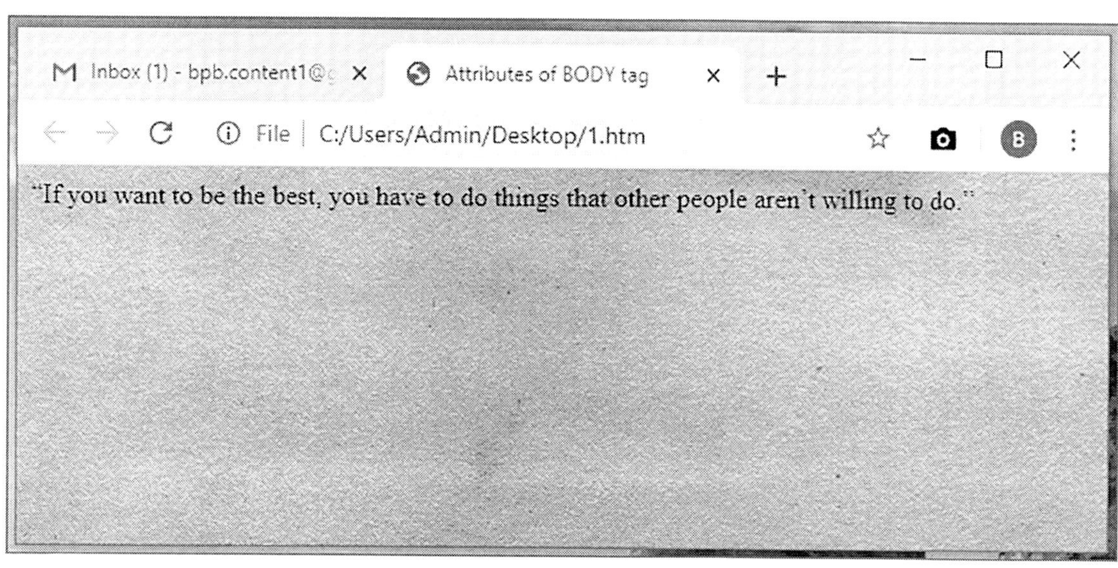

Figure 3.2: Using <Body> tag with its attributes

Internet and Web Services

The above web page is showing the following:

1. The TITLE bar shows the TITLE as "**Attributes of BODY tag**".
2. Image "**perspective.jpg**" is set on a web page over the background color.
3. The color of the text appears as blue.
4. All margins are set to 150 pixels.
5. As there is no hyperlink, therefore the output is not showing any type of link color.

Extra Byte

The attributes alink, background, bgcolor, link, text, leftmargin and topmargin are not supported by HTML 5. You need to use CSS instead.

Note: If the attributes bgcolor and background are used simultaneously, then the browser will hide the background color and set the background image over it.

RGB color values for predefined colors

Sometimes the browser Window does not display the exact color that you have set by specifying the color name with bgcolor attribute. In such case, you can use the RGB values of the color with the bgcolor attribute.

RGB is a combination of **three** colors: **Red**, **Green** and **Blue**. It is a size digit combination of letters and numbers. The size digits are usually three sets of two-digit numbers in hexadecimal format ranging from **00** to **FF** which represent the amount of red, green, and blue colors.

Some Basic RGB Color Codes are:

Color	HTML / CSS Name	Hex Code #RRGGBB	Decimal Code (R, G, B)
	Black	#000000	(0,0,0)
	White	#FFFFFF	(255,255,255)
	Red	#FF0000	(255,0,0)
	Lime	#00FF00	(0,255,0)
	Blue	#0000FF	(0,0,255)
	Yellow	#FFFF00	(255,255,0)
	Cyan / Aqua	#00FFFF	(0,255,255)
	Magenta / Fuchsia	#FF00FF	(255,0,255)
	Silver	#C0C0C0	(192,192,192)
	Gray	#808080	(128,128,128)
	Maroon	#800000	(128,0,0)
	Olive	#808000	(128,128,0)
	Green	#008000	(0,128,0)
	Purple	#800080	(128,0,128)
	Teal	#008080	(0,128,128)
	Navy	#000080	(0,0,128)

3.8.5 The FONT tag

Font tag is used for formatting the text with respect to font size, font color, and font style. It is a container tag and therefore the text which is written between this paired tag will get affected.

Font tag has three attributes viz. size, color, and face and all these attributes can be used in combination. However, it is not mandatory to use all the three tags simultaneously.

Table 3.3: The various attributes of Font tag are:

S. No	Attribute Name	Function	Example
1	Size	Sets the font size of the text.	<FONT size="10">Welcome to the world of HTML</FONT>
2	Color	Sets the color of the text.	<FONT color="Green"> Welcome to the world of HTML</FONT>
3	Face	Sets the look of the text.	<FONT face="Arial" color="Orange"> Welcome to the world of HTML</FONT>

Syntax of using FONT tag is:

```
<FONT size ="value" color ="color name" face ="list of font types"> text </font>
```

Definition

Font is the graphical representation of a text that may include a different typeface, color and size of the text.

Program 3.2: To create a web page that will make the use of Font tag and its attributes.

```
<HTML>
<HEAD>
<TITLE>HTML Font Tag</TITLE>
</HEAD>
<BODY bgcolor="Yellow">
<FONT face = "Courier" color = "red" size = "14"> When you change the quality of your
thinking, you change the quality of your life, sometimes instantly. </FONT>
</BODY>
</HTML>
```

Output of the program is given below:

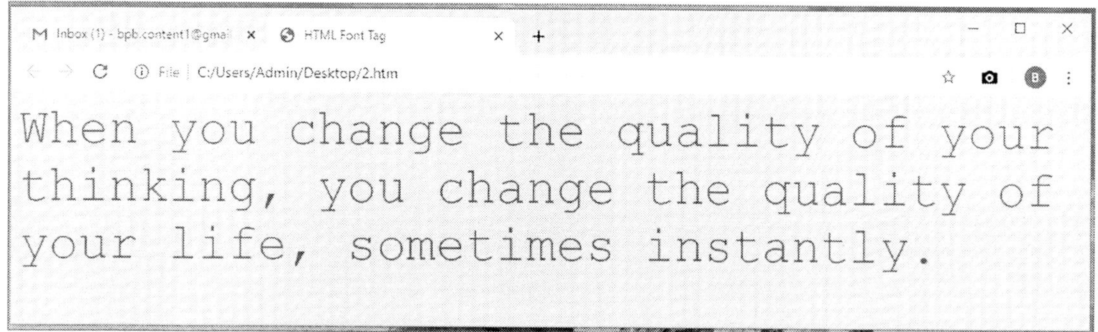

Figure 3.3: Using <Font> tag with its attributes

MEMORIZE

Size of the font is typically measured in a point (pt) which is the vertical measurement of the letters. There are approximately 72 points per inch or 2.54 cm.

3.8.6 The BASEFONT tag

BASEFONT tag is used to define the default size of the text. Sometimes, when the browser does not display the text in a specific font size which you have set it while writing the HTML code. You can use base font tag in your HTML code. It is used to change the default font properties such as font size, color, and face of the entire text in a HTML document. BASEFONT is an **empty element** i.e. it is not mandatory to close this tag.

The HTML<BASEFONT> tag is used to specify a base font for the document to use. This BASEFONT is applied to complete a document. It is to be remember that most web browsers use a relative model for sizing fonts which ranges from 1 (**smallest**) to 7 (**largest**).

However, this tag is depreciated now.

Table 3.4: The various attributes of BASEFONT tag

S. No	Attribute Name	Function	Example
1	**Size**	Sets the default text size.	<BASEFONT size="10">Welcome to the world of HTML.
2	**Color**	Sets the default color of the text.	<BASEFONT color="Green"> Welcome to the world of HTML.
3	**Face**	Sets the default font face of the text.	<BASEFONT face="Arial" color="Orange"> Welcome to the world of HTML.

Syntax of using BASEFONT tag:

```
<BASEFONT size="value" color="color name" face="list of name of font type">
```

Program 3.3: To create a web page that will make the use of BASEFONT tag and its attributes.

```
<HTML>
<HEAD>
<TITLE>HTML Basefont Tag</TITLE>
</HEAD>
<BODY bgcolor="Purple" text="White">
<BASEFONT face = "cursive,serif" color = "#ff9900" size = "4"/>
<P>Basefont tag is used to set the default color, size and font
face of the text</P>
</BODY>
</HTML>
```

BASEFONT tag works only with internet explorer.

Output of the program is given below:

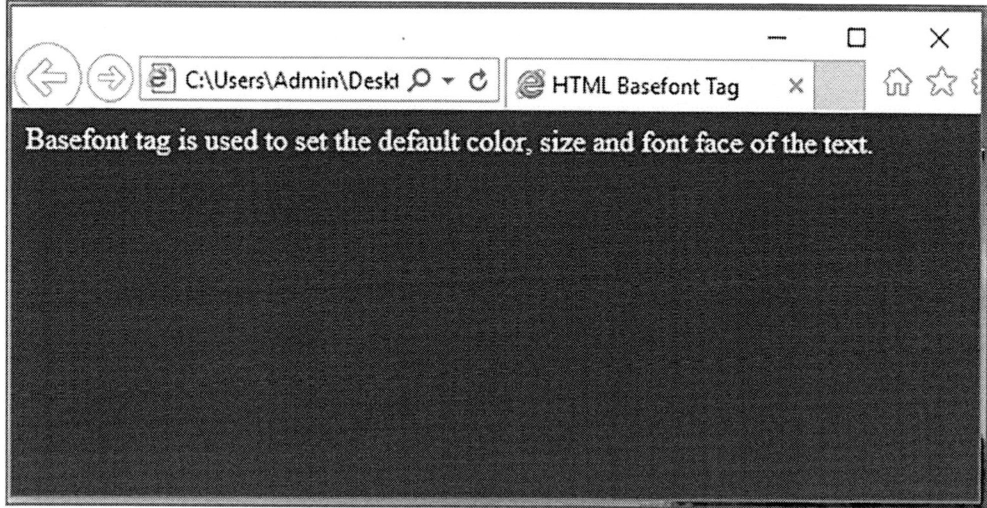

Figure 3.4: Using <BASEFONT> tag with its attributes

3.8.7 The <P> Tag

<P> tag is used for writing paragraphs. A paragraph is formed by writing several sentences which together express a single unit of information. In HTML, whenever you press **enter** key and start writing a new paragraph, a web browser does not understand it and combine this text with the previous text. Therefore, whenever you want to display different paragraphs in different lines, always use <P> tag.

<P> tag is used to mark a block of text as a paragraph. It divides your HTML document in different sections. It is a **container tag**.

<P> tag has only one attribute i.e. **align**. Align attribute is used to set the alignment of the text.

There are four different values of align attribute:

1. **align=" left"**: Aligns the text to the left side of the Window.
2. **align=" center"**: Aligns the text to the center of the Window.
3. **align=" right"**: Aligns the text to the right side of the Window.
4. **align=" justify"**: Aligns the text to the left and right side of the Window.

Syntax of using <P> tag

```
<P align="value"> paragraph </P>
```

Program 3.4: To create a web page by using <P> tag and its attribute align.

```
<HTML>
<HEAD>
    <TITLE>HTML Paragraph Tag</TITLE>
</HEAD>

<BODY bgcolor="purple" text="white">
```

```
<p align="left"> Strive for progress, not perfection." <p>

<p align="center"> "You've got to get up every morning with determination if you're going to go to bed with satisfaction." </p>

<p align="right"> "To be successful you must accept all challenges that come your way. You can't just accept the ones you like."</p>

</BODY>
</HTML>
```

The output of the program is given below:

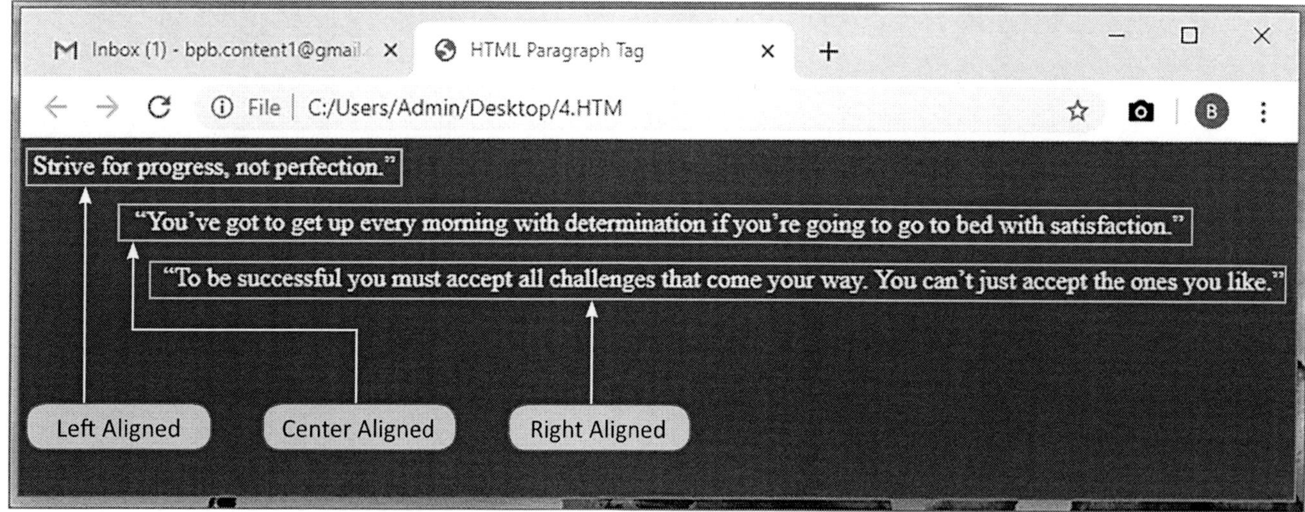

Figure 3.5: Using <p> tag with all types of alignments

Definition

Alignment is the arrangement of text or graphics relative to a margin. Left margin means the text is lined up along the left margin. Right margin means the text is lined up along the right margin. Centre alignment means the text is aligned around a midpoint. Justified alignment means that text is lined up along both margins.

3.7.8 The <PRE> tag

In HTML web browser ignores the spaces and lines within the text while displaying it as a web page. In order to retain these spaces and lines, <PRE> tag is used. Pre stands for **preformatted text**. This tag not only displays the text in a fixed width font but also displays the text in the same way as you have typed it in HTML program.

The <PRE> tag displays the text with all blanks and tabs. It is a **container tag** and therefore needs to be closed.

<PRE> tag has only one attribute i.e. **width**. It is used to set the maximum number of characters to be displayed in one line.

Syntax of using <PRE> tag is:

```
<PRE> type your text </PRE>
```

MEMORIZE

The HTML <pre> tag is used for indicating preformatted text. Browsers normally render pre text in a fixed-pitched font, with whitespace intact, and without word wrap.

Program 3.5: To create web page that will use <PRE> tag.

```
<HTML>

<HEAD>
   <TITLE>HTML Pre Tag</TITLE>
</HEAD>

  <BODY bgcolor="pink" text="black">

<PRE> "Coming together is a beginning;
                keeping together is progress;
                               working together is success." </PRE>
</BODY>
</HTML>
```

Output of the program is given below:

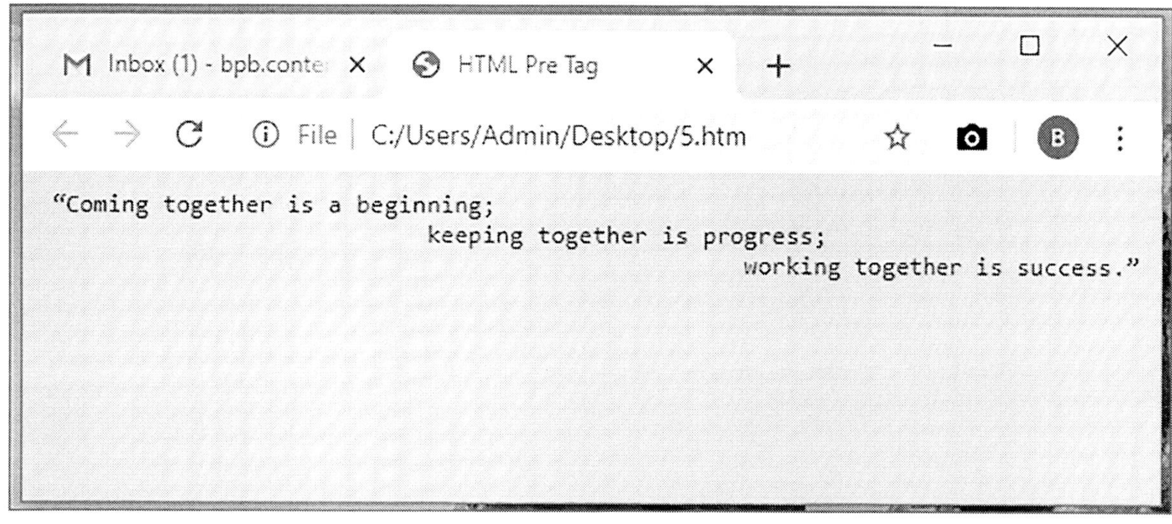

Figure 3.6: Using <pre> tag

Difference between <P> tag and <PRE> tag

The <p> tag is used for defining paragraph whereas <pre> tag defines pre-formatted text. Browsers automatically add some space (margin) before and after each <p> element while, whereas text in a <pre> element is displayed in a font (usually Courier), and it preserves both spaces and line breaks.

3.7.9 <B>, <I> and <U> tags

<B>, <I>, and <U> tags are the physical text styles that are used to change the physical appearance of the text.

- <B> tag is used to display the text in **bold**.
- <I> tag is used to *italicize* the text.
- <U> tag is used to underline the text.

All these tags are container tags and therefore must be closed. All these tags can be used in a nested manner i.e. one inside the other tag. However, all nested tags are closed in reverse order in the way they are opened.

These tags do not have any attribute.

Syntax of using <B>, <I>, and <U> tags are:

```
<B> type any text here </B>
<U> type any text here </U>
<I> type any text here </I>
```

Program 3.6: To create a web page that will make the use of <B>, <I>, <U> tags.

```
<HTML>
  <HEAD>
    <TITLE>HTML Tag</TITLE>
  </HEAD>
  <BODY bgcolor="purple" text="white">
 <PRE>
<B>Action is the foundational key to all success. </B>
<I>Action is the foundational key to all success. </I>
<u>Action is the foundational key to all success. </u>
<B><I><U>Action is the foundational key to all success. </U></I></B>
<PRE>
</BODY>
</HTML>
```

Output of the program is given below:

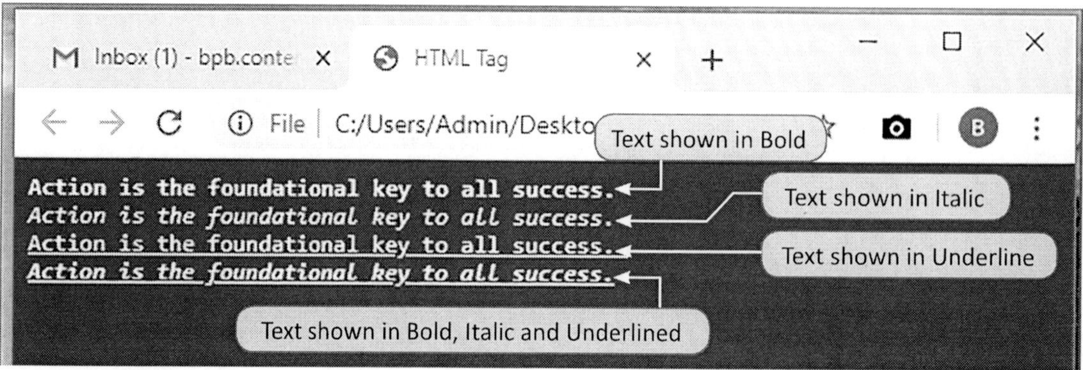

Figure 3.7: Using <B>, <I>, <U> tags

3.7.10 Making Text as Superscript and Subscript

HTML provides the tags for writing various mathematical and chemical equations.

For Example,

x^2+y^2: It is a mathematical equation.

$H_2+CO_{2:}$ It is a chemical equation.

In equation x^2+y^2 , you have seen that the number 2 is displayed little bit higher than the normal text. This feature is known as **superscript**.

In equation H_2+CO_2, 2 is displayed little lower than the normal text. This feature is known as **subscript**.

Using <SUP> tag for Mathematical Equations.

Superscripted text is displayed by using <SUP> tag. It is a container tag and does not have any attribute. The text which is written inside this paired text will be displayed little higher than the normal text.

Syntax of using <SUP> tag

```
<SUP> type your text here </SUP>
```

Program 3.7: To create a web page that will make the use of <SUP> tag.

```
<HTML>

  <HEAD>
    <TITLE>HTML Superscript Tag</TITLE>
  </HEAD>

  <BODY bgcolor=”purple” text=”white”>
<pre>
x<SUP>2</SUP> + y<SUP>2</SUP>

This program uses <SUP> superscript </SUP>tag</pre>

</BODY>
</HTML>
```

Output of the program is given below:

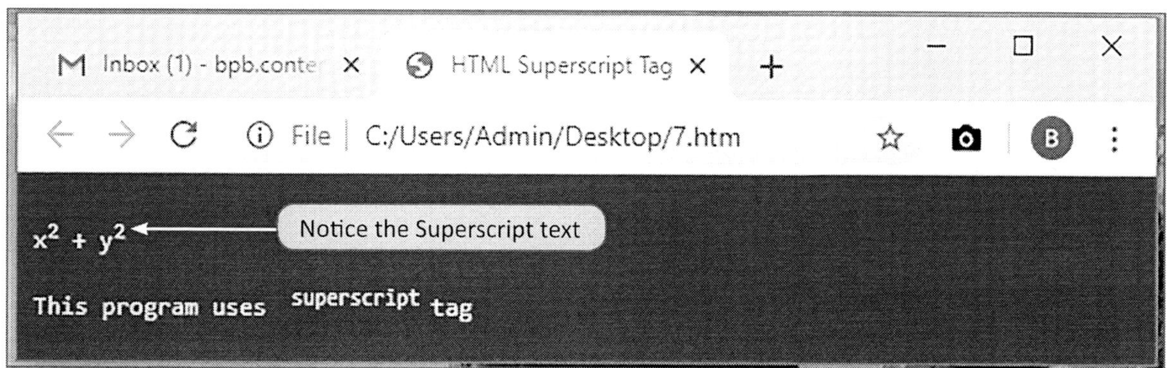

Figure 3.8: Using <Superscript> tag

Using <SUB> tag for Chemical Equations

Subscript text can be displayed by using <SUB> tag. It is a container tag and does not have any attribute.

Syntax of using <SUB> tag:

```
<SUB> type your text here </SUB>
```

Program 3.8: To create a web page that will use <SUB> tag.

```
<HTML>

  <HEAD>
    <TITLE>HTML Subscript Tag</TITLE>
  </HEAD>

  <BODY bgcolor="Purple" text="White">
  H<SUB>2</SUB>O + CO<SUB>2</SUB>

This program uses <SUB> subscript </SUB>tag

</BODY>
</HTML>
```

Output of the program is given below:

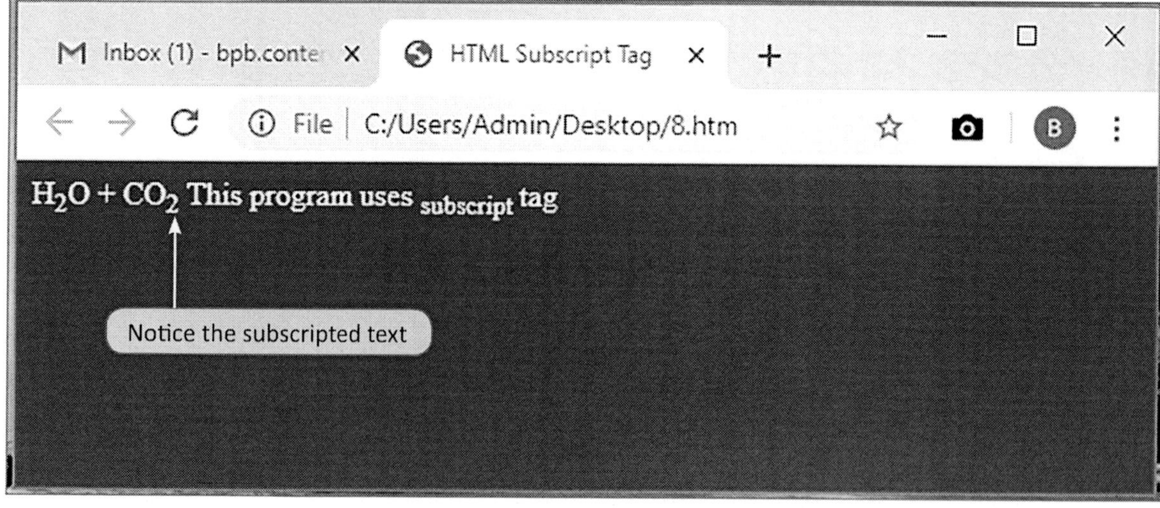

Figure 3.9: Using <Subscript> tag

MEMORIZE

Superscript: A character or symbol that is written little bit above the normal text. To make the text as superscript, <SUP> tag is used.

Subscript: A character or a symbol that is written little bit lower than the normal text. To make the text as subscript, <SUB> tag is used.

3.7.11 Creating Headings in HTML

Headings are used to emphasize the text. In HTML, there are six levels of inserting Headings from **H1** to **H6**. H1 tag displays the text in largest size. As the level increases from H1 to H6, the Headings size becomes smaller and smaller. Therefore, H6 displays the text in smallest size.

This tag is a container tag and therefore must be closed.

Syntax of using Heading tag:

```
<H1> Type your text </H1>
```

Program 3.9: To create a web page that will insert Headings in different sizes.

```
<HTML>

  <HEAD>
    <TITLE>HTML Heading Tag</TITLE>
  </HEAD>

  <BODY bgcolor="Purple" text="White">

<H1> Reading is to the mind, as exercise is to the BODY. </H1>
<H2> Reading is to the mind, as exercise is to the BODY. </H2>
<H3> Reading is to the mind, as exercise is to the BODY. </H3>
<H4> Reading is to the mind, as exercise is to the BODY. </H4>
<H5> Reading is to the mind, as exercise is to the BODY. </H5>
<H6> Reading is to the mind, as exercise is to the BODY. </H6>
</BODY>
</HTML>
```

Output of the program is given below:

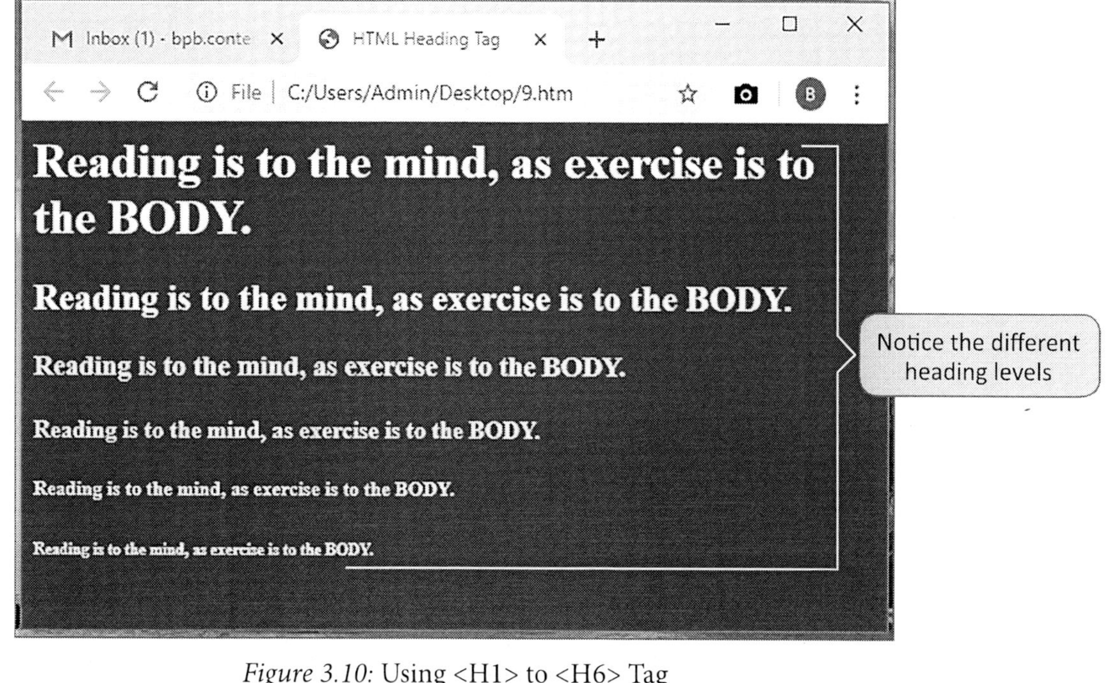

Figure 3.10: Using <H1> to <H6> Tag

3.7.12 The
 Tag for Breaking Line

Sometimes, it is required to break a paragraph i.e. remaining text to be appeared on next line.
 tag does this job.
 is an **empty tag** and therefore does not require to be closed. It provides a single line space between two lines. To provide multiple line space, use <BR> as many times as required.

For Example,

```
<p> Hello! Everybody ..... <BR> How are you</p>
```

Program 3.10: To create a web page that will show the effect of <BR> tag.

```
<HTML>
<HEAD>
<TITLE>USE OF BR TAG</TITLE>
</HEAD>
<BODY BGCOLOR="TEEL">
I WANDERED lonely as a cloud <BR>
That floats on high over vales and hills,<BR>
When all at once I saw a crowd,<BR>
A host, of golden daffodils;<BR>
Beside the lake, beneath the trees,<BR>
Fluttering and dancing in the breeze.<BR>
</BODY>
</HTML>
```

Output of the program is given below:

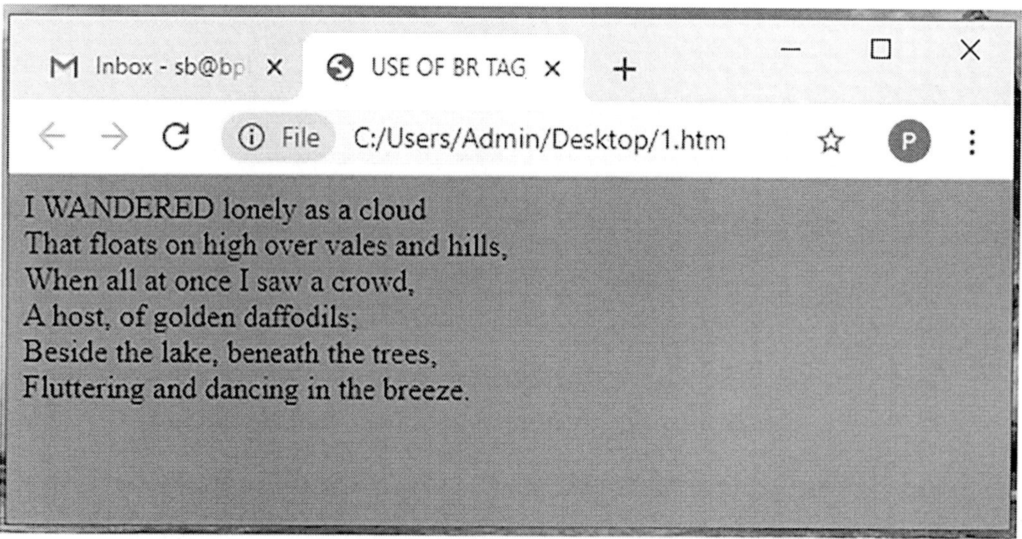

Figure 3.11(a): Using <BR> tag

See the usage of <BR> after every line. But what would happen if <BR> not used.

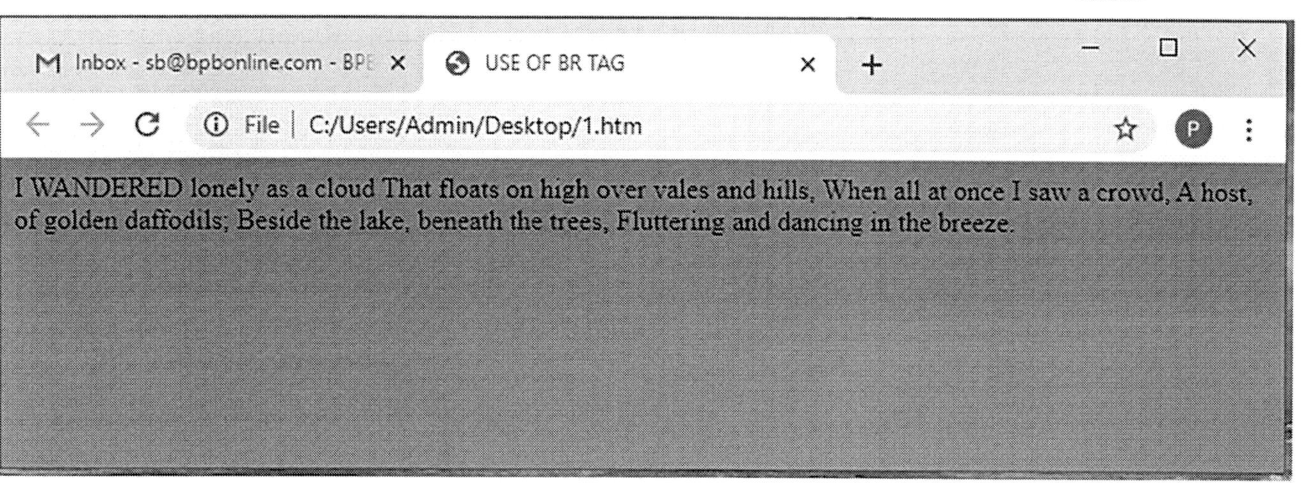

Figure 3.11(b): The output without <BR> tag

As it is clear from the above output, all lines are wrapped into a single line if the <BR> tag is not used.

3.7.13 The <HR> Tag for inserting Horizontal Line

<HR> tag is a **horizontal ruler.** This tag produces a Horizontal line spread across the width of the Browser window. The <HR> element is used to separate content (or define a change) in an HTML page. It is useful to separate sections or different paragraphs by inserting lines in a web page. The web browser starts a new line to insert horizontal rule and any text after this tag is displayed in a new line. It is an **empty tag**. The thickness, width and color; can be defined by the following attributes.

Table 3.5: The various attributes of <HR> tag

Attributes	Value	Description
Size	Values	Specifies the size (thickness) of the line. Default is 3.
Color	Color	Specifies the color of the line.
Width	Number or %	Specifies the width of the line. It may be absolute value or certain % of the Browser Window width.
NoShade	-	Specifies the shade to be appear or not. If NOSHADE option is not given 3-D lines appears.

Syntax of HR tag is:

```
<HR size=value width=value color=value Noshade>
```

For Example,

- <HR> Type a new text.
- <HR Size =5 color = Red Width = 80%> Type a new text.
- <HR Size = 4 Color= Yellow Width = 80% Noshade> Type a new text.

By default, the size of horizontal rule is 3 pixels.

A pixel represents a single dot on the screen.

Program 3.11: To create a web page that will make the use of <HR> tag with all its attributes.

```
<HTML>
<HEAD>
<TITLE>USE OF HR TAG</TITLE>
</HEAD>
<HTML>
  <H1>Learn HTML</h1>
  <P>This HTML tutorial will teach you the basics of the (Hyper Text Markup Language)
     and how to make your website from the scratch. </P>
 <HR size=”10%” color =”Red” width=”100%” Noshade>
 <H1>Learn CSS</h1>
 <P>In our CSS tutorial you will learn how to use CSS to control the style and layout
of multiple Web pages all at once. </p>
</BODY>
</HTML>
```

Output of the program is given below:

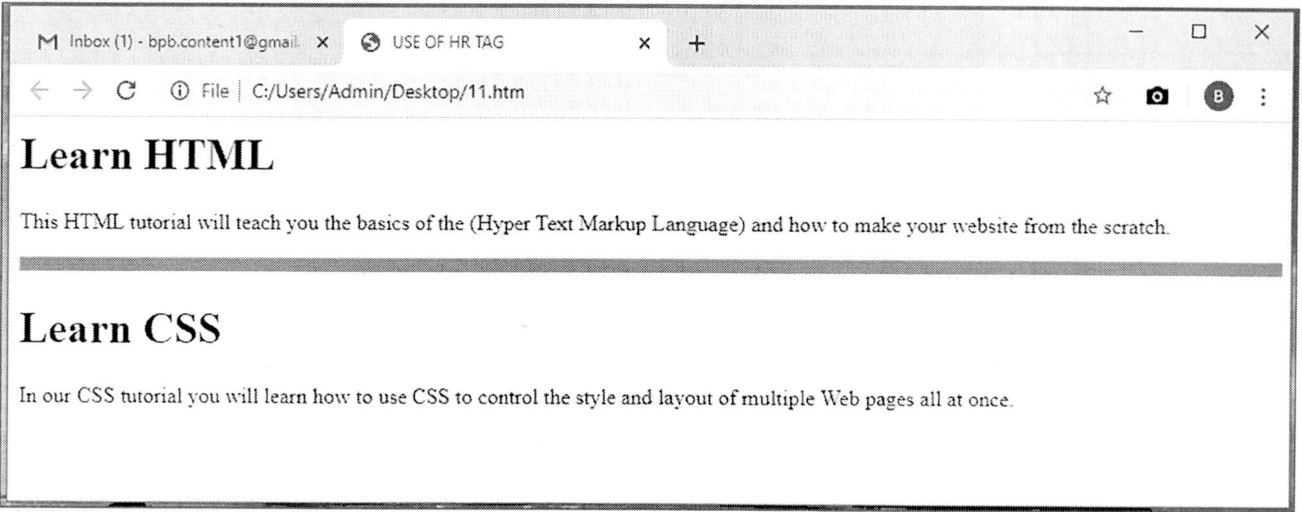

Figure 3.12: Using <HR> tag with its attributes

Check Your Progress

Answer the following questions.

1. Which tags are used for raising and lowering the text than the normal text?
2. How can you set the size and thickness of a horizontal ruler?
3. Differentiate between `<PRE>` and `<P>` tags.

3.8 SPECIAL CHARACTERS IN HTML

In HTML, there are some special characters which have some special meaning and therefore cannot be used "*as it is*" in HTML.

These characters are:

- Less than : <
- Greater than : >
- Ampersand : &
- Quote : " "
- Non-breaking space :

Extra Byte

The   tag creates a space that does not break into a new line. Instead it creates a space before, after or in-between of the text.

This tag allows you to create multiple spaces in a row, something that cannot be done by only pressing the spacebar.

Table 3.6: List of Escape Sequence for using special characters

Special character	Escape sequence	Example	Output
<	<	A<B	A<B
>	>	A>B	A>B
&	&	A&B	A&B
"	"e;	"e;A"e;	"A"
Whitespace		This is	This is

Program 3.12: To create a web page that will describe the use of Special Characters.

```
<HTML>
<HEAD>
  <TITLE>HTML Nested Lists</TITLE>
</HEAD>
<BODY bgcolor="Green">
The salary of Mohan is &lt; than the salary of Sohan
<Br><br>
The height of Yash is &gt; than the height of Agrima
<Br><br>
Agrima&amp; Yash are good friends.
<BR>
<BR>
&quot;Heena&quot; is my good friend.
<BR><BR>
This    is an example    of good friendship.
</BODY>
</HTML>
```

Output of the program is given below:

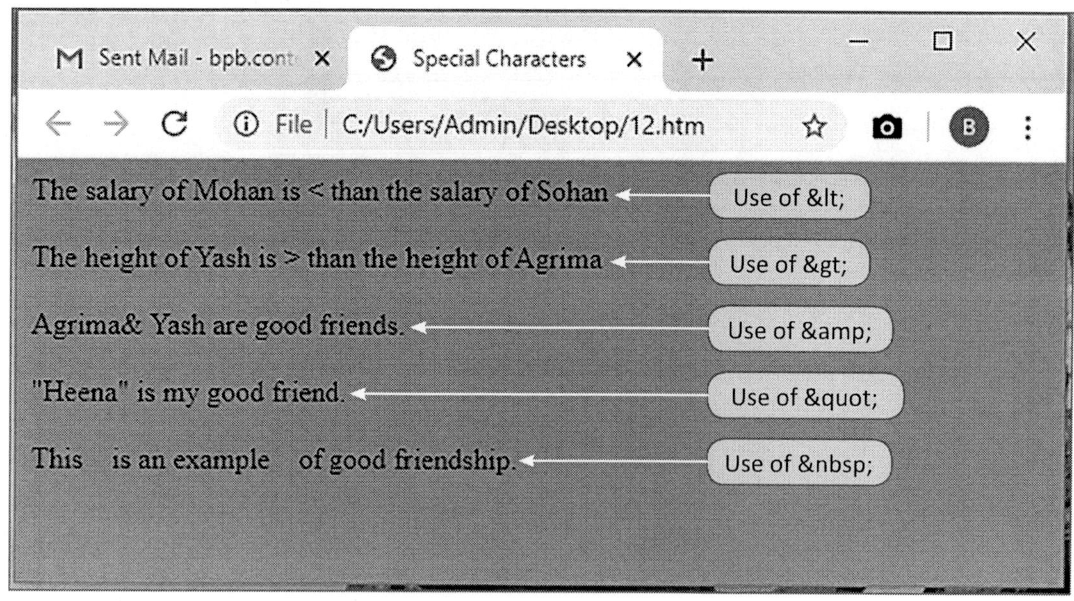

Figure 3.13: Using special characters tags

3.9 LOGICAL AND PHYSICAL TEXT STYLES

In HTML, there are two different styles for formatting the text, which can be applied either on a single word or a sentence.

Styles for formatting the text are:

a. Logical Text Styles b. Physical Text Styles

3.9.1 Logical Text Styles

Logical tags are structural tags that describe the nature and type of the content they enclose. They do not determine how the text will appear. The advantage of using the logical tags is that the meaning of the enclosed text is more precisely conveyed.

Each browser has its own technique to indicate to its viewer that the text between the tags are different.

An example of a logical tag is the <**strong**> tag**.**

By placing text in between this tag you are telling the browser that the text has some greater importance.

The Syntax for using a Logical Tag is:

```
<Tag Name> Character/s to be formatted. </Tag Name>
```

Table 3.7: Various Logical Tags Styles

Tag Name	Tag Description	Example
<strong>	Strong Emphasis	I am strong inside a <strong> tag.
<em>	Emphasis	I am emphasized inside a <em> tag.
<abbr>	Abbreviation	I am an abbreviation inside a <abbr> tag.
<cite>	Citation	I am a citation inside a <cite> tag.

Tag Name	Tag Description	Example
<code>	Code	I am programming code inside a <code> tag.
<dfn>	Definition	I am a definition inside a <dfn> tag.
<kbd>	Keyboard	I am quite like keyboard strokes inside a <kbd>tag.
<samp>	Sample	I am a sample inside a <samp> tag.
<var>	Programming Variable	I am a programming variable inside a <var> tag.

Program 3.13: To create a web page that will use all logical text styles.

```
<HTML>
<HEAD>
<TITLE>HTML LOGICAL TEXT STYLES </TITLE>
</HEAD>
<BODY>
I am strong inside a <strong> tag <BR>
I am emphasized inside a <em> tag<BR>
I am an abbreviation inside a <abbr> tag<BR>
I am a citation inside a <cite> tag<BR>
I am programming code inside a <code> tag<BR>
I am a definition inside a <dfn> tag<BR>
I am quite like keyboard strokes inside a <kbd>tag<BR>
I am a sample inside a <samp> tag<BR>
I am a programming variable inside a <var> tag<BR>
</BODY>
</HTML>
```

Output of the program is given below:

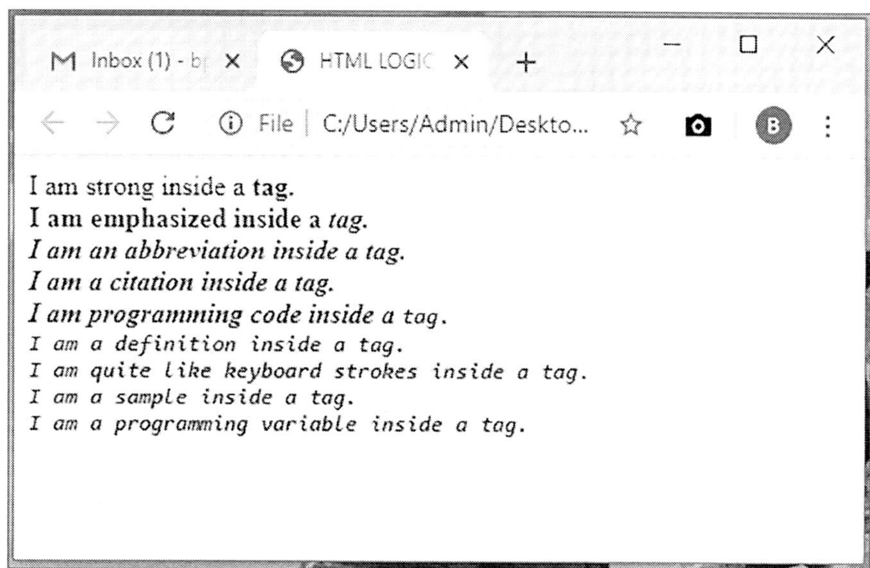

Figure 3.14: Using logical text style tags

3.9.2 Physical Text Styles

Physical tags define the physical appearance of the text i.e. how the text should be displayed in the browser. They control the physical characteristics of the text. Physical tags don't provide meaning beyond physical appearance.

Physical tags are used to indicate exactly how specific characters are to be formatted.

Extra Byte

The use of physical tags creates unnecessary limitations and problems for developers. To overcome these limitations and problems Web developers use Cascading Style Sheets to change the visual appearance of Web pages.

The Syntax for using a physical tag is:

```
<Tag Name> Characters to be formatted. </Tag Name>
```

There are many physical tags, some of which are listed in the following table. Note that these are all two sided-tags.

Table 3.8: List of Physical Tags

Tag Name	Tag Description	Example
<i>	Italics	I am in italics inside an <i> tag.
<b>	Bold	I am bold inside a <b> tag.
<u>	Underline	I am underlined inside a <u> tag.
<strike>	Strikethrough	I am in strikethrough inside a <strike> tag.
<sup>	Superscript	I am superscript inside a <sup> tag.
<sub>	Subscript	I am subscript inside a <sub> tag.
<tt>	Keyboard	I am in typewriter form in a <tt> tag.
<big>	Bigger Font	I am bigger font inside a <big> tag.
<small>	Smaller Font	I am bigger font inside a <small> tag.
<font>	Font Face	I am an inside a <font face="arial"> tag.

Program 3.14: To create a web page that will use all physical text styles tags.

```
<HTML>
<HEAD>
<TITLE> Physical text styles tags </TITLE>
</HEAD>
<BODY bgcolor="pink">
<p>
I am using <B>bold</B> tag.<br>
I am using <I>italics</I> tag.<br>
I am using <U>underline</U> tag.<br>
I am using <Strike>Strike</strike> tag.<br>
I am using <TT>typewriter</TT> tag.<br>
I am using <small>Small</small> tag.<br>
I am using <Big>Big</Big> tag.<br>
</body>
</html>
```

Output of the program is given below:

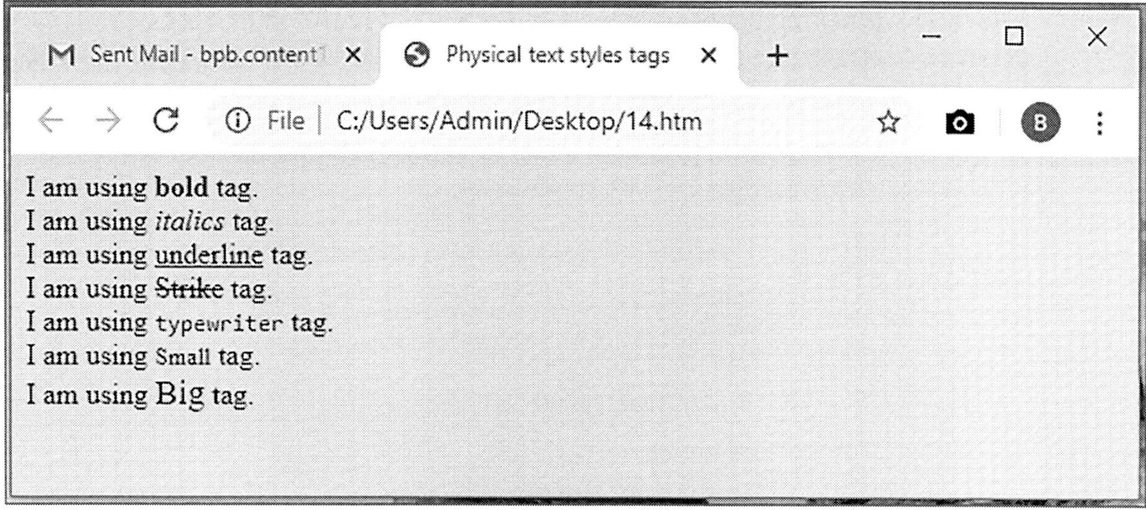

Figure 3.15: Using physical text style tags

Check Your Progress

State whether the following statements are True or False.

1. Physical tags are used to indicate exactly how specific characters are to be formatted.
2. The < tag creates a space that does not break into a new line.
3. The advantage of using the physical tags is that the meaning of the enclosed text is more precisely conveyed.

3.10 LISTS IN HTML

HTML lists are used to group the related pieces of information together. The items inside the list are known as **list elements**. All the lists contain one or more list elements. A list can be **ordered list**, **unordered list**, and **definition list**. Apart from that, there can be nested list which is a list inside another list.

The three types of lists are:

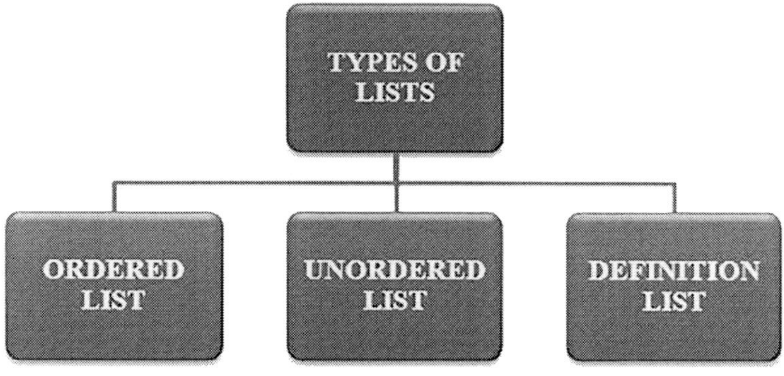

Figure 3.16: Types of Lists

* **Let's have a look on all these types of lists.**

3.10.1 Ordered list

Ordered html list is used for listing items marked with numbers. It is also known as **numbered lists.** The tag used for ordered list is <OL>. It is a **container tag** and therefore the content is written between opening <OL> and closing </OL> tags.

Each item in the ordered list starts with opening <li> tag and ends with </li> closing tag.

<OL> tag has two attributes: **Start** and **Type**.

Start attribute is used to define the starting number of the list.

The possible options of start tag are:

- <OL type = "1" start = "2"> // Numerals starts with 2.
- <OL type = "I" start = "2"> // Numerals starts with II.
- <OL type = "i" start = "2"> // Numerals starts with ii.
- <OL type = "a" start = "2"> // Letters starts with b.
- <OL type = "A" start = "2"> // Letters starts with B.

Type attribute specifies the type of numbering for listed items. By default, it is a number.

The possible options of type attribute are:

- <OL type = "1"> - Default-Case Numerals.
- <OL type = "I"> - Upper-Case Numerals.
- <OL type = "i"> - Lower-Case Numerals.
- <OL type = "A"> - Upper-Case Letters.
- <OL type = "a"> - Lower-Case Letters.

Note: It is to be noted here that both attributes are optional. Start value can begin with any number.

Program 3.15: To create a web page that will create ordered list in HTML <HTML>.

```
<HEAD>
<TITLE>HTML ordered list tag</TITLE>
</HEAD>
<BODY>
    <h3>A numbered list with start value 1:</h3>
    <OL start=1>
        <li>Apple</li>
        <li>Mango</li>
        <li>Banana</li>
        <li>Strawberry</li>
    </ol>
    <h3>An alphabetized list with start value 2:</h3>
    <ol type="A" start=2>
        <li>Red</li>
        <li>Blue</li>
```

```
    <li>Orange</li>
    <li>Pink</li>
  </OL>
  <h3>An alphabetized list with start value 3 (lowercase letters):</h3>
  <ol type="a" start=3>
    <li>Peach</li>
    <li>Apricot</li>
    <li>Banana</li>
    <li>Strawberry</li>
  </OL>
  <h3>A numbered list with start value 4(Roman numerals):</h3>
  <ol type="I" start=4>
    <li>Potato</li>
    <li>Tomato</li>
    <li>Brinjal</li>
    <li>Bottleguard</li>
  </OL>
  <h3>A numbered list with start value 5 (lowercase Roman numerals):</h3>
  <OL type="i" start=5>
    <li>Lilly</li>
    <li>Rose</li>
    <li>Sunflower</li>
    <li>Lotus</li>
  </OL>
 </BODY>
</HTML>
```

Output of the program is given below:

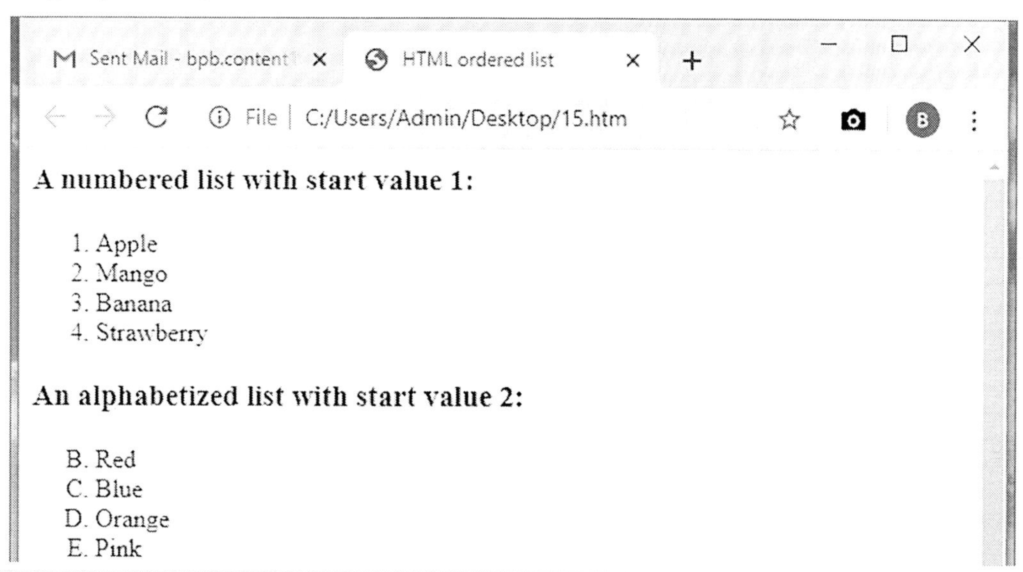

An alphabetized list with start value 3 (lowercase letters):

c. Peach
d. Apricot
e. Banana
f. Strawberry

A numbered list with start value 4(Roman numerals):

IV. Potato
V. Tomato
VI. Brinjal
VII. Bottleguard

A numbered list with start value 5 (lowercase Roman numerals):

v. Lilly
vi. Rose
vii. Sunflower
viii. Lotus

Figure 3.17: Using <OL> tag with its attributes

MEMORIZE

An ordered list is also known as numbered list. By default, HTML displays the list in ascending order of numbers.

3.10.2 Unordered List

An unordered html list is used for listing items marked with bullets. It is also known as **bulleted lists.** The tag used for unordered list is <UL>. It is a container tag and therefore the content is written between opening <UL> and closing </UL> tags.

Each item in the ordered list starts with opening <li> tag and ends with </li> closing tag.

The default bullet type for most web browsers is a full disc (black circle), but this can be adjusted by using an HTML attribute called **type**.

<UL> tag uses only one attribute i.e. type that defines the type of bullet.

Three types of bullets which can be used are: **circle**, **disc** and **square**.

Following are the possible options:

1. <UL type = "square">
2. <UL type = "disc">
3. <UL type = "circle">

Note: These is no start attribute.

Program 3.16: To create a web page that will create an unordered list in HTML.

```
<HTML>
<HEAD>
<TITLE>HTML Unordered List</TITLE>
```

```
</HEAD>
<BODY>
    <h2>Unordered List with Square Bullet</h2>
    <ul type="square">
        <li>Pizza</li>
        <li>Burger</li>
        <li>Noodles</li>
    </ul>
<h2>Unordered List with Disc Bullet</h2>
<ul type="disc">
        <li>Coke</li>
        <li>Fanta</li>
        <li>Dew</li>
    </ul>
<h2>Unordered List with Circle Bullet</h2>
<ul type="circle">
        <li>Hot Tea</li>
        <li>Ice Tea</li>
        <li>Coffee</li>
    </ul>
</BODY>
</HTML>
```

Output of the program is given below:

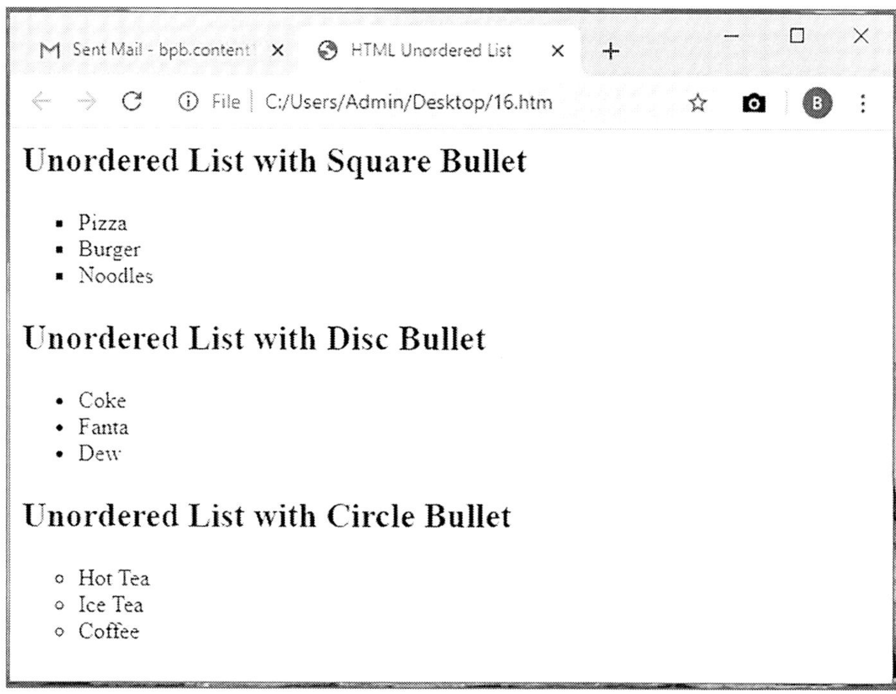

Figure 3.18: Using <UL> tag with its attributes

MEMORIZE

An unordered list is also known as bulleted list as it creates bullets before the list item. By default, it displays the list with solid circle bullet.

Check Your Progress

Fill in the blanks.

1. The expanded form of <OL> is _______________.
2. The expanded form of <UL> is _______________.
3. <OL> uses _______________ attributes.

3.10.3 Nested Lists

Lists can be inserted one inside the other and this concept is known as **nested lists**. A nested list or a sublist is a list within a list. ***For example***, you can insert ordered list inside unordered list and vice-versa.

To make nested list, you should make another list inside the <li> and </li> as created in the following example:

Program 3.17: To create a web page that will use nested lists.

```
<HTML>
<HEAD>
   <TITLE>HTML Nested Lists</TITLE>
</HEAD>
<BODY>
   <h4>HTML Nested Lists</h4>
   <ul>
      <li>Books Written By Khushwant Singh
         <ul>
            <li>Train to Pakistan</li>
            <li>I Shall never Hear a Nightingale </li>
      <li>The Portrait of a Lady: Collected Stories</li>

         </ul>
      </li>
<br>
      <li>Books Written By Mahatma Gandhi</li>
<ul>
         <li>An Autobiography or The Story of My Experiments with Truth</li>
         <li>The Essential Gandhi </li>
         <li>The Words of Gandhi</li>

      </ul>
```

```
    </ul>
</BODY>
</HTML>
```

Output of the program is given below:

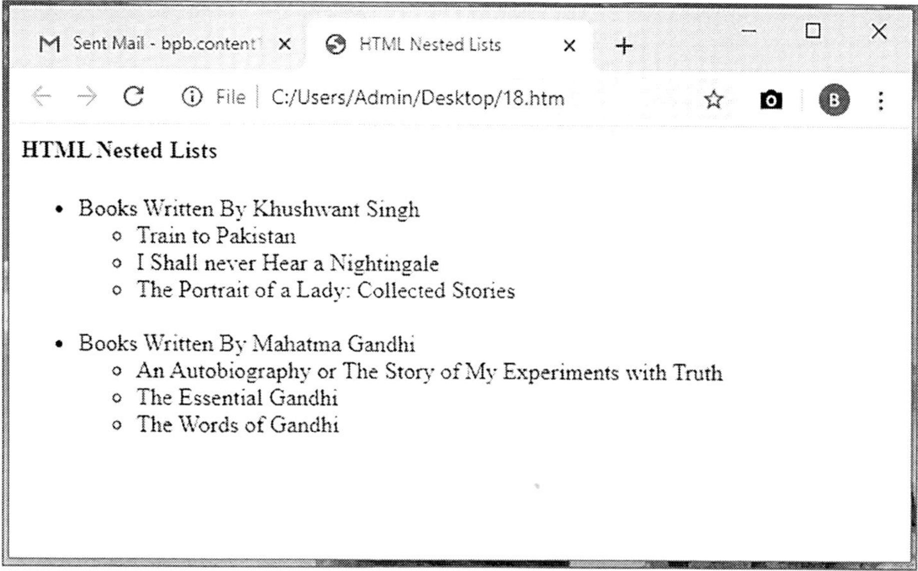

Figure 3.20: Output of the nested list

Program 3.18: To create a web page by using nested lists.

```
<HTML>
<HEAD>
   <TITLE>HTML Nested Lists</TITLE>
</HEAD>
<BODY>
   <h4>HTML Nested Lists</h4>
   <ul>
      <li>Chapter 1
         <ul>
            <li>Section 1</li>
            <li>Section 2 </li>

         </ul>
      </li>
      <li>Chapter 2</li>
<ul>
         <li>Section 1</li>
         <li>Section 2 </li>

      </ul>
      <li>Chapter 3</li>
<ul>
            <li>Section 1</li>
```

Internet and Web Services

```
            <li>Section 2 </li>

        </ul>

    </ul>
</BODY>
</HTML>
```

Output of the program is given below:

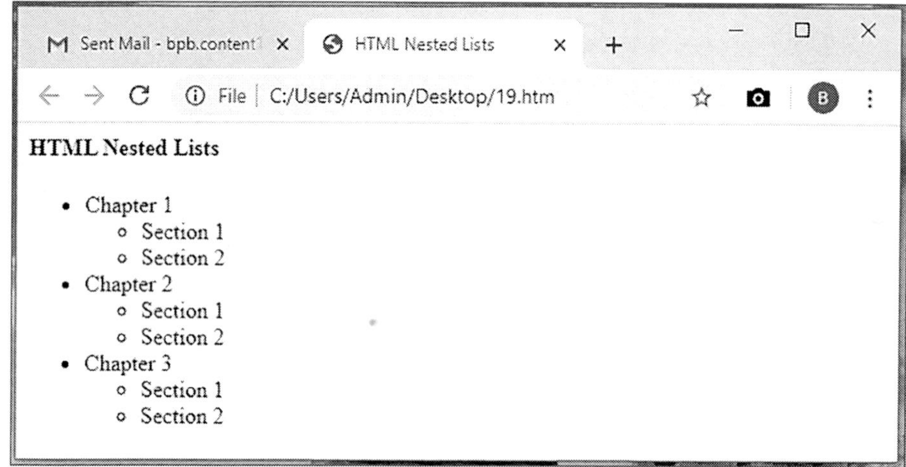

Figure 3.21: Output of the program

Check Your Progress

Answer the following questions.

1. Which tag is used for defining lists?
2. Which tag is used for describing the definition?
3. How <DL> is different from<OL>?

3.10.4 Definition lists

Using HTML, you can also create list of definition terms with their definitions. A description, or definition, list is used to arrange terms or names with a description in the same way as they are arranged in a dictionary.

Three tags are used for Definition list:

- <DL> tag is used for creating definition list and is a **container tag**.
- <DT> tag is used for listing definition term and is an **empty tag**.
- <DD> tag is used for describing the definition and is an **empty tag**.

Syntax of using <DL> tag along with <DT> and <DD> tags is:

```
<DL>

<DT> Definition term </DT>

<DD> Description of definition term</DD>

</DL>
```

The <DL> tag is a container tag & is written with the <DT> and <DD> elements inserted between the start and end tag. The number of those elements will depend on the number of definition terms and descriptions in the list.

Program 3.19: To create a web Page that will describe the use of definition list tag.

```
<HTML>
<HEAD>
<TITLE>HTML font Tag</TITLE>
</HEAD>
<BODY>
<H2> Use of Definition List tag</h2>
<DL>
<DT>Bookmark</DT>
<DD>A bookmark is a saved link to a particular Web page. Microsoft Internet Explorer denotes bookmarks as "favourites."</DD>

<DT>Cookie</DT>
<DD>A piece of code or data created by a web server and stored on a user's computer. It is used to keep track of the user's usage patterns and preferences. </DD>

<DT>Firewall</DT>
<DD>A firewall is a barrier that acts as a security system to protect trusted computer systems and networks from outside connections and untrusted networks, such as the Internet.</DD>
</DL>
</BODY>
</HTML>
```

Output of the program is given below:

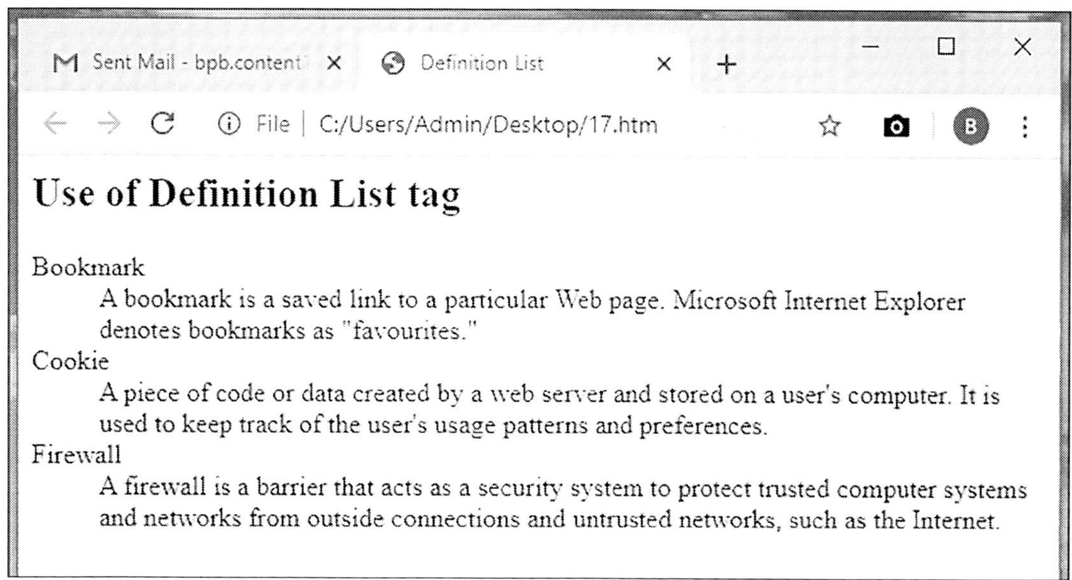

Figure 3.19: Using <DL> tag with its attributes

MEMORIZE

Definition list is used to create a list of definition with their description. It is an indented list without any number or bullet preceded the text.

Comments in HTML

- Comment are one type of textual content which appear in your HTML code, but are not rendered by user's browser.
- Comments are given between special <!-- and --> characters.
- Browsers ignore the text between the comment characters.
- Comments are also useful for debugging HTML code, because you can comment out HTML lines of code, one at a time, to search for errors:

For Example,

This Code	Would Display
<p> This html comment would <! - - This is a comment - - > be displayed like this. <p>	This html comment would be displayed like this.

Note: You don't see the text between the tags <!-- and -->. If you look at the source code, you would see the comment. To view the source code for this page, in your browser Window, select **View** and then select **Source**.

Program 3.20: Design a web page that will use comment tag.

```
<HTML>
<HEAD>
<TITLE>Use of comment tag </TITLE>
</HEAD>
<BODY bgcolor="pink">
<!--This is a comment. Comments are not displayed in the browser-->
<p>This is a paragraph. </p>
</body>
</html>
```

Output of the program is given below:

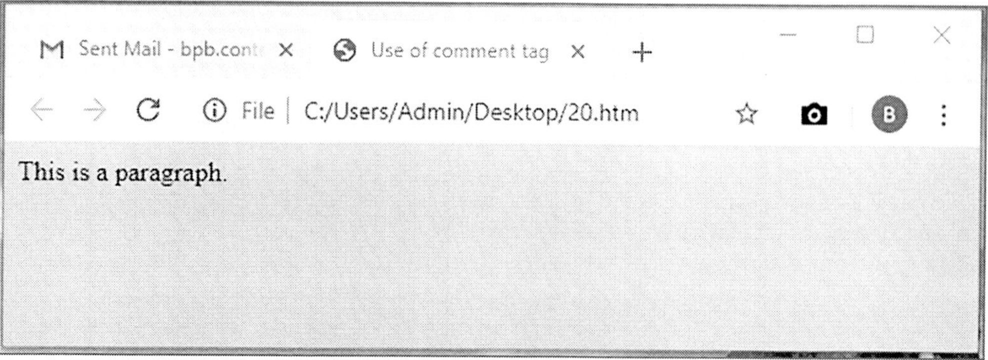

Figure 3.22: Inserting comments

Let's Revise

- Hyper Text Markup Language (HTML) is a document-layout and hyperlink-specification language i.e., a language used to design the layout of a document and to specify the hyperlink.
- HTML tells the browser how to display the contents of a hypertext document i.e., a document including text, images, and other support media.
- A Tag is a coded HTML command that indicates how part of web page should be displayed. You can type HTML in capital letters as well as in small letters.
- An Attribute is a special word used inside tag to specify additional information to tag such as color, alignment etc.
- HTML container elements require a starting as well as an ending tag.
- HTML Empty elements require a starting tag and not an ending tag.
- The HTML Tag is used to mark the beginning and end of an HTML document.
- The HEAD tag is used to define the document header. Tag contains information about the document, including its TITLE and document description.
- The BODY tag defines the document's BODY. It contains all the contents of an HTML document, such as text, images, lists, table.
- HTML has six levels of headings, numbered 1 through 6, with 1 being the largest. Headings are typically displayed in larger or bolder fonts than normal BODY text.
- To start a new paragraph, <P>tag is used. It is a container tag.
- BR tag is used to end one line.
- Horizontal Rules <HR> tag produces a horizontal line spread across the width of the browser window.
- <FONT> tag lets you change the size, style and color of the text. It is generally used for changing the appearance of a short segment of the text.
- <BASEFONT> tag lets you define the basic size for the font, the browser will use to render normal document text.
- Comment are one type of textual content which appear in your HTML code, but are not rendered by user's browser.
  - Comments are given between special <!-- and--> characters.
  - Browsers ignore the text between comment characters.
- Subscript and Superscript
  - To write something like H20, you can write it as H ₂O.
  - Similarly, to write something like X2, you can write it as X².
- Three types of lists are unordered, ordered and definition lists.
  - Unordered list is a bulleted list.
  - Ordered list is a numbered list.
  - Definition list creates a list of definitions.

Learning Zone

SECTION A: OBJECTIVE TYPE QUESTIONS

A. MULTIPLE CHOICE QUESTIONS.

1. Which brackets are used to start the tag?

   a. [ ] b. { } c. < > d. ( )

2. Which HTML tag is used to change the size, color, and face of the text?

   a. <FONT> b. <MOD> c. <F> d. <TEXT>

3. Which HTML tag would you apply the bgcolor attribute to in order to change the background color of the web page?

   a. <HTML> b. <HEAD> c. <BODY> d. <p>

4. In which section of an HTML document do you enter the <TITLE> element?

   a. The BODY section b. The footer section

   c. The style section d. The HEAD section

5. An unordered list can be created by using ___________ tag.

   a. <UL> b. <OL> c. <BL> d. <NL>

6. Which attribute is used to align the headings?

   a. Align b. Right c. Right d. Center

7. Which tag is used to write chemical equations?

   a. Sup b. Sub c. Subscript d. Superscript

8. Which of the following heading tags will cause a browser to render text at the largest default size?

   a. <H3> b. < H2> c. < H5> d. <H4>

9. Which of the following is the proper syntax to start an HTML comment?

   a. <!!> b. <!> c. <Comment> d. <Notate>

10. Which of the following is the HTML tag used to insert a horizontal rule?

    a. <H1> b. <HR> c. <RULE> d.

11. What HTML container tags do you apply to text to format the text as a paragraph?

    a. <PARA></PARA> b. <TEXT></TEXT> c. <p> </p> d. <STYLE></STYLE>

12. The attribute used with the <HR> tag having 2D rule is:

    a. Width b. Size c. Noshade d. None of these

Ans. 1. c 2. a 3. c 4. d 5. a 6. a
7. b 8. b 9. c 10. b 11. c 12. c

B. FILL IN THE BLANKS.

1. HTML stands for ___________.
2. The full form of <sub> tag is ___________.
3. The lowest level of heading is ___________.

4. HTML tags are not ____________.
5. ____________ and ____________ are two types of tags.
6. Unordered list is also known as ____________.
7. Ordered list is also known as ____________.
8. The three attributes used with font tag are ____________, ____________ and ____________.
9. The RGB value of a color is a ____________ digit combination of letter and number.
10. The ____________ attribute is used to add background color of a web page.

Ans. 1. Hypertext Markup Language 2. Subscript 3. H6
4. Case sensitive 5. Container, Empty
6. Bulleted list 7. Numbered list
8. Face, color, size 9. 6-Digit 10. bgcolor

C. STATE WHETHER THE FOLLOWING STATEMENTS ARE TRUE OR FALSE.

1. The full form of HTML is Human Text Markup Language.
2. Web pages on your computer screen are also known as E-pages.
3. Website is a collection of several web pages.
4. Software used to display and retrieve web pages is known as interpreter.
5. Charles Babbage is the inventor of HTML language.
6. The first website in the history of internet was published by Tim Berners Lee.
7. HTML5 has a standard interface and it works with computer and mobile phones.
8. Empty tags are not required to be closed.
9. In HTML, you use enter key to start a new paragraph.
10. <H6> tag is the second level heading tag.
11. Text typed within <!—and--> tag will be displayed by the browser.
12. White is the default background color of a web page.
13. Logical tags are mostly used for writing mathematical equations.
14. <BASEFONT> tag is supported only by the internet explorer.
15. An ordered list by default shows the list items in ascending order.
16. Creating new list inside a main list to display sub items is known as definition list.
17. It is not required to close <SUP> and <SUB> tags.
18. <DT> is expanded as definition term.
19. <UL> is expanded as unique list.
20. There is no difference between <p> tag and <pre> tag.

Ans. 1. False 2. True 3. True 4. False 5. False
6. True 7. True 8. True 9. False 10. False
11. False 12. True 13. False 14. True 15. True
16. False 17. False 18. True 19. False 20. False

SECTION B: SOLVED THEORY QUESTIONS

1. **What is the extension of HTML documents?** **(Delhi 2012)**

Ans: The HTML documents/files are saved with extension .HTML or .htm.

2. **What do you mean by tag?**

Ans: A tag is defined as the building block of codes in an HTML documents. Tags are also known as coded elements.

3. **Give some examples of container elements and empty elements used in HTML.**

Ans: Container elements: <HEAD>, <TITLE>, <BODY>, <OL>, <UL>.
Empty elements: <BR>, <HR>, <LI>.

4. **Write HTML code to set the image 'flower. gif' stored in 'My Pictures' folder in D: drive as the background image of your Web page.**

Ans: The HTML code is <BODY background="D:\My Pictures \Flower.gif">.

5. **Write one basic difference between bgcolor and background attributes.**

Ans: The bgcolor attribute is used to set the background color of a web page whereas background is used to set the background image of a web page.

6. **Name two common graphic files formats that most browser recognize. (CBSE 2007)**

Ans: **The two common graphic file formats are: .gif and .jpg.**

7. **Explain the following statement: <BODY bgcolor="yellow" text ="red" alink="Purple">**

Ans: The statement says that the background color of a web page is yellow, the color of the text is red and active link color is purple.

8. **What is the use of <FONT> tag in HTML code? What are its three attributes?**

Ans: The <FONT> tag is used to change the size, color, and type face of the text on HTML page. The three attributes of FONT tag are: size, color, and face.

9. **Write the expansions of the following tags used in HTML.**

a.
 b. <OL> c. <HR> d. <DL>

Ans: a.
: Break line b. <OL>: Ordered list
c. <HR>: Horizontal Rule d. <DL>: Definition list

10. **What are the different forms of lists used in HTML?**

Ans: The different forms of list are:
a. Ordered List b. Unordered List c. Definition List

11. **What is the purpose of using <LI> tag in an unordered list?**

Ans: <LI> creates bulleted points for each list item.

12. **What is the purpose of using HTML?**

Ans: Hyper Text Markup Language (HTML) is used to create Web pages and tells the browser how to display them. It designs the basic layout and formatting of Web pages. HTML is made up of elements or tags and attributes, which work together to identify document parts and tell browser how to display them.

13. **What do you mean by an attribute in HTML?**

Ans: Attributes provide some additional information about HTML elements. Attribute name come inside the opening tag after tag name. These come in name/value pairs like name="value".
The syntax of using attribute is:
<Tag_name attribute_name="value">

For Example, <BODY bgcolor="red">

Here, the attribute is bgcolor that specify the background color of a web page.

14. What are the two categories of HTML elements? Define them.

Ans: All HTML elements can be categorized into two categories. Container elements and empty elements.

Container elements are those elements that require a start as well as an end tag.

For example: <HTML>, <HEAD>, <BODY>.

Empty elements are those elements that require only a starting tag and not an ending tag.

For example: <BR>, <HR>, <LI> etc.

15. List any two types of alignment that can be applied to a paragraph in HTML.

Ans: The two types of alignment that can be applied to a paragraph are:

a. Left alignment: This type of alignment aligns text in left. This is the default alignment.

   Syntax:

   <P align="left"></P>

b. Right alignment: This type of alignment aligns text in right within the paragraph.

   Syntax:

   <P align="right"></P>

16. Differentiate between <BR> and <HR> tags.

Ans:
 tag is used to insert a line break which means the text/image following the tag will be moved to the next line while <HR> tag is used to insert horizontal line that can divide the information into sections.

17. How is <OL> tag is different from <UL> tag?

Ans: <OL> tag is used to create ordered list which is also known as numbered list. By default, ordered lists are marked with numbers, such as 1, 2, 3.

For example:

```
<OL>
    <li> Breakfast</li>
    <li> Lunch </li>
</OL>
```

Output of the above code is:

1. Breakfast
2. Lunch

<UL> tag is used to create unordered list which is also known as bulleted list. By default, every item in the HTML list is marked by a plain black dot.

For example:

```
<UL>
    <li>Apples</li>
    <li>Oranges</li>
</UL>
```

Output of the above code is:

- Apples
- Oranges

18. What is the purpose of using type and start attributes used in ordered lists?

Ans: type attribute specifies the type of numbers or bullets depending on whether the list item is inside an ordered list or unordered list.

size attribute is used to change the beginning value of an ordered list. Normally, the ordered list begins with 1. It lets us to /further customize an HTML ordered list by setting a new starting digit or alphabet for the ordered list element.

Syntax:

<OL start="value" type = "value">

For example:

```
<h1> List of Computer Books</h1>
<OL type='A' start=1>
<li>HTML</li>
<li>C++</li>
<li>Networking</li>
<li>JAVA Core</li>

</OL>
```

19. What is definition list?

Ans: Definition List is a list of items, with a description of each item. HTML definition lists (<DL>) are indented list without any bullet symbol or any number in front of each item. This list elements have a unique array of tags and elements; the resulting lists are like those we would see in a dictionary. Tags used in definition lists are as follows:

a. <DL>: Opening tag that defines the start of the list.

b. <DT>: List item that defines the definition term.

c. <DD>: Definition of the list item.

d. </DL>: Closing tag that defines the end of the list.

20. What is a <BASEFONT> tag? Name the attributes used with this tag.

Ans: <BASEFONT> tag specifies a default font size, color, and face for the font, the browser will use to render normal document text, i.e. the text, for which no other font setting has been provided. It occurs only for one time in the document. Attributes hold with basefont are: size, color and face.

23. Where can a comment be placed in an HTML document? How is it useful?

OR

How do you give a comment in HTML?

OR

Why are comment included in HTML document? With the help of an example, explain how they are included in HTML code?

OR

How are comments inserted in HTML code? Explain with an example. (CBSE 2007, 2006, 2005)

Ans: Comments are inserted in HTML code with the help of <!—....—> tag. To insert the text as comment, type the text between <!– and —> tag, then that text will be ignored by the browser and invisible for the user.

Example:

```
<HTML><BODY>
<!--This is a comment.-->
This is a book
</BODY><HTML>
```

21. Distinguish between <P> tag and <BR> tag with the help of an example. (Delhi 2018)

Ans:

<P> tag	 tag
It is a container element.	It is an empty element.
It is used to define a paragraph of the text on the web page.	It is used to insert line break.
It inserts line break with extra space in the beginning.	It does not insert any extra space.
This tag has an attribute align.	This tag has no attribute.
Example: <HTML> <BODY> <P> This is a paragraph.</P> </BODY> </HTML>	Example: <HTML> <BODY> This is a 1ine break into the Web document. </BODY> </HTML>

22. Write HTML code to display the unordered list (with square bullets) of two cities "DELHI" and "MUMBAI". The web page should have a yellow background and the title of the page should be 'My Cities'. (Sample paper 2019-20)

Ans:
```
<HTML>
<HEAD>
<TITLE> My Cities</TITLE>
</HEAD>
<BODY bgcolor="yellow">
<UL type="square">
<LI> DELHI </LI>
<LI> MUMBAI </LI>
</UL>
</BODY>
</HTML>
```

23. Write HTML code to display an ordered list (with uppercase roman numbers) listing any three subjects being taught in your school. The web page should have a red background and the title of the page should be 'My Subjects'. (Sample paper 2019-20)

Ans:
```
<HTML>
<HEAD>
<TITLE> My Subjects</TITLE>
</HEAD>
<BODY bgcolor="red">
<OL type="I">
<LI> Science</LI>
<LI> Maths</LI>
<LI> Computers</LI>
</OL>
</BODY>
</HTML>
```

24. How can the font size of a single line on a web page be changed?

Ans: The font size of a single line on a web page can be changed by using the <FONT> tag or using the Heading levels.

25. **What is the method of viewing the source code of the current page in web Page?**

Ans: To view the HTML source code behind a web page, follow these simple steps:

1. Go online and open a web browser, such as Mozilla Firefox or Internet Explorer.
2. Go to any website by typing the URL of any web page whose HTML source code you'd like to see.
3. Look at the HTML source of the page:
1. In Firefox, choose View→Page Source from the menu bar.
2. In Internet Explorer, choose View→Source.

26. **Which heading level gives the most prominent heading?**

Ans: H1 heading level is the most prominent heading.

27. **Expand the following tags used in HTML:**

a. <HR> b. < SUB > c. <UL> d. < A >

Ans: a. <HR>: Horizontal Rule b. < SUB >: Subscript

c. <UL>: Unordered List d. < A >: Anchor

28. **How would you preview changes made in an HTML code without closing the HTML document in the text editor?**

Ans: We can preview the changes by refreshing the HTML page.

SECTION C: APPLICATION ORIENTED QUESTIONS

1. **Write a code that will produce the following output:**

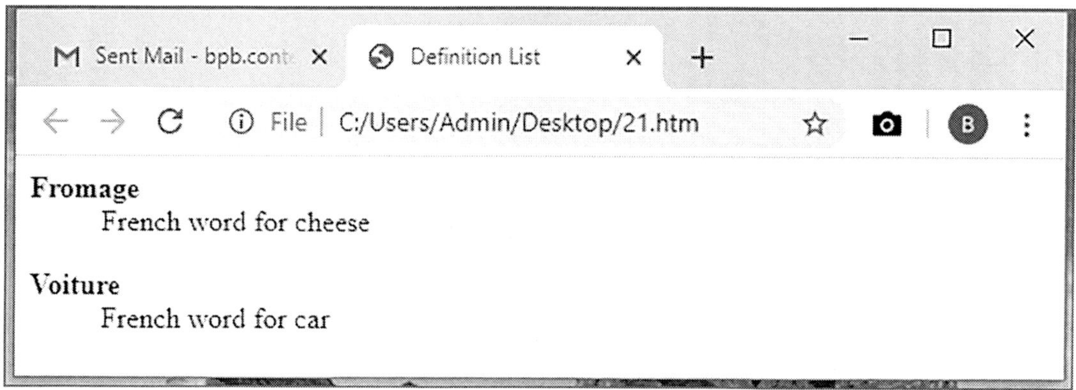

Ans:

```
<HTML>
<HEAD>
<TITLE>Definition List </TITLE>
</HEAD>
<BODY>
<DL>
<B> <DTXB> Fromage</B>
<DD> French word for cheese
</DL>
<DL>
<B> <DTXB> Voiture</B>

<DD> French word for car
</DL>
</BODY>
</HTML>
```

2. **Write HTML program that make body text appear 60 pixels away from the top edge of page and 75 pixels away from left edge of page.**

Ans:

```
<HTML>
<HEAD>
 <TITLE>Usage of Margins </TITLE>
</HEAD>
<BODY topmargin = "60" leftmargin = "75">
Information Technology is an important subject of Engineering.
</BODY>
</HTML>
```

3. **Identify the error(s) in the following HTML code. Also, write the correct code and underline the correction.**
<BODY color="red" background ="logo.jpg">

Ans: Error is: use bgcolor attribute in place of color attribute.
The correct code is:
<BODY bgcolor = "red" background ="logo.jpg">

4. **Identify error(s) in the following HTML code. Also, write the correct code.** **(CBSE 2008)**
<OL> type="a" start="d">

Ans: <OL> tag's attributes should be placed in between <and>. In <OL> list, the start attribute must be set to a numeric value and type attribute specifies 'A', 'a', T 'i' or '1'. So, the correct code is:
<OL type="a" start="4">

5. **Palvi is planning to open her bakery shop. She is not computer savvy so she has requested you to help her. What all steps you will use to create a simple web page for the bakery.**

Ans: Steps for creating a web page for her bakery is:
   a. Write a paragraph about the bakery shop.
   b. Give address, contact details and opening and closing time of shop.
   c. Add <H1> tag heading to the title.
   d. Use the <body> tag and its attributes in the beginning of the text.
   e. Set the background color of a web page or an image as a wallpaper.

6. **Muneesh is creating a web page using html. While developing web page, he found the following html codes written incorrectly. Help him to correct these following html codes:'**
   a. H <sub> 4 </sup>
   b. <ol type="Square>
   c. <font size="Green" color="Blue">
   d. </u> This is my book<u>

Ans: The corrections in the above code is:
   a. H ₄
   b. <UL type = "Square">
   c. <font size="10" color="Green">
   d. <u>This is my book</u>

7. **Consider the given output and answer the questions:**

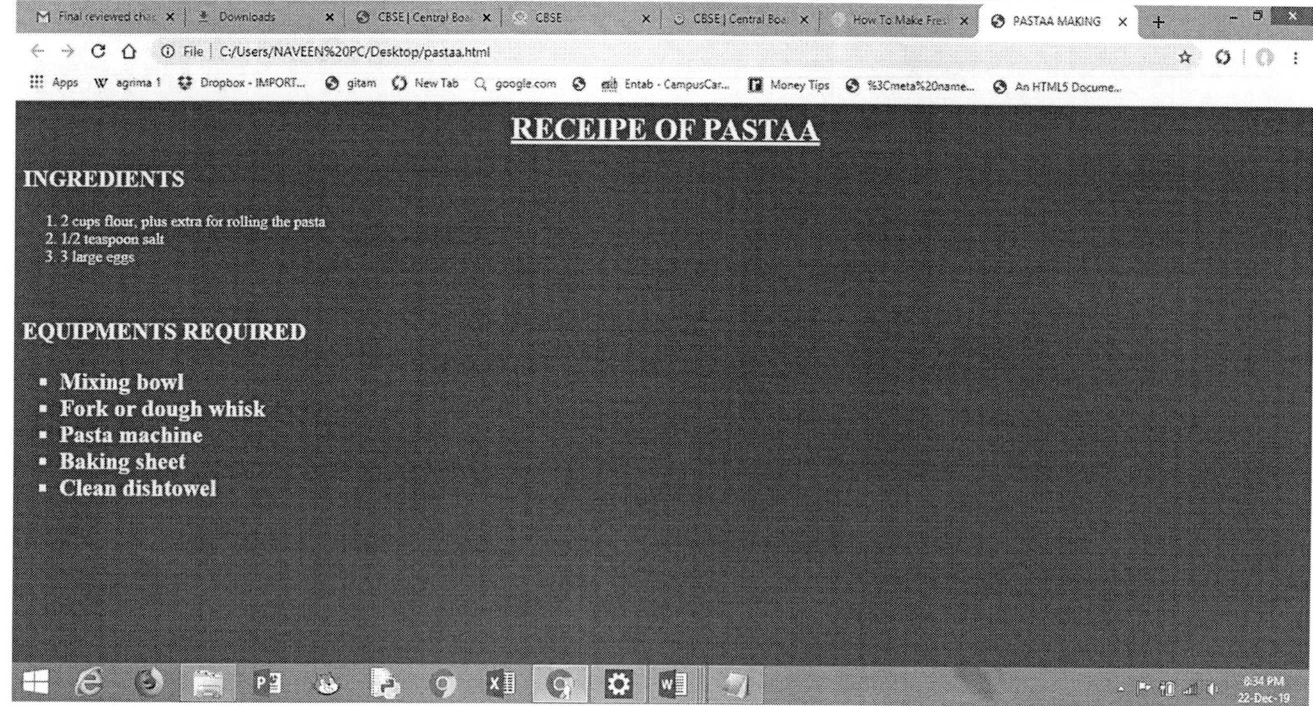

a. Name the tag used to create the heading of the page.

b. Name the tag used to create the line under the line recipe of pasta.

c. Name the tag used to create the ingredient list.

d. Name the tag used to create the bulleted list.

e. Which type of attribute is used with unordered list.

Ans: a. <H1> tag is used to create the heading of a page.

b. <U> tag is used to underline the heading.

c. <OL> tag is used to create the ordered list.

d. <UL> tag is used to create the unordered list.

e. Square attribute is used with the <UL> tag marked with C.

8. **Sidharth has to create a home page for his school web site. Help him to write the correct html code for the following:**

a. Insert the title as "ABC Public School".

b. Insert the comment as "this is a comment".

c. Insert the heading as MY HOME PAGE.

d. Leave 100 pixels margin between the text of the document and the left edge of the browser.

e. Create horizontal rule of blue color with thickness of 4 after the heading.

f. Set the background image of your school. The name of the image is "logo.gif" stored in c:\my pictures.

Ans: a. <title> ABC Public School</title>

b. <Comment> this is a comment</comment>

c. <H1> MY HOME PAGE</H1>

d. <Body leftmargin="100">

e. <HR color=blue" size="4">

f. <Body background="c:\my pictures\logo.gif">

SECTION D: SELF - ASSESSMENT

A. FILL IN THE BLANKS.

1. The latest version of html is ____________.
2. The secret codes used to create web pages is called ____________.
3. ____________ version of html was officially released by W3C.
4. ____________ delivers the web pages to the web browsers through the internet.
5. ____________ is the default text editor in the Linux operating system.
6. ____________ tag comes between the opening and closing of the head tag.
7. ____________ tag is used to create a numbered list.
8. The two attributes used with <OL> tag are ____________ and ____________.
9. There is only ____________ attribute used with <UL> tag.
10. The expanded form of <LI> is ____________.
11. ____________ tag is used to insert your comments or remarks to explain your code.
12. ____________ is the hexadecimal value used for the white color.
13. By default, the paragraph is ____________ aligned in a web page.
14. <font size = ____________ > will set the size to the largest font size value.
15. ____________ tag defines subscripted text.
16. ____________ tag inserts a single line break.
17. ____________ code will set the color of the line yellow.
18. ____________ tag makes the text appear italicized or slant as compared to the normal text.
19. ____________ tag is used to define the list of definitions.
20. ____________ tag defines the important text.

B. STATE WHETHER THE FOLLOWING STATEMENTS ARE TRUE OR FALSE.

1. Other than <i> tag, <em> tag can be used to display the text in italics.
2. It is not essential to close the <ol> tag.
3. <DT> tag is used to insert the definition term.
4. <SUB> tag is used to display the term as x2.
5. <font size=10> is used to change the style of the font.
6. <U> tag is used to underline the heading of a web page.
7. <Bold> tag is used to emphasize the text.
8. There are three types of bullets used with unordered list.
9. <SUB> text is used to display the text little lower than the normal text.
10. The default font size of the internet explorer is 3.
11. A logical tag <strong> that is preferred over a <b> a physical tag.
12. You cannot use multiple line breaks on a web page.
13. Heading tag is an empty tag.

14. When background attribute is used, then bgcolor attribute of the <body> tag has no effect.
15. The width attribute of <hr> tag specifies the horizontal width of the line.

C. TICK THE CORRECT ANSWER.

1. Which of the following is not an example of WYSIWYG editor?
   a. Microsoft FrontPage b. Adobe Dreamweaver
   c. WordPad d. MS-word
2. Which of the following is not an example of notepad?
   a. Notepad b. Microsoft expression web
   c. Both a and b. d. WordPad
3. which of the following is not a valid attribute of <body> tag?
   a. Background color b. bgcolor c. Leftmargin d. Text
4. The <hr> tag inserts ____________ on a web page. (Outside Delhi 2012)
   a. Straight line b. Circle c. Border d. None of these
5. Choose correct HTML tag for the largest heading. (Delhi 2014)
   a. <H1> b. <H6> c. <Big heading> d. <H size=1>
6. Three essential tags to create HTML document:
   a. <html>, <head> and <body> b. <html>, <title> and <body>
   c. <head>, <title> and <body> d. <head>, <<html> and <title>
7. This provides additional information about the tag.
   a. Extension b. Attribute c. Tags d. Elements
8. In text editor, the file extension used to save html documents is:
   a. .html b. .txt c. .doc d. none of these
9. Align attribute is associated with the following tags except one:
   a. <P> tag b. <HR> tag c. <Hn> tag d.
 tag
10. The tag namely used for mathematical equations:
    a. <Superscript> tag b. <SUP> tag c. <MATH> tag d. <SUB> tag
11. This list also called as bullet list.
    a. Unordered list b. Ordered list c. Circle list d. Any of these
12. This tag represents the list items within the ordered and unordered list
    a. <LIST> b. <LI> c. <LISTITEM> d. none of these
13. Select the available bulleted type options with unordered list:
    a. Square, circle, triangle b. Square, disc, circle
    c. Square, rectangle, circle d. Polygon, square, disc
14. The tag used to change the font style, color and size of the text is:
    a. <BASEFONT> b. <FONT> c. <STYLE> d. <COLOR>
15. The default start value of the ordered list is:
    a. 1 b. i c. A d. a

D. ANSWER THE FOLLOWING QUESTIONS.

Type A: Very Short Answer Questions.

1. Write the extension of html program file. (Delhi 2005)
2. What is the purpose of using html? (outside Delhi 2009)
3. What is the use of align attribute with <p> tag? (Delhi 2011, 2012)
4. Which tag is used to insert a heading of third level on a web page? (Delhi 2007)
5. Differentiate between background and bgcolor attributes of body tag. (Delhi 2014)
6. Which tags are used to display the text in superscript and subscript? (Delhi 2016)
7. Identify which of the following is a tag or an attribute: (Outside Delhi 2019)

   a. hr b. br c. p d. align
8. How can one insert horizontal line a web page? (Delhi 2008)
9. What is the purpose of using <h1>.... <h6> tags? (Delhi 2006)
10. Define the term tag and attribute.
11. What is the use of <li> tag? (Delhi 2012)
12. Differentiate between <ol> and <ul> tag. (Outside Delhi 2013)
13. How can you set the left and right-side margin of a web page?
14. What is the full form of RGB?

Type B: Short Answer Questions.

1. Mention the difference between an attribute and tag.
2. How can you display the 2D and 3D horizontal rule in a web page?
3. List the different logical and physical text styles with their description.
4. What is the difference between subscript and superscript tags used in HTML? Also, give one program to illustrate the same.
5. What is nested list?
6. Why are the attributes important in a list? Explain with the help of an example.
7. Explain the importance of type attribute with <OL> tag.
8. What is the significance of start attribute with <OL> tag?
9. Write a short note on Definition list.
10. How can you differentiate between container tag and empty tag?

Type C: Long Answer Questions.

1. Write the difference between <H1> and <H6> heading tag. Give suitable example. (Outside Delhi 2006)
2. Identify the error(s) in the following html code. Also, write the correct code. (Outside Delhi 2006)

   <body color="Red" background ="school.jpg">
3. What is RGB code? (Delhi 2011, 2012)
4. Distinguish between <BASEFONT> and <FONT> tag with the help of example of each. (Outside Delhi 2008)
5. Where can a comment be placed in an html document? How is it useful? (Delhi 2008)
6. Consider the given code and answer the following questions:

```
<html>
<head>
<title>My First Webpage</title>
</head>
<body bgcolor=”#EDDD9E”>
<h1 align=”center”>My First Webpage</h1>
<p align=” center”>Welcome to my <strong>first</strong> webpage. I am writing this
page using a text
editor and plain old html. </p>
<p>By learning html, I’ll be able to create web pages like a pro....<br>
which I am of course. </p>
Here’s what I’ve learned:
<ul>
<li>How to use HTML tags</li>
<li>How to use HTML colors</li>
<li>How to create Lists</li>
</ul>
</body>
</html>
```

a. Name the various tags used in the above code.

b. Which attribute is used to align the paragraph at the center of a web page?

c. Which type of list is used in the above code?

7. Find the error in the following HTML codes:

```
<HTML>
<HEAD>
</HEAD>
<BODY>
<U> <I> HTML stands for Hyper Text Markup Language. </I></U>
<BODY>
</HTML>
```

8. Find the error in the following HTML codes:

```
<HTML>
<HEAD>
</HEAD>
<BASEFONT SIZE=10>
<BODY>
I am in 10th Standard
</BODY>
```

```
</BASEFONT>
</HTML>
```

9. Find the error in the following HTML codes:

```
<HTML>
<HEAD>
</HEAD>
<BODY><p color=blue>
<H3>
I am in 10th Standard.
</H3>
</P>
</BODY>
</HTML>
```

10. Find the error in the following HTML codes:

```
<HTML>
<HEAD>
</HEAD>
<BODY topmargin=45 left margin =60>
Hypertext Markup Language
</BODY>
</HTML>
```

11. Find the error in the following HTML codes:

```
<HTML>
<HEAD>
</HEAD>
<BODY background=”C:\Users\Public\Pictures\Sample Pictures\Desert.jpg”>
< FONT type =”Verdana”>
Hypertext Markup Language
</FONT>
</BODY>
</HTML>
```

12. Find error(s) in the following HTML code segment. Rewrite the correct code and underline the corrections made.

```
<UL STYLE: Square >
<LI> Water Bottles
<LI> Lunch box
<LI> Handkerchief
</OL>
```

SECTION E: LAB EXERCISE

1. **Write HTML code to display an unordered list (with square) listing any three books being used in your school. The web page should have a pink background and the title of the page should be 'My Books'.**
2. **Write a program to display the web page as given below using html lists.**

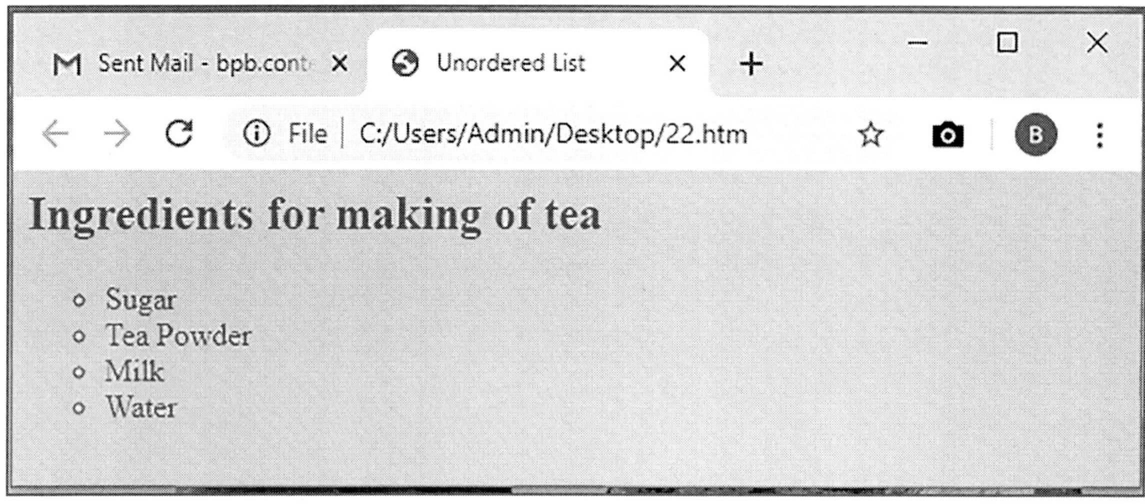

3. **Write html code to list the various services provided by the internet using ordered list considering the following points:**
   a. Title of a web page is Internet services.
   b. The background color of a web page should be yellow.
   c. The heading of a web page should by services provided by the internet.
   d. The heading should be underlined.
4. **Write the html code to display the following:**

   $a^2 + b^2 = c^2$ and $6CO_2 + 6H_2O \rightarrow C_6H_{12}O_6 + 6O_2$
5. **Create a webpage with HTML describing your hobbies. Use paragraph and list tags.**

Activity Zone

1. Tell students to design a web page of their own hobbies.
2. Tell students to make a presentation that will describe all the tags which they have studied so far.
3. Students can create a list of logical text styles and physical text styles and make a poster on it.

Images, Links, Tables

Outline of the Chapter

✦ Introduction ✦ Inserting images ✦ Inserting external links internal link, e-mail link ✦ Inserting tables

Learning Objectives

- To know how to insert hyperlinks using <A> tag
- To know how to insert images and link images
- To know the different attributes used with <img> tag
- To know the difference between internal and external link
- T know how to display data in tabular format by using <table> tag
- To know the different attributes used with <table> tag
- To know the purpose of using <TR>, <TD> and <TH> tags

INTRODUCTION

HTML provides us various tools for inserting images, to show data in tabular form and to link html documents with each other.

For example, when you open a website of any school, it displays the images of the school, laboratories, canteen and libraries etc. along with some textual information that have a long-lasting impact to memorize these things. On clicking of any image or text, you may be taken to some other web page.

Take another ***example*** where the school result or the list of all major activities organized by the school is displayed in tabular format

All these facilities i.e. linking one web page to another web page, inserting images on web page and store the data in a tabular format are provided by HTML tags.

This chapter is completely dedicated to all those HTML tags that help us to achieve this target.

4.1 INSERTING IMAGES

Images not only make the web page more attractive and interesting; it also helps in understanding the basic purpose of the web page.

In HTML, you can insert images by using <IMG> tag. Web browsers display the images in the following formats:

- GIF (**Graphics Interchange Format**)
- JPEG/JPG (**Joint Photographic Experts**)
- X-Bitmap (XBM)

Other supported file types can also be used such as **.TIFF**, **.PNG** etc.

Key features of <IMG> tag:

- <IMG> is an **empty tag** and therefore it is not required to close it.
- It can be used anywhere in a web page wherever it is required.
- It uses a specific location as a URL of an image to be inserted.

Tips for adding images

If you have images that are not in .jpg or .gif format, then use image editor to convert them. Such programs are Adobe Photoshop or PaintShop Pro programs.

*** Let's discuss various attributes of <IMG> tag.**

Table 4.1: Attributes of <IMG> tag

Attributes	Value	Description
Src	URL	Specifies the URL of an image.
Alt	text	Specifies an alternate text for an image.
Align	Top, bottom, middle, left, right	Specifies the alignment of an image according to surrounding elements.
Border	pixels	Specifies the width of the border around an image.
Height	pixels	Specifies the height of an image.
Width	pixels	Specifies the width of an image.

The syntax of using <IMG> tag:

```
<IMG src="url of an image" alt="text" border="pixels"
height="pixels" width="pixels" align="alignment">
```

Note: It is not mandatory to use all attributes simultaneously except src attribute, otherwise an image cannot be inserted.

Extra Byte

In the src attribute, specify the exact path/ location of an image where it is stored. If it does not exist, a Crossmark will appear in a box in place of that image.

Program 4.1: To create a web page that will insert an image.

```
<HTML>
<head>
<title>Inserting Images</title>
</head>
<body>
Charles Babbage was the father of computers.
<br>
<IMG src="CharlesBabbage.jpg" alt="Charles Babbage" height="150" width="150" border="5">
</body>
</HTML>
```

Output of the program is given below:

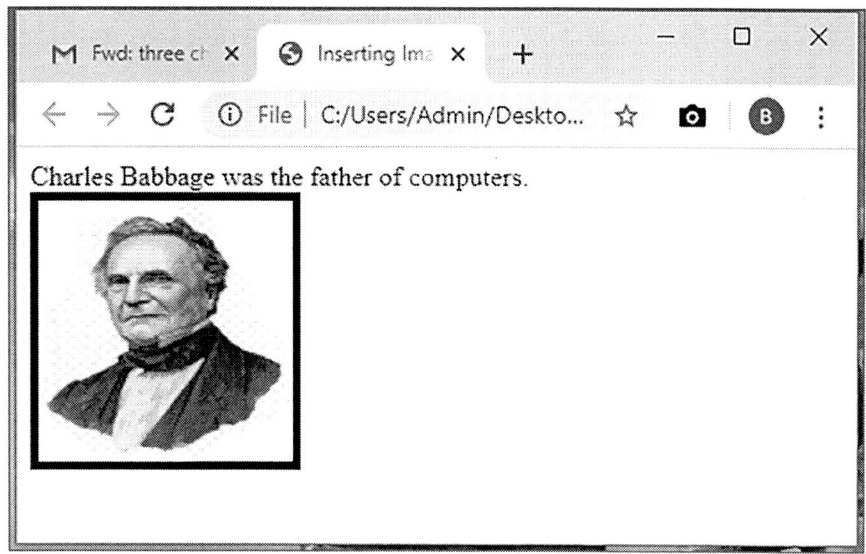

Figure 4.1: ***Inserting Image on a web page***

In figure 4.1, you have seen that the image **CharlesBabbage.jpg** is left aligned with height and width 150 pixels and the thickness of border is 5. However, it is not displaying any alternative text because the picture is located successfully on a system.

4.1.1 Aligning Images at different locations on a web page with respect to text

An image can be aligned **top**, **bottom**, **left**, **middle** and **right** of the text. The align attribute can take any one value from these values.

To see the effect of all these alignments, consider the given program.

Program 4.2: A program that shows different alignment of an image.

```
<HTML>
<body>
<h1>Alignment of Image</h1>
<h2>align="bottom" (default):</h2>
<p>Save trees, save life <img src="trees1.jpg" alt="trees" width="50" height="50"> Save trees, save life. </p>
<h2>align="middle":</h2>
<p>Save trees, save life. <img src="trees1.jpg" alt="trees" width="50" height="50" align="middle"> Save trees, save life. </p>
<h2>align="top":</h2>
<p>Save trees, save life. <img src="trees1.jpg" alt="trees" width="50" height="50" align="top"> Save trees, save life. </p>
<h2>align="right":</h2>
<p>Save trees, save life. <img src="trees1.jpg" alt="trees" width="50" height="50" align="right"> Save trees, save life. </p>
```

```
<h2>align="left":</h2>
<p>Save trees, save life. <img src="trees1.jpg" alt="trees" width="50" height="50" align="left"> Save trees, save life. </p>
</body>
</HTML>
```

Output of the program is given below:

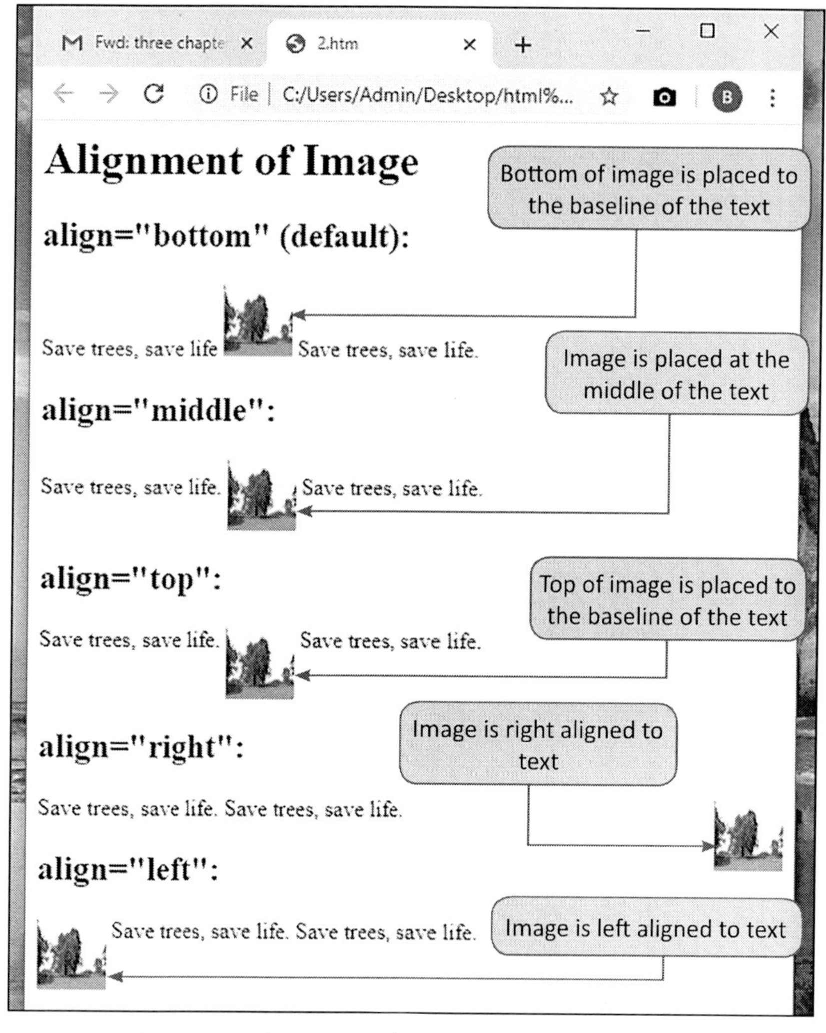

Figure 4.2: Showing Different alignments of image

Extra Byte

- **Top Alignment:** When the top alignment is used, the top of an image is aligned to the top edge of the tallest item (assume it as another image) in the next line. But, if there is no other image, then the image is aligned to the top of the text.
- **Bottom Alignment:** When the bottom alignment is used, the bottom of an image is aligned to the same horizontal plane as the baseline of the text.
- **Middle Alignment:** Different web browser displays the image in the middle in different ways. The internet explorer aligns the image to the middle of the tallest item in the next line. Whereas, Mozilla Firefox displays the image to the baseline of the text in which it is placed.
- **Left and Right Alignment:** By default, an image is always aligned to the left of a web page. However, if attribute align is set to right, then the image is placed at the right side of the text.

4.1.2 Aligning Image at the Center of a Web Page

If you want to align an image that will appear at the center horizontally in the browser window, then use **<center>** tag before using **<img>** tag.

Program 4.3: To create a web page that inserts an image and aligned it in center of a web page.

```
<HTML>
<body>
<center>
<img src="mytree.png" alt="Trees are life" width="200" height="200" ></center>
</body>
</HTML>
```

Output of the program is given below:

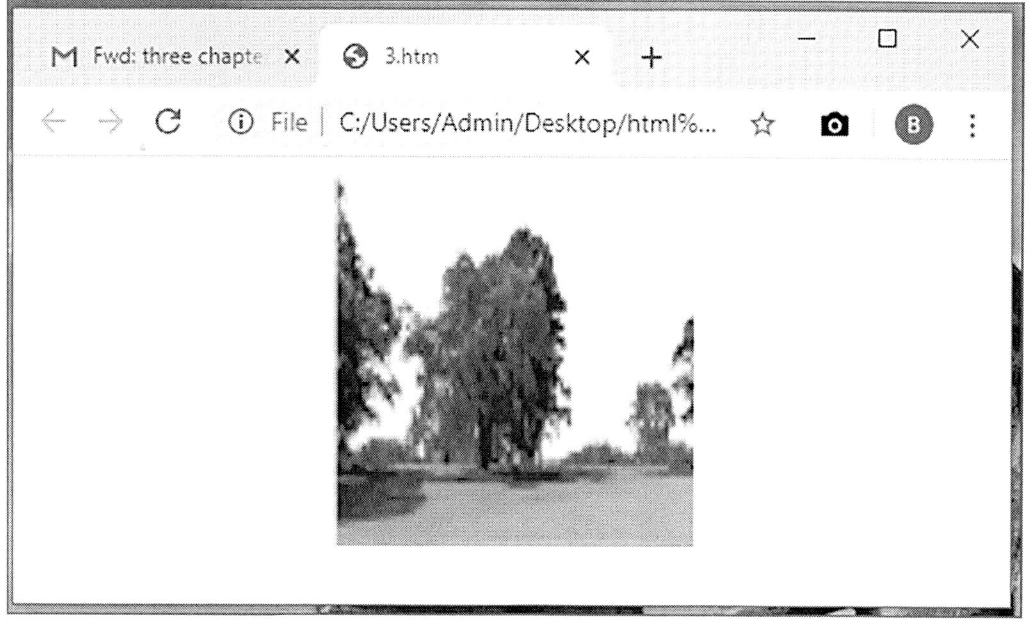

Figure 4.3: Aligning image at center of web page

In the above *figure 4.3*, the image is displayed at the center of a web page.

4.1.3 Displaying Alternate Text for an Image

There are situations when a web browser does not display an image, this is the case when the location of an image is not specified correctly. ***For example***, if your image is saved at location "C:\my pictures", but you set the location as C:\ then the browser will not display an image. Similarly, if the name of an image is not correct or if the proper file format is not used, then the browser will not display the image.

In such cases, you can set an alternate text that will show a brief description about an image which is to be inserted.

For setting alternate text, **alt attribute** is used inside an <IMG> tag.

Program 4.4: To insert an image where the alternate text is set by using alt attribute.

```
<HTML>
<body>
<img src="mytrees.jpg" alt="Trees are life" width="150"
height="150" >
</body>
</HTML>
```

The value of alt is displayed as a tooltip in a web browser. While specifying the alternate text, the length of the text must not be more than 1024 characters.

Output of the program is given below:

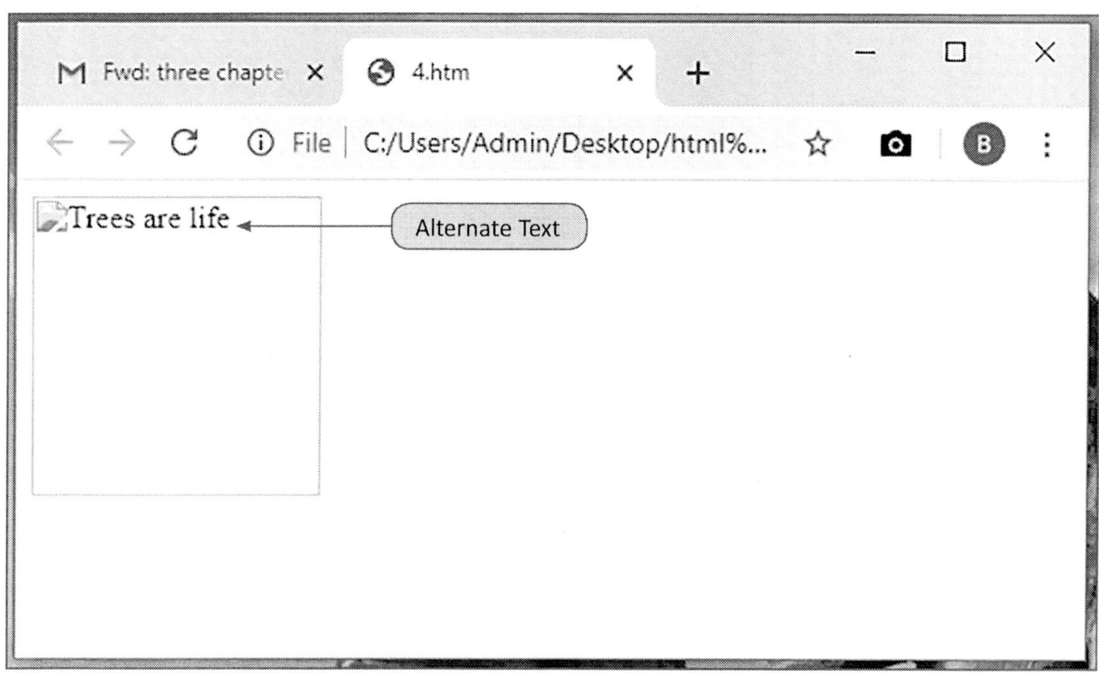

Figure 4.4: Displaying alternate text for image

In the above *figure 4.4*, an alternate text is displayed as the web browser is not able to locate the image from a specified location.

MEMORIZE

<IMG> tag is used for inserting images in HTML. Various attributes of <img> tag are: **src**, **alt**, **align**, **height** and **width**. **src** attribute is used for setting path/location of an image. **Align** attribute is used to align an image w.r.t text. **Height** and **width** attributes are used to set the height and width of an image. **Border** attribute is used to set the thickness or the width of the border.

Check Your Progress

Fill in the blanks.

1. _____________ tag is used to display an image at the center of a web page.
2. There are _____________ types of alignment for an image.
3. _____________ attribute is used inside an <IMG> tag.

4.2 INSERTING LINKS IN HTML

Consider the situation where you search for a specific information through the internet. It displays various links. When you click on one link it may contains several other texts known as **hypertext** which are related to another web pages. It is called **linking of web pages**.

Links are used to connect one web page to another web page or to the different sections of the same web page or with an image. A link is highlighted and underlined to differentiate it from the normal text in a web page.

Definition

Hyperlinks: Links that take you directly to other pages and even specific parts of a given page are known as hyperlinks.

HTML provides the facility to link one web page with another web page by using **Anchor <A>** tag with attribute **HREF** that tells the **URL/Location** of a link to be inserted.

Recall the attributes of **<BODY>** tag where you have used **link**, **alink** and **vlink** color. These are used to set the color of hyperlinks.

Note: The default color of a hyperlink is always blue. The default color of alink is red and vlink is purple.

Key features of Anchor <A> tag:

- <A> tag is a **container tag** and therefore it must be closed.
- Inside <A> tag, use attribute HREF that specifies the URL/location of the link.

An anchor can point to any resource on the Web: an HTML page, an image, a sound file, a movie, etc. HREF stands for Hypertext Reference.

The syntax of using <A> tag is:

```
<A HREF="URL">Text to be displayed </A>
```

For example,

<A HREF="Net.html"> Click to Know the Terms in Networking </A>

MEMORIZE

The anchor element <A> is used to create hyperlinks between a source anchor and a destination anchor. The source is the text, image, or button that links to another resource and the destination is the resource that the source anchor links to.

Do's and Don'ts:

- Always set the exact location or path of a file which is to be linked.
- Do not forget to use HREF attribute with <A> tag else the file will not be linked.

4.2.1 Types of Linking

HTML provide two types of linking, i.e. **External linking** and **Internal linking**.

a. **External Linking:** The external linking links two documents or web pages.

b. **Internal Linking:** The internal linking links different sections of a same web page. On clicking a specific text/image, a different section of a same document will be visible in the browser Window.

* **Let's discuss these types of linking in detail.**

External Linking----- Linking to different documents

For external linking, use HREF attribute with <A> tag that will specify the URL of a document which is to be linked.

The syntax for creating external link is:

```
<A href="URL">Text to be displayed</A>
```

Program 4.5: To create a web page that will link it with some other web page.

```
File: Main.HTML Linked to File "Net.HTML"
<HTML>
<head>
<title> Inserting Links in HTML</title>
</head>
<body>
<A href="Net.HTML"> Click to Know The Terms in Networking </A>
</body>
</HTML>
```

```
File: Net.HTML
<HTML>
<body>
<h2> Network</h2>A network is a collection of computers, servers, mainframes, network devices, peripherals, or other devices connected to one another to allow the sharing of data.
<br>
<br>
<h2> Ring Topology</h2> A ring topology is a network configuration in which device connections create a circular data path.
</body>
</HTML>
```

Output of the program is given below:

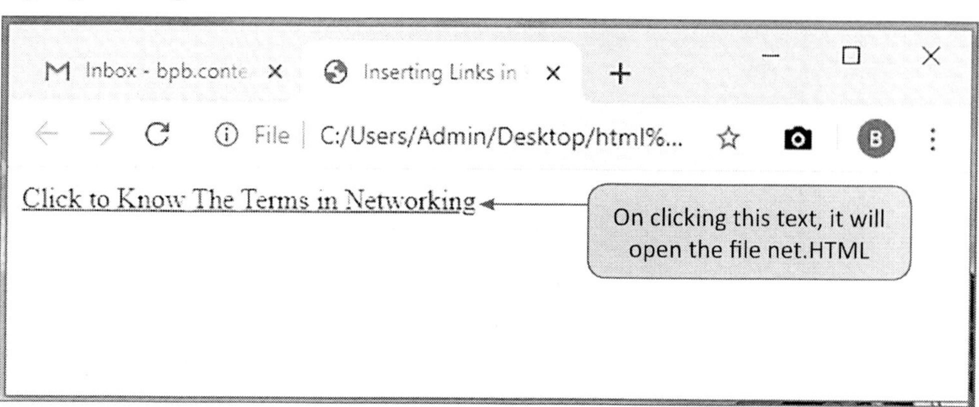

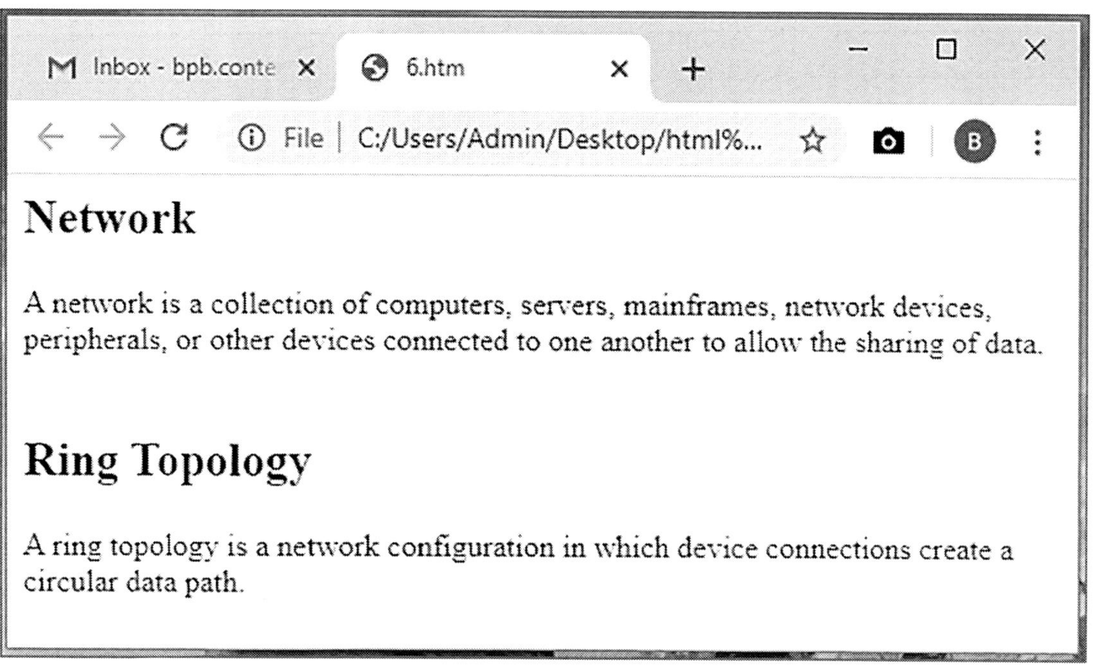

Figure 4.5: Showing linking of two different documents

It is an example of External Linking because in the above *Program 4.5*, **main.html** file contains a link which is inserted by using anchor <A> tag. A link is established with the file **net.html**. **HREF** attribute in main. html use this URL for the successful linking of two web pages.

Linking Images with the document

You can also link images with your web page. For this set the path/location/URL of an image with SRC attribute of <IMG> tag. Use <IMG> along with anchor <A> tag.

Program 4.6: To create a web page that will make image as a link.

Main.HTML	Picture.HTML

<HTML>
<head>
<title> Inserting Links in HTML</title>
</head>
<body>
<A Href="picture.HTML">Click on an image <img src="flower.jpg" align="top"></A>
</body>
</HTML>
	<HTML>
	<body>
	<pre>
	DESCRIPTION OF ROSE FLOWER
	The rose is a type of flowering shrub. Its name comes from the Latin word Rosa.
	The flowers of the rose grow in many different colors, from the well-known red rose or yellow roses.
	Sometimes white or purple roses.
	Roses belong to the family of plants called Rosaceae.</pre>
	</body>
	</HTML>

Output of the program is given below:

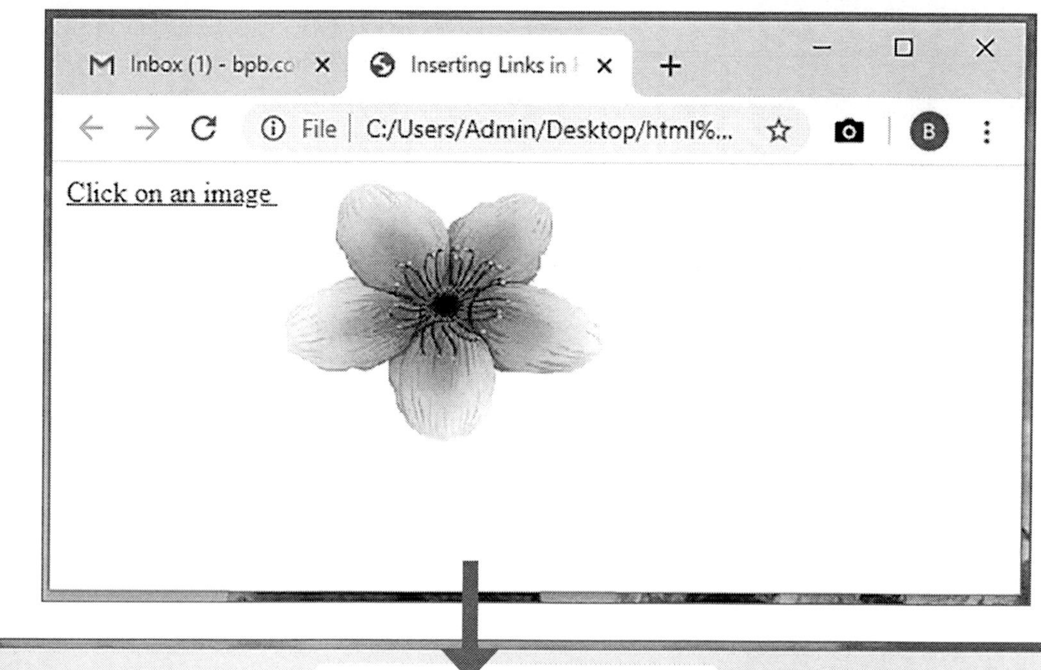

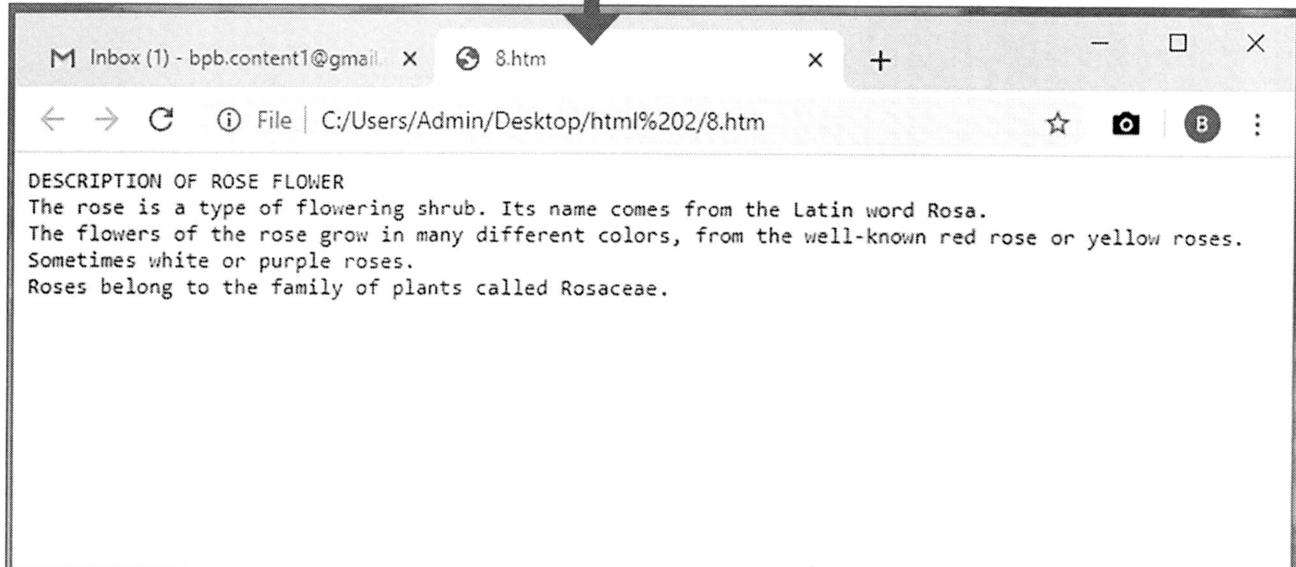

Figure 4.6: Linking image on a web page

In the **Program 4.6**, **main.html** contains an image "*flower.jpg*" which when clicked opens another web page that contains the description of a flower stored in a file **picture.html**.

Using Title Attribute as Alink

Title attribute can be used to display the title of the link. With title attribute, specify a string of text that will appear when you place a mouse pointer over a link.

The syntax of using title attribute with <A> tag is:

```
<A HREF="URL" title="text"> hyperlinked text</A>
```

Extra Byte

The main advantage of using title attribute is that it helps in displaying the information related to the hyperlinked text.

Program 4.7: To create a web page by using Title attribute as Alink.

```
<HTML>
<head>
<title> Inserting Links in HTML</title>
</head>
<body>
<A HREF="picture.HTML" Title="Hyperlink Created to know the description">Click here </
A>
</body>
</HTML>
```

Output of the program is given below:

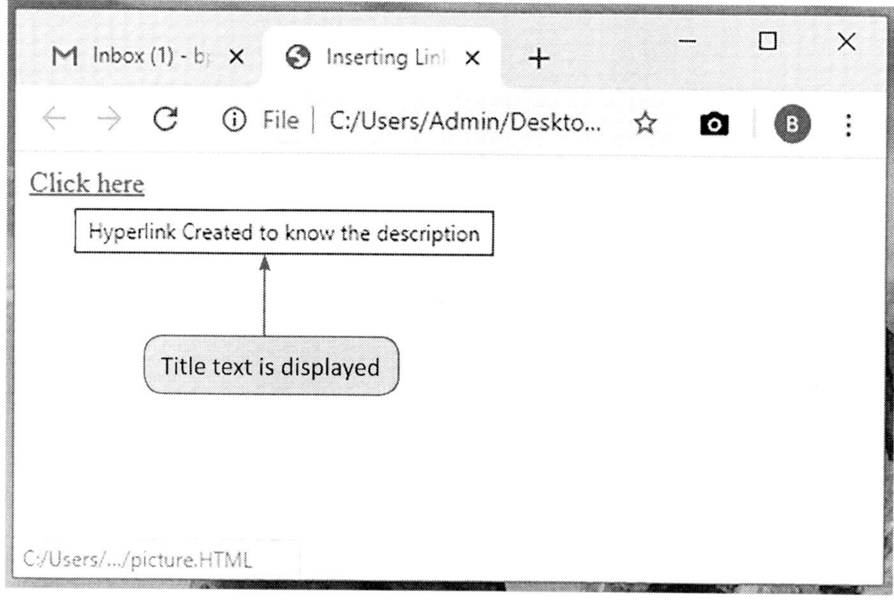

Figure 4.7: Title is showing as a link

E-mail Links

HTML also provides the facility to link an e-mail account for sending e-mail messages over the internet. To create an e-mail link, you will use **mailto:** along with your e-mail address with **HREF** attribute.

The syntax for creating e-mail as a link is:

```
<A href="mailto:email address ? Subject="Text">Type text here</A>
```

To add a subject for the e-mail message, you would add ?subject= after the e-mail address.

For example,

<A HREF="mailto:helpdesk@campuscare?subject=Report Card Assistance">Help Desk</A>

Internal Linking -------- Link Different Sections of a same web page

Internal links are also known as **fragment identifier links** that helps the user to jump from one section of a document to other section of the same document.

For inserting internal links follow the given steps:

1. Give a name to a section of a web page which is to be linked. For this, use the given syntax:
   <A name="name of the section"> Type the text related to a section </A>
2. Then, provide the hyperlink to the above-mentioned named section of a document by using **href** attribute with <A> tag.

For this, follow the given syntax:

```
<A HREF="#name of the section"> Type text for hyperlinking</A>
```

Program 4.8: To create a web page that will make you to understand the use of internal linking.

```
<HTML>
<head>
</head>
<body>
<A href="#Languages"> Languages in India</A><br>
<A Href="#Festivals"> Festivals of India</A><br><br><br>
<A name="Festivals"><b> List of Most Famous Festivals of India </b></A>
<Pre>
Diwali <br>
Holi<br>
Dussehra<br>
Ramadan/ Eid -Ul-Fitr<br>
Christmas<br>
Ganesh Chaturthi<br>
Durga Pooja<br>
Baishakhi.v
</pre>
<A name="Languages"><b> List of some of the Indian languages</b></A>
<pre>
Sanskrit <br>
Hindi<br>
English<br>
Gujarati <br>
Punjabi<br>
Bengali<br>
Assamese<br>
</pre>
</body>
</HTML>
```

Extra Byte

You can also use ID attribute in place of Name attribute in internal linking.

Extra Byte

The **hash symbol (#)** tells the browser that it's a section of a page it's looking for, and not a separate page or older.

The # goes in the **href** attribute's value, ***not*** in the name attribute.

Output of the program is given below:

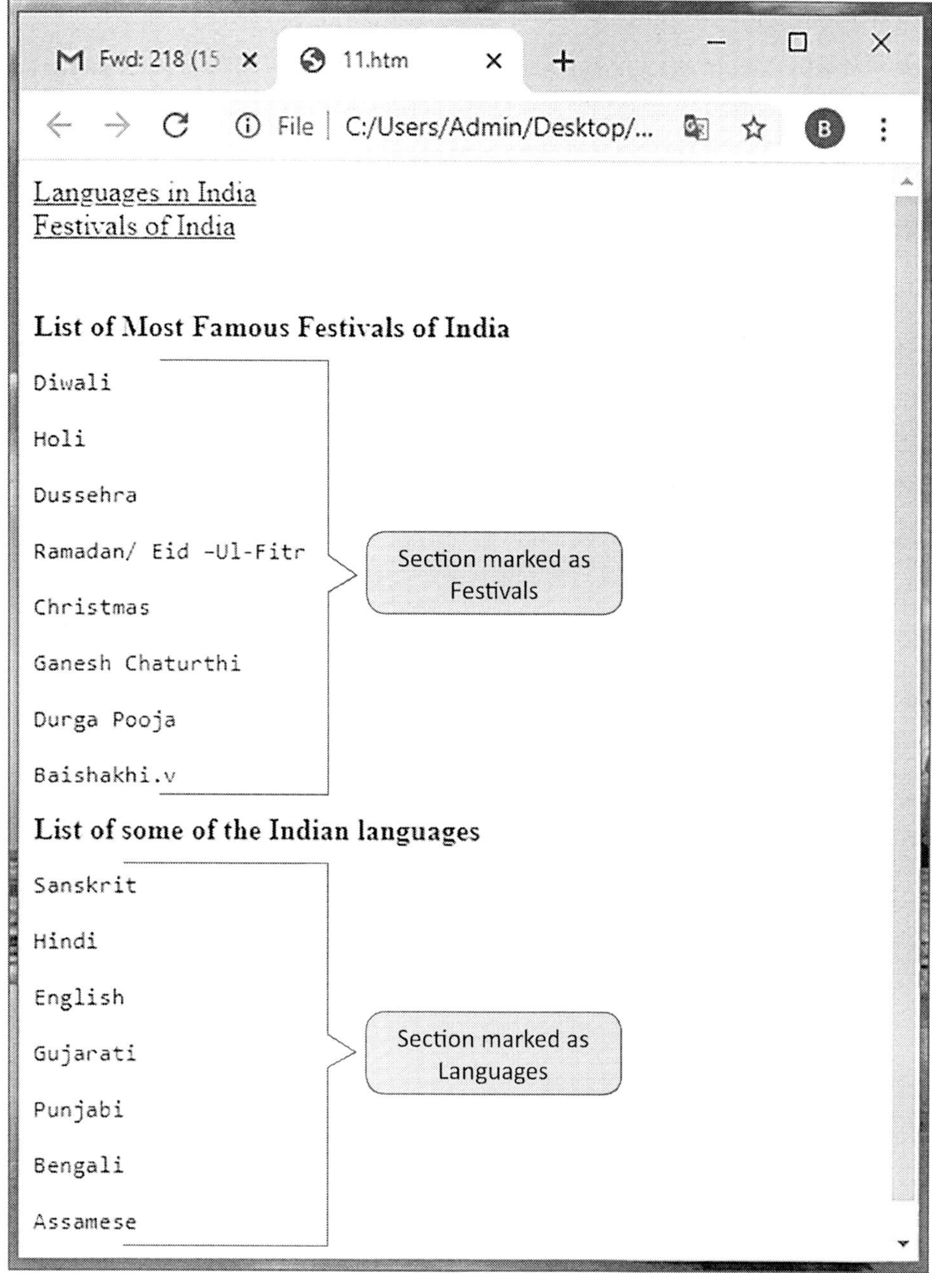

Figure 4.8: Section of same web page is linked through Internal Linking

In the *figure 4.8*, there are two sections namely, list of festivals of India and list of some of the Indian languages. These two sections have been given a name as **Festivals** and **Languages** respectively which are then later on be linked by using <A> tag with HREF attribute.

The statements:

<A HREF="#Languages"> Languages in India</A>

and

<A HREF="#Festivals"> Festivals of India</A>

are used to set the links to two different sections (#Festivals and #Languages) of a same web page.

Advantage of using Internal Linking

The advantage of using Internal Linking are:

1. It helps to link back to the top of the page from the bottom. This is because once you have scrolled down a bit, all the **navigation** links that are usually placed at the top of the page are lost.
2. It eliminates scrolling completely on long pages by splitting it up and having a row of links to the main headlines on the page.

Linking Different Sections of Different Web Pages

In HTML, you can also link different sections of different web pages with each other. To do this, you have to name a section of one web page and give its link in another web page.

For example, suppose you have two HTML files namely **one.html** and **two.html**. In **one.html**, you name a section link by using NAME attribute as:

<A NAME="link"> It creates a link between two documents</A>

Now, to provide its link in the file **two.html**, you have to give a statement like this:

<A HREF="two.html#link">

In this way, a hyperlink is created between different sections of different web pages.

Program 4.9: To create a web page that will create a link between different sections of different web pages.

Main.HTML	Fest.HTML

<HTML>
<head>
<title> Creating link between different sections</title>
</head>
<body>
<A Href="fest. HTML#Gandhi"> Mahatma Gandhi</A>
 	
<A href="fest. HTML#Nehru"> Pt. Jawahar Lal Nehru</A>
</body>
</HTML>
	<HTML>
	<head>
	</head>
	<body>
	<A name="Gandhi"><b> About Mahatma Gandhi </b></A>
	<pre>
	1) The complete name of Gandhi ji was 'Mohandas Karamchand Gandhi' a.k.a 'M.K. Gandhi'
	
	2) Mahatma Gandhi was born on 2nd October, 1869 at Porbandar in Gujrat State of India.
	
	3) Gandhiji's father's name was 'Karamchand Uttamchand Gandhi' & Mother was 'PutliBai Gandhi'
	
	4) Gandhiji's wife was 'Kasturba Gandhi' also known as 'Ba'.
	
	5) Mahatma Gandhi and Kasturba Gandhi were married at a very young age, Gandhi ji were 13 years old and Kasturba was 14 years old.
	
	6) Gandhi ji and Kasturba had four sons – Harilal, Manilal, Ramdas and Devdas.
	
	7) The Title of 'Mahatma' was given to Gandhi ji by Rabindranath Tagore at Shantiniketan Ashram.
	
	8) Gandhiji completed his studies in Law from London.</pre>

Main.HTML	Fest.HTML
	<A name="Nehru"><b> About Pt. Jawaharlal Nehru <b></A> <pre> 1) Nehru was born on 14th November 1889 at Allahabad in United Province. 2) Belonged to a community of Kashmiri Pandits. Father Motilal Nehru (1861-1931) and Mother, Swarooprani Thussu (1968-1938). 3) Joined Theosophical society formed by Annie Besant when he was 13. 4) Graduated from Trinity College, Cambridge in 1910 with an Honors degree in Natural Science. </body> </HTML>

Output of the program is given below:

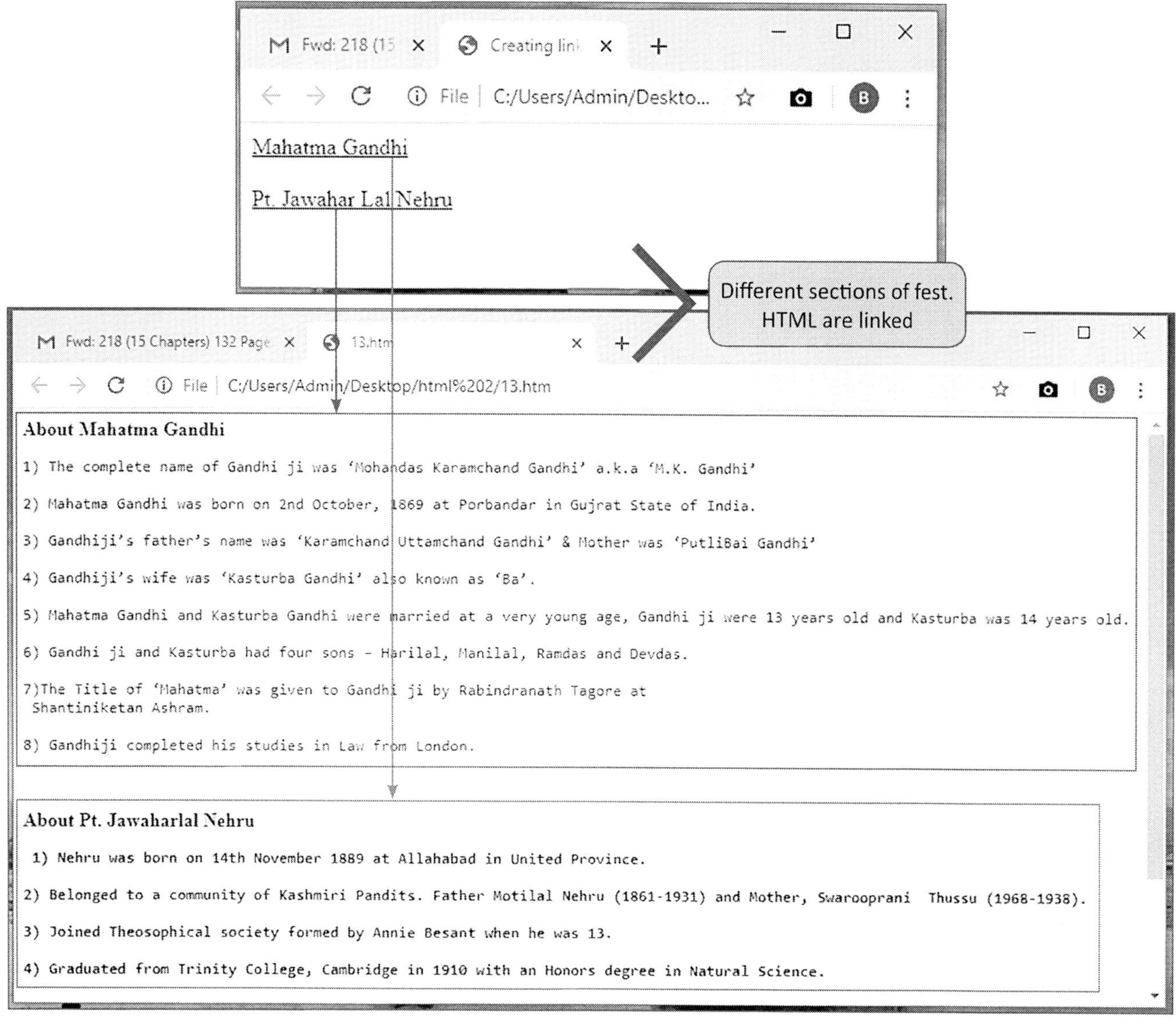

Figure 4.9: Internal linking of different documents

MEMORIZE

There are two types of linking: **External linking** (links different documents or images to a web page) and **Internal linking** (links different sections of a same web page).

Check Your Progress

Answer the following questions.

1. What is the advantage of using hyperlinking in a document?
2. Name two different types of linking.
3. Can you link your e-mail address by using <A> tag?

4.3 INSERTING TABLES IN HTML

Table: A table is nothing but a means of arranging data in rows and columns. Each row and column consist of group of cells where you store the data.

For example,

To store the marks of students in 5 subjects, a table could have been like this:

MARKS OF STUDENTS – CLASS-X

NAME	ENGLISH	MATHS	PHYSICS	CHEMISTRY	COMPUTER SCIENCE
ANKITA	78	65	80	90	97
SIDHARTH	70	87	85	90	98
YASHVARDHAN	80	98	67	89	95
NAVEEN	85	89	78	85	89
PALVI	50	90	89	76	88

The HTML tables allow users to arrange data like text, images, links into rows and columns of cells.

This kind of arrangement of data can be created in HTML using <TABLE> tag.

The various other tags which are used with <table> tag are:

<TR> : Defines table rows in table.

<TD> : The data in the cells of the rows are inserted by using either the TH tag or the TD tag. The TD keeps the data in regular font and left aligned by default.

<TH> : Defines currently selected cell as table header. The TH tag encloses the Header object and makes the data **boldface** and **center** aligned.

<CAPTION> : Defines the title or caption of the table.

* **Let's know the various attributes of <table> tag.**

4.3.1 Attributes of <Table> tag

Table 4.2: Attributes of <Table> Tag

Attribute Name	Description
Border	Sets the border of cells.
Bordercolor	Sets the color of the border of cells.
Bgcolor	Sets the background color of table or cells.
Background	Sets the image for a table or table rows.
Frame	Sets which outside border line should be displayed.
Rules	Sets which inside border line should be displayed.
Align	Sets the alignment of the table with respect to browser window.
Height & width	Sets height and width of the table.
Cellspacing	Sets the space between the cells and table border.
Cellpadding	Sets the space between the cell content and cell border.
Summary	Define the introduction of a table.

*** Let's discuss all these attributes in detail.**

1. Border Attribute

- Border attribute is used to set the inside and outside lines of cells inside a table. The inside lines show the rows and columns of the table and the outside lines displays the dimensions of the table.
- The border attribute can take value from 1 upto any number. If the border value is 1, then it displays one-pixel line on inside and outside of the table. However, it is omitted, neither inside nor outside lines are visible.
- If the value is larger than one, then it only thickens the outer lines of a table (giving a 3D effect) leaving the inside lines to one-pixel point.

Program 4.10: To create a web page that will use the border attribute in table.

```
<HTML>
<HEAD><TITLE></TITLE></HEAD>
<BODY>
Table 1 with border value=1 <br>
<TABLE border = 1>
<TR>
<TD> Thinner border</TD>
<TD> Thinner border </TD>
</TR>
<TR>
<TD> Thinner border </TD>
<TD> Thinner border </TD>
</TR>
</TABLE>
<br><br>
Table 2 with border value=5 <br>
<TABLE border = 5>
<TR>
```

```
<TD> Thicken border</TD>
<TD> Thicken border </TD>
</TR>
<TR>
<TD> Thicken border </TD>
<TD> Thicken border </TD>
</TR>
</TABLE>
<br><br>
Table 3 without border attribute <br>
<TABLE >
<TR>
<TD> Thicken border</TD>
<TD> Thicken border </TD>
</TR>
<TR>
<TD> Thicken border </TD>
<TD> Thicken border </TD>
</TR>
</TABLE>
<br>
<br>
</BODY>
</HTML>
```

Output of the program is given below:

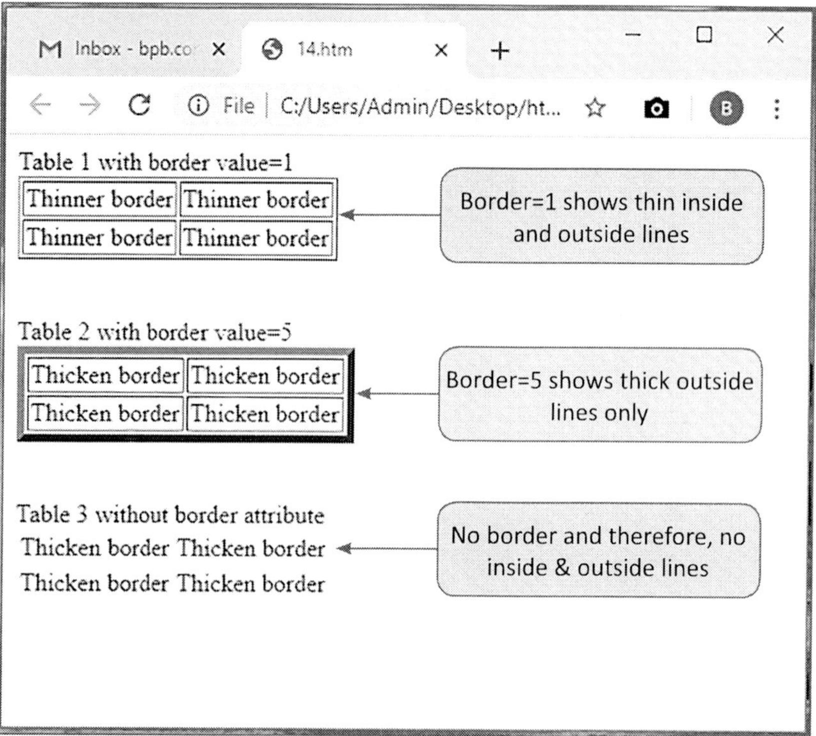

Figure 4.10: Showing Different borders

2. Bordercolor Attribute

This attribute is used to set the color of the border i.e. inside and outside lines of the table. The value of bordercolor can be the name of any color which you want to set. If you omit this attribute, the color of the table border is set to its default grey.

Program 4.11: To create a web page that will set bordercolor of a table as Red.

```
<HTML>
<HEAD><TITLE></TITLE></HEAD>
<BODY>
<TABLE border = 2 bordercolor="Red">
<TR>
<TD> Team</TD>
<TD> Ranking </TD>
</TR>
<TR>
<TD> India </TD>
<TD> 1 </TD>
</TR>
<TR>
<TD> Australia </TD>
<TD> 2 </TD>
</TR>
</TABLE>
<br><br>
<TABLE border = 2>
<TR>
<TD> Country</TD>
<TD> Player Name </TD>
</TR>
<TR>
<TD> India </TD>
<TD> M.S. Dhoni </TD>
</TR>
<TR>
<TD> Australia </TD>
<TD> Smith </TD>
</TR>
</TABLE>

</BODY>
</HTML>
```

Output of the program is given below:

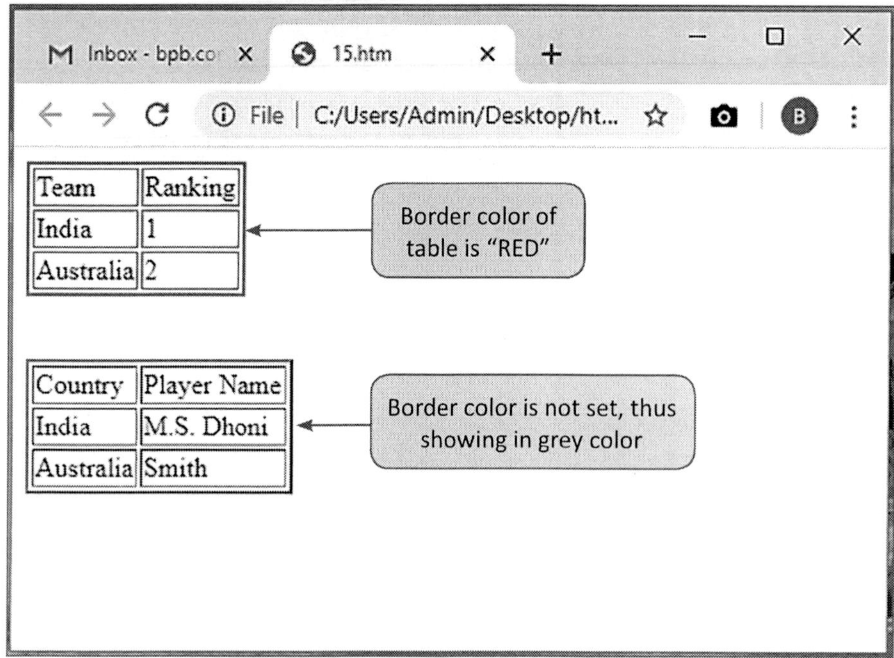

Figure 4.11: Showing Different border colors

3. Frame Attribute

Frame attribute is used along with border attribute. It decides as to which border line will render (display) that is left or right or both edges, top or bottom or both edges, all borders or no border.

The various values that frame attribute can take are:

Table 4.3: Values of Frame Attributes of <Table> Tag

Value	Description
void	The outside borders are not displayed.
above	The top outside border is displayed.
below	The bottom outside border is displayed.
hsides	The top and bottom outside borders are displayed.
vsides	The left and right outside borders are displayed.
Lhs	The left outside border is displayed.
Rhs	The right outside border is displayed.
box	The outside borders are displayed on all four sides.
border	The outside borders are displayed on all four sides/same as box.

Program 4.12: To create a web page that will show display border lines at different edges of a table.

```
<HTML>
<head>
<title> Frame Attribute </title>
</head>
<body>
<table border=2 Frame=”above”>
```

```
<tr>
<th>Employee code </th>
<th>Basic Salary</th>
</tr>
<tr>
<td>EM001</td>
<td>10000</td>
</tr>
<tr>
<td>EM002</td>
<td>10500</td>
</tr>
</table>

<br>
<table border=2 Frame="below">
<tr>
<th>Employee code </th>
<th>Basic Salary</th>
</tr>
<tr>
<td>EM001</td>
<td>10000</td>
</tr>
<tr>
<td>EM002</td>
<td>10500</td>
</tr>
</table>
<br>
<table border=2 Frame="all">
<tr>
<th>Employee code </th>
<th>Basic Salary</th>
</tr>
<tr>
<td>EM001</td>
<td>10000</td>
</tr>
<tr>
<td>EM002</td>
```

```
<td>10500</td>
</tr>
</table>
<br>

<table border=2 frame="hsides">
<tr>
<th>Employee code </th>
<th>Basic Salary</th>
</tr>
<tr>
<td>EM001</td>
<td>10000</td>
</tr>
<tr>
<td>EM002</td>
<td>10500</td>
</tr>
</table>
<br>
<table border=2 frame="lhs">
<tr>
<th>Employee code </th>
<th>Basic Salary</th>
</tr>
<tr>
<td>EM001</td>
<td>10000</td>
</tr>
<tr>
<td>EM002</td>
<td>10500</td>
</tr>
</table>

<br>
<table border=2 frame="void">
<tr>
<th>Employee code </th>
<th>Basic Salary</th>
</tr>
```

```
<tr>
<td>EM001</td>
<td>10000</td>
</tr>
<tr>
<td>EM002</td>
<td>10500</td>
</tr>

</table>
</body>
</HTML>
```

Output of the program is given below:

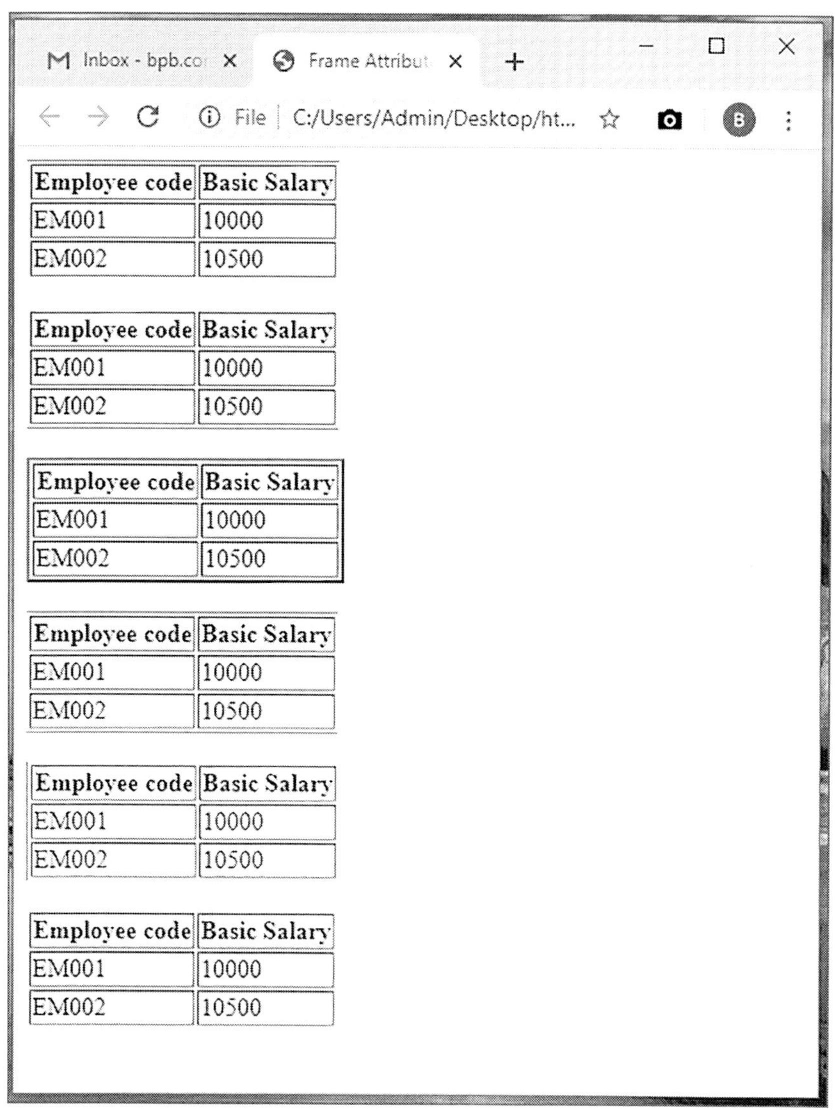

Employee code	Basic Salary
EM001	10000
EM002	10500

Employee code	Basic Salary
EM001	10000
EM002	10500

Employee code	Basic Salary
EM001	10000
EM002	10500

Employee code	Basic Salary
EM001	10000
EM002	10500

Employee code	Basic Salary
EM001	10000
EM002	10500

Employee code	Basic Salary
EM001	10000
EM002	10500

Figure 4.12: Showing Frame values of a table

Note: It is to be noted that frame attribute works only with outside border.

4. Rules Attribute

It also works with border attribute except that it works with inner border of cells of table.

Table 4.4: Values of Rules Attributes of <Table> Tag

Values	Description
all	Displays all borders.
cols	Displays vertical borders between cells.
groups	Displays borders between all cells groups.
none	No border will be shown.
rows	Displays horizontal borders between rows only.

Program 4.13: To create a web page that will use RULES attribute in table.

```
<HTML>
<head>
<title>Rules Attribute </title>
</head>
<body>
<table border=2 rules="all">
<tr>
<th>Employee code </th>
<th>Basic Salary</th>
</tr>
<tr>
<td>EM001</td>
<td>10000</td>
</tr>
<tr>
<td>EM002</td>
<td>10500</td>
</tr>
</table>

<br>
<table border=2 rules="cols">
<tr>
<th>Employee code </th>
<th>Basic Salary</th>
</tr>
<tr>
<td>EM001</td>
```

If you want to set an individual cell of the table with different background colour, the attribute bgcolor can be used with either <TH> tag or <TD> tag.

```
<td>10000</td>
</tr>
<tr>
<td>EM002</td>
<td>10500</td>
</tr>
</table>
<br>
<table border=2 rules="groups">
<tr>
<th>Employee code </th>
<th>Basic Salary</th>
</tr>
<tr>
<td>EM001</td>
<td>10000</td>
</tr>
<tr>
<td>EM002</td>
<td>10500</td>
</tr>
</table>
<br>

<table border=2 rules="none">
<tr>
<th>Employee code </th>
<th>Basic Salary</th>
</tr>
<tr>
<td>EM001</td>
<td>10000</td>
</tr>
<tr>
<td>EM002</td>
<td>10500</td>
</tr>
</table>
<br>
```

```
<table border=2 rules="rows">
<tr>
<th>Employee code </th>
<th>Basic Salary</th>
</tr>
<tr>
<td>EM001</td>
<td>10000</td>
</tr>
<tr>
<td>EM002</td>
<td>10500</td>
</tr>
</table>

</body>
</HTML>
```

Output of the program is given below:

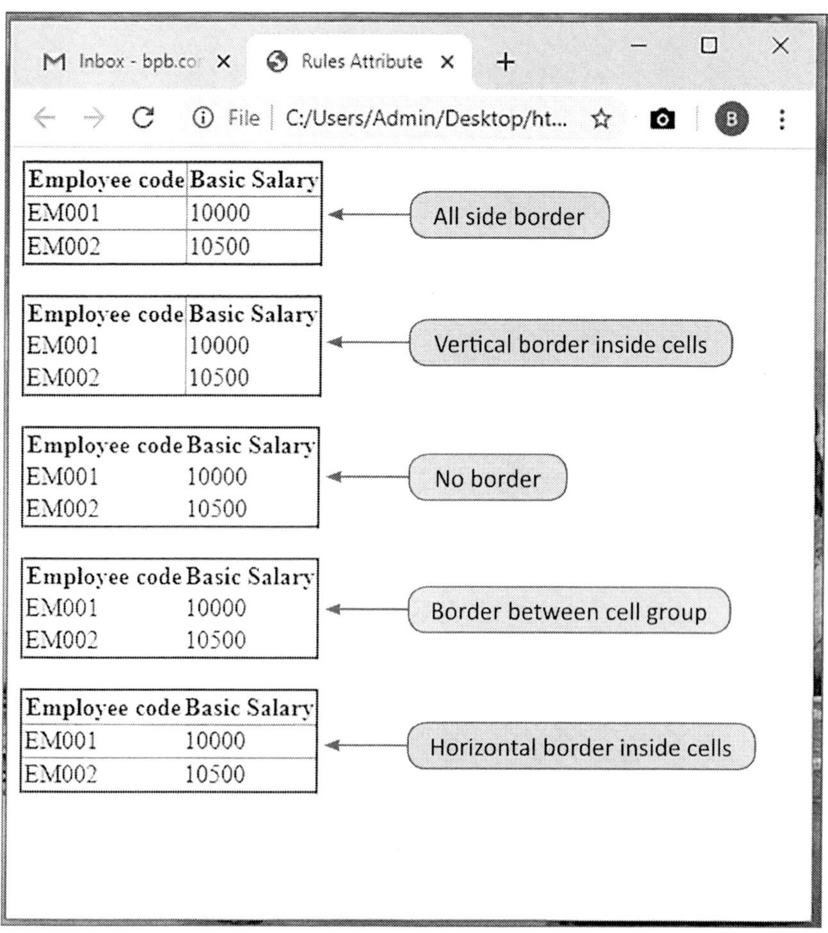

Figure 4.13: Showing Different RULES values of a table border

5. Align Attribute

Align attribute helps in placing the table on the webpage. Align attribute takes three values i.e. **left**, **center** and **right**.

- To place the table at left side of the web page, use align="left".
- To place the table at the right side of a web page, use align="right".
- To place the table at the center of a web page, use align="center".
- If you omit this attribute in the tag, then the table will be aligned left which is the default alignment.

Program 4.14: To create a web page which will set the table by using different alignments.

```
<HTML>
<BODY>
<TABLE border = 2 align="left">
<TR>
<TD> Item Code</TD>
<TD> Item Name </TD>
</TR>
<TR>
<TD> 101 </TD>
<TD> Salt </TD>
</TR>
<TR>
<TD> 102 </TD>
<TD> Sugar </TD>
</TR>
</TABLE>
<br><br>
<TABLE border = 2 align="center">
<TR>
<TD> Item Code</TD>
<TD> Item Name </TD>
</TR>
<TR>
<TD> 101 </TD>
<TD> Salt </TD>
</TR>
<TR>
<TD> 102 </TD>
<TD> Sugar </TD>
</TR>
</TABLE>
```

```
<TABLE border = 2 align="right">
<TR>
<TD> Item Code</TD>
<TD> Item Name </TD>
</TR>
<TR>
<TD> 101 </TD>
<TD> Salt </TD>
</TR>
<TR>
<TD> 102 </TD>
<TD> Sugar </TD>
</TR>
</TABLE>

<br>
<br>

</BODY>
</HTML>
```

Output of the program is given below:

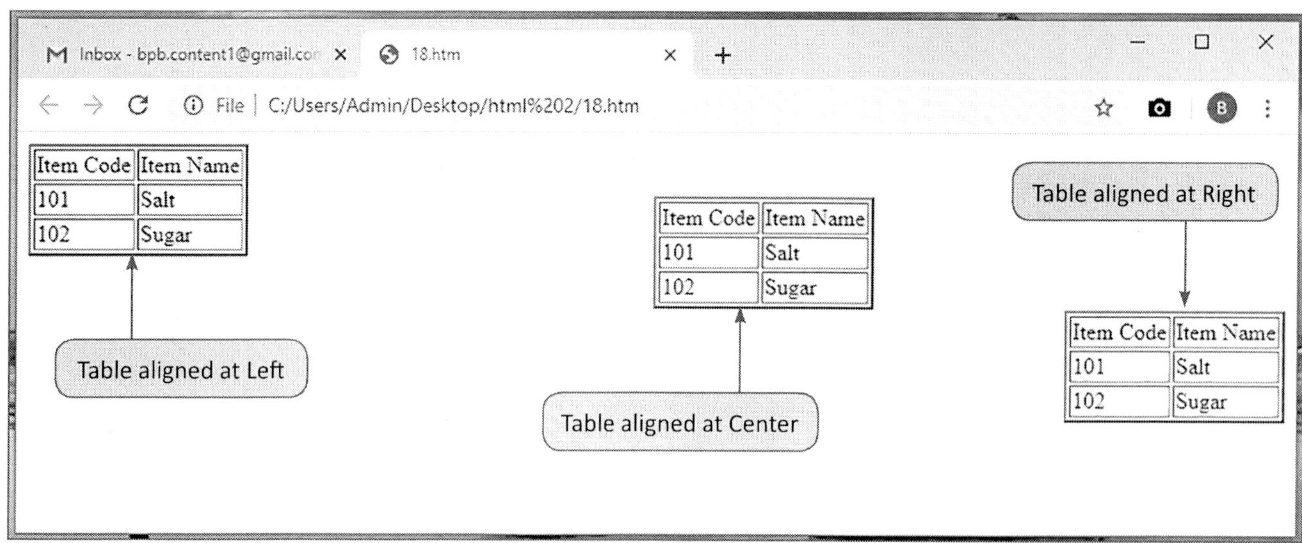

Figure 4.14: Showing Different Alignments of table

6. Bgcolor Attribute:

You can also set the background color of a table by using bgcolor attribute. This attribute takes the name of the color or hexadecimal number as value.

Program 4.15: To create a web page that will use background color for rows in a table.

```
<HMTL>
<HEAD><TITLE></TITLE></HEAD>
<BODY>
<TABLE border = 2 bgcolor="pink">
<TR>
<TD> Roll no</TD>
<TD> Student Name </TD>
</TR>
<TR>
<TD> 1 </TD>
<TD> John Walter </TD>
</TR>
<TR>
<TD> 2 </TD>
<TD> Aakash Gandhi </TD>
</TR>
</TABLE>
<br><br>
<table border=2>
<TR>
<TD bgcolor="blue"> Roll no</TD>
<TD bgcolor="yellow"> Student Name </TD>
</TR>
<TR>
<TD bgcolor="pink"> 1 </TD>
<TD bgcolor="green"> John Walter </TD>
</TR>
<TR>
<TD bgcolor="red"> 2 </TD>
<TD bgcolor="orange"> Aakash Gandhi </TD>
</TR>
</TABLE>

</BODY>
</HTML>
```

Extra Byte

The image can be set to individual cells as well by using the background attribute in the <TH>and <TD> tag.

Output of the program is given below:

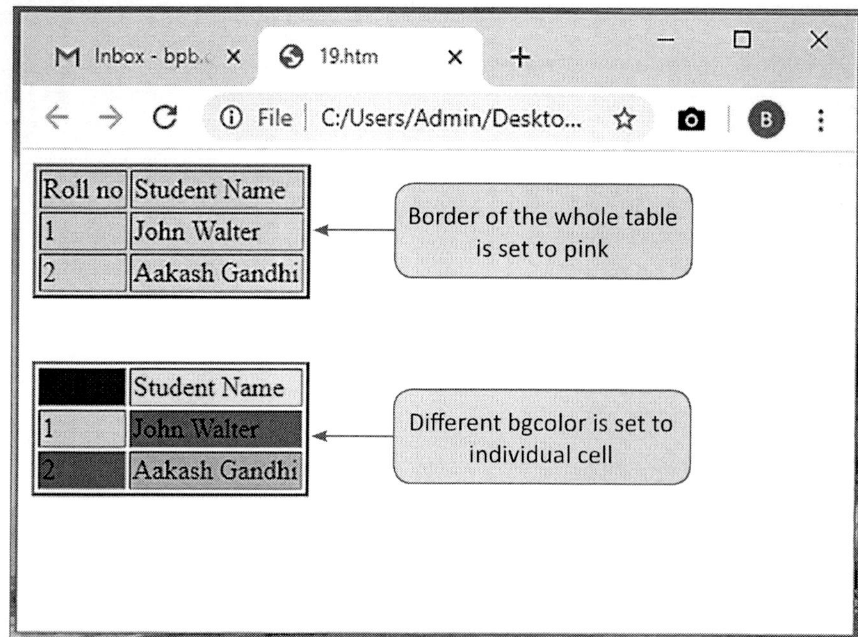

Figure 4.15: Showing Different border colors for rows

7. Background Attribute

If you want to insert an image or a picture at the background of the table, you can do so by using the background attribute. This attribute takes the value as the address or the path of the picture. The picture may be a bitmap or a graphic image.

In the following code, the image named **butterfly.jpg** is set as background to the entire table.

Program 4.16: To create a web page that will insert an image as a background of a table.

```
<HTML>
<BODY>
<TABLE border ="1" background="butterfly.jpg">
<TR>
<TH>Spring</TH>
<TH>Summer</TH>
<TH>Winter</TH>
</TR>
<TR>
<TD>Orchid</TD>
<TD>Galdiolus</TD>
<TD>Rose</TD>
</TR>
<TR>
<TD>Lilly</TD>
<TD>Lilac</TD>
```

```
<TD>Cyclamen</TD>
</TR>
<TR>
<TD>Tulip</TD>
<TD>Freesia</TD>
<TD>Amaryllis</TD>
</TR>
</TABLE>
</BODY>
</HTML>

</BODY>
</HTML>
```

Output of the program is given below:

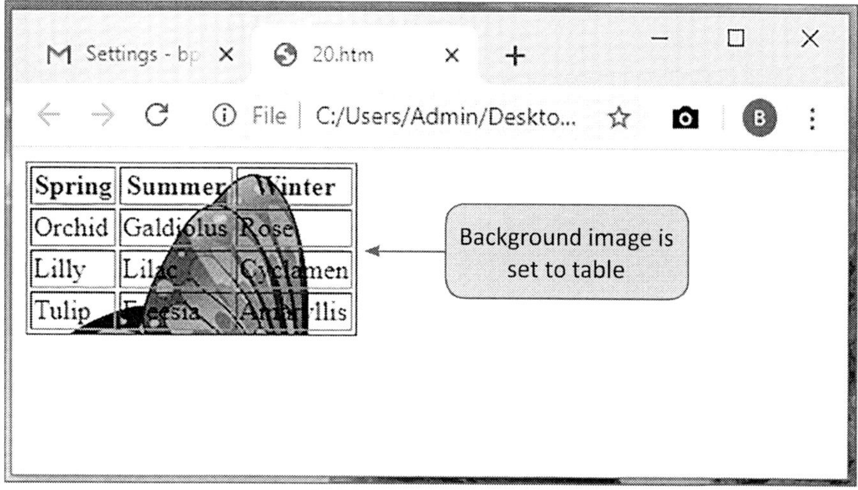

Figure 4.16: Inserting image as a background of a table

8. Width Attribute

The width attribute helps in identifying the breadth of the table in comparison to the webpage. It accepts the value as a number (in pixels) or in percentage (in proportion to the width of the webpage). If you omit this attribute, the width of the table is set according to the length of the characters inside the cells.

Program 4.17: To create a web page that will change the width of a table w.r.t browser Window.

```
<HTML>
<BODY>
<TABLE border ="1" width="30%">
<TR>
<TH>Spring</TH>
<TH>Summer</TH>
<TH>Winter</TH>
```

```
</TR>
<TR>
<TD>Orchid</TD>
<TD>Galdiolus</TD>
<TD>Rose</TD>
</TR>
<TR>
<TD>Lilly</TD>
<TD>Lilac</TD>
<TD>Cyclamen</TD>
</TR>
<TR>
<TD>Tulip</TD>
<TD>Freesia</TD>
<TD>Amaryllis</TD>
</TR>
</TABLE>
</BODY>
</HTML>

</BODY>
</HTML>
```

Output of the program is given below:

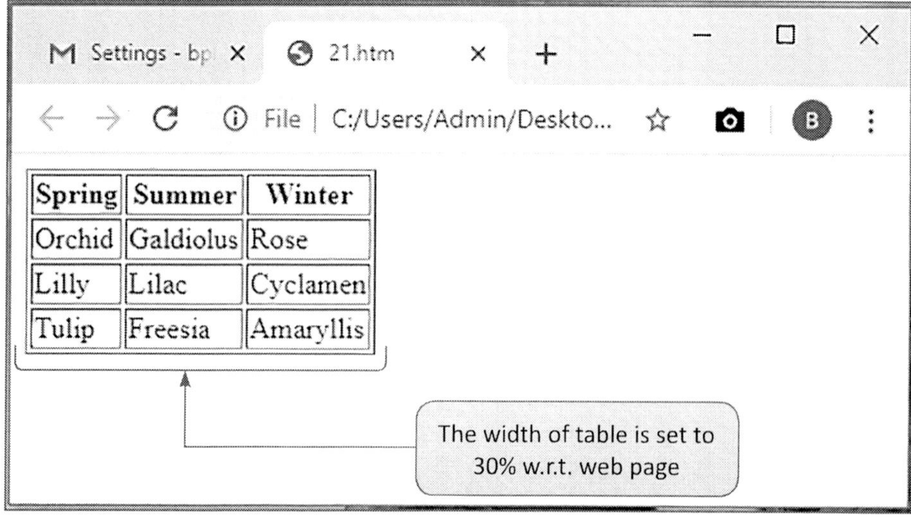

Figure 4.17: Setting width of table

9. Height Attribute

Height attribute is used to set the height of the table in pixels or in percentage with respect to browser Window.

Program 4.18: To create a web page that will use height attribute of a table.

```
<HTML>
<BODY>
<TABLE border ="1" height="50%">
<TR>
<TH>Spring</TH>
<TH>Summer</TH>
<TH>Winter</TH>
</TR>
<TR>
<TD>Orchid</TD>
<TD>Galdiolus</TD>
<TD>Rose</TD>
</TR>
<TR>
<TD>Lilly</TD>
<TD>Lilac</TD>
<TD>Cyclamen</TD>
</TR>
<TR>
<TD>Tulip</TD>
<TD>Freesia</TD>
<TD>Amaryllis</TD>
</TR>
</TABLE>
</BODY>
</HTML>

</BODY>
</HTML>
```

Output of the program is given below:

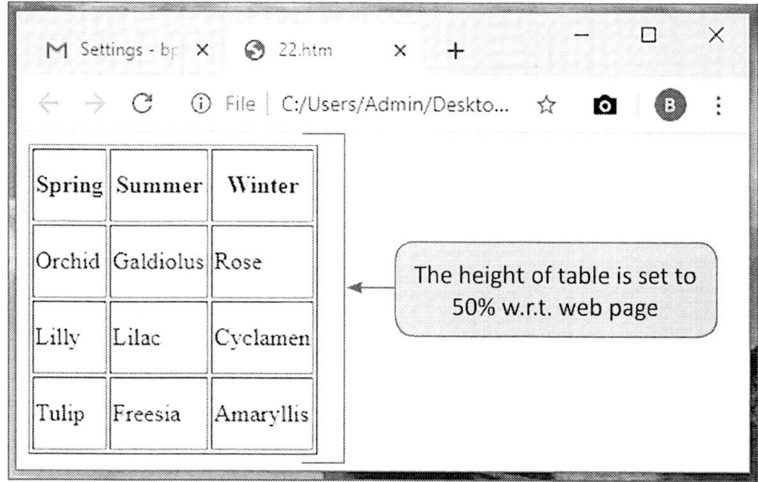

Figure 4.18: Setting height of a table

Images, Links, Tables

10. Cellspacing and Cellpadding Attributes

These attributes ae used to control the spacing in cells. **Cellspacing Attribute** controls the space between cells whereas **Cellpadding attribute** controls the space between the cell content and cell border/wall. (*Figure 4.19*)

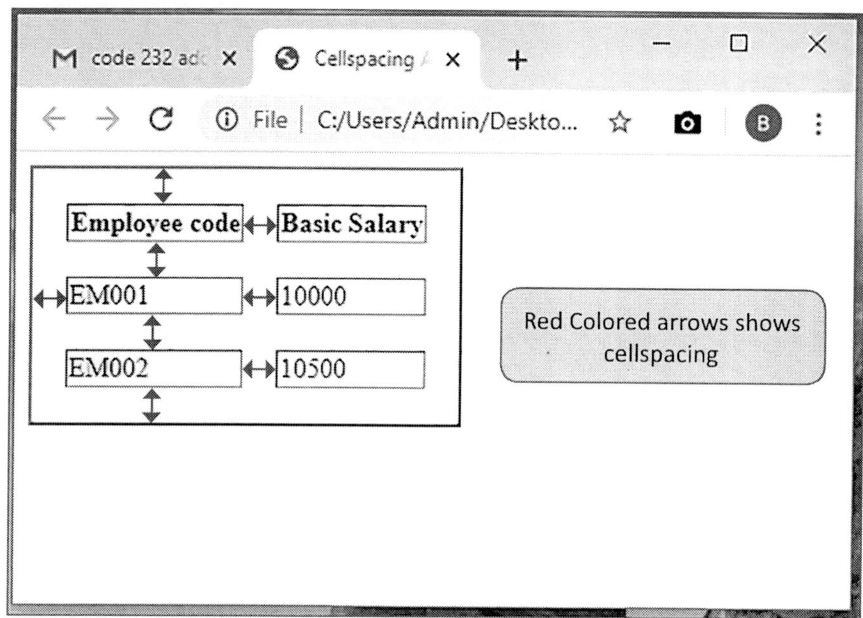

Figure 4.19: Cellspacing between cells

In this figure 4.19, all red colored arrows show cellspacing between cells. Cellspacing is the amount of space between the border of each cell and table border. (*figure 4.20*)

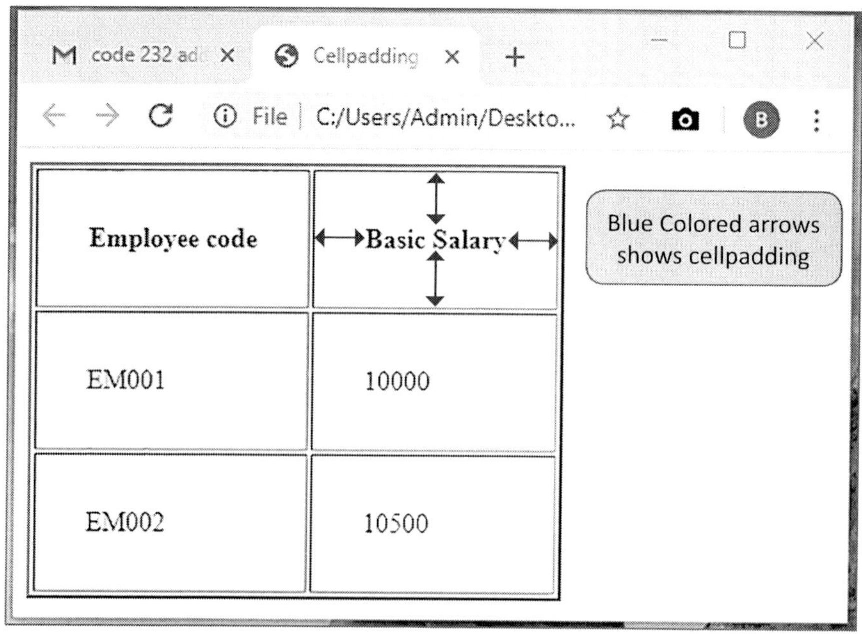

Figure 4.20: Cellpadding in table

In *figure 4.20*, all blue colored arrows show cellpadding between cells and cell content. Cellpadding is actually the amount of space between the cell borders and the content written inside cells.

Program 4.19: To create a web page that will show spanning of rows and columns in a table.

```
<HTML>
<head>
<title>Cellpadding and Cellspacing Attribute </title>
</head>
<body>
<table border=2 cellspacing=10 cellpadding=20>
<tr>
<th>Employee code </th>
<th>Basic Salary</th>
</tr>
<tr>
<td>EM001</td>
<td>10000</td>
</tr>
<tr>
<td>EM002</td>
<td>10500</td>
</tr>
</table>

</body>
</HTML>
```

Output of the program is given below:

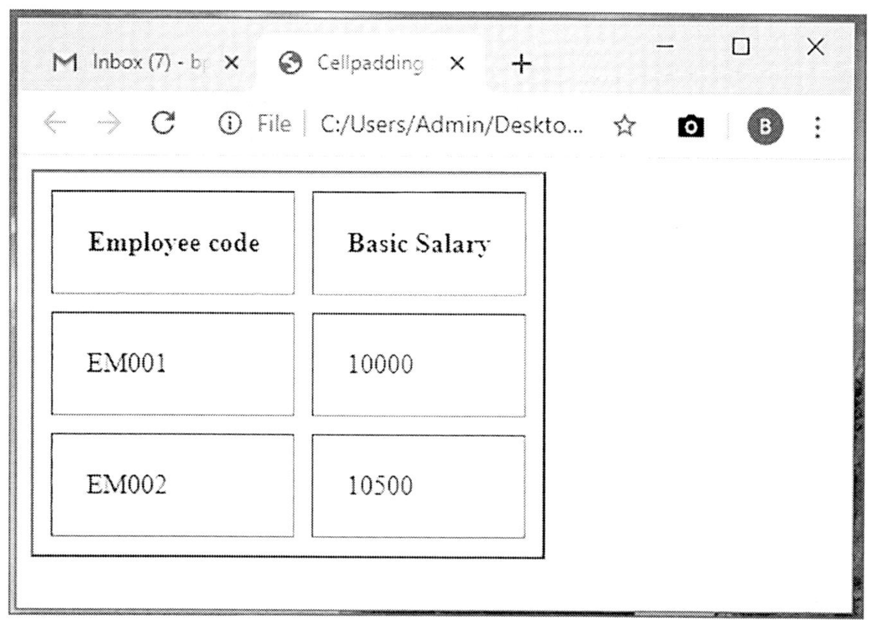

Figure 4.21: Cellspacing and Cellpadding in table

11. Summary Attribute

Summary attribute is used to provide information about a table. ***For example***, if you want to store the details of students, then to provide an information as: **Details of Students** about that table can be given by using summary attribute to know that the inserted table shows the information of students.

Program 4.20: To create a web page that will use summary attribute on table.

```
<HTML>
<BODY>
<table border=2 summary="Students' Details">

<TR>
<TD> Roll No</TD>
<TD> Student Name </TD>
</TR>
<TR>
<TD> 1 </TD>
<TD> John Walter </TD>
</TR>
<TR>
<TD> 2 </TD>
<TD > Aakash Gandhi </TD>
</TR>
</TABLE>

</BODY>
</HTML>
```

Output of the program is given below:

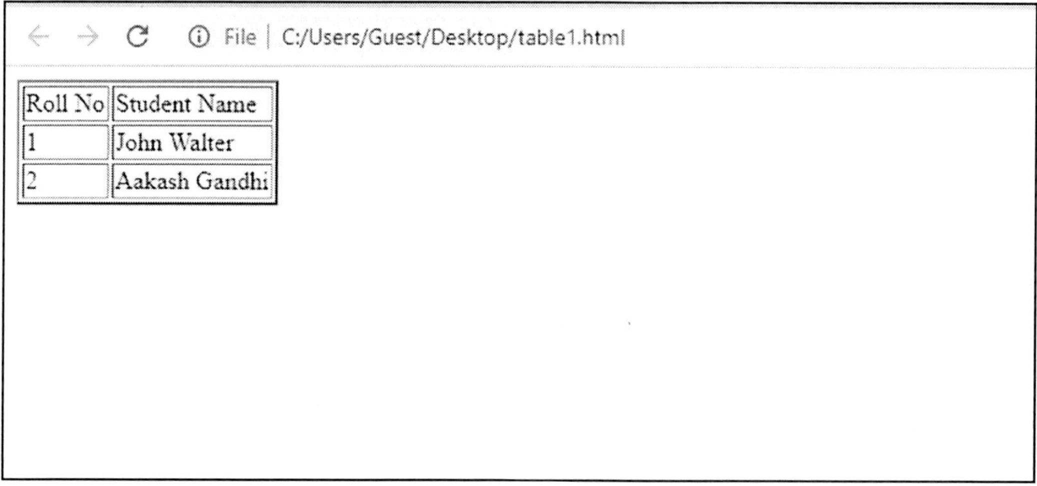

Figure 4.22: Not displaying Summary of a table

It is to be noted here that the **summary attribute** makes no visual difference in ordinary web browsers. This **attribute** can be used by users with visual impairment through non-visual browsers such as **BrailleSurf**.

Check Your Progress

State whether the following statements are True or False.

1. Summary attribute is used to provide information about a table.
2. Background attribute accepts the value as a number (in pixels) or in percentage.
3. Frame attribute is used along with border attribute.

4.3.2 The <TH>and <TD>Elements

The expanded form of <TH> tag is **table Header**. It is used to define the table header as a first row in the table. It is used inside the table tag. The text which is written using <TH> tag is displayed in boldface and centered by default.

The expanded form of <TD> tag is table data. It is used to create the table cells. The text inserted using the TD element is displayed in a regular font size and left aligned by default.

The attributes used with <TH> and <TD> tags are: **Align**, **Colspan**, **Rowspan**, No wrap and Valign.

* **Let's discuss various attributes of <TH> and <TD> elements.**

4.3.3 Attributes of <TD> and <TH> Elements

1. **Align Attribute:** Align attribute is similar to that of table, except that it aligns the text inside the cell rather than the table.
2. **NoWrap Attribute:** The NoWrap attribute does not allow the text to flow to the next line in the cell. If the sentence is wider than the width of the cell, no wrap will show the sentence in one straight line.
3. **COLSPAN Attribute:** The Colspan attribute helps in merging two or more columns of a table. This attribute is used with the <TD> or <TH> tag.
4. **ROWSPAN Attribute:** The Rowspan attribute helps in merging two or more rows of a table. This attribute is used with the <TD> or <TH> tag.

For example,

Consider the table employee that consists of 4 rows and 3 columns. Now, the cells of first row have been merged into 1 column and cell 3 of second row has merged with cell 3 of third row resulting into one row as shown in *figure 4.23*:

Program 4.21: Program to merge rows and column.

```
<HTML>
<head>
<title> Colspan Attribute </title>
</head>
<body>
```

```
<table border=2 bgcolor= "Pink" width="30%" height="30%">
<tr>
<th colspan=3> Employee Details</th>
</tr>
<tr>
<td>Employee code </td>
<td>Basic Salary</td>
<td> Country</td>
</tr>
<tr>
<td>EM001</td>
<td>10000</td>
<td rowspan=2>India</td>
</tr>
<tr>
<td>EM002</td>
<td>10500</td>
</tr>
</table>
</body>
</HTML>
```

Output of the program is given below:

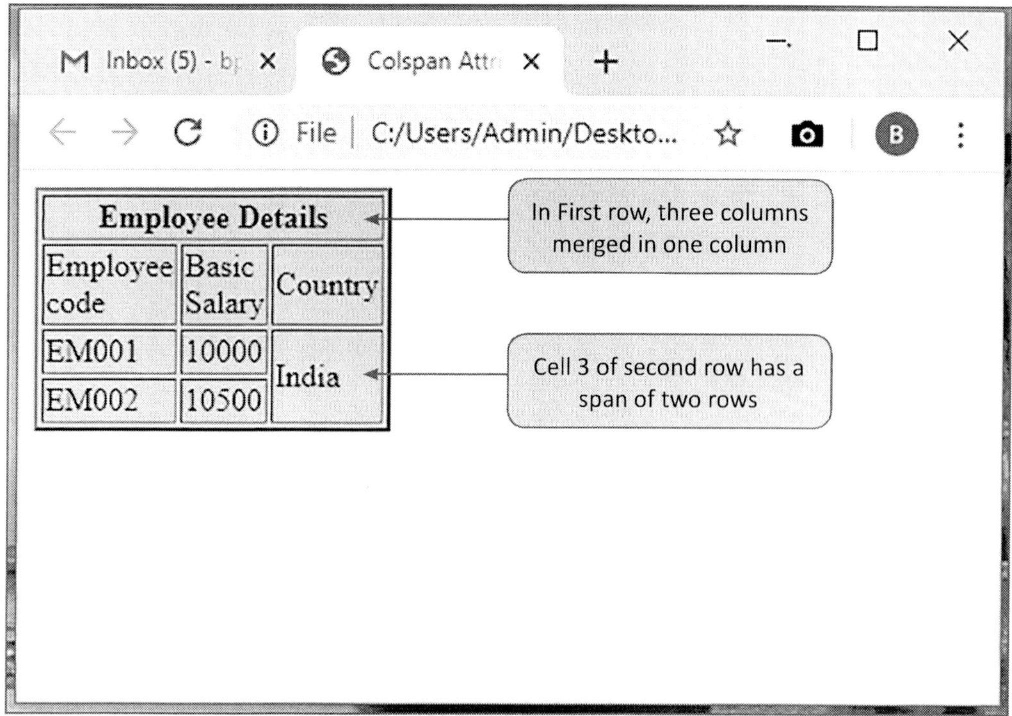

Figure 4.23: Merging of rows and columns

Program 4.22: To create a web page that will show different rowspan and colspan of rows and columns respectively.

```
<HTML>
<head>
<title> Colspan & Rowspan Attributes </title>
</head>
<body>
<table border=2 bgcolor= "Pink" >
<tr>
<Td rowspan=2> A</td>
<td> data 1</td>
</tr>
<tr>
<td> data 2</td>
</tr>
</table>
<br>
<table border=2 bgcolor= "Green" >
<tr>
<Td colspan="2"> A</td>
</tr>
<tr>
<td> data 1</td>

<td> data 2</td>
</tr>
</table><br>
<table border=2 bgcolor= "orange" >
<tr>
<Td rowspan=2> A</td>
<td> data 1</td>
<td rowspan=2> data 3</td>
</tr>
<tr>
<td> data 2</td>
</tr>
</table>
<br>
</body>
</HTML>
```

Output of the program is given below:

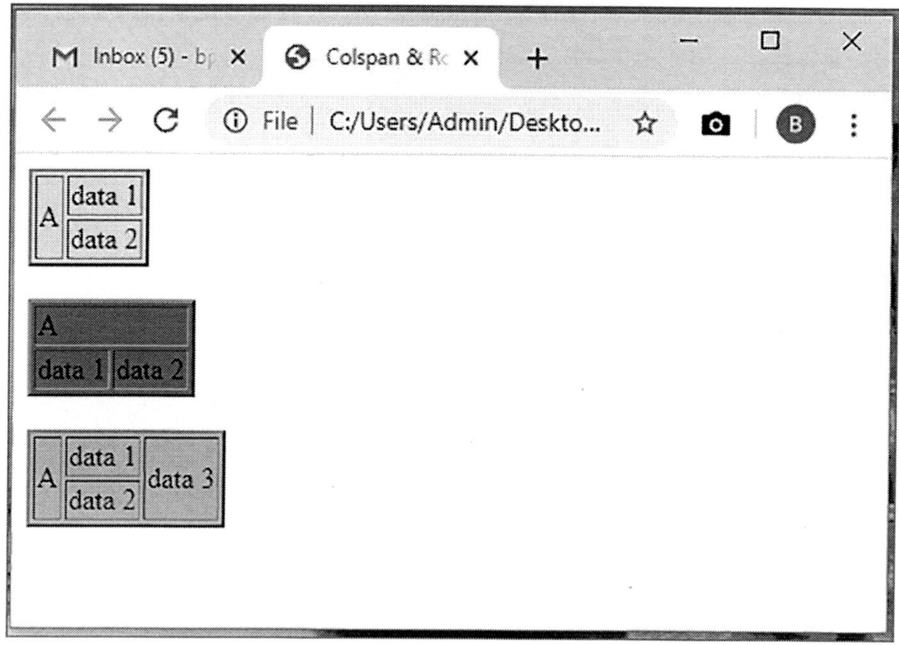

Figure 4.24: Showing Different Merging of rows and columns

5. **Valign Attribute:** In cells that have span of more than one row, data can also be aligned vertically by using VALIGN attribute. The possible values of valign attribute are: **top**, **middle** and **bottom**.

   By default, the vertical alignment of cell is **middle**.

Program 4.23: To create a web page that will show the vertical alignment of a text while row are merged.

```
<HTML>
<head>
<title>Valign Attribute </title>
</head>
<body>
<table border=2 bgcolor= "Pink" width="30%" height="30%">
<tr>
<th colspan=3> Employee Details</th>
</tr>
<tr>
<td>Employee code </td>
<td>Basic Salary</td>
<td> Country</td>
</tr>
<tr>
<td>EM001</td>
<td>10000</td>
<td rowspan=2 valign="bottom">India</td>
</tr>
```

```
<tr>
<td>EM002</td>
<td>10500</td>
</tr>
</table>
</body>
</HTML>
```

Output of the program is given below:

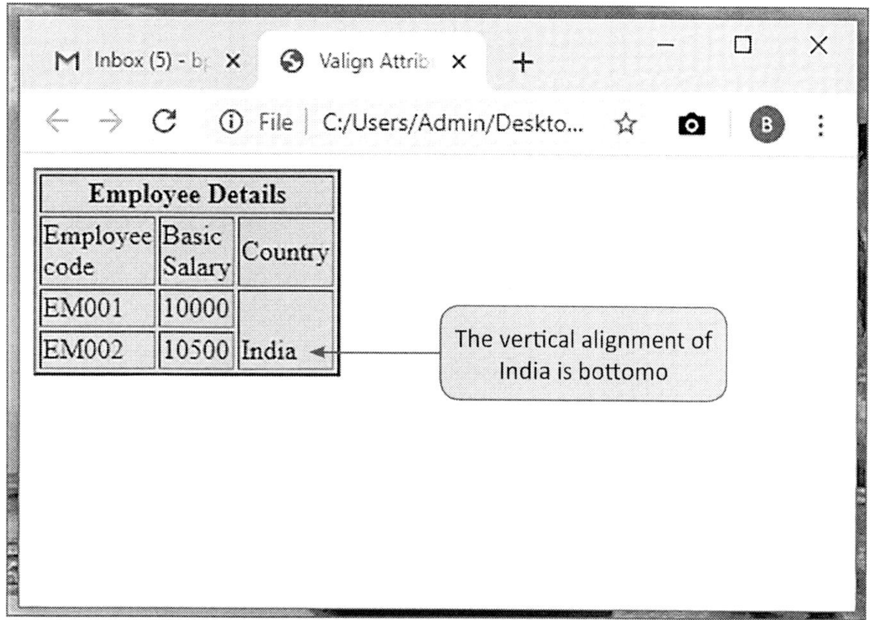

Employee Details		
Employee code	Basic Salary	Country
EM001	10000	
EM002	10500	India

Figure 4.25: Vertically aligning the text

Extra Byte

It is to be noted here that if you want to merge fist row with second, third and so on, then specify rowspan attribute with <TD> of first row and do not use <TD> with second and other rows. Similarly, to merge third row with fourth, fifth and so on, then specify rowspan with <TD> of third row and do not use <TD> with third and other rows.

4.5 THE <CAPTION> TAG

The <Caption> tag is like a title, used to provide a text to the table to explain the contents of the table. It is generally in **bold**, at center with respect to the table. However, the position of the caption can be on either the top or the bottom of the table using the **align** attribute as shown in *program 4.24*:

Program 4.24: To create a web page that will use caption tag in table.

```
<HTML>
<HEAD><TITLE></TITLE></HEAD>
<BODY>
<table border=2>
```

```
<Caption align="top"> Students' Details</Caption>
<TR>
<TD bgcolor="blue"> Roll no</TD>
<TD bgcolor="yellow"> Student Name </TD>
</TR>
<TR>
<TD bgcolor="pink"> 1 </TD>
<TD bgcolor="green"> John Walter </TD>
</TR>
<TR>
<TD bgcolor="red"> 2 </TD>
<TD bgcolor="orange"> Aakash Gandhi </TD>
</TR>
</TABLE>
</BODY>
</HTML>
```

Output of the program is given below:

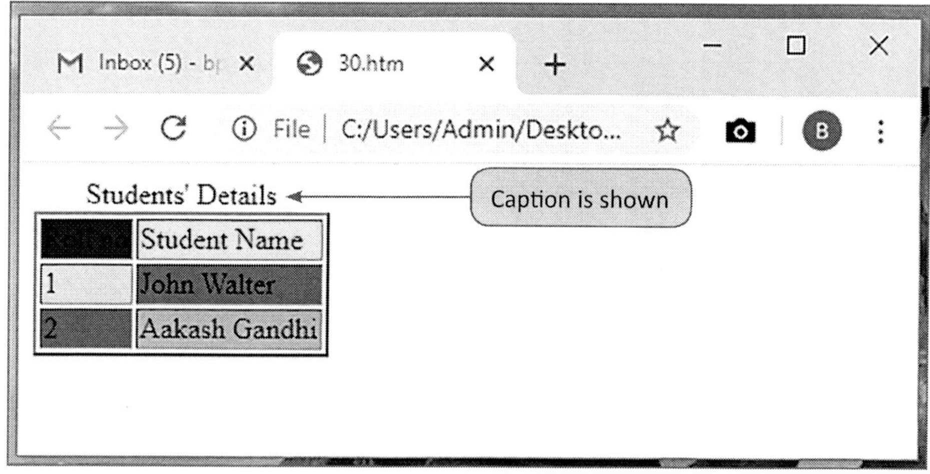

Figure 4.26: Showing Caption of a table

MEMORIZE

<Table> tag is used to create tables in html in order to display data in tabular format. It is in the form of matrix hat, which consist of rows and columns. Rows are formed by using **<TR>** tag and cells are created by using **<TD>** tag.

Let's Revise

- The <img> tag is used to insert images in a web page.
- <img> uses src as a main attribute. The format of image should be .jpeg, .jpg or .gif only.

- Linking provides several web pages to be connected with each other.
- Two types of linking are: internal and external.
- External linking helps in linking different documents with each other.
- Internal linking helps in linking different sections of a same web page.
- Name attribute is used for internal linking.
- The <Table > tag arranges the data items on the web page in rows and columns.
- <Table> tag is used along with <TR> and <TD> tags.
- <TR> tag is used to create rows in a table and <TD> tag is used to create cells in a table.
- The <TH> tag encloses the Header object and makes the data boldface and center aligned.
- The <TD> keeps the data in regular font and left aligned by default.
- <TR> tag in turn is nested within the TABLE tag and is used to define rows in a table.
- The colspan attribute helps in merging the columns of a row. This attribute is not used with table tag but with the <TH> or the <TD> tag.
- When the table's cells span across more than one row, it is called ROWSPAN. If we want to give the table a nice sidebar, this attribute is used. The rowspan appears as merged cells.
- The <caption> tag is used to provide a text to the table so as to explain the contents of the table. It is generally in bold, at center with respect to the table.

Learning Zone

SECTION A: OBJECTIVE TYPE QUESTIONS

A. MULTIPLE CHOICE QUESTIONS.

1. Which one of the following is not an attribute of <A> tag?
   a. NAME b. HREF c. Source d. Both a. & b.
2. Which is the correct HTML statement for creating a hyperlink?
   a. <a name="">A</a> b. <a>B</a>
   c. <a href="http://www.example.com">example</a>
   d. <a url="http://www.example.com">example</a>
3. How can you create an e-mail link?
   a. <mail href="a@b"> b. <mail>a@b</mail>
   c. <a href="a@b"> d. <a href="mailto:a@b.com">
4. Which of these tags are all <table> tags?
   a. <table><head><tfoot> b. <table><tr><td>
   c. <table><tr><tt> d. <thead><body><tr>
5. Choose the correct HTML statement to left-align the content inside a table cell.
   a. <td valign="left"> b. <tdleft> c. <td leftalign> d. <td align="left">
6. What is the correct HTML statement for inserting an image?
   a. <image src="image.gif" alt="MyImage" > b. <img href="image.gif" alt="MyImage" >
   c. <img src="image.gif" alt="MyImage" > d. <img alt="MyImage">image.gif</img>

7. Colspan=n can be added to only which tag?

a. <table> b. <td> c. <tr> d. <caption>

8. Which property tells how many rows a cell should span? (Delhi 2017)

a. Colspan = n b. Rowspan =n c. Both a. and b. d. None of these

9. Border, cellspacing, cellpadding, align are the attributes of:

a. <body> b. <img> c. <table> d. None of these

10. Which sequence of HTML tags are correct?

a. <HTML><head><title></<title></head><body></body></HTML>

b. <HTML><head></head><body><title></<title></body></HTML>

c. <HTML><head><title></<title><body></body></head></HTML>

d. <HTML><title></<title><head></head><body></body></HTML>

11. Web browsers display images in the following format:

a. GIF b. XBM c. JPEG d. All of the above

12. The attribute of the <IMG> tag is used to provide alternate text for an image.

a. ALT b. SRC c. IMG d. None of these

13. In VLINK Attribute, V Stand for: (Delhi 2018, 2019)

a. Visited b. Very c. Victory d. Visitor

14. Which of these tags is/are used with <Table> tag? (Delhi 2017)

a. <TR> b. <TD> c. <TH> d. All of the above

15. Which of the following is/are attributes of <TR> Tag?

a. Text b. Colour c. Align d. All of the above

Ans.	1. c	2. c	3. d	4. b	5. d
	6. c	7. b	8. b	9. c	10. a
	11. d	12. a	13. a	14. d	15. c

B. FILL IN THE BLANKS.

1. ____________ tag is used for storing data in tabular format.
2. The expanded form of TR tag is ____________.
3. TD tag can only be used inside ____________ tag.
4. ____________ and ____________ are two types of linking in HTML.
5. The default alignment of an image is ____________. (Delhi 2017)
6. ____________ is used to change the active link color.
7. ____________ attribute is used to align the text vertically in a cell.
8. ____________ tag is used to provide the heading of a table.
9. ____________ tag is used to give title to a table.
10. Images can also be inserted as a ____________ in html.
11. In HTML, while creating a table, you cannot use background attribute with ____________ tag. (Delhi 2017)

12. To increase space between two cells, ____________ attribute should be used. (Delhi 2017)

13. To use an image as a table's background, write ____________.

14. ____________ tag is used to add columns to a table. (Outside Delhi 2014)

15. ____________ attribute is used to add border color of a row.

16. An image that is displayed inline with the text on a web page is called ____________.

Ans. 1. <table> 2. Table row 3. TR 4. Internal & External
5. Left 6. alink 7. Valign 8. <TH>
9. Caption 10. Link 11. <table> 12. Cellspacing
13. <table background="image"> 14. <TD> 15. bordercolor 16. Hotspot

C. STATE WHETHER THE FOLLOWING STATEMENTS ARE TRUE OR FALSE.

1. A table's background color can be specified using background color attribute.
2. <TD> is a container tag.
3. <CAPTION> tag gives heading to a table.
4. The HTML tag for inline image is <img>.
5. The absence of <TR> tag will create the table structure.
6. <TH> tag is used to define the header cell of a table.
7. <TD> tag is used to define the table data. (Delhi 2014)
8. Bordercolor attribute is used to set the table border.
9. Rowspan attribute is used to merge two columns together.
10. Colspan attribute is used to merge rows together.
11. The default value of the table border is 1.
12. If you do not specify the height and width of an image, it will be displayed in actual size.
13. Align attribute specifies the vertical alignment of cell content.
14. <TR> tag is used to specify the individual table data in a table. (Delhi 2011)

Ans. 1. False 2. True 3. True 4. False 5. True
6. True 7. True 8. True 9. False 10. False
11. False 12. True 13. False 14. False

SECTION B: SOLVED THEORY QUESTIONS

1. What is the expanded form of URL?

Ans: The expanded form of URL is: Uniform Resource Locator.

2. What is the significance of using<IMG> tag? Mention it's any two attributes along with their purpose. (Delhi 2019)

Ans: <IMG> tag is used to insert images in a webpage.
Its two main attributes:

a. SRC: It specifies the URL or the location of the image.

b. ALT: It specifies an alternate text for an image in case the browser does not display the image.

3. **What are the various types of image alignment? The following code is written to align the image in the center of the browser's window. However, the desired result is not achieved. Mention the reason.**

<IMG SRC="house.gif " ALIGN= "center">

Ans: In HTML, there are five types of alignments available to align an image. These alignments are top, bottom, middle, left, and right. Therefore, firstly, in the above code, the value center of attribute align is invalid here.

Secondly, if we want to center align an image, we need to use the <CENTER> tag because the middle alignment cannot align an image at the center of a web page. Instead, it aligns the image in between of the text.

4. **Consider the following HTML statement:**

<body bgcolor ="Blue" alink ="red" vlink="yellow">

In the above statement, what do you mean by 'alink' and 'vlink'?

Ans: Alink stands for active link while vlink stands for visited link. When the cursor is positioned on the hyperlinked text, the coloured specified in alink attribute (red) is seen. When the link has been clicked once, the colour changes to the one specified in vlink attribute (yellow)

5. **Name the following with respect to HTML.**
   a. **Attribute for changing bullet type of list tag.**
   b. **Element to create a hyperlink.**

Ans: a. type, b. <A> Anchor tag

6. **Identify which of the following is a tag or an attribute:** **(Delhi 2017)**

a. img b. a c. align d. Color e. font f. noshade

Ans:

Tags	Attributes
Img	align
A	color
Font	noshade

7. **Define hypertext and hyperlink?**

Ans: Hypertext is simply a text or a phrase that links to another text. These links are references that redirect us to other web pages and these references are called hyperlinks. Hypertext documents interlink various websites or web pages through the use of hyperlinks, which are activated when clicked.

8. **Which attributes are used to change the visited and active link color in a web page?**

Ans: alink attribute is used to change the color of active link.

Vlink attribute is used to change the color of visited link.

9. **Which tag is used to insert the link? Name the attribute which is mandatory for linking.**

Ans: Anchor <A> tag is used to insert the link. HREF i.e. hyper reference is the mandatory attribute which is used to link the specified document/image or a web page.

10. **Explain the command <A HREF="auto.HTML"> Click here for autobiography</A>**

Ans: This command will open the "auto.HTML" Web page in the browser when we click the hypertext "Click here for autobiography".

11. **Consider the given HTML code and answer the following:**
<A HREF=#intro> Introduction </A>
In the above code:
   a. **What is the purpose of #?**
   b. **What will happen when the user clicks "Introduction"?**

Ans: a. The # symbol is used to tell the Web browser that this link is in the same Web page.
   b. When we click Introduction, we are redirected (or sent) to the section named 'intro' in the Web page.

12. **What is the difference between cellspacing and cellpadding?** **(Delhi 2017)**

Ans: CELLSPACING is used to set the space between the cells of a table.
CELLPADDING is used to set the amount of space between the contents of the cell and the cell wall.

13. **What is the purpose of the mailto function?**

Ans: The mailto function is used to send e-mail messages to multiple recipients. For this, type the e-mail address in the same link, separated by commas.

14. **What is the purpose of using VALIGN attribute in tables?**

Ans: The VALIGN attribute vertically aligns the data in a table. It is used with <TD> tag.
Valign attribute takes three values that is top, middle and bottom. It is basically used when there is a span of two or more than two rows and you have to align the data vertically either at the top, middle or bottom.

SECTION C: APPLICATION ORIENTED QUESTIONS

1. **Write the HTML code to do the following:**
   a. **To display a horizontal line of green colour.**
   b. **To create a hyperlink on the word CLICK to an image named testimage.jpeg.**

Ans: a. <hr color="green">
   b. < a href="testimage.jpeg"> CLICK </a>

2. **Gaurav, a web designer in a company named "International Designers" has just created a webpage in which different sections of the webpage are linked and can be traversed by clicking on the text as "Top", "Middle" and "Bottom". Is its internal linking or external linking and why? Additionally, tell him about the suitable tag and its attribute(s) to open another webpage named 'second. html' by clicking on the text "Next".**

Ans: Internal linking, because the links are used to traverse different sections in the same webpage.
The tag and attributes to open another webpage named 'second.html' by clicking on the text "Next" is:
<a href="second.html">Next</a>

3. **Write output of the following HTML code.**

```
<html> <head> <title> Table </title> </head>
<body>
<table border="1">
<tr> <th align="center" rowspan="3"> ONE </th> <th> TWO </th>
<th>THREE </th> </tr>
<tr> <td> Rose </td> <td> Lily </td> </tr>
<tr> <td align="center"> Pansy </td> <td align="center"
colspan="2"> Dahlia </td> </tr>
</table> </body> </html>
```

Ans: 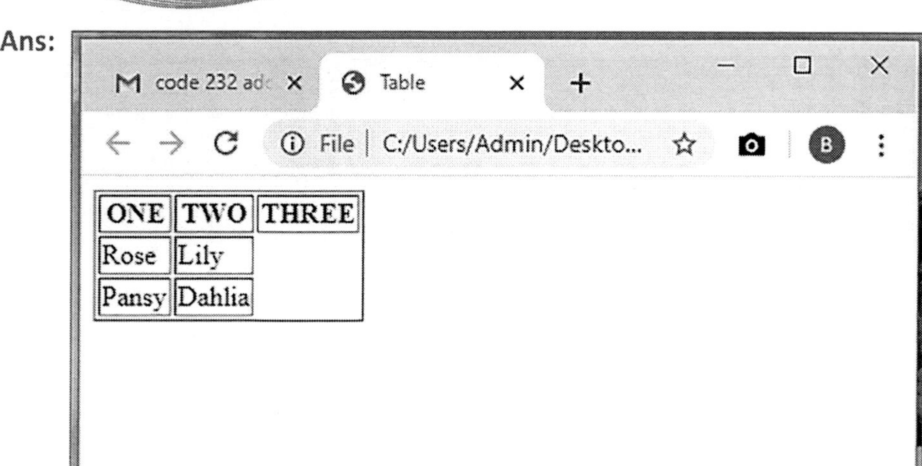

ONE	TWO	THREE
Rose	Lily	
Pansy	Dahlia	

4. **Palvi is inserting links in her web page. She wants to change the color of the links that have not been visited yet to green colour. The links that have been viewed to red and the link that is currently being clicked by the user in a document to cyan. Help her in doing so.**

Ans: She can write the code as:

```
<body link=”green” alink=”cyan” vlink=”red”>
```

5. **Observe the following table and write the HTML code to generate it:**

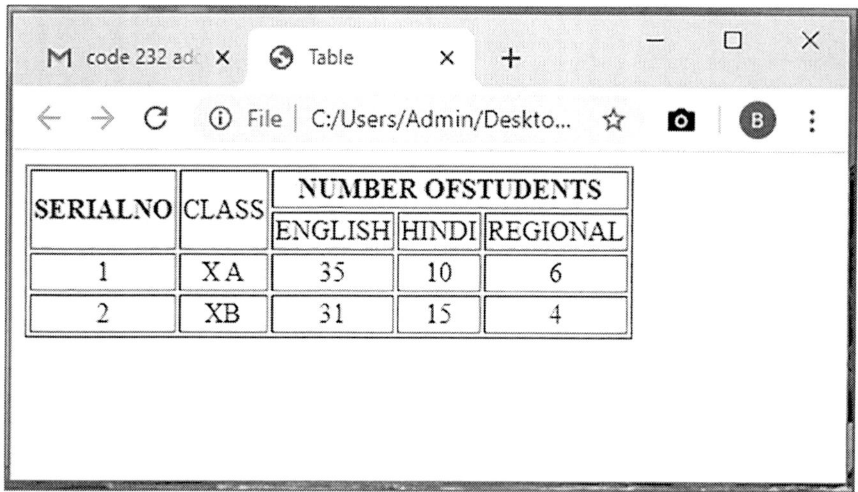

SERIALNO	CLASS	NUMBER OFSTUDENTS		
		ENGLISH	HINDI	REGIONAL
1	XA	35	10	6
2	XB	31	15	4

Ans:

```
<html> <head> <title> Table </title> </head>
<body>
<table border=”1”>
<tr> <th align=”center” ROWSPAN=”2”> SERIALNO</th>
<td ROWSPAN=”2”> CLASS</th> <th COLSPAN=”3”>NUMBER OFSTUDENTS </th> </tr>
<tr> <td> ENGLISH </td> <td> HINDI </td>
<td>REGIONAL</td></tr>
<tr align=”center”> <td align=center”> 1 </td>
<td align=”center”> X
A </td> <td>35</td><td>10</td><td>6</td></tr>
<tr align=”center”> <td align=center”> 2 </td>
<td align=”center”> XB </td> <td>31</td><td>15</td><td>4</td></tr>
</table> </body> </html>
```

6. **Create the following table in HTML by using suitable tags:**

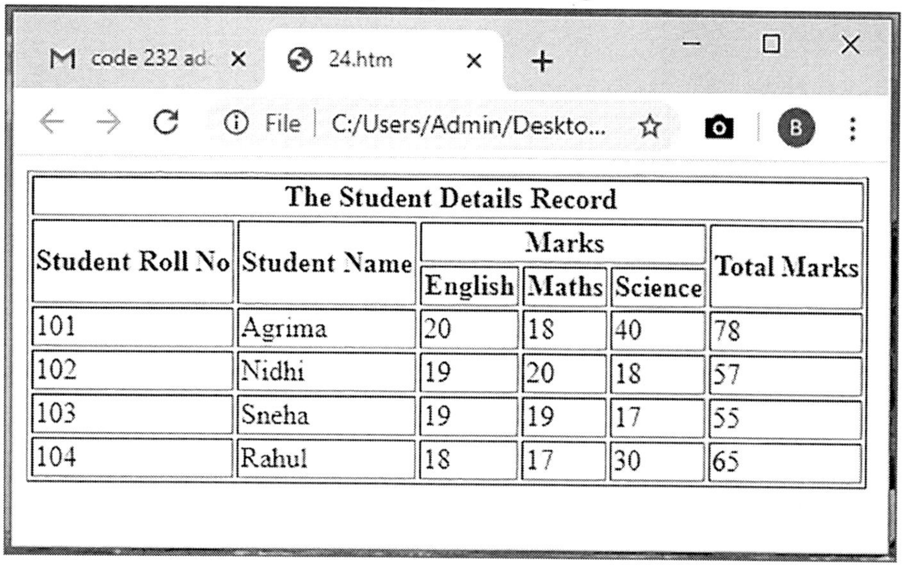

The Student Details Record					
Student Roll No	**Student Name**	**Marks**			**Total Marks**
		English	**Maths**	**Science**	
101	Agrima	20	18	40	78
102	Nidhi	19	20	18	57
103	Sneha	19	19	17	55
104	Rahul	18	17	30	65

Ans:
```
<HTML>
<HEAD>
<TITLE>
</TITLE>
</HEAD>
<BODY>
<TABLE BORDER=1>
<TR>
<TH COLSPAN=6 ALIGN="center"> The Student Details Record</TH>
</TR>
<TR>
<TH ROWSPAN=2>Student Roll No</TH>
<TH ROWSPAN=2> Student Name</TH>
<TH COLSPAN=3> Marks </TH>
<TH ROWSPAN=2>Total Marks</TH>
</TR>
<TR>
<TH>English</TH>
<TH>Maths</TH>
<TH>Science</TH>
</TR>
<TR>
<TD>101 </TD>
<TD> Agrima </TD>
<TD> 20 </TD>
<TD> 18 </TD>
<TD> 40 </TD>
<TD> 78 </TD>
</TR>
<TR>
<TD>102 </TD>
```

```
<TD> Nidhi </TD>
<TD> 19 </TD>
<TD> 20 </TD>
<TD> 18 </TD>
<TD> 57 </TD>
</TR>
<TR>
<TD>103 </TD>
<TD> Sneha </TD>
<TD> 19 </TD>
<TD> 19 </TD>
<TD> 17 </TD>
<TD> 55 </TD>
</TR>
<TR>
<TD>104 </TD>
<TD> Rahul </TD>
<TD> 18 </TD>
<TD> 17 </TD>
<TD> 30</TD>
<TD> 65 </TD>
</TR>
</TABLE>
</BODY>
</HTML>
```

7. **Write HTML code to display the following table:**

Specifications:

- The title of the webpage is "Schedule"
- The Caption of the Table is Duty Chart.
- AM, 10 AM, 12 AM are Headings given to the table.

Ans:

```
<HTML>
<HEAD>
<TITLE>
Schedule
</TITLE>
</HEAD>
<BODY>
<TABLE Border = 1>
<CAPTION>Duty Chart</CAPTION>
<TR>
<TH> 8 AM </TH>
<TH> 10 AM </TH>
<TH> 12 AM </TH>
</TR>
<TR>
<TD> KEVIN</TD>
```

```
<TD> KHUSHBOO </TD>
<TD> AMARJEET </TD>
</TR>
</TABLE>
</HTML>
```

8. Write the HTML code to generate the following web page with the given below specifications:

a. Bordered table should have background color in pink.

b. Table's header row with a heading "INCOME TAX SLABS 2021-22" should spread over four cells.

c. After heading row, first cell of next row should spread over five rows with an image named "it.jpg" stored in d: drive.

d. Set the space between the cell wall and the cell content to 10 pixels and set the space between the cells to 10 pixels.

e. At the bottom of the page, a link to next page is there which is linked to another webpage named "next.HTML".

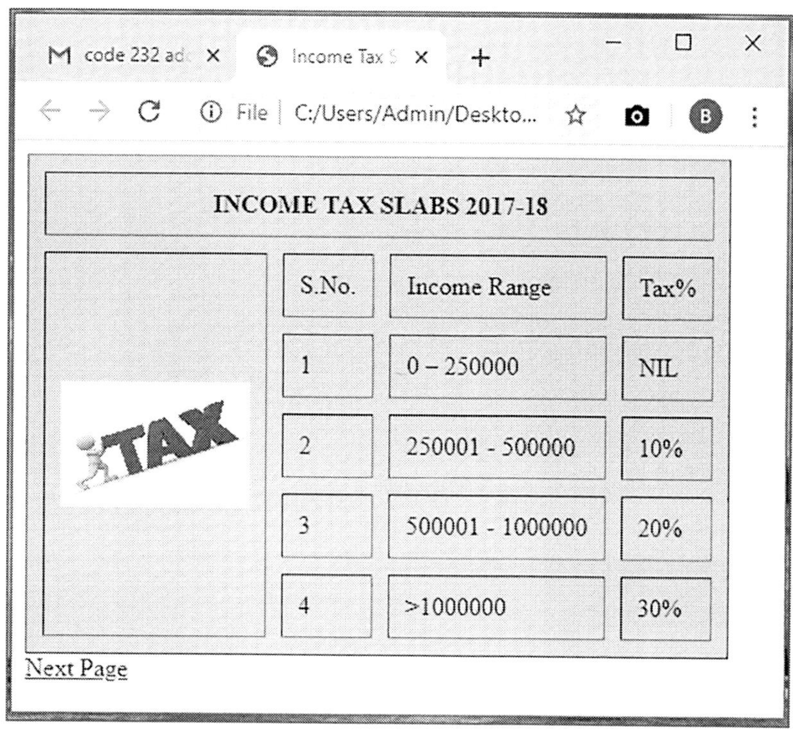

INCOME TAX SLABS 2017-18			
	S.No.	Income Range	Tax%
	1	0 – 250000	NIL
	2	250001 - 500000	10%
	3	500001 - 1000000	20%
	4	>1000000	30%

Next Page

Ans:

```
<HTML>
<head><title>Income Tax Slabs 2021-22</title></head><body>
<table bgcolor="pink" border=1 cellspacing=10 cellpadding=10>
<tr>
<th colspan=4>
INCOME TAX SLABS 2021-22
</th>
</tr>
<tr>
<td rowspan=5><img src="d:\it.jpg"></td>
<td>S.No.</td>
<td>Income Range</td>
<td>Tax%</td>
```

```
</tr>
<tr>
<td>1</td>
<td>0 - 250000</td>
<td>NIL</td>
</tr>
<tr>
<td>2</td>
<td>250001 - 500000</td>
<td>10%</td>
</tr>
<tr>
<td>3</td>
<td>500001 - 1000000</td>
<td>20%</td>
</tr>
<tr>
<td>4</td>
<td>>1000000</td>
<td>30%</td>
</tr>
</table>
</table>
<a href=”next.HTML”>Next Page</a>
</body>
</HTML>
```

9. **Write the HTML code to generate the following output:**

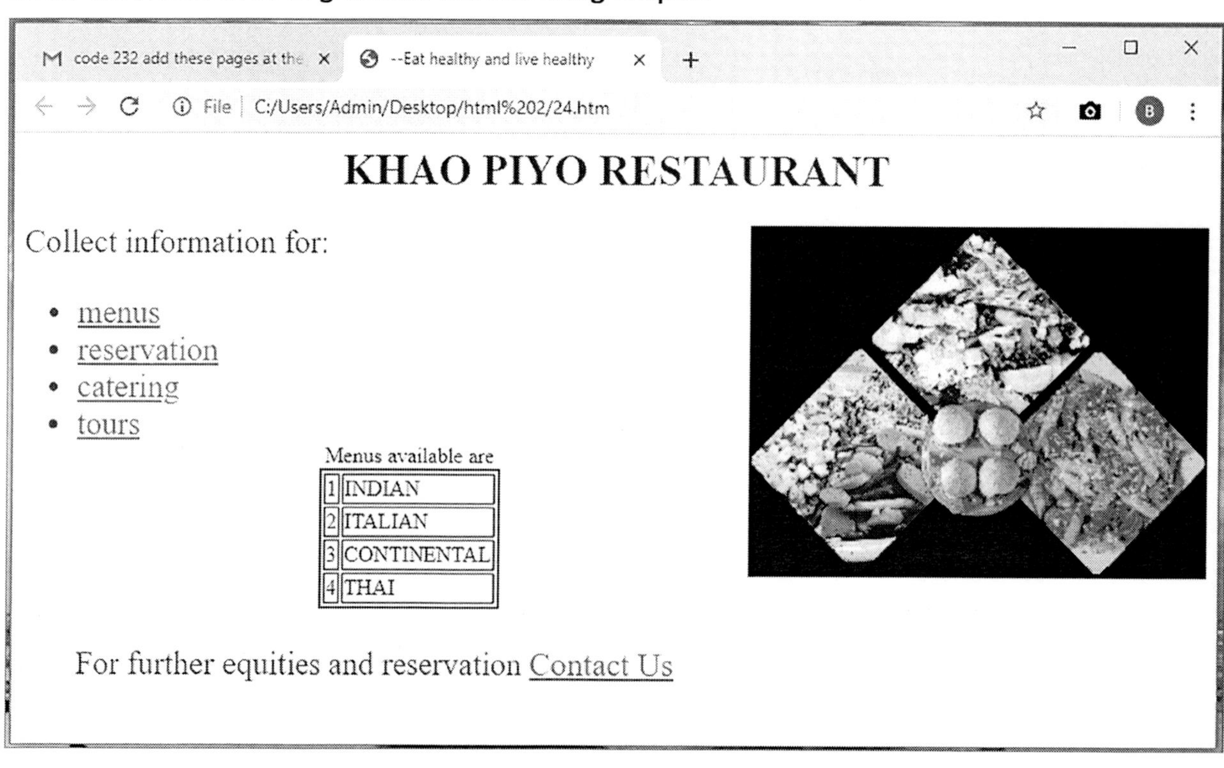

Note the following points while generating the webpage:

a. Link color is green, active link color is blue and visited link color is red.

b. Title of the page is "Eat healthy, live healthy".

c. Heading of the page is Maroon.

d. Image used is "restaurant.jpg".

e. Caption of table is blue.

f. Table border is blue and size 2.

g. The links are one.HTML, two.HTML, three.HTML and four.HTML.

h. The e-mail id for contact is abc@xyz.com.

Ans:

```
<HTML>
<HEAD>
<TITLE> --Eat healthy and live healthy</TITLE></HEAD>
<BODY LINK ="Green" ALINK "Blue"VLINK = "Red">
<CENTER>
<H1><FONT COLOR = "maroon">KHAO PIYO RESTAURANT</FONT></H1></center>
<IMG SRC = "resturant.png" ALIGN = "right" HEIGHT = "255" WIDTH = "250">
<FONT COLOR = "purple" SIZE = "5">
<FONT color="purple" size="5">
Collect information for:
<UL>
<LI><A HREF = "one.HTML">menus</A>
<LI><A HREF = "two.HTML">reservation</A>
<LI><A HREF = "three.HTML">catering</A>
<LI><A HREF = "four.HTML">tours</A>
</U L>
</FONT>
<FONT SIZE = 5>
<CENTER>
<TABLE BORDER = 2 BORDERCOLOR = "blue">
<FONT color = blue><CAPTION>Menus available are </CAPTION></font>
<TR><TD> 1 <TD> INDIAN
<TR><TD>2 <TD> ITALIAN
<TR><TD> 3 <TD> CONTINENTAL
<TR><TD> 4 <TD> THAI
</TABLE></CENTER><BR>
For further equities and reservation
<A HREF = "mailto:abc©xyz.com">Contact Us</A></font>
</BODY></HTML>
```

10. **Shreya has just started e-learning html. She has made a list of few html tags which she will be using in creating a web page but by mistake she has mentioned wrong attributes in front of the tags. Help her in selecting correct attributes from 'Column B' for the tags given in 'Column A'.**

(Delhi 2019)

Column A (TAGS)	Column B (ATTRIBUTES)
BODY	NAME
IMG	TEXT
OL	ALT
A	START

Ans: The correct tags with their attributes are:

1. BODY: TEXT
2. IMG: ALT
3. OL: START
4. A: ALT

11. Observe following output and write HTML code to generate it. **(Delhi 2018)**

Consider the following points while generating the web page:

- The title of the page is "FOOTBALL CLUB".
- The heading is blue color.
- Font of entire documents is Arial.
- Image Used is "football.jpeg".
- The page is linking to:
  - o Proud history to "history.html".
  - o Bottom message is of size 2.

Ans:

```
<HTML>
<BODY>
<HEAD>
<TITLE>FOOTBALL CLUB</TITLE>
```

```
<!-- OR <TITLE>Manchester Football Club Website</TITLE> -->
</HEAD>
<BODY>
<FONT FACE="Arial">
<CENTER>
<!-- OR <P ALIGN="Center"> -->
<H1><FONT COLOR= "Blue" >FOOTBALL CLUB</H1></FONT>
<BR>
<IMG SRC="football.jpeg" >
</CENTER>
<B>
Welcome to the website of the Manchester Football Club
</B>
<BR>
The Manchester Football Club is based in United States of
America and has a long and
<A HREF="history.html">proud history</A>.
We have several teams in various age groups from kids to grown- ups so there is a
team to suit any player
<BR><BR>
<U>This year's motto:</U>
<BR>
<I>We are the BEST: </I>
<HR>
<B>If you have any questions about us, send us a mail at manr@football.us</B>
<BR>
<FONT SIZE=2>
<P ALIGN="Right">© ManchesterFootball Club Last updated 30<SUP>th</SUP> July 2017
</P>
</FONT>
</FONT>
</BODY>
</HTML>
```

12. **Observe the following table and generate the following code in HTML.** **(Delhi 2015)**

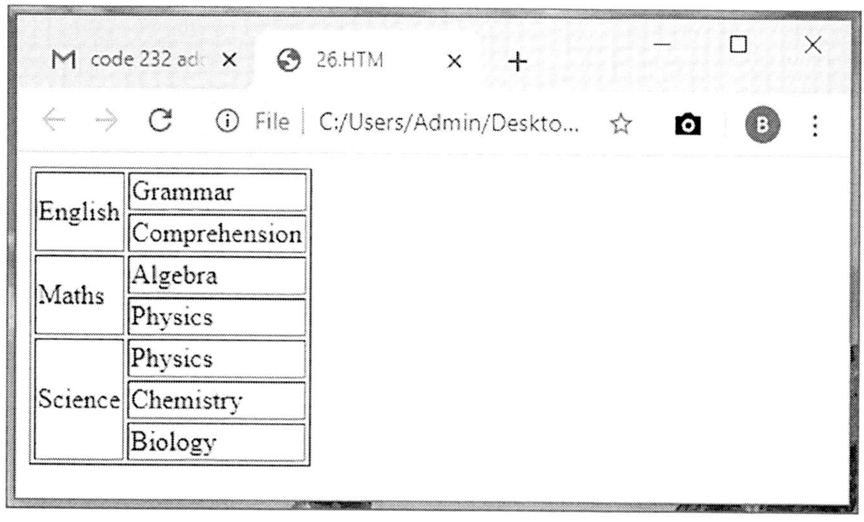

English	Grammar
	Comprehension
Maths	Algebra
	Physics
Science	Physics
	Chemistry
	Biology

Ans:

```
<HTML>
<BODY>
<HEAD>
</HEAD>
<BODY>
<TABLE BORDER = 1>
<TR>
<TD ROWSPAN = 2> English </TD>
<TD> Grammar </TD>
</TR>
<TR>
<TD> Comprehension </TD>
</TR>
<TR>
<TD ROWSPAN = 2> Maths </TD>
<TD> Algebra </TD>
</TR>
<TR>
<TD> Physics </TD>
</TR>
<TR>
<TD ROWSPAN = 3> Science </TD>
<TD> Physics </TD>
</TR>
<TR>
<TD> Chemistry </TD>
</TR>
<TR>
<TD> Biology </TD>
</TR>
</TABLE>
</BODY>
</HTML>
```

13. Carefully study the Web page given here. Identify 10 tags (Structural as well as formatting tags) that have been utilize in creating this Web page and write usage of each of them. (CBSE 2013)

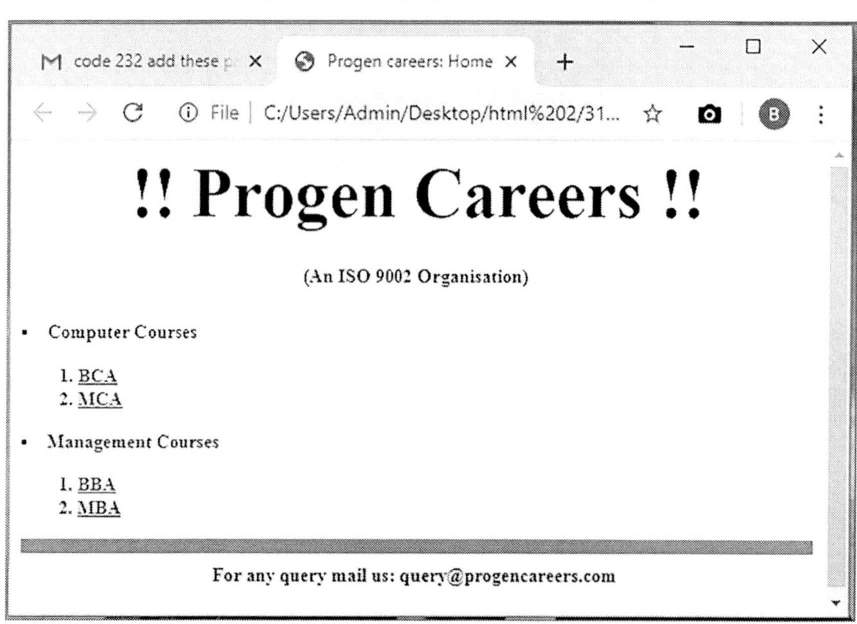

Ans: 1. <HTML>..........</HTML> It encloses the entire HTML document and tells the browser that it is reading an HTML document and to display as such.

2. <HEAD>.........</HEAD> It encloses the head of the HTML document and it is used to contain face information about the document.
3. <TITLE>.....</TITLE> It indicates the title of the document and appears in a browser's bookmark file.
4. <BODY>......</BODY> It is used to enclose the body (text, images, tags, links) of the HTML document.
5. <H1>.........</H1> It is used to define the heading level 1.
6. <UL>.......</UL> It is used to create an unordered list.
7. <LI>.....</LI> It is used to define each list item in the list.
8. <U>.....</U> It is used to underline the text.
9. <HR> It is used to insert a horizontal line.
10. <CENTER>..... </CENTER> This tag is used to align the text centrally.

14. Which of the following is the correct code of HTML page?

a.
```
<HTML>
<TITLE> Hello
</TITLE>
</HTML>
```
b.
```
<HTML>
<HEAD>
<TITLE> Hello
</TITLE>
</HEAD>
</HTML>
```
c.
```
<HTML>
<BODY> Hello
</HTML>
```
d.
```
<HTML><HEAD> Hello
<BODY>
</HTML>
```

Ans: b. Because <TITLE> tag must be closed inside the <HEAD> tag.

15. If you want to create a link of the document having URL as www.computerapplications.com/practicequestions.html then how can you create a link to this document with your document?

Ans: The code can be written as:

<A href="www.computerapplications.com/practicequestions.html"> Online Assignment</A>

16. Differentiate between the following with respect to Tables in HTML with suitable html program. (Delhi 2018)

a. Cellspacing and Cellpadding.

b. Rowspan and Colspan.

Ans: a. Cellspacing: The cellspacing attribute specifies the space, in pixels between cells.

Example:
```
<body>
<p>Table without cellspacing:</p>
<table border = 1>
<tr>
<th>Month</th>
```

```
<th>Savings</th>
</tr>
<tr>
<td>January</td>
<td>Rs100</td>
</tr>
</table>
<p>Table with cellspacing:</p>
<table border =
1cellspacing="10">
<tr>
<th>Month</th>
<th>Savings</th>
</tr>
<tr>
<td>January</td>
<td>Rs100</td>
</tr>
</table>
</body>
```

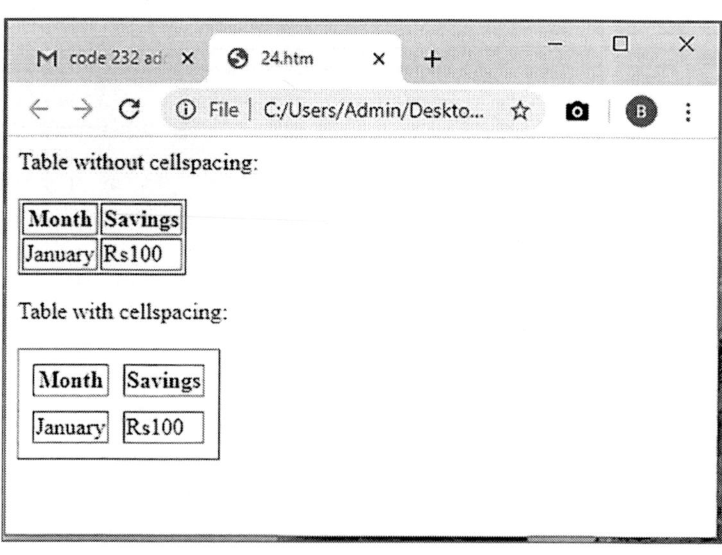

Cellpadding: The cellpadding attribute specifies the space, in pixels between the cell wall and the cell content.

Example:

```
<body>
<p>Table without cellpadding:</p>
<table>
<tr>
<th>Month</th>
<th>Savings</th>
</tr>
<tr>
<td>January</td>
<td>Rs100</td>
</tr>
</table>
<p>Table with cellpadding:</p>
<table cellpadding="10">
<tr>
<th>Month</th>
<th>Savings</th>
</tr>
<tr>
<td>January</td>
<td>Rs100</td>
</tr>
```

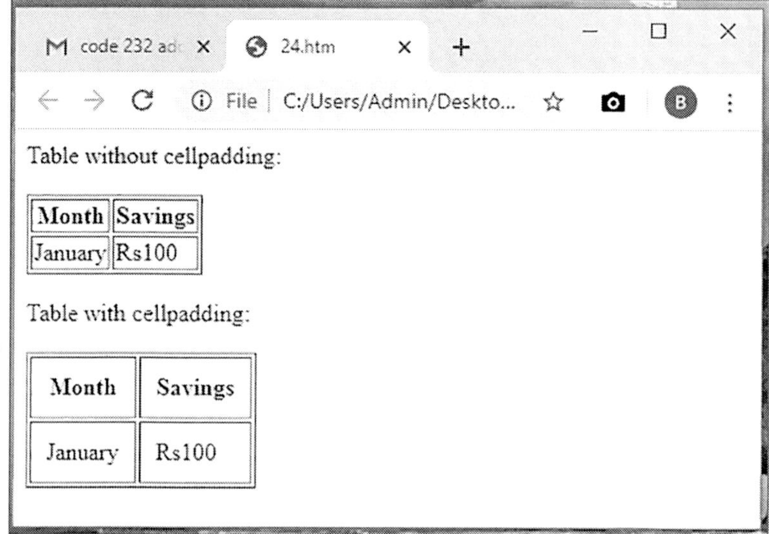

```
</table>
</body>
```

b. Rowspan: The rowspan attribute specifies the number of rows a cell should span. It is used to merge multiple rows

Example:

```
<table>
<tr>
<th>Month</th>
<th>Savings</th>
<th>Savings for holiday!</th>
</tr>
<tr>
<td>January</td>
<td>Rs100</td>
<td rowspan="2">Rs50</td>
</tr>
<tr>
<td>February</td>
<td>Rs80</td>
</tr>
</table>
```

Month	Savings	Savings for holiday!
January	Rs100	Rs50
February	Rs80	

Colspan: The colspan attribute defines the number of columns a table cell should span. It is used to merge multiple columns

Example:

```
<table>
<tr>
<th>Month</th>
<th>Savings</th>
</tr>
<tr>
<td>January</td>
<td>Rs100</td>
</tr>
<tr>
<td>February</td>
<td>Rs80</td>
</tr>
<tr>
<td colspan="2">Sum:Rs180</td>
</tr>
</table>
```

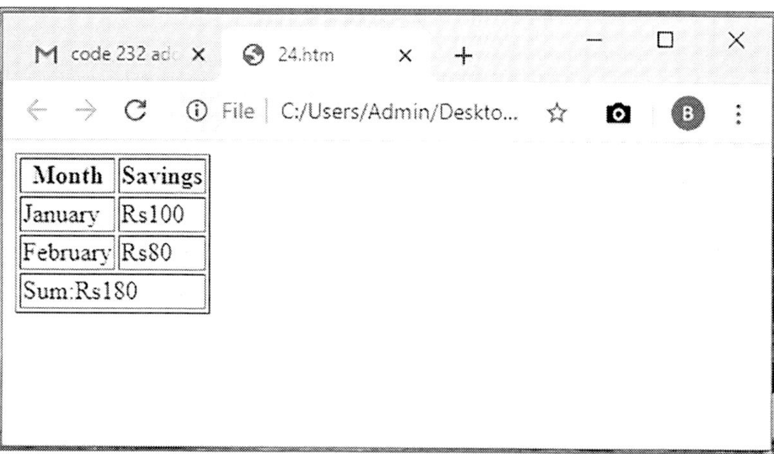

Month	Savings
January	Rs100
February	Rs80
Sum:Rs180	

SECTION D: SELF - ASSESSMENT

A. FILL IN THE BLANKS.

1. Images on the web slows down the ____________ speed of a web page.
2. There are ____________ types of alignment options available in HTML to align an image.
3. The color of hyperlinked text is always ____________.
4. The image file with ____________ format is larger than in memory size as compared to ____________ format graphics.
5. Web browser can accept the web addresses with the help of ____________ protocol.
6. The ____________ tag is used to insert images in the web page.
7. The most important attribute used with image is ____________.
8. The full form of src is ____________.
9. The ____________ element defines a table row.
10. The ____________ tag defines a table header.
11. For internal linking, the section names are provided by ____________ attribute.
12. To set the background color of a table ____________ attribute is used.
13. ____________ is used to set the distance between the table border and cell content.
14. ____________ is used to set the distance between two cells of a table.
15. The tag used to create a hyperlink is ____________.
16. Combining two or more cells of a table is called ____________.
17. Combining rows of a table is called ____________.
18. Combining columns of a table is called ____________.
19. A link used to navigate or open other web pages on a web site on internet is called ____________.
20. ____________ attribute is used with <A> tag to link other web pages.

B. STATE WHETHER THE FOLLOWING STATEMENTS ARE TRUE OR FALSE.

1. The <IMG> tag is an empty tag.
2. The middle value is a type of align attribute of <img> tag.
3. By default, the color of the hyperlink is blue.
4. Alink is defined as active link color.
5. Vlink is defined as visited link color.
6. The <A> tag is used to insert hyperlink in a web page.
7. Alink and vlink are the attributes of table tag.
8. The <table> tag is used to insert tables in a web page.
9. <tr> tag is used to create cells in a table.
10. Cellpadding is an attribute of table tag.
11. <caption> tag used to give heading to a table. (Delhi 2017)

12. If border attribute is not set with table tag, then the outlines of the cells will be invisible.
13. Height and width attributes can be used to set the height and width of a table.
14. Center is an attribute to align images at the center of a web page.
15. SRC attribute is used to make the text hyperlink.

C. TICK THE CORRECT ANSWER.

1. <img> tag has no end tag.
   a. True b. False c. None d. Can't say
2. Which of the following pair of attributes is required for <img> tag?
   a. src and alt b. img and src c. src and a d. img and alt
3. In order to add border to a table, border attribute is specified in which tag? (Outside Delhi 2014)
   a. <th> b. <table> c. <td> d. <tr>
4. Which tag is used to insert image in an HTML page?
   a. <img> b. <image> c. <imge> d. <pic>
5. Which attribute is used to display an image?
   a. source attribute b. srs attribute c. src attribute d. val attribute
6. If the image cannot be displayed then ____________ specifies an alternate text for an image. (Outside Delhi 2015)
   a. value attribute b. text attribute c. caption attribute d. alt attribute
7. Cell of the table is defined by using ____________.
   a. <tr> b. <td> c. <th> d. <thead>
8. If you want to make image as an hyperlink, then the correct syntax is: (Outside Delhi 2015)
   a. <img src="flower.gif"><a href="try.html"> click</a>
   b. <a href=try.html><img src=image.gif>click</a>
   c. <a href=image src=try.html>click</a>
   d. <img src=try.html>
9. For heading you can use ____________.
   a. <td> b. <tr> c. <thead> d. <th>
10. Headings of table lies inside ____________.
    a. <thead> b. <tfoot> c. <th> d. <tbody>
11. For adding caption to the table, you use ____________.
    a. <caption> b. <thead> c. <th> d. <tr>
12. Border-spacing in a table is given in ____________.
    a. Pixels b. cm c. mm d. Inch
13. Borders cannot be applied on ____________.
    a. <th> b. <td> c. <tr> d. <thead>

14. Which attribute defines numbers of columns in a group?

a. Width b. Span c. Scope d. Headers

15. Which of the following does not specify a column width?

a. Fixed b. Percentage c. Proportional d. Pixels

16. Which of the following is not the valid value for align attribute of <img>? (Outside Delhi 2014)

a. Justify b. Char c. Middle d. Left

17. Valign attribute of a table does not take the value ____________.

a. Justify b. Middle c. Baseline d. Bottom

18. Which tag tells where a link start? (Outside Delhi 2014)

a. <l> b. <a> c. <start> d. None of the above.

19. The tag used to insert hyperlink is: (Outside Delhi 2013)

a. <a> b. <h> c. <u> d. <l>

20. Find the correct syntax to create an e-mail link from the given below:

a. <a href=abc@gmail.com> b. <a href=abc@xyz.com>

c. <mail = abc@xyz.com> d. <a href=mailto:abc@xyz.com>

D. ANSWER THE FOLLOWING QUESTIONS.

Type A: Very Short Answer Questions.

1. Which tag ends one line and jumps to the next line?
2. Write the full forms of the following tag: (Outside Delhi 2008)

   a. <a> b. <img>
3. Name the attributes of the <table> tag that specify the dimensions of a table. (Outside Delhi 2014)
4. Write the HTML code to display the table with border of 5px. (Delhi 2014)
5. Mention the suitable HTML tag and the attribute to insert an image named globe.jpg in the background of a webpage. (Delhi 2019)
6. Write the html code to send an email at abc@xyz.com through your web page. (Delhi 2016)
7. Write the HTML code to display an image on the right side of a page. (Delhi 2017)
8. Which tag is used for inserting rows and creating columns in a table?
9. Which attribute is used for naming different sections of a web page?
10. Expand the terms HREF and SRC.
11. Name any three attributes of table tag.
12. What happens when you set border =3 of a table?
13. What is the significance of alt attribute?
14. How can you give caption of the table?
15. Give one example to set a link to an e-mail address cbse@gmail.com.
16. How can you align an image at the center of a web page?

Type B: Short Answer Questions.

1. Discuss various advantages and disadvantages of html.
2. Write the name of the tag used for the following:
   a. Inserting images
   b. Inserting external and internal link
   c. Inserting table.
3. Differentiate between external and internal link.
4. What is the difference between align and valign attribute of a <TD> tag?
5. Can you set height and width of an image? If yes then how? Give an example to illustrate the same.
6. Observe the following table and write the HTML code to generate it: (Outside Delhi 2014)

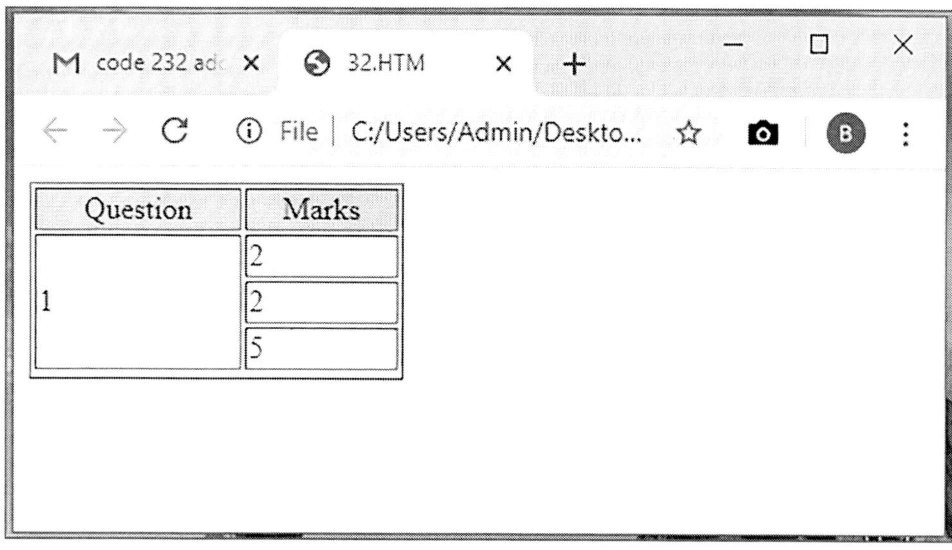

<table>
<tr><th>Question</th><th>Marks</th></tr>
<tr><td rowspan="3">1</td><td>2</td></tr>
<tr><td>2</td></tr>
<tr><td>5</td></tr>
</table>

Type C: Long Answer Questions.

1. Rachit, a beginner in web designing is not able to understand that how internal linking is different from external linking. Explain him about the same. Additionally, tell him about the suitable tag and its attribute(s) for creating internal linking. (Delhi 2018)
2. Observe the following table and write the HTML code to generate it: (Delhi 2017)

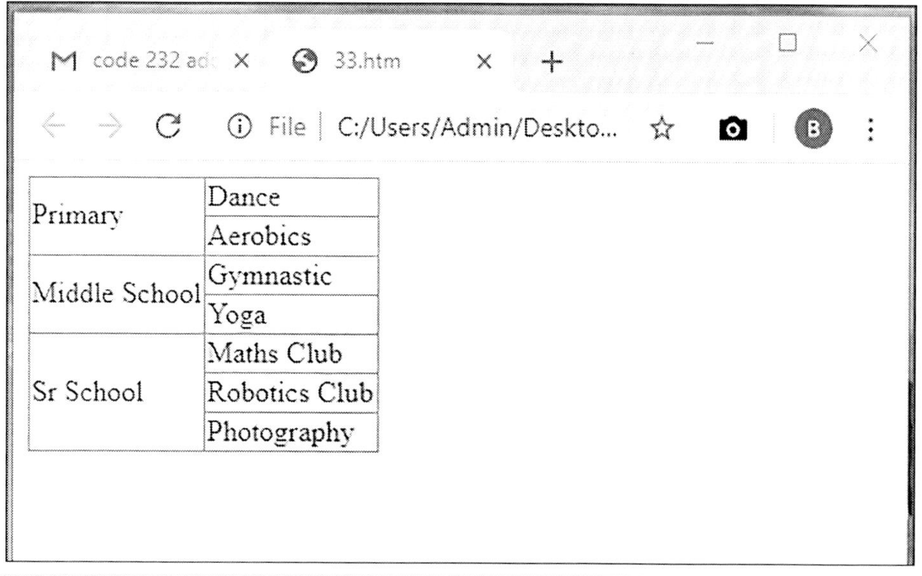

<table>
<tr><td rowspan="2">Primary</td><td>Dance</td></tr>
<tr><td>Aerobics</td></tr>
<tr><td rowspan="2">Middle School</td><td>Gymnastic</td></tr>
<tr><td>Yoga</td></tr>
<tr><td rowspan="3">Sr School</td><td>Maths Club</td></tr>
<tr><td>Robotics Club</td></tr>
<tr><td>Photography</td></tr>
</table>

3. Observe the following output and write the HTML code to generate it:

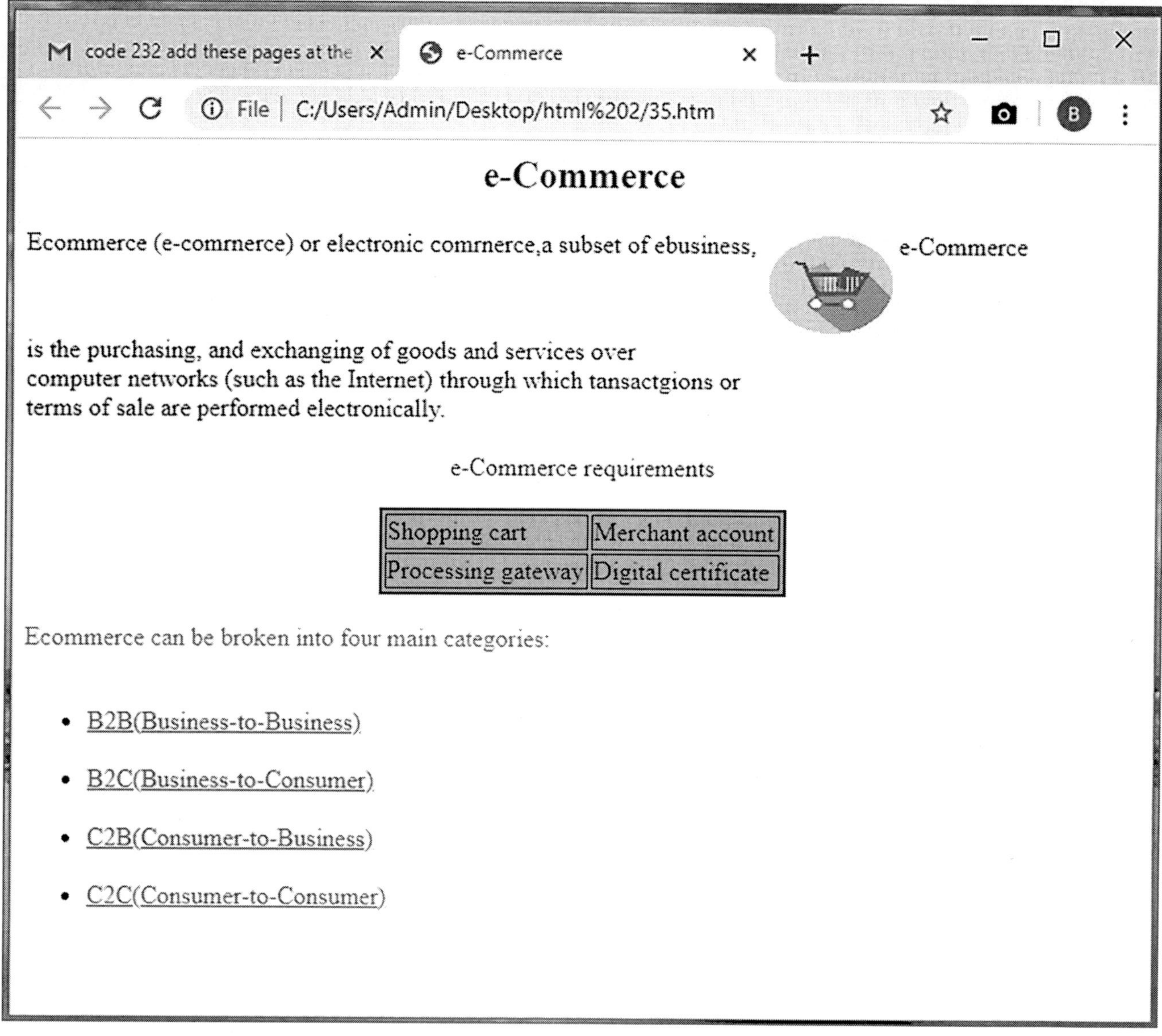

Note the following points while generating the Webpage:

- Link colour is green, active link colour is blue and visited links colour is red.
- Title of the page is "eCommerce".
- Heading of the page is maroon.
- Image used is "ecommerce.jpg"
- Caption of table is blue.
- Background of table is "cyan".
- Table border is blue and of size 2.
- The 4 links are one.html, three.html and four.html.
- List Heading is red.
- Heading should be in centre of the page.

4. Observe the following output and write the HTML code to generate it:

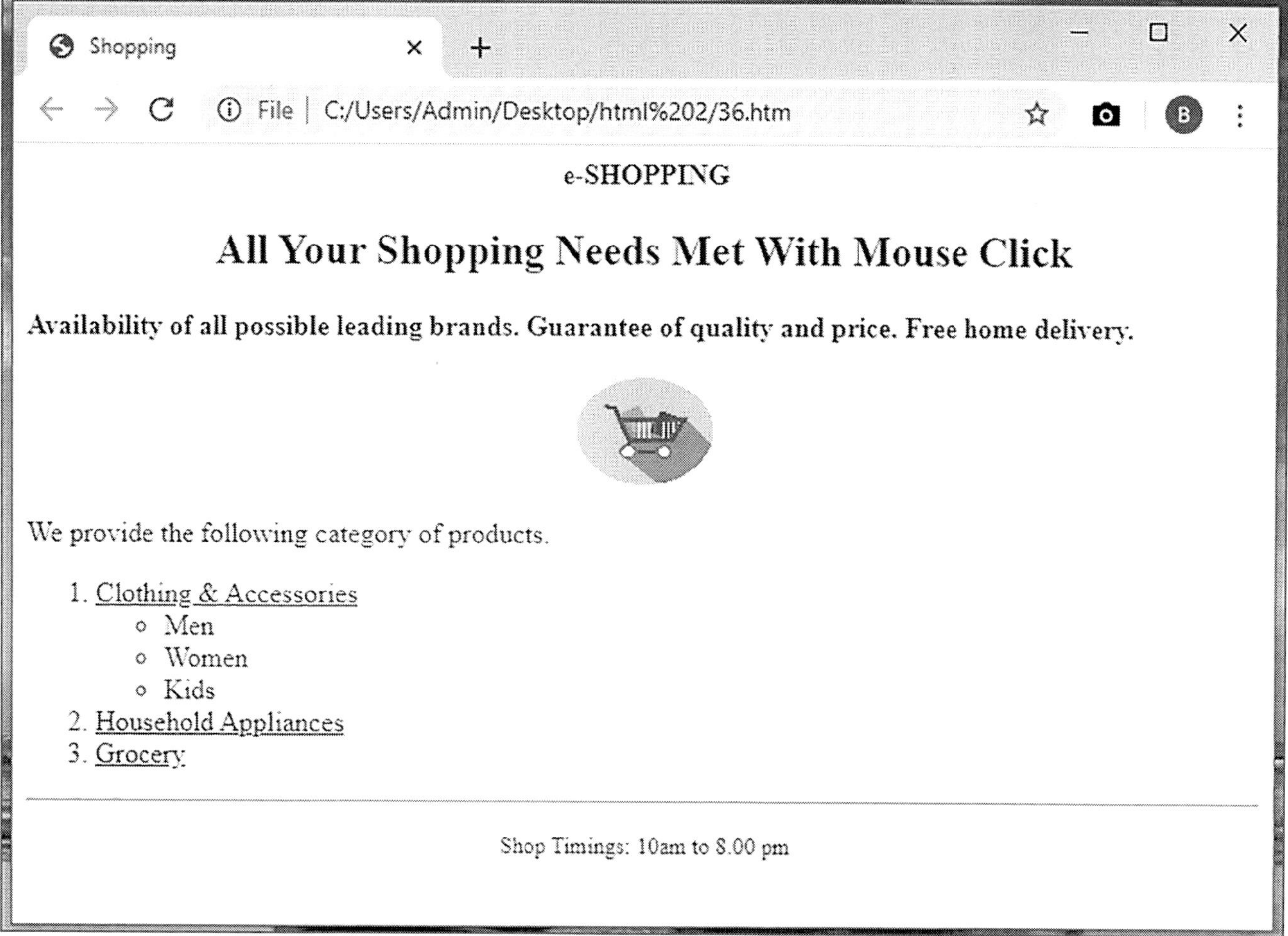

Consider the following points while generating the web page:

- The title of the page is "e-Shopping".
- The heading is in red color.
- Text colour is maroon.
- Font of the entire document is Arial.
- Image used is "images.jpg".
- The pages linked are:
- Clothing & Accessories to "cloth.html".
- Household Appliances to "house.html".
- Grocery to "grocery.html".
- Bottom message is of size 2.

5. Observe the following web page and write HTML code to generate it.

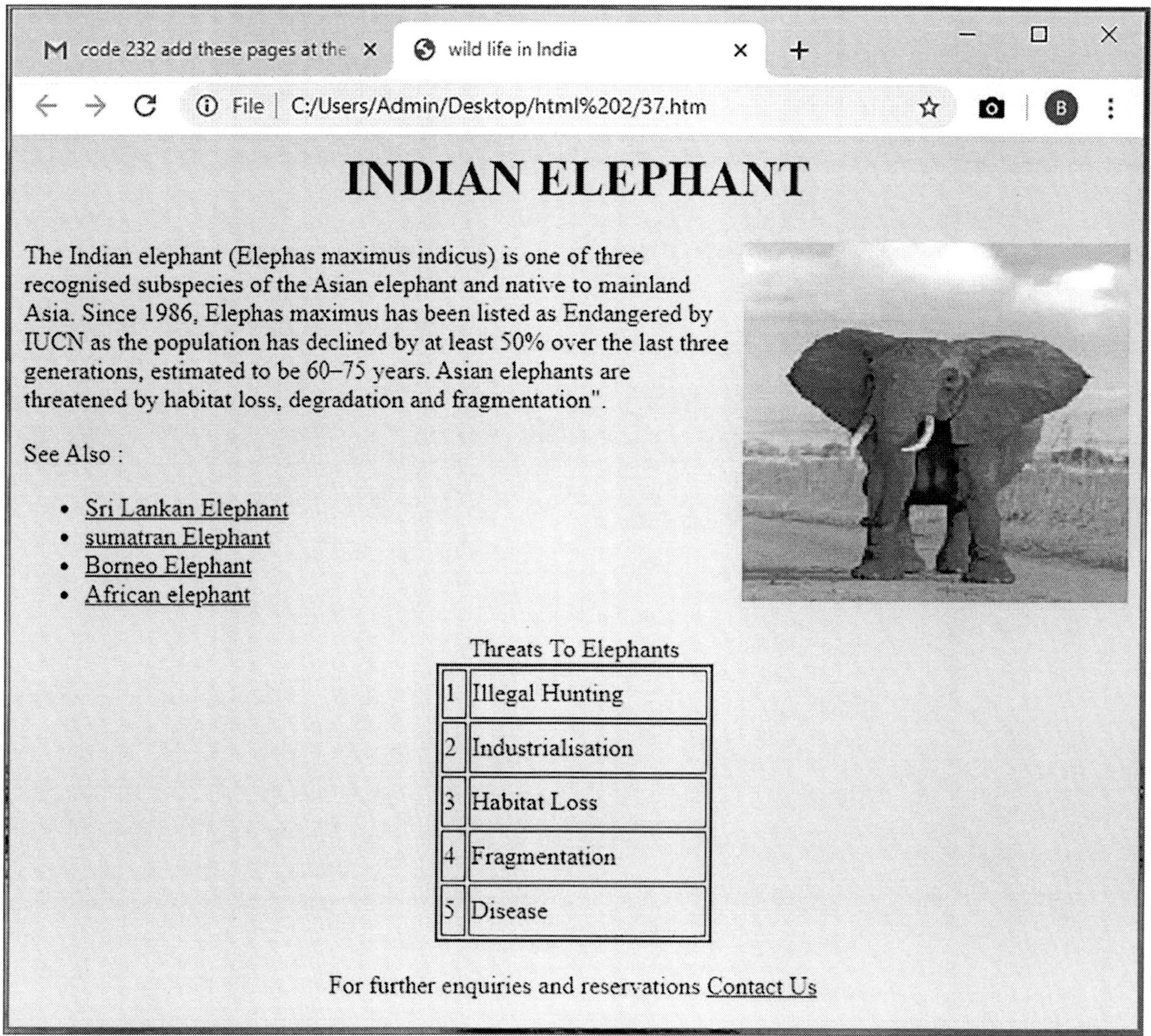

Note the following points while generating the Webpage:

- Link colour is black, background colour is yellow and visited link colour is green.
- Title of the page is "Wild life in India".
- Heading of the page is maroon.
- Image used is "elephant.png".
- Caption of table is blue.
- Table border is blue and of size 2.
- The 4 links are one.html, two.html, three.html and four.html.
- The e-mail id for contact us is abc@xyz.com.

SECTION E: LAB EXERCISE

1. Write the HTML code to send an e-mail at abc@xyz.com through your webpage.
2. Name the attributes of <A> tag which are used for internal linking in a webpage.
3. Observe the following table and write the HTML code to generate it: (Delhi 2016)

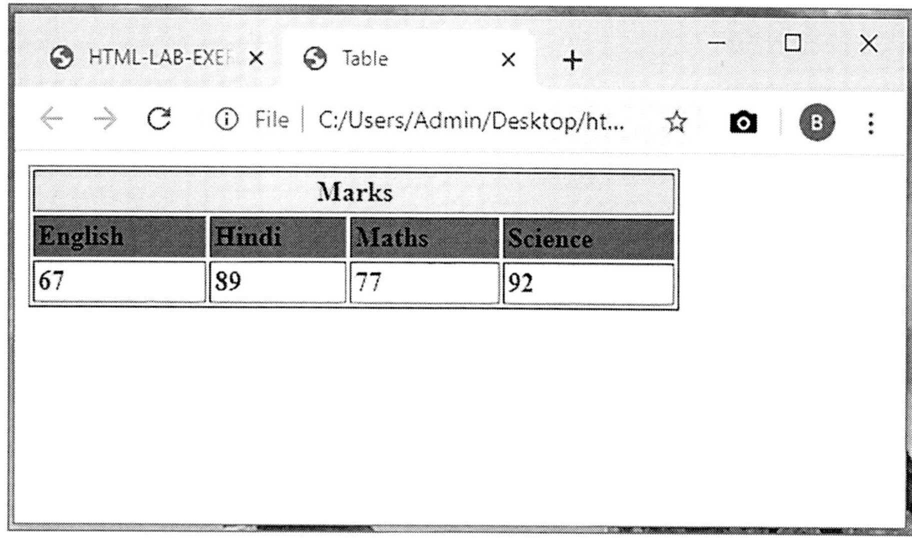

Marks			
English	Hindi	Maths	Science
67	89	77	92

Note: First row has yellow background and 2nd row has green background.

4. Write the names of two attributes for each tag:

   a. <HR> b. <Body> c. <img> d. <Table>

   e. <A>

5. Observe the following web page and write the html code to generate it.

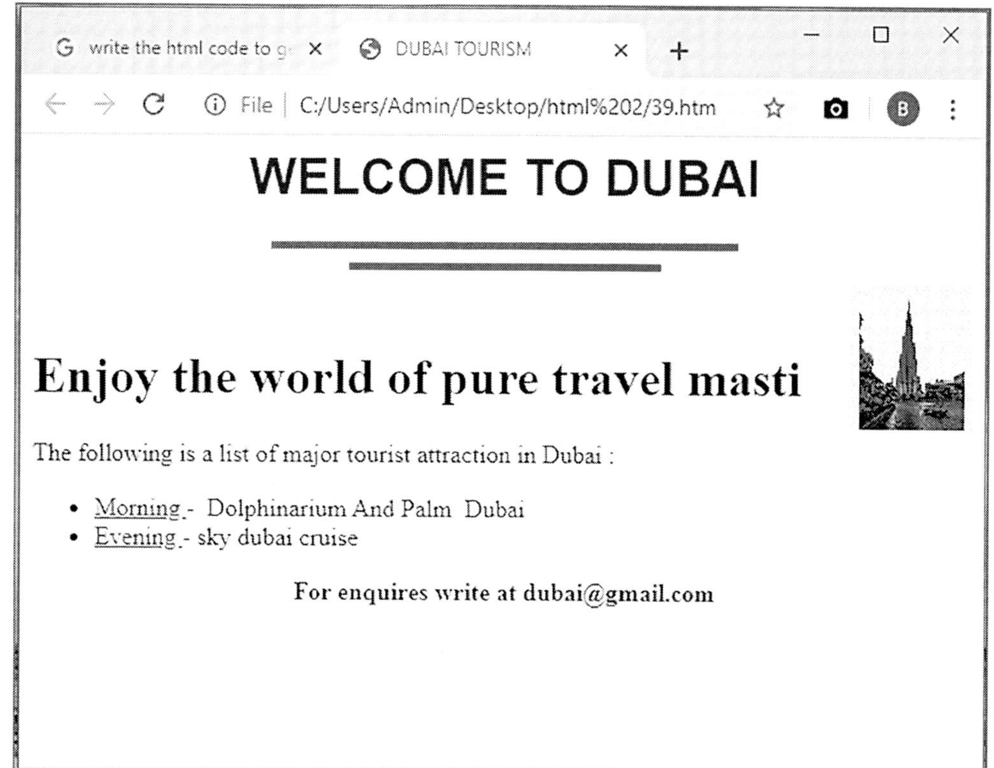

Note the following points while generating the web page:

- Title of the page is "DUBAI TOURISM".
- The heading text" Welcome to Dubai" is in Arial font and is of Maroon color.
- The horizontal line below the heading are 5 pixels thick and of red color.
- Image used in the page is "burg.jpg".
- The bulleted list contains links as specified below:
- The text Morning is a link to the webpage" morning.html".
- The text Evening is a link to the webpage" evening.html".

6. Write an HTML code to generate the given table in web page exactly as given.
(Sample Paper 2013)

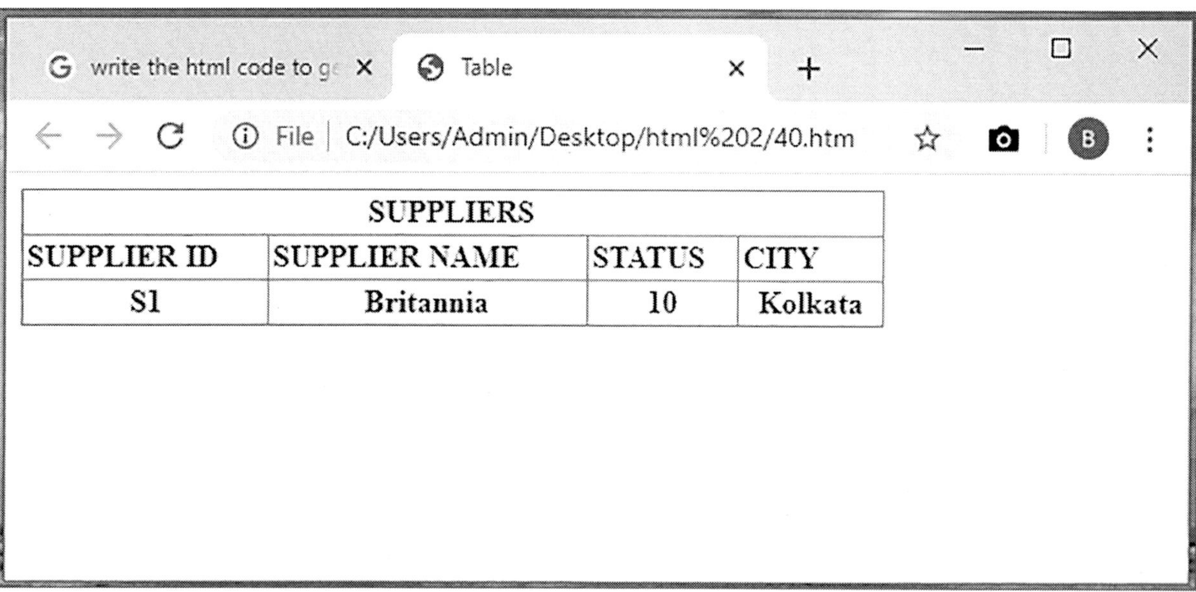

SUPPLIERS			
SUPPLIER ID	SUPPLIER NAME	STATUS	CITY
S1	Britannia	10	Kolkata

7. Write the HTML code to generate the following output of a table with the content exactly in the same format as shown within the table: (Sample paper 2013)

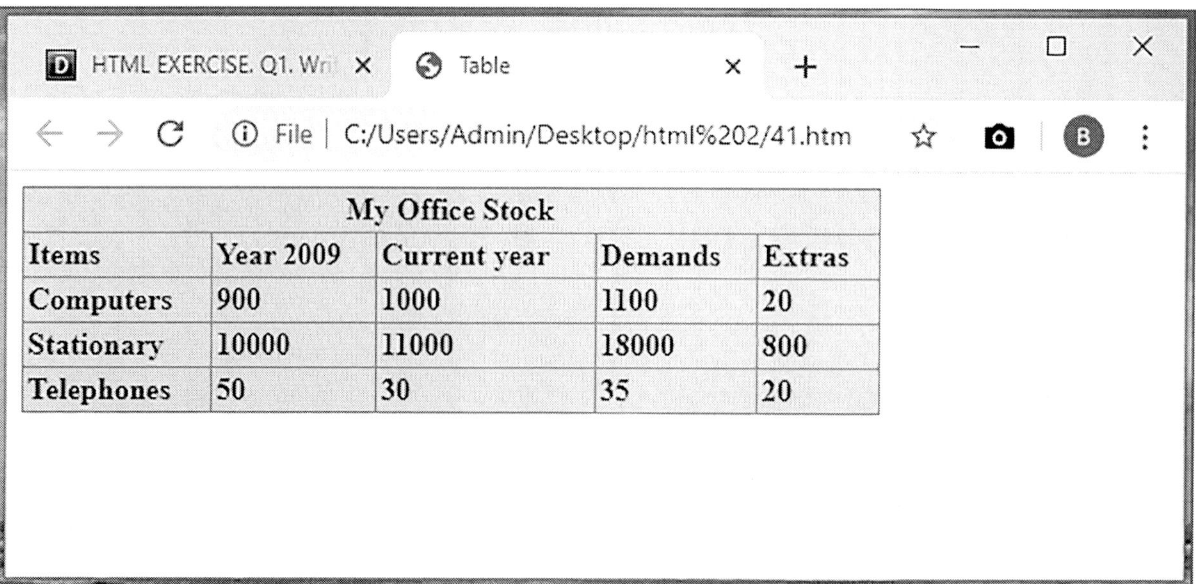

My Office Stock				
Items	Year 2009	Current year	Demands	Extras
Computers	900	1000	1100	20
Stationary	10000	11000	18000	800
Telephones	50	30	35	20

8. Write the HTML code to generate the following output.

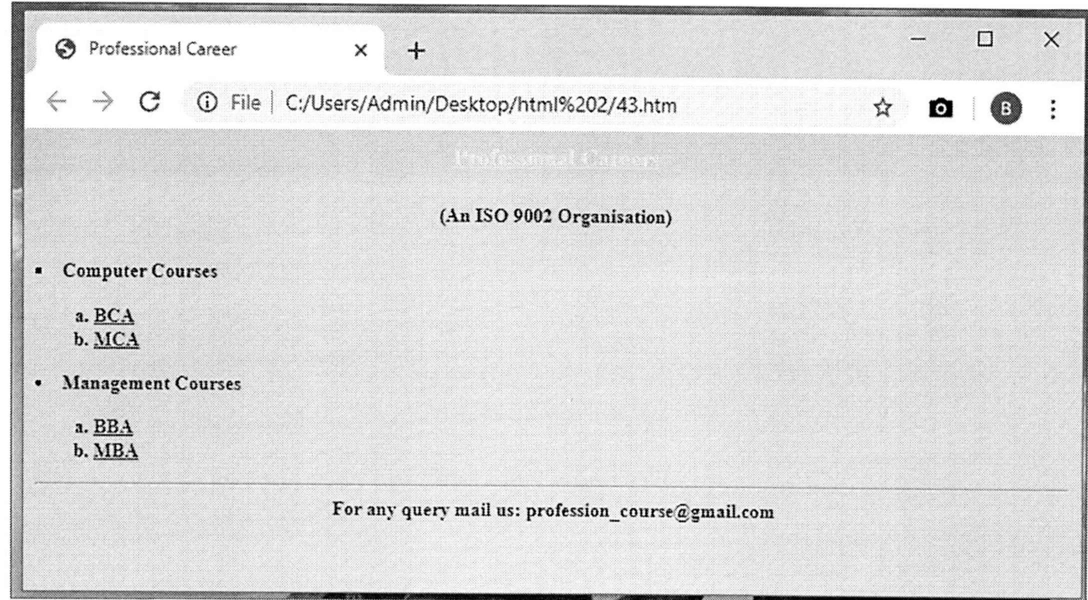

Note the following points while generating the webpage.

- Title of the page is "Professional Career".
- Heading of the page is Yellow.
- Image used is "image1.jpg".
- The links are BCA.html, MCA.html, BBA.html, MBA.html, A.html respectively.
- Background color is "Pink".

Activity Zone

1. Make a presentation on various html table tags.
2. Tell students to make a web page on "Artificial Intelligence is a boon to human life".
3. Tell students to make a web page on "Managing Security in Mobile Phones**".**
4. Make an online quiz on various html tags.
5. Students can create a web page to make their class time table as:

TIME TABLE							
DAYS	Period I	Period II	Period III		Period IV	Period V	Period VI
MON	English	Maths	Hindi	BREAK	Science	So. Studies	Computer
TUE	English	Maths	Hindi		Science	So. Studies	Computer
WED	English	Maths	Hindi		Science	So. Studies	Computer
THUR	English	Maths	Hindi		Science	So. Studies	GK
FRI	English	Maths	Hindi		Science	So. Studies	GK
SAT	English	Maths	Hindi		Science	So. Studies	GK

6. Tell students to write the code for the following web page. Also tell them to insert images of all dishes to the right of the text.

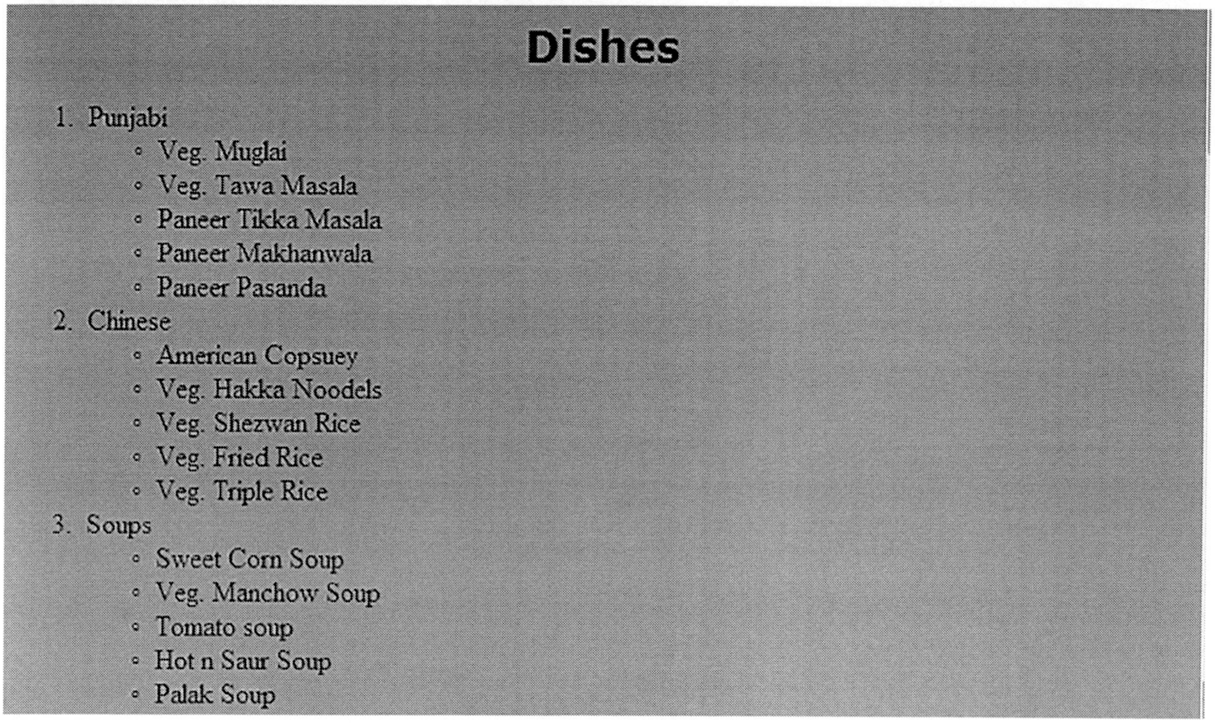

Dishes

1. Punjabi
   - Veg. Muglai
   - Veg. Tawa Masala
   - Paneer Tikka Masala
   - Paneer Makhanwala
   - Paneer Pasanda
2. Chinese
   - American Copsuey
   - Veg. Hakka Noodels
   - Veg. Shezwan Rice
   - Veg. Fried Rice
   - Veg. Triple Rice
3. Soups
   - Sweet Corn Soup
   - Veg. Manchow Soup
   - Tomato soup
   - Hot n Saur Soup
   - Palak Soup

5 Creating Forms, inserting Audio and Video in HTML

Outline of the Chapter

- Introduction
- Form tag and its attributes
- INPUT element
- Programs related to each form control
- Embedding Video files in HTML document
- What is FORM?
- Working of HTML form
- Attributes of Input element/ Form controls
- Embedding Audio files in HTML document

Learning Objectives

- To know how to create forms in HTML
- To know the Purpose of using forms
- To know about the form tag and its related attributes
- To know the various controls placed on forms and difference between them
- Assign attributes to the <input> element to create the different FORM objects
- To know how to insert audio and video in HTML

INTRODUCTION

In daily life, you come across various websites which are asking you to enter some details in a displayed form on the screen. All these forms are the objects that are used for collecting data from the user. ***For example***, if you want to register yourself as a member of sports academy online, then you enter your details in a respective form.

5.1 WHAT IS FORM?

In HTML, a form is a window that consists of the elements of a form called the **form fields**. HTML Forms are required when you want to collect some data from the site visitor. ***For example***, during user registration you would like to collect information such as name, e-mail address, credit card, etc.

All those types of forms are created by using HTML special tag known as **FORM** element. Web forms allow you to receive feedback, to make orders or other kind of information from the people who visit and read your web pages.

Consider the given form,

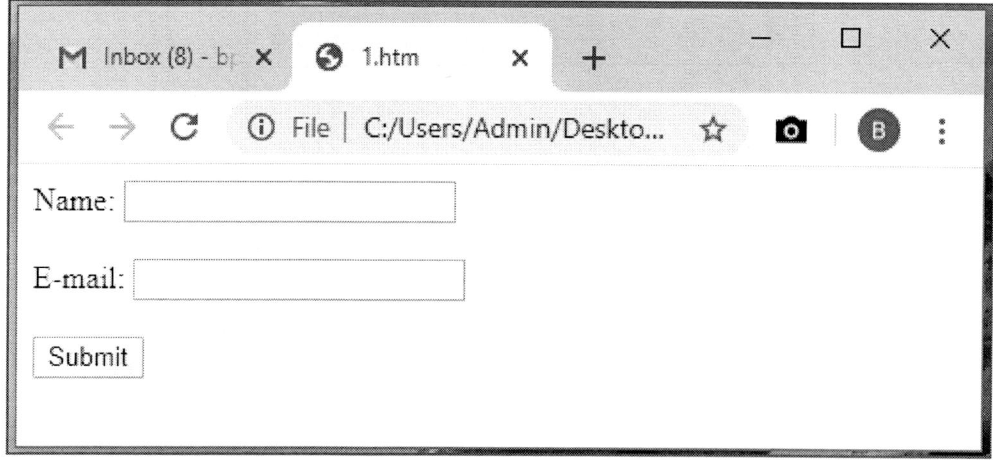

Figure 5.1: Form Entry

The above form requests the user to enter the name and e-mail address. When the required data is entered by the user and click on submit button the form is submitted to the web server.

Definition

Form is the element that allows user to take input or information from users and to process the request. For example, to take name, age and e-mail-id of the user.

5.2 WORKING OF HTML FORM

When you load a page, you are making an **HTTP request** (a GET request, usually). This request is sent by your browser to the server, and the server responds with the web page you are looking for. This interaction is one of the most fundamental concepts of the internet. It is how HTML forms are designed to work.

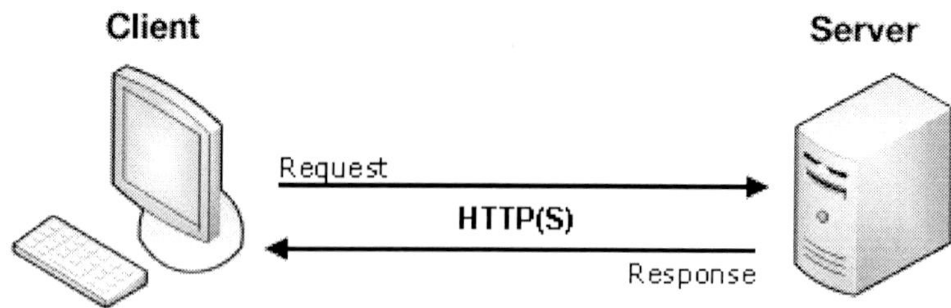

Figure 5.2: Processing of form

It is clear from the above picture that the user (client) is making HTTP request which is sent by the web browser to the server. The server on the other end process the request and respond to client.

5.3 CREATING FROM USING FORM ELEMENT

Web forms are created by using <FORM> element. Form element is a **container element** that begins with <FORM> tag and end by </FORM> tag. All html forms contain some controls that enables the user to enter and submit data.

For example,

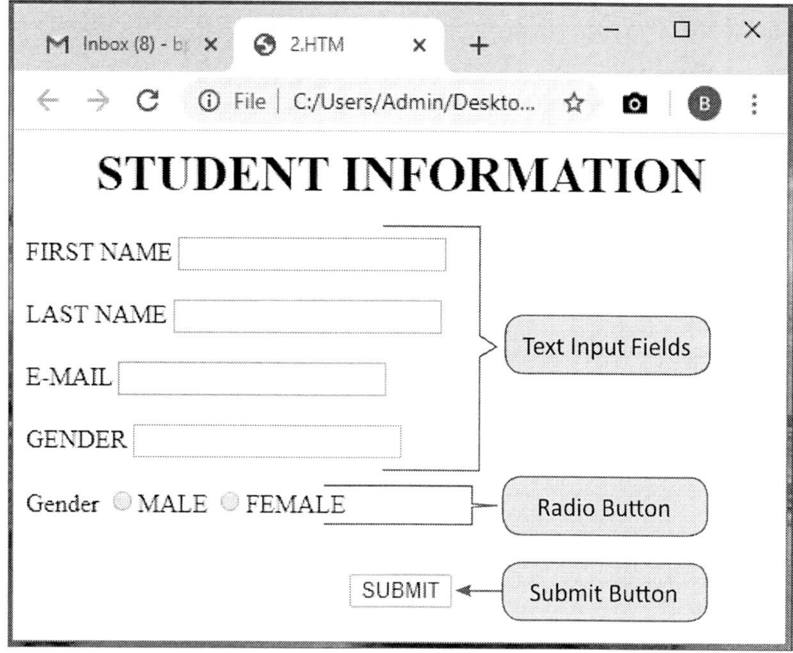

Figure 5.3: Controls on HTML form

In the above student information form, there are six controls where the user has to enter first name, last name, e-mail address, select gender and then submit the form.

Note: Controls are like text input fields, radio button and submit button.

5.4 ATTRIBUTES OF FORM TAG

The FORM tag normally has three attributes: (*Figure 5.4*)

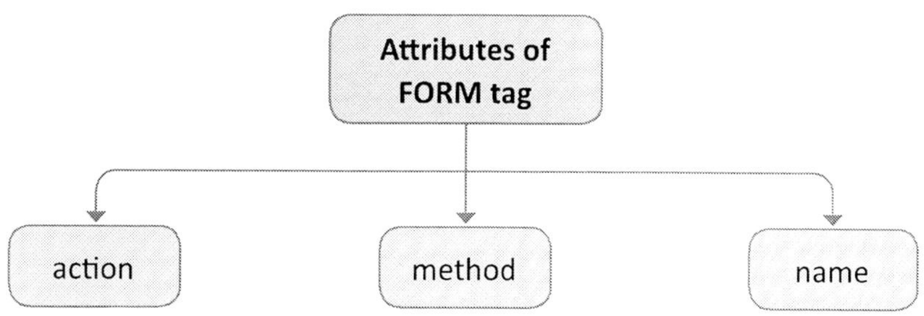

Figure 5.4: Attributes of Form Tag

* **Let's explain these attributes with their purpose.**

Table 5.1: Attributes of FORM tag

Attribute	Value	Description
action	URL	This attribute specifies the URL where the form data is sent when the form is submitted. The URL is called the **destination of the form.**
method	get post	Specifies the HTTP method to use when the form is submitted. • **get:** The form data is submitted as URL variables. • **post:** The form data is submitted as HTTP post.

Attribute	Value	Description
name	form name	This attribute defines a unique name for the form as there can be multiple forms on a web page. However, the form name will not be displayed on the form. The name attribute is optional if there is only one form on the web page.

The syntax of using form tag:

```
<Form name= "formname" action = "URL" method="type of method">
```

For example,

```
<form name="order" action="post" method=mailto:abc@gmail.com>
```

MEMORIZE

A form is an object that is used for collecting data from the user. HTML forms are used to pass data to a server. A form can be inserted in HTML documents by using the HTML form element which acts as a container for all the input elements.

Difference between GET and POST method:

Get Method	Post Method
All the data sent through get method is visible in the browser's address bar i.e. on URL.	The data sent through post method is not visible to the user.
Using Get method, it is possible to bookmark the page with specific query string values.	Using Post method, you cannot bookmark the page with specific query.
The GET method is not suitable for passing sensitive information such as the username and password, because these are fully visible in the URL query string.	It is more secure than GET because user-entered information is never visible in the URL query string or in the server logs.

Note: The name attribute represents the form's name within the forms collection. Its value must be unique among the forms in a document, and must not be an empty string.

The <input> tag inside the form tag does not have an end tag.
There can be as many <input> tags as form fields you want in your web page.

Check Your Progress

Fill in the blanks.

1. ________________ and ________________ are the two methods for submitting form on a web server.
2. ________________ attribute represents the form name within the form tag.
3. The ________________ tag inside the form tag does not have an end tag.

5.5 THE INPUT ELEMENT

Form controls are also known Input elements that are used to make choices and text can be entered by using the interface elements defined with <INPUT> tag. The <input> element is the most important form element. Using input elements, a form can be submitted to a destination point whenever required.

Input element is an **empty element** specified by <INPUT> tag. It is used to provide an input field in a form where the user can enter the data.

MEMORIZE

<Form> tag is a container tag whereas **<input>** tag is an empty tag. It contains attributes only.

5.6 ATTRIBUTES OF INPUT ELEMENT OR FORM CONTROLS

The various attributes of INPUT element are:

Table 5.2: Attributes of Input element

Attribute	Description	Example
maxlength	Number	maxlength="200"
type	Specifies the type of control to be used. For example, checkbox, radio button, text field etc.	type="radio"
value	Specifies the initial or starting value for the control.	value="male"
size	Specifies the number of characters for input field.	size="30"
name	Specifies the name of the type of control.	name="first name"

Note: The <input> element can be displayed in several ways, depending on the type attribute.

For example,

Type	Description
<input type="text">	Defines a one-line text input field.
<input type="radio">	Defines a radio button (for selecting one of many choices).
<input type="submit">	Defines a submit button (for submitting the form).

All these elements/controls are defined as attributes of input tag. Each form must include one button to submit the details on a web. When someone clicks on that button, all the information filled in is sent to an internet address that you specify in the form itself.

Consider the given form which is created in HTML *(figure 5.5)*:

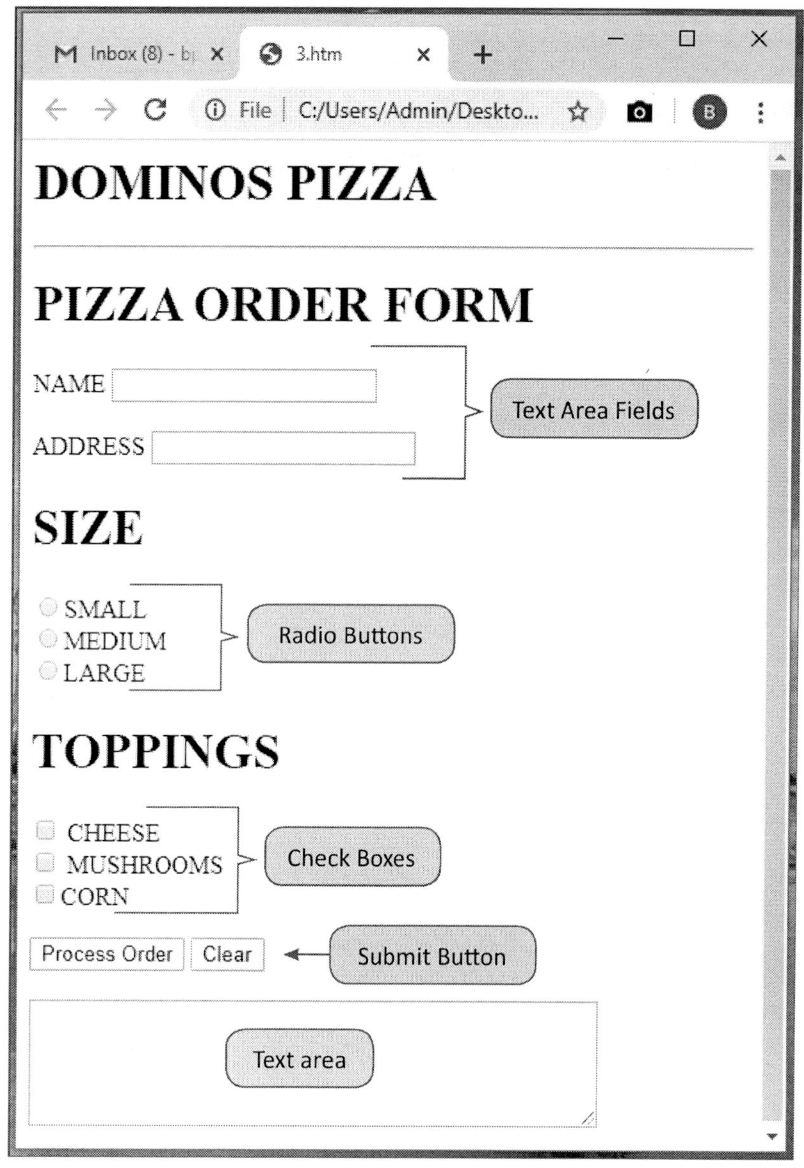

Figure 5.5: HTML form contain various controls

Program 5.1: The source code for the above HTML form (*figure 5.5*) is:

```
<html>
<body>
<P ALIGN =RIGHT>
<RIGHT><H1>DOMINOS PIZZA </H1></RIGHT>
<form method="post">
<p align=right>
<right><h1><hr>PIZZA ORDER FORM</hr></h1></right>
NAME <input type="text"name="name"/>
<br>
<br>
ADDRESS <input type="text"name="address"/>
<br>
```

```
<p align=right>
<right><h1>SIZE</h1></right>
</p>
<input type="radio" name="size" value ="small"/>SMALL
<br>

<input type="radio" name="size" value ="medium"/>MEDIUM
<br>

<input type="radio" name="size" value ="large"/>LARGE
<br>

<p align=right>
<right><h1>TOPPINGS</h1></right>
</p>

<input type ="checkbox"name="s1" value="CHEESE"> CHEESE
<br>

<input type ="checkbox"name="s2" value="MUSHROOMS"> MUSHROOMS
<br>

<input type ="checkbox"name="s3" value="CORN">CORN
<br>

<p>
<input type="submit" name="request" value="Process Order">
<input type ="reset" name="clear" value="Clear">
<br>
<br>
<textarea rows="5" cols="50"name="">
</textarea>
</p>
</form>
</body>
</html>
```

In this way, you can create html forms by using various input controls and attributes.

5.7 EXPLAINING DIFFERENT TYPES OF FORM ELEMENTS

The different types of FORM controls that you can use to collect data using HTML form are:

- Text Input Control
- Checkboxes Control
- Radio Box Control

- Listbox Control
- Combobox Control
- Password field Control
- Submit and Reset Button Control

⁎ Let's know about the various attributes used by input element.

1. Textbox Control

The Textbox control is a common form input field. It creates a place where in one-line information can be typed.

Following is the list of attributes which is used for creating text field.

Table 5.3: Attribute of Text Field

Attributes used by input element for textbox control	Description
Type	Indicates the type of input control and for text input control it will be set to text.
Name	Used to give a name to the control which is sent to the server to be recognized and get the value.
Value	This can be used to provide an initial value inside the control.
Size	Allows to specify the width of the text-input control in terms of characters.
Maxlength	Allows to specify the maximum number of characters a user can enter into the text box.

Syntax of using textbox control:

```
<INPUT type="text" name="value" value="initial value" size="width in number"
maxlength="length in numbers" >
```

Program 5.2: To create a web page that will use a single-line text input used to take Name and e-mail address of a user.

```
<html>
<head>
<title> Textbox control</title>
</head>
<form method="post">
Name:
<INPUT type="text" name="firstname" size=20 maxlength=100 ><BR><BR>
E-mail:
<input name="text" type="text" name="E-mail" size=20 maxlength=100 >
</form>
</body>
</html>
```

Output of the program is given below:

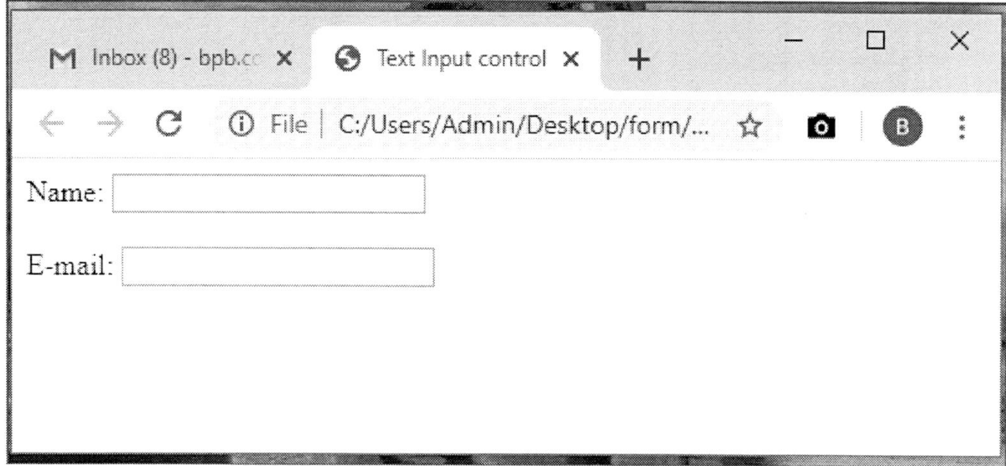

Figure 5.6: Form showing text fields

2. Textarea

Textarea is the field that displays several text lines at a time. Textarea field is generally used to prepare the body of the e-mail or use it to take comment from the user.

Following are the attributes of textarea:

Table 5.4: Attribute of Textarea Field

Attribute Name	Description
Cols and Rows	It takes the value as number. While cols indicate the length of the textarea, the rows indicate the number of rows with text that will be visible at a time.
Name	It provides an internal name to the textarea field as understood by the computer.
Tabindex	It defines the order number of activations of this field when the visitor clicks on the tab key.
Wrap	It helps in flowing the text to the next row in a paragraph when the text reaches the right-hand border of the text area. **It can take three types of values as discussed below:** (a) If the text is not wrapped, i.e. its value is set to "wrap off", it will be placed in the first row of the text area. In such case if the sentence doesn't get completed at the right-hand border of the text area, the text after the border will not be visible (b) The value Virtual recognizes the text with line breaks when textarea is loaded on the web page.

Syntax of using textarea control is:

```
<textarea rows="no. of rows" cols="no. of cols." wrap="physical" name="value of name">
Type text here
</textarea>
```

Program 5.3: To create a web page that will make use of textarea control

```
<HTML>
<HEAD>
<TITLE> Textarea Control</TITLE>
</HEAD>
<BODY>

<form method=”post” action=”mailto:youremail@gmail.com”>
<textarea rows=”5” cols=”30” wrap=”physical” name=”comments”>
Enter Comments Here
</textarea>

</form>
</BODY>
</HTML>
```

Output of the program is given below:

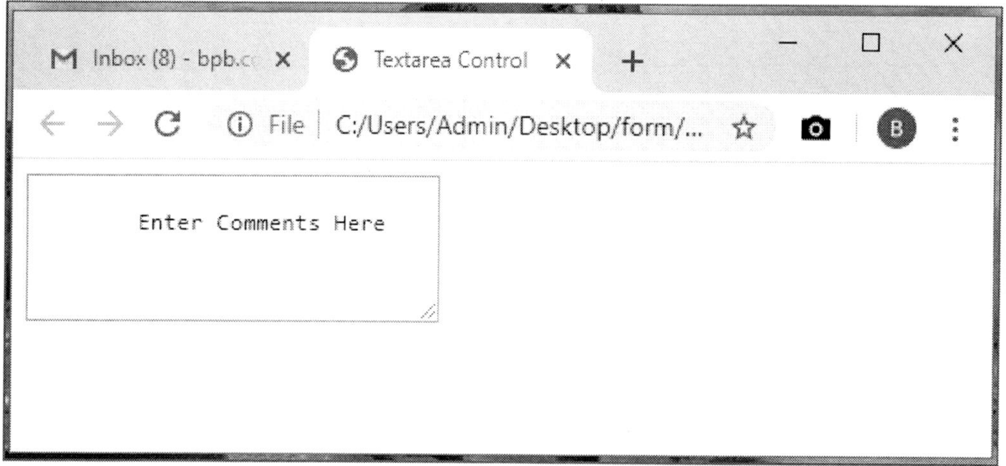

Figure 5.7: Form showing textarea control

3. Password Control

It provides a single line text input filed to enter the password. Password filled shows a single dot for each entered character to prevent from seeing the password by other user.

Following is the list of attributes used for creating password field.

Table 5.5: Attributes of Password Field

Attributes of Password control	Description
Type	Indicates the type of input control and for password input control it will be set to password.
Name	Used to give a name to the control which is sent to the server to be recognized and get the value.

Attributes of Password control	Description
Value	This can be used to provide an initial value inside the control.
Size	Allows to specify the width of the text-input control in terms of characters.
Maxlength	Allows to specify the maximum number of characters a user can enter into the text box.

Syntax of using textbox control:

```
<INPUT type=" password " name="value" value="initial value" size="width in number" maxlength ="length in numbers" >
```

Program 5.4: To create a web page that will use password field control.

```
<html>
<head>
<title>Password Control</title>
</head>
<body>
<form>
User ID: <input type="text" name="user id">
<br><BR>
Password: <input type="password" name="password">
</form>
</body>
</html>
```

Output of the program is given below:

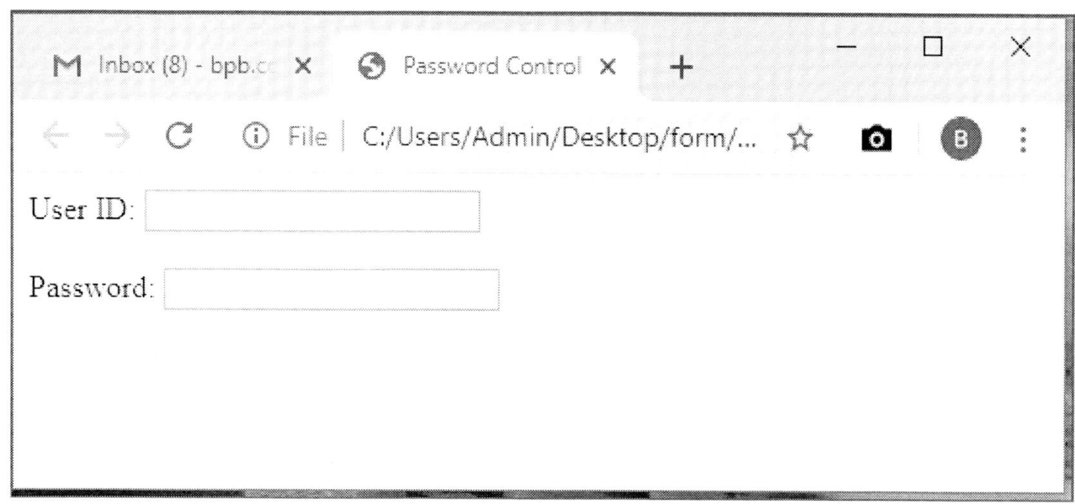

Figure 5.8: Form showing text and password field

MEMORIZE

A password field is a special type of control that does not display what the user types. Each keystroke is represented on the screen either by an asterisk or a bullet, so that it won't display the password to other users.

4. Radio button

It provides a radio button on the form. Multiple radio buttons can have the same name that belongs to one radio group only. If in the group, one radio button is selected. Then all other radio buttons of that group will be deselected.

Extra Byte

Radio button enables the selection of one of the options out of the many. This button is also called **toggle button**.

Following is the list of attributes used for creating radio button.

Table 5.6: Attribute of Radio button control

Attributes for radio button	Description
type	Indicates the type of input control and for checkbox input control it will be set to radio.
name	Used to give a name to the control which is sent to the server to be recognized and get the value.
value	The value that will be used if the radio box is selected.
checked	Set to checked if you want to select it by default.

Syntax of using Radio button control:

```
<Input  type="radio" name="name_value" value="Value"  Checked>
```

It is to be noted here, that if checked is written, then that radio button will be selected by default while opening a web page.

Program 5.5: Write a program that will use radio buttons control in a form.

```
<html>
<head>
<title>Radio Button </title>
</head>
<body>
<form>
<b>Select Subject:</b> <BR><BR>
<input type="radio"name="subject" value="maths" checked> Mathematics <BR>
<BR>
<input type="radio"name="subject" value="cs"> Computer Science
</form>
</body>
</html>
```

Extra Byte

Every checkbox does not get a different name, rather a collection of checkboxes gets the same name so as to refer to a group. As compared to radio button, a checkbox allows for multiple selections of items.

Output of the program is given below:

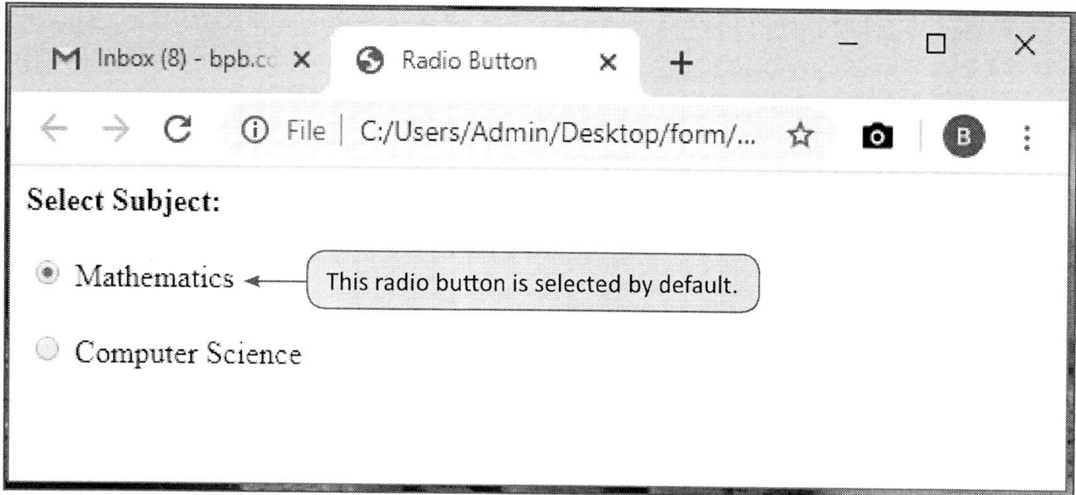

Figure 5.9: Form showing Radio button control

5. Checkbox control

It provides a checkbox control on the form. The user can choose more than one item from the list of items. You can make a group of checkboxes, by giving them the same name.

The check box's attributes namely, **name**, **align**, **value**, **type** and **checked** behave the same as a radio button's attributes.

Following is the list of attributes for <checkbox> tag.

Table 5.7: Attribute of Checkbox control

Attributes for checkbox control	Description
type	Indicates the type of input control and for checkbox input control it will be set to checkbox.
name	Used to give a name to the control which is sent to the server to be recognized and get the value.
value	The value that will be used if the checkbox is selected.
checked	Set to checked if you want to select it by default.

Syntax of using Checkbox control is:

```
<Input type="checkbox" name="name_value" value="Value" Checked>
```

It is to be noted here, that if checked is written, then that checkbox will be selected by default while opening a web page.

Program 5.6: To create a web page that will use checkbox control.

```
<html>
<head>
<title>Checkbox Control</title>
</head>
```

```
<body>
<form>
<b>Status of Employee</b> <br><br>
<input type="checkbox"name="married "value="on"> Married
<input type="checkbox"name="Employed"value="on"> Employed
<input type="checkbox"name="post graduate"value="on" checked> Post-Graduate
</form>
</body>
</html>
```

Output of the program is given below:

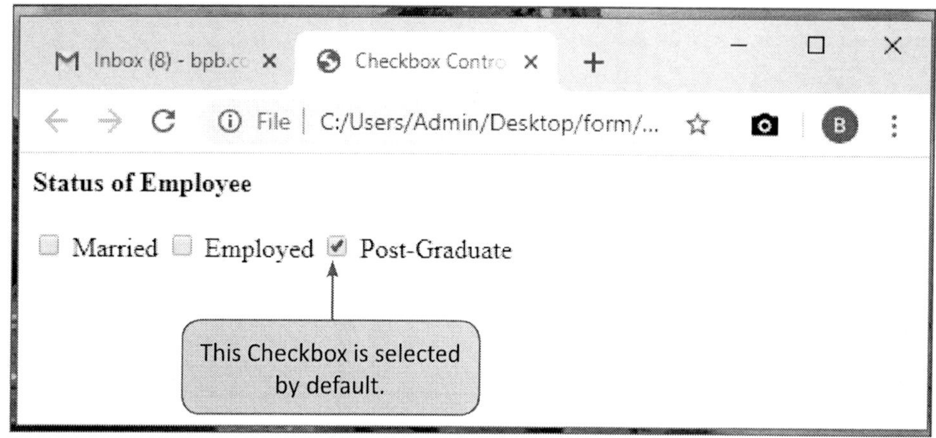

Figure 5.10: Form showing Checkbox control

5. Select Box Control

A select box, is also called as **drop-down box** or **listbox** which provides option to list down various options in the form of drop-down list, from where a user can select one or more options.

Note: Select element is used in conjunction with Option element.

You can use select control for listing drop down list and for making list as a group.

1. **Select Element with Optgroup:** Optgroup element is used to group multiple options in select dropdown. The name of optgroup is set by using label attribute in optgroup.
2. **Select Dropdown:** Select or select dropdown is used to fetch single or multiple options in dropdown list. Select options are fixed, thus user can choose only given option or options. To select city, country, date, month, year etc., Select Dropdown is used.

Following is the list of important attributes used with select control.

Table 5.8: Attributes of Select Box control

Attributes used for select box control	Description
name	Used to give a name to the control which is sent to the server to be recognized and get the value.
size	This can be used to present a scrolling list box.
multiple	If set to "multiple" then allows a user to select multiple items from the menu.

Following is the list of important attributes used with option element.

Table 5.9: Attributes of Option button Field

Attributes used with option element	Description
value	The value that will be used if an option in the select box is selected.
selected	Specifies that this option should be the initially selected value when the page loads.
label	An alternative way of labelling options.

Program 5.7: To create a web page that will use a simple drop down select box control.

```
<html>
<head>
<title>Select Box Control</title>
</head>
<body>
<form>
<b>Select any one item from the list<b><br><br>

<select name="Item" size=5 multiple>
<option selected disabled>--Select Item---</option>
<option value="Pizza" >Pizza</option>
<option value="Burger" >Burger</option>
<option value="Chowmein" >Chowmein</option>
<option value="Momos" >Momos</option>
</select>
</form>
</body>
</html>
```

Output of the program is given below:

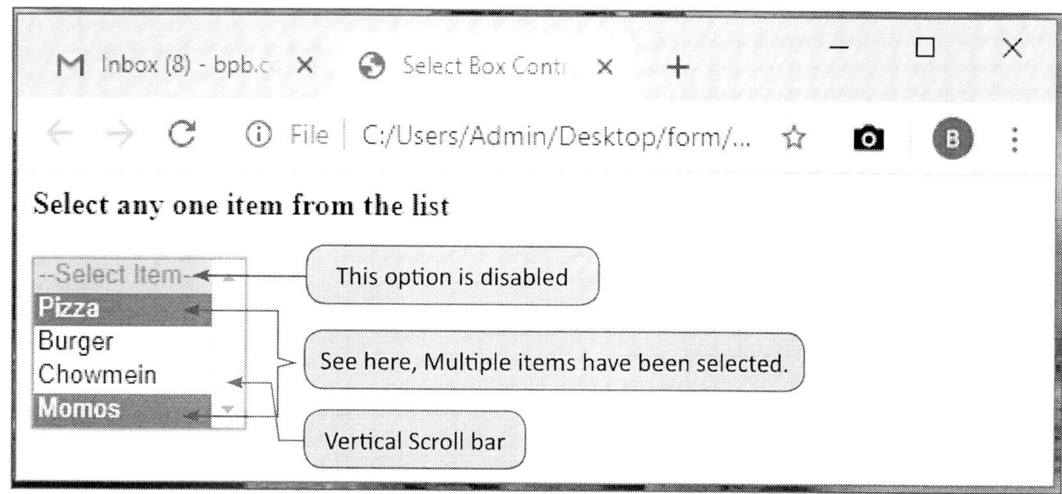

Figure 5.11: Form showing select control

Creating Forms, inserting Audio and Video in HTML

Program 5.8: To create a web page that will use a select box control with optgroup.

```
<html>
<head>
<title>Select Box Control</title>
</head>
<body>
<form>
<b>Current City:</b><br>
<select name="city">
   <option selected disabled>--Select City--</option>
   <optgroup label="Metros">
   <option>New Delhi</option>
   <option>Kolkata</option>
   <option>Mumbai</option>
   <option>Chennai</option>
   </optgroup>
<optgroup label="Others">
      <option>Noida</option>
      <option>Gurugram</option>
      <option>Faridabad</option>
      <option>Ghaziabad</option>
   </optgroup>
</select>
</form>
</body>
</html>
```

Output of the program is given below:

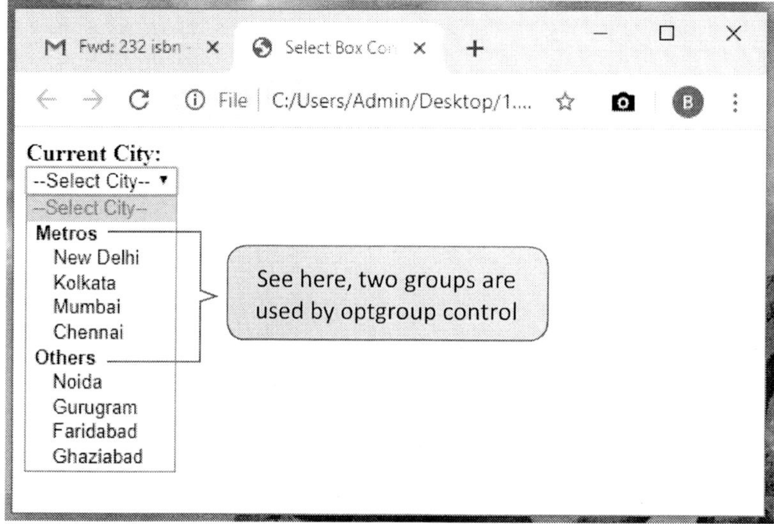

Figure 5.12: Form showing select box control with optgroup

6. Button Controls

There are various ways in HTML to create clickable buttons. You can also create a clickable button using <input> tag by setting its type attribute to button. The type attribute can take the following values:

Table 5.10: Attributes of Button Control

Attributes used for button controls	Description
submit	This creates a button that automatically submits a form.
reset	This creates a button that automatically resets form controls to their initial values.
button	This creates a button that is used to trigger a client-side script when user clicks that button.
image	This creates a clickable button and we can use an image as background of the button.

Syntax of using button control:

```
<input type="submit/reset/button/image" name="value of type" value="value">
```

Program 5.9: To create a web page that will use button control.

```
<html>

<head>
<title>File Upload Box</title>
</head>

<body>
<form>
<b> Enter basic details</></br><br>
Name:
<INPUT type="text" name="firstname" size=20 maxlength=100 ><BR><BR>
Email:
<input name="text" type="text" name="email" size=20 maxlength=100 >
<br><br>
<b>Select Subject:</b> <BR><BR>
<input type="radio"name="subject" value="maths"> Mathematics <BR>
<BR>
<input type="radio"name="subject" value="cs"> Computer Science
<br><br>
<input type="submit" name="submit"value="Submit">
<input type="reset" name="reset" value="Reset">
```

```
<input type="button" name="ok" value="OK">

</form>
</body>

</html>
```

Output of the program is given below:

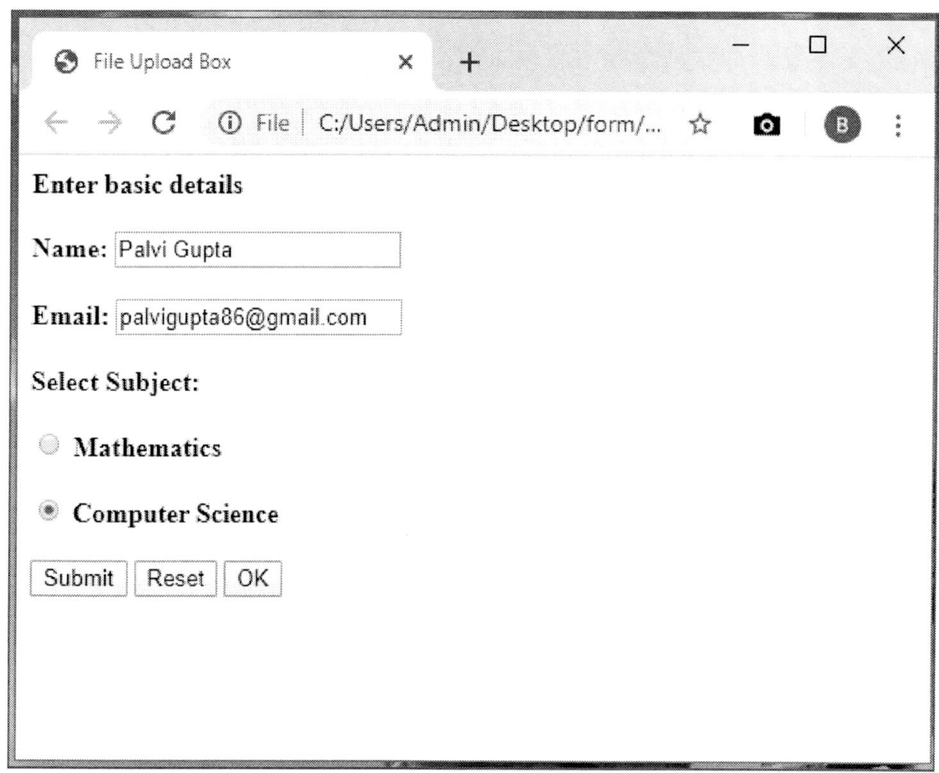

Figure 5.13: Form showing submit, reset and OK buttons

Check Your Progress

Multiple choice questions.

1. ______________ creates a button that automatically resets form controls to their initial values.
   a. Reset   b. Submit   c. Button
2. ______________ is used to group multiple options in select dropdown. The name of optgroup is set by using label attribute in optgroup.
   a. Optgroup element   b. Select box   c. Select drop down

5.7 EMBEDDING AUDIO AND VIDEO IN HTML WEB PAGE

To make a web page more interesting and interactive, you can also insert audios and videos in HTML document.

5.7.1 The <audio> tag

The <audio> tag defines sound, such as music or other audio streams. Audio tag is used to add sound and music in the html page. It is used in conjunction with source tag.

The audio tag, supports three types of audio files:

1. **mp3:** MIME-type audio/mpeg 2. **wav:** MIME-type audio/wav 3. **ogg:** MIME-type audio/ogg

Source tag uses two attributes:

1. **src:** It provides the URL of the audio file which is to be inserted.
2. **type:** It provides the file format of audio file.

Program 5.10: To create a web page that will insert audio in different file formats.

```
<html>
<body>
<audio controls>
<source src="sample.ogg" type="audio/ogg">
<source src="kalimba.mp3" type="audio/mpeg">
<source src="jazz.wav" type="audio/wav">
</audio>
</body>
</html>
```

5.7.2 Embedding video files

A video file can be inserted in an HTML page in three ways:

1. By using <**embed**> tag 2. By inserting **video** link 3. By using <**video**> tag

∗ **Let's learn all these types for inserting videos in HTML document**

1. <Embed> Tag

The first way would be using the <embed> tag. It is an **empty** tag.

Various File types supported by embed tag are:

- **.swf:** Made by Macromedia Flash
- **.wmv:** Microsoft Windows Media Video
- **.mov:** Quick Time Movie, belongs to Apple
- **.mpeg:** Created by Moving Pictures Expert Group

Most commonly used embed tag are **.mpeg** and **.swf**, because of the compact format.

Attributes used with embed tag are:

Table 5.11: Attributes of Embed tag for inserting video files

Attribute	Description
Src	It provides the URL of the video to be inserted
Height	Height of the video
Width	Width of the video
Autostart	Value may be false or true

The syntax for inserting video using embed tag:

```
<embed src="URL of the video" autostart="false/true "height="value"width="value" />
```

2. Inserting link for video

The second way is to insert a video file using a link.

Consider an example:

```
<a href="example.mpeg" title="Download movie">film name</a>
```

3. Using <video> tag

The third way of inserting video is by using <video> tag.

Video tag is used to add a video to the html page. The **HTML5 video tag**, supports three types of video files:

- **mp4:** MIME-type video/mp4
- **webm:** MIME-type video/webm
- **ogg:** MIME-type video/ogg

Attributes used by video tag are:

Height and Width that defines the height and width of a video to be inserted.

Program 5.11: To create a web page that will insert video by using video tag.

```
<html>
<body>
<video width="320"height="240"controls>
<source src="sample-video.mp4"type="video/mp4">
<source src="sample-video.ogg"type="video/ogg">
<source src="sample-video.webm"type="video/webm">
</video>
</body>
</html>
```

Check Your Progress

Fill in the blanks.

1. ____________ tag is used to insert sound in HTML.
2. .mp3 is a ____________ type of file.
3. .mp4 is a ____________ type of file.

Let's Revise

- The HTML <form> element defines a form that is used to collect user input.
- Form elements are the different types of input elements, like text fields, checkboxes, radio buttons, submit buttons.

- The <input> element is the most important form element that can be displayed in several ways, depending on the type attribute.
- <input type=»text»> defines a one-line input field for text input.
- Password input control is a single-line text input but it masks the character as soon as a user enters the text.
- <input type="radio"> defines a radio button. Radio buttons let a user to select ONE of a limited number of choices.
- Checkboxes are used when more than one option is required to be selected.
- Textarea field creates a text area that is much like a two-dimensional text field where user can enter or edit text in.
- A Submit buttons, when activated submits a form. A form may contain more than one submit button.
- Reset buttons, when activated, resets all controls to their initial values
- The <audio> tag defines sound, such as music or other audio streams. Audio tag is used to add sound and music in the html page. It is used in conjunction with source tag.
- A video file can be inserted in an HTML page in three ways.
  - By using <embed> tag
  - By inserting video link
  - By using <video> tag

Learning Zone

SECTION A: OBJECTIVE TYPE QUESTIONS

A. MULTIPLE CHOICE QUESTIONS.

1. What is the default type of 'type' attribute of <input> element?
   a. Text b. Password c. Numerals d. Special Characters
2. Which of the following is not used with password attribute?
   a. name b. size c. maxlength d. min
3. Which element is used to create multi-line text input?
   a. Text b. Textarea c. Submit d. Radio button
4. Which attribute is not used for the radio type button?
   a. name b. value c. checked d. selected
5. Which attribute is used with <select> element?
   a. multiple b. selected c. name d. value
6. The attribute of <form> tag is:
   a. Method b. Action c. Both a. and b. d. None of above
7. <input type="reset"> defines a:
   a. Link to reset all the form values b. Reset button
   c. Reset field d. Reset radio button

8. Which tag creates a check box for a form in HTML?

a. <checkbox>
b. <input type="checkbox">
c. <input=checkbox>
d. <input checkbox>

9. To create a combo box (drop down box) which tag will you use?

a. <select>
b. <list>
c. <input type="dropdown">
d. all of the above

10. Which tag creates a check box for a form in HTML?

a. <checkbox>
b. <input type="checkbox">
c. <input=checkbox>
d. <input checkbox>

11. Which of the following tag is used for audio in HTML?

a. <bgsound> b. <audio> c. <video> d. <canvas>

12. Which of the following browser does not support .wav file format?

a. Opera b. Firefox c. Chrome d. Internet Explorer

13. We mask the input typed into a text field by specifying an <input> tag as:

a. Password b. Secure c. Invisible d. Hidden

14. In order to clear the values in a form, the developer specifies an <input> tag as:

a. Empty b. Clear c. Refresh d. Reset

15. Which of the following is true?

a. The <option> tag does not have a value attribute. If selected, it passes its displayed value
b. The <option> tag only passes values through its value attributes. The displayed value is never displayed
c. The <option> tag passes values through the value tag if it is present, and passes the value displayed if the value attribute is not given
d. The purpose of the <option> tag is to specify the type of control to use, not to pass values

Ans.	1. a	2. d	3. b	4. d	5. a
	6. c	7. b	8. b	9. c	10. b
	11. b	12. d	13. a	14. b	15. a

B. FILL IN THE BLANKS.

1. A ____________ can be inserted in HTML document which can act as a container for all the input elements.
2. ____________ method is used to send form data as URL variables.
3. ____________ control displays several text lines at a time.
4. If the value of the type attribute is "radio" then the form will show ____________.
5. ____________ enables the selection of one of the options out of the many.
6. A ____________ allows for multiple selections of items.
7. If the value of the type attribute is "Submit" i.e., the form will show ____________.
8. A "select" element must contain at least one ____________ element.

9. ____________ allows for the creation of groups of options in a select menu.

10. ____________ tag is used for inserting audio in html document.

Ans. 1. Form 2. Get 3. Textarea 4. Radio button
5. Option button 6. Checkbox 7. Submit Button 8. Option
9. Optgroup 10. <audio>

C. STATE WHETHER THE FOLLOWING STATEMENTS ARE TRUE OR FALSE.

1. < form> tag is used to insert form in html document.
2. maxlength attribute of textfield sets the minimum number of characters a field can take.
3. <form> tag is an empty tag.
4. Form controls are placed by using input tag with type attribute.
5. Reset button is used to clear all inputs entered previously by the user.
6. Submit button submits the data in the form.
7. The two methods of posting form are getform and postform.
8. <select> tag is used for drop-down list
9. The <choice> tag inside the <select> element defines the available options in the list.
10. Combo box is a combination of drop-down list and text input.
11. To set the password field, a password type input should be taken.
12. <form> tag can be nested within another <form> tag.
13. size attribute is valid for the submit button.
14. The attribute data with <input> tag specifies the kind of data to be entered in a particular field.
15. Radio buttons and check boxes are different from each other in terms of functionality.

Ans.					
	1. True	2. False	3. False	4. True	5. True
	6. True	7. False	8. True	9. False	10. True
	11. True	12. False	13. False	14. False	15. True

SECTION B: SOLVED THEORY QUESTIONS

1. **Define forms in HTML.**

Ans: Forms are the means to collect the user information whenever a user fills any form or provides any details and then save it into the database.

2. **Name the different attributes used with form tag.**

Ans: The various attributes used with form tag are action, method and name.

3. **What is the difference between the methods get and post?**

Ans: get method appends the form-data to the URL in name/value pairs. The length of a URL is limited (about 3000 characters). post method Sends the form-data as an HTTP post transaction. It has no size limitations.

4. What do you mean by form controls? Name the various form controls.

Ans: A form is a window that consists of the elements of a form called the form fields. These fields are also known as form controls.

Various types of form controls are: Text field, text area, drop-down box, radio buttons, checkbox, Password field, Select and/or a command button.

5. Differentiate between text field and textarea field.

Ans: The TEXT BOX is a single line box. They are generally used for collecting information such as names, e-mail addresses, URLs, etc. The TEXTAREA is a multiple line box. TEXTAREAs are generally used to gather feedback or comments.

6. What are the limits of the text field size?

Ans: The default size for a text field is around 13 characters. However, if we include the size attribute, we can set the size value to be as low as 1. The maximum size value will be determined by the browser width. If the size attribute is set to 0, the size will be set to the default size of 13 characters.

7. Differentiate between radio button and checkbox control.

Ans: Radio button enables the selection of one of the options out of the many. Radio buttons operate as a group and provide mutually exclusive selection values. As compared to radio button, a checkbox allows for multiple selections of items. Each checkbox operates individually, so a user can toggle each response "on" and "off."

8. What happens when submit or reset button get activated?

Ans: A Submit buttons, when activated, submits a form. A form may contain more than one submit button. Reset button, when activated, resets all controls to their initial values.

9. What are the different methods of inserting video in html document?

Ans: The different methods of inserting videos in html are:

a. By using <embed> tag
b. By using <video> tag
c. By inserting YouTube video link

10. How can you insert audio in html document?

Ans: Audio can be inserted by using <audio> tag in HTML document.

11. If you want to enter information which is long enough to fit in a single sentence, then which type of control should be used?

Ans: Use <textarea> control for multi-line input.

12. What happens when you are using check boxes for the stream (science, humanities, commerce) instead of radio button?

Ans: If we are using check boxes instead of radio button then we can select more than one stream which is not logically correct.

13. What is the utility of reset button in a form?

Ans: Reset button is used to clear all inputs by the user which he has entered previously.

14. What is the purpose of using submit button on a form?

Ans: Submit button submits the data in the form. It is usually sent to a web page on the server when the user clicks on the Submit button.

SECTION C: APPLICATION ORIENTED QUESTIONS

1. **Write HTML code to generate the form as shown in the above given screenshot.**

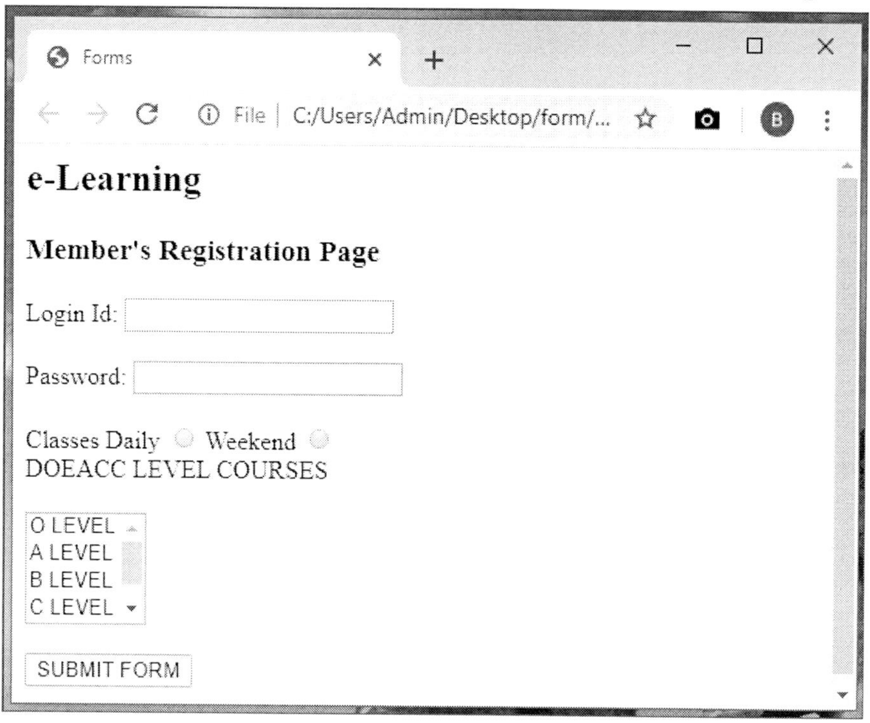

Ans:

```
<html>
<head><title>Forms</title></head>
<body>
<h2>e-Learning</h2>
<h3>Member’s Registration Page</h3>
<form method=”post” action=”Forms.html”>
Login Id: <input type=”text” name=”id”><br> <br>
Password: <input type=”password” name=”pswd”><br> <br>
Classes Daily <input type=”radio” name=”classes” value=”Daily”>
Weekend <input type=”radio” name=”classes” value=”Weekend”>
<br>
DOEACC LEVEL COURSES<br> <br>
<select name=”cType” multiple>
<option value=”OL”>O LEVEL</option>
<option value=”A”>A LEVEL</option>
<option value=”B”>B LEVEL</option>
<option value=”C”>C LEVEL</option>
<option value=”D”>D LEVEL</option>
</select>
<br> <br>
<input type=”submit” value=”SUBMIT FORM”>
</form>
</body>
</html>
```

2. **Which form elements have been used to create controls having labels as "Login Id", "Classes", "DOEACC COURSES", and "Submit" as shown in the above given screenshot of "e-Learning Member's Registration Page". Also mention how form element given for "Classes" is different from form element given for "Course Type".**

Ans:

Login Id element is	Text box
Classes element is	Radio button
DOEACC COURSES element is	Drop down box
Submit element is	submit button
The form element for classes is	Radio button
The form element for course Type is	drop down box

3. **Write the HTML code for the given output**

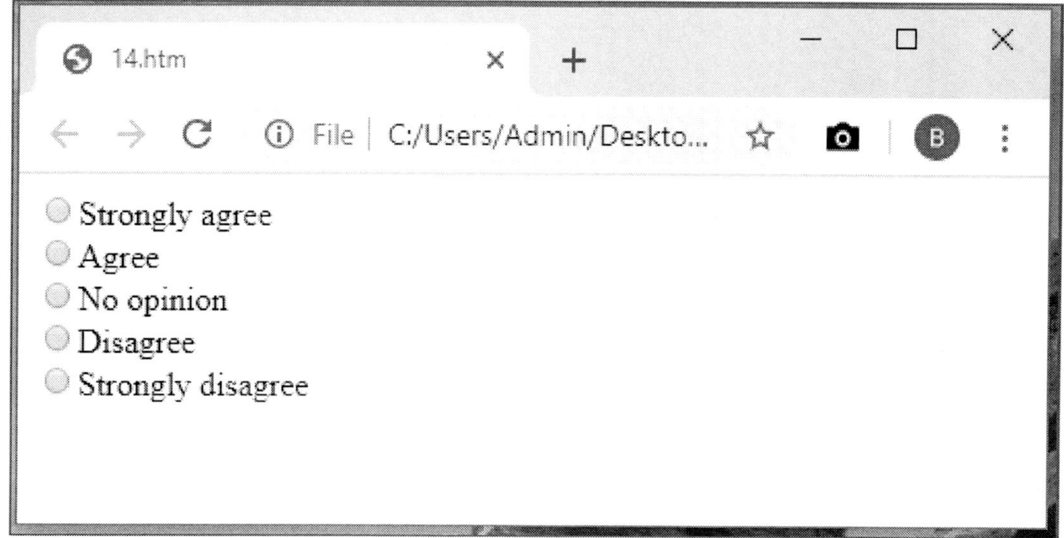

Ans:

```
<html>
<body>
<form method="post">
<INPUT TYPE="radio" NAME="orbits" VALUE="strongly_agree">Strongly agree<BR>
<INPUT TYPE="radio" NAME="orbits" VALUE="agree">Agree<BR>
<INPUT TYPE="radio" NAME="orbits" VALUE="no_opinion">No opinion<BR>
<INPUT TYPE="radio" NAME="orbits" VALUE="disagree">Disagree<BR>
<INPUT TYPE="radio" NAME="orbits" VALUE="strongly_disagree">Strongly
disagree<BR>
</form>
</body>
</html>
```

4. **Carefully observe the following labeled screenshot and answer the questions that follow:**

a. Identify the form element labeled as 1 and 2?

b. Why has the form element labeled as 2 used to input the Address?

c. Write HTML code to create the form element labeled as 3.

d. Differentiate between the form element labeled 3 and the form element labeled

e. How can any one item be highlighted in the Dropdown box labeled as 5?

Ans: a. Form element labeled as 1 is a Textbox and Form element labeled as 2 is a Textarea.

b. Text areas are the fields that display multiple text lines at a time. Hence, it has been used to accept Address which also contains multiple lines of text.

c.
```
<input type="radio" name="Ltype" value="DND">Do Not Disturb <br>
<input type="radio" name="Ltype" value="Vib">VIBRATE <br>
<input type="radio" name="Ltype" value="Act">Active <br>
```

d. Form element labeled as 3 is a Radio button. It enables the selection of one of the options out of the many.
Whereas, form element labeled as 4 is a checkbox. As compared to radio button, a checkbox allows for multiple selections of items.

e. To highlight one item in a dropdown box, "selected" clause is used in the <option> tag as follows:
```
<option selected>
```
Example:
```
<select>
<option>SINGAPORE</option>
<option selected>JAPAN</option>
<option>MALAYSIA</option>
</select>
```

5. Observe the following code and answer the questions that follow:

```
<html>
<head>
<title>
Find Output
</title>
</head>
<body>
<select Multiple>
<Option> Science</Option>
<Option> Commerce</Option>
<Option> Humanities</Option>
</select>
</body>
</html>
```

a. What is the use of <select> tag in the above code?

b. Explain the purpose of Multiple attribute of <select> tag.

c. What output will be produced when the above code is executed?

Ans: a. <select> tag is used to create a dropdown box that prompts the user to select item / item(s) from the list.

b. Multiple attribute of <select> tag allows multiple selection from the list.

c.

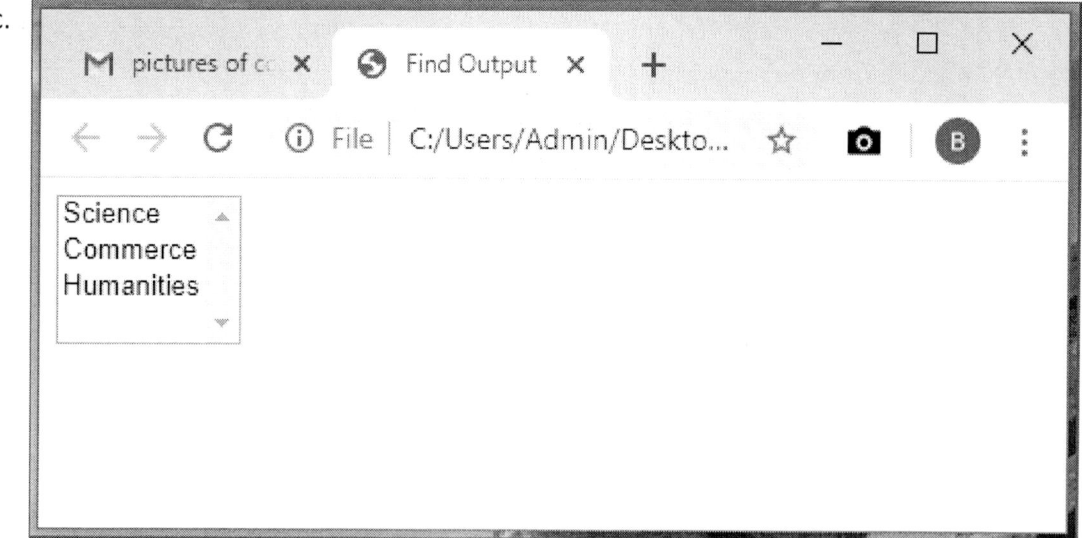

6. Aayush wants to send highly sensitive form data such as username and password which method out of get/post should he use to send the form data? Why?

Ans: post method

a. Appends form-data inside the body of the HTTP request (data is not shown in URL)

b. Form submissions with POST cannot be bookmarked

7. **Write the HTML code for the following for the following output.**

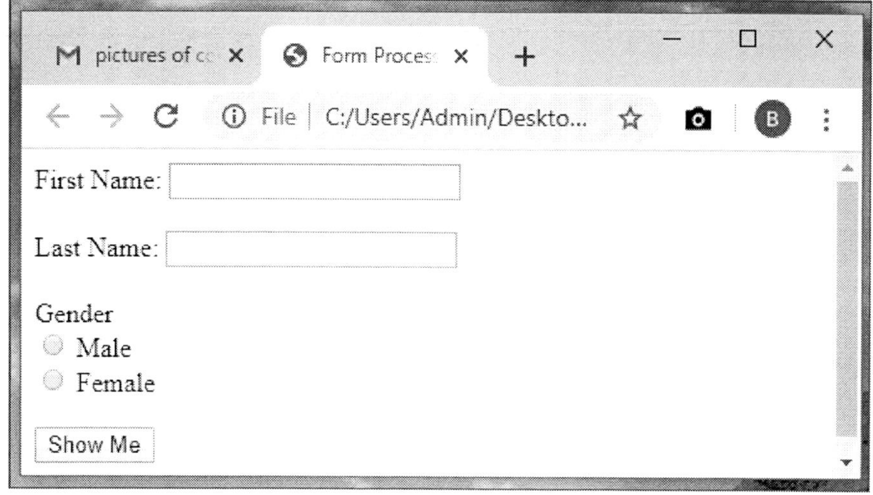

Ans:

```
<html>
<head><title>Form Processing</title>
</head>
<body>
<form action=”Forms.html”>
<p>First Name: <input type=”text” name=”fname”><br> <br>
Last Name: <input type=”text” name=”lname”><br> <br>
Gender <br>
<input type=”radio” name=”gender” value=”male”>
Male<br>
<input type=”radio” name=”genders” value=”female”>
Female <br></p>
<p>
<label>

<input type=”button” value=”Show Me”>
</label>
</p>
</form>
</body>
<html>
```

8. **Write the HTML code for the following for the following output.**

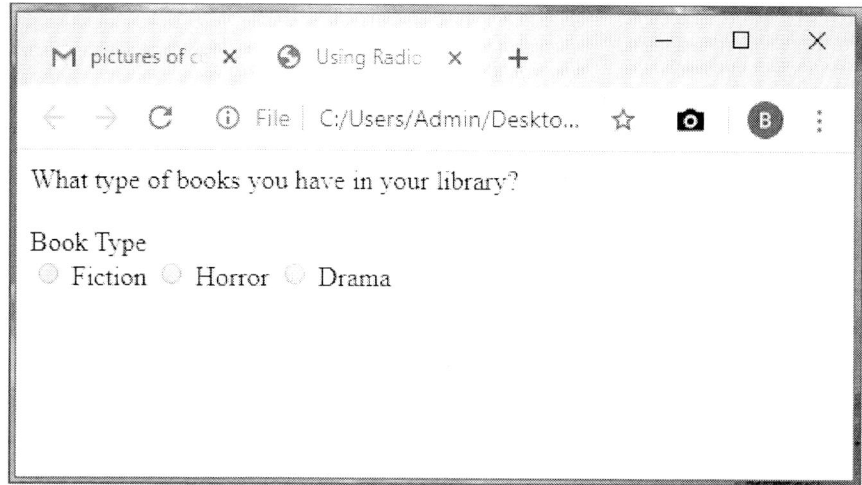

Ans:
```
<html>
<head><title>Using Radio Buttons</title>
</head>
<body>
<form>
What type of books you have in your library? <br> <br>
Book Type<br>
<input type= “radio” name= “ftype” value= “Fiction”> Fiction
<input type= “radio” name= “htype” value= “Horror”> Horror
<input type= “radio” name= “dtype” value= “Drama”> Drama
</form>
</body>
<html>
```

9. **Write the HTML code for the following for the following output:**

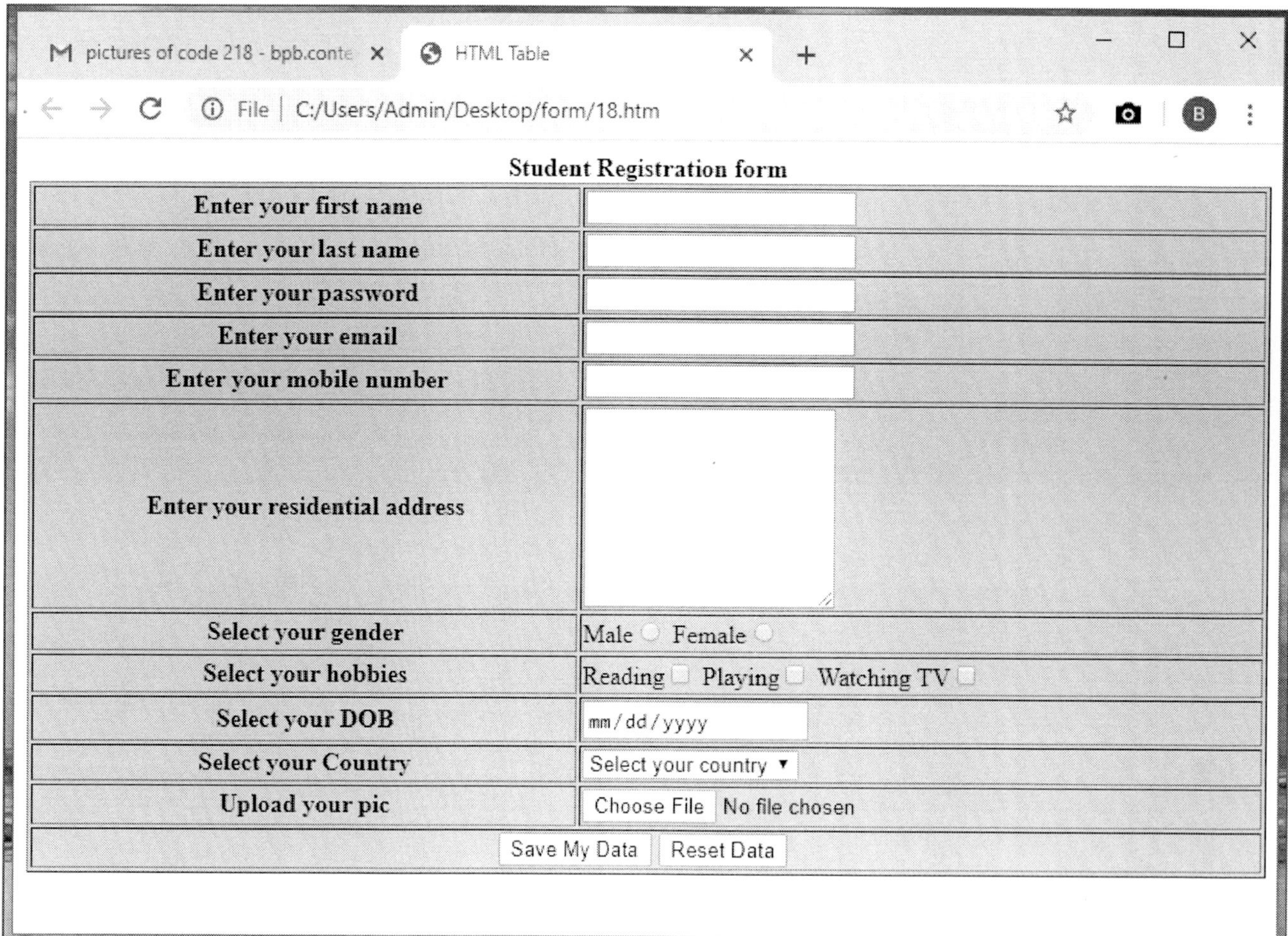

Ans:
```
<html>
<head>
<title>HTML Table</title>
</head>
<body>
<form method=”” action=””>
<table border=”1” align=”center” width=”800” bgcolor=”#CCCCCC” >
<caption> <b>Student Registration form</b></caption>
<tr>
```

```
<th>Enter your first name</th>
<td><input type="text" name="fn" maxlength="10"  ></td>
</tr>
<tr>
<th>Enter your last name</th>
<td><input type="text"/></td>
</tr>
<tr>
<th>Enter your password</th>
<td><input type="password"/></td>
</tr>
<tr>
<th>Enter your email</th>
<td><input type="email"/></td>
</tr>
<tr>
<th>Enter your mobile number</th>
<td><input type="number"/></td>
</tr>
<tr>
<th>Enter your residential address</th>
<td><textarea rows="8" cols="20"></textarea></td>
</tr>
<tr>
<th>Select your gender</th>
<td>
Male<input type="radio" name="g" value="m"/>
Female<input type="radio" name="g" value="f"/>
</td>
</tr>
<tr>
<th>Select your hobbies</th>
<td>
Reading<input type="checkbox" name="x" value="h1"/>
Playing<input type="checkbox" name="x" value="h2"/>
Watching TV<input type="checkbox" name="x" value="h3"/>
</td>
</tr>
<tr>
<th>Select your DOB</th>
<td><input type="date"/></td>
</tr>
<tr>
<th>Select your Country</th>
<td>
<select name="country">
<option value="" selected="selected" disabled="disabled">Select your country</
option>
<option value="1">India</option>
<option value="2">England</option>
</select>
```

```
</td>
</tr>
<tr>
<th>Upload your pic</th>
<td><input type=”file”/></td>
</tr>
<tr>
<td colspan=”2” align=”center”><input type=”submit” value=”Save My Data”/>
<input type=”reset” value=”Reset Data”/>
</td>
</tr>
</table>
</form>
</body>
</html>
```

10. Write the HTML code for the following for the following output.

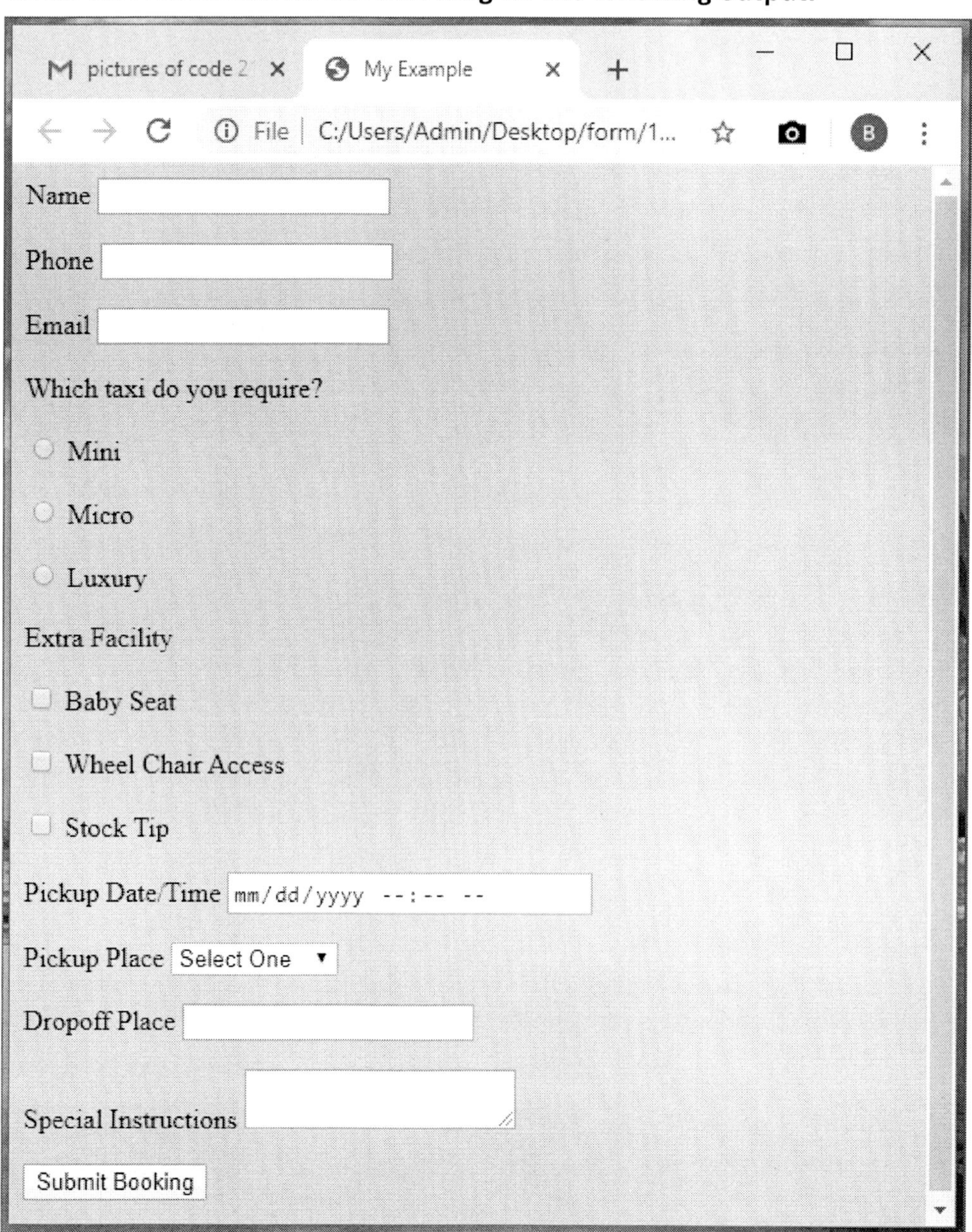

Ans:
```
<html>
<title>My Example</title>
<body bgcolor="pink">
<form method="get" enctype="application/x-www-form-urlencoded" action="/html/codes/
html_form_handler.cfm">
<p>
<label>Name
<input type="text" name="customer_name" required>
</label>
</p>
<p>
<label>Phone
<input type="tel" name="phone_number">
</label>
</p>

<p>
<label>Email
<input type="email" name="email_address">
</label>
</p>

<p>Which taxi do you require?</p>
<p><label> <input type="radio" name="min" required value="mini"> Mini </label></p>
<p><label> <input type="radio" name="mic" required value="micro"> Micro </label></
p>
<p><label> <input type="radio" name="lux" required value="luxury"> Luxury </label></
p>
<p> Extra Facility</p>
<p><label> <input type="checkbox" name="extras" value="baby"> Baby Seat</label></p>
<p><label> <input type="checkbox" name="extras" value="wheelchair"> Wheel Chair
Access</label></p>
<p><label> <input type="checkbox" name="extras" value="tip"> Stock Tip </label></p>
<p>
<label>Pickup Date/Time
<input type="datetime-local" name="pickup_time" required>
</label>
</p>

<p>
<label>Pickup Place
<select id="pickup_place" name="pickup_place">
<option value="" selected="selected">Select One</option>
<option value="office" >Taxi Office</option>
<option value="town_hall" >Town Hall</option>
<option value="telepathy" >We'll Guess!</option>
</select>
```

```
</label>
</p>

<p>
<label>Dropoff Place
<input type="text" name="dropoff_place" required list="destinations">
</label>

<datalist id="destinations">
<option value="Airport">
<option value="Beach">
<option value="Fred Flinstone's House">
</datalist>
</p>

<p>
<label>Special Instructions
<textarea name="comments" maxlength="500"></textarea>
</label>
</p>

<p><button>Submit Booking</button></p>

</form>
</body>
</html>
```

SECTION D: SELF - ASSESSMENT

A. FILL IN THE BLANKS.

1. ____________ identifies where on a web page the form control elements will appear.
1. ____________ tag uses the type attribute to define the type of information to be captured within the control.
2. ____________ tag differs from the input tag as it can accept larger passages of text spanning multiple lines.
3. ____________ button allows the user to put information into action, after the user has input the requested information.
4. ____________ and ____________ are the two required attributes of form tag.
5. ____________ type of control is used when only one option has to be selected out of many options.
6. <input type=" ____________ " > clears all inputs by the user in a form.
7. The ____________ type attribute creates a button that automatically submits a button.
8. Multi-line control is created using ____________ tag.
9. ____________ control does not give the user the opportunity not to choose anything.

B. STATE WHETHER THE FOLLOWING STATEMENTS ARE TRUE OR FALSE.

1. You can create clickable buttons using <input> tag.
2. You can give comments using multi-line input.
3. Radio buttons are used when you have to choose multiple options at a time.
4. The checkboxes are used when you want to select more than one option.
5. A select box is also called a drop-down box.
6. The <form> tag is a container tag.
7. The <input> tag is an empty element.
8. size attribute is valid for the submit button.
9. In forms, images can't be used in a submit button.
10. <form> tag can be placed anywhere in the html document.

C. TICK THE CORRECT ANSWER.

1. Which form tag would be best for getting someone's country?

   a. <select> b. <input type="radio">
   c. <input type="checkbox"> d. <textarea>

2. When should you use GET as the method for submitting your form? (choose all that apply)

   a. Top of Form
   b. Sensitive data (like passwords)
   c. Search results that people may want to bookmark
   d. Large form with lots of data

3. What is the default type of 'type' attribute of <input> element?

   a. Text b. Password c. Numerals d. Special Characters

4. Which of the following is a new input attribute introduce by HTML5?

   a. Text b. Checkbox controls c. Submit buttons d. Date

5. Which of the following is not used with password attribute?

   a. name b. size c. maxlength d. min

6. Which element is used to create multi-line text input?

   a. Text b. Textarea c. Submit d. Radio button

7. an attribute with <input> tag that specifies the kind of data to be entered in a particular field.

   a. Data b. Declare c. Type d. None of them

8. An object on the form page which submits the form data to the web server is:

   a. Go button b. Submit button c. Save button d. Reset button

9. An attribute of the <form> tag that specifies the URL to which the data is sent is:

   a. Address b. URL c. Action d. Method

10. The type of control used when only one option is to be selected from the set of alternatives:

    a. Check boxes b. Radio buttons c. Submit button d. Text input

D. ANSWER THE FOLLOWING QUESTIONS.

Type A: Very Short Answer Questions.

1. What do you understand by html forms?
2. Name the attributes used with form tag.
3. What re the two methods used with method attribute?
4. Differentiate between get and post method.
5. Differentiate between submit button and clear button.
6. What do you mean by maxlength in input tag?
7. Define textarea with its utilty.
8. What are radio buttons?
9. Which control should be used when you want to enter remarks for a student?
10. Which control should be used to select more than one hobby?
11. Which control should be used to opt one of the gender as either male or female?
12. What if the name attribute is omitted?

Type B: Short Answer Questions.

1. How will you create a custom button?
2. Explain the difference between textual input boxes and password input boxes.
3. Write the code to get the following output.

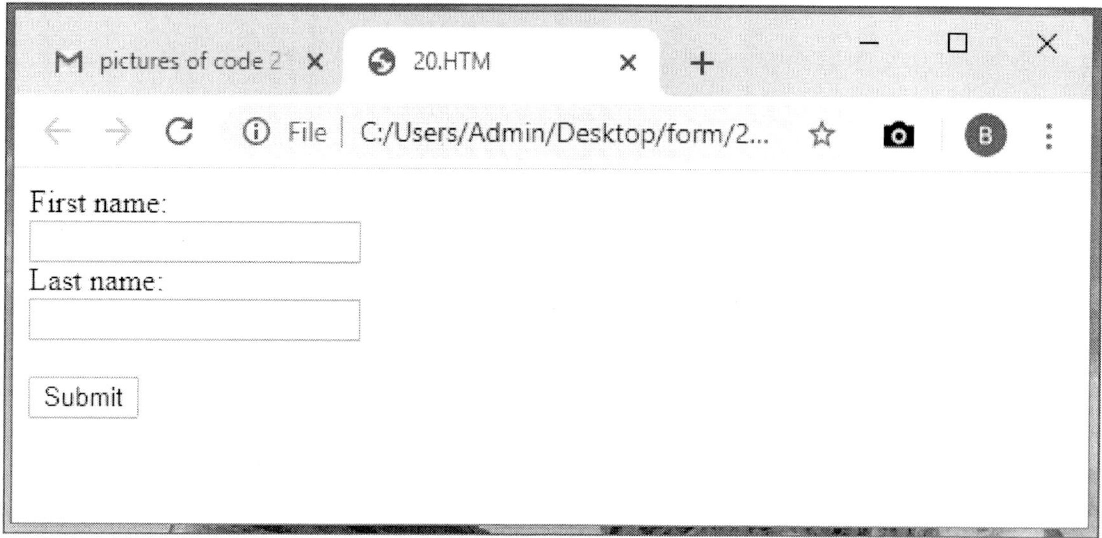

4. What is the output of the following code?

```
<html>
<body>
First name:<br>
   <input type="text" name="firstname"><br>
   Last name:<br>
   <input type="text" name="lastname">
<br> Gender
<input type="radio" name="gender" value="male"
```

```
checked> Male
   <input type="radio" name="gender" value="female">

Female
   <input type="radio" name="gender" value="other">

Other<br>
<input type="submit" value="Submit">
</html>
</body>
```

5. Write the html code to generate the following output.

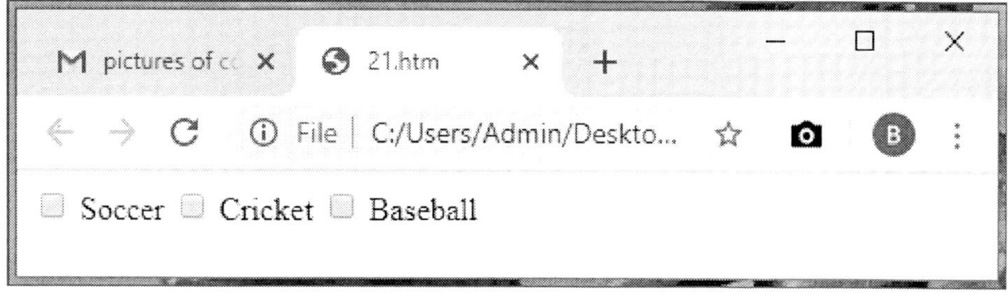

6. Compare the following controls:
   a. Radio button and submit button
   b. Radio button and checkboxes
   c. Checkboxes and drop-down list
   d. Drop-down list and combo box
   e. Submit and Reset button

Type C: Long Answer Questions.

1. Write HTML code to generate the following form. Save it as task1.html.

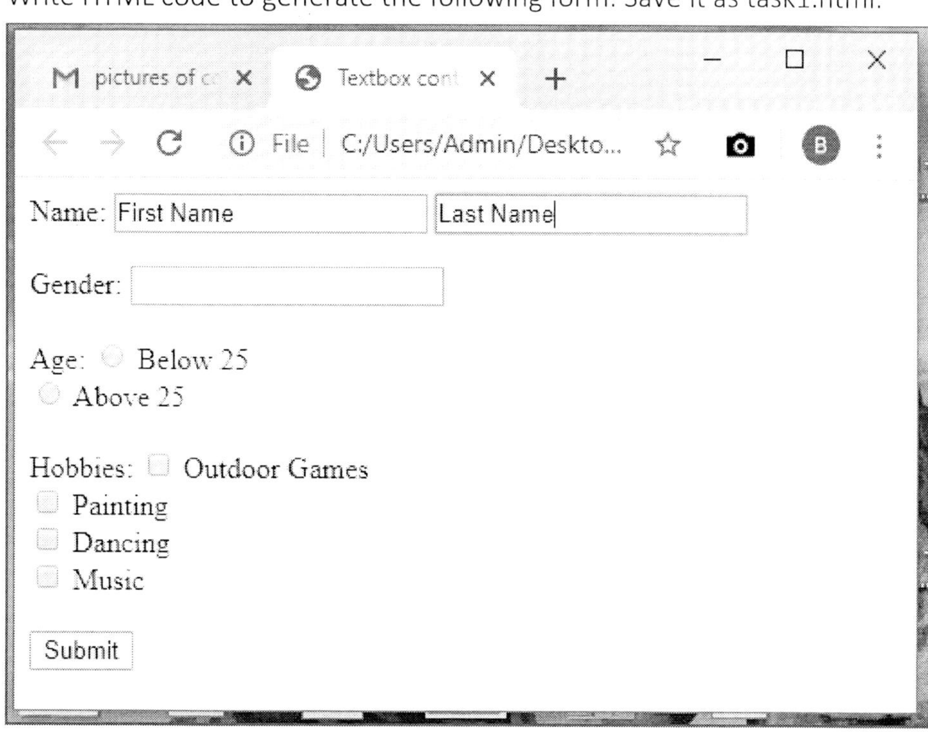

2. Write code to create the following HTML Form to accept User's Information as part of a Magazine Survey.

   Note: Address accepts multiline text.

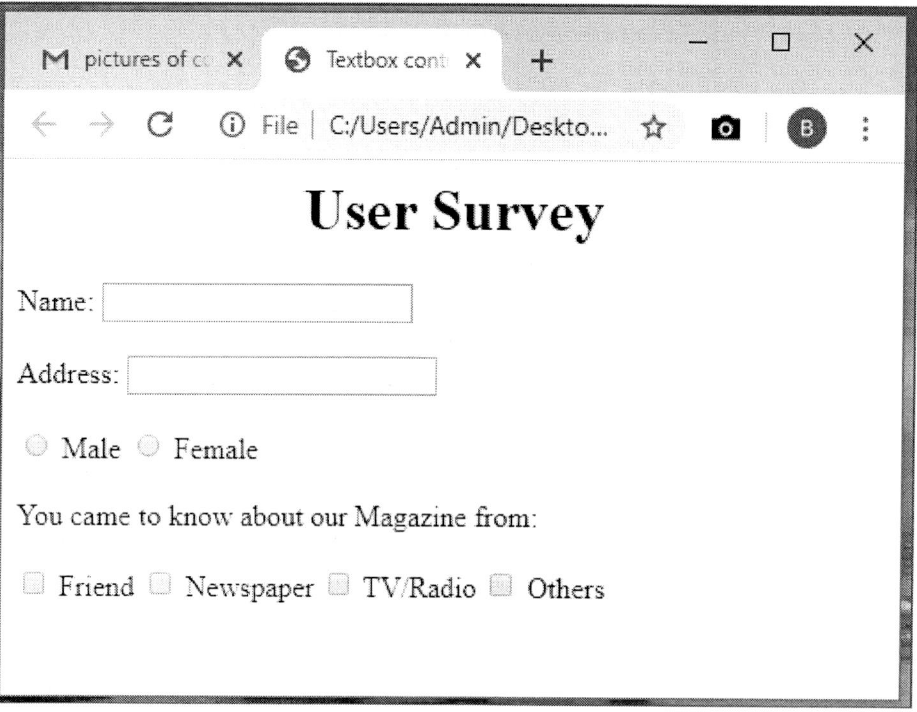

3. Write html program using form tag to generate the given output.

Inbox - sb@bp

Textbox control

File | C:/Users/Admin/Documents/class...

Create an Account

E-mail:

Password:

Age:

Select Age ▼

Tell us a little about yourself:

I agree to the terms of service

Sign up

4. Observe the given output and answer the questions:

a. Which input control is used in the above form?

b. How many times the input control is used in the form?

c. What do you mean by option control?

5. Palvi is creating a customer's feedback form for her e-learning course website. Suggest her to choose correct form control which she should use for the following:

a. She wants to get the firstname and lastname of the customer.

b. To define an area where user can enter his comments.

c. To select the name of the city out of 20 cities.

d. To provide the option where the user can select his gender.

Activity Zone

1. Tell students to find the output of the following HTML code and paste it on A4 size sheet.

```
<HTML>
<body>
</p>
<form name="form1" method="post" action="">
<p>Outdoor Games You Play</p>
<p>
<input type="checkbox" name="game1" value="table tennis"> Table Tennis<br>
<br>
<input type="checkbox" name="game2" value="football">Foot Ball<br>
<br>
<input type="checkbox" name="game3" value="swimming">Swimming<br>
<br>
</p>
</form></form>
</body>
```

2. Tell students to design a web page that will ask the user to select items from pizza, burger and chowmein and then submit the button.

3. Tell students to make a presentation that will describe all the form controls which they have studied so far.

6 Cascading Style Sheet (CSS)

Outline of the Chapter

- Introduction
- Advantages and limitations of CSS
- In-line, internal and external methods of CSS
- What is CSS?
- Methods of applying CSS
- Various properties of CSS

Learning Objectives

- To know the meaning of CSS and its purpose to use
- To know various advantages and limitations of CSS
- To know the difference between in-line, internal and external methods
- To know the various FONT, COLOR, BACKGROUND, BORDER and MARGIN properties of CSS

INTRODUCTION

In previous chapters, you have learnt about html tags and their usage. For each tag, you apply formatting feature which is cumbersome at some point. What if there is a facility to use all formatting features for the entire web page at one place and all html tags will be stored at one place. It would become easier with the use of cascading style sheet that makes our work easier.

This chapter will completely focus on CSS and its usage along with simple programs.

* **So, let's start with the meaning of CSS.**

6.1 WHAT IS CSS?

The expanded form of CSS is **Cascading Style Sheet**. It is a simple language that is used to describe the formatting features of web pages. It defines the style, design and layout for your web pages.

For example, you can control the font color, font style, the spacing between paragraphs, how columns are sized and laid out, what background images or colors are used, layout designs etc. to be displayed in different screen sizes for different devices.

Most commonly, CSS is combined with the markup languages HTML or XHTML.

CSS was originated by **Håkon Wium Liein** 1994. Its first version came out in December 1996.

Version 2 i.e. CSS Level-2 came in May 1998 and builds on CSS1.

Definition

CSS is expanded as cascading style sheet which is used to describe look, define styles and format web pages across internet. CSS is always used in combination with HTML.

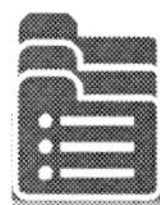

MEMORIZE

CSS is a way to provide style to HTML. Cascading Style Sheets (CSS) is a simple mechanism for adding style (e.g., fonts, colors, spacing) to Web documents. CSS describes how HTML elements are to be displayed on screen, paper, or in other media.

* **Let's discuss the various advantages and limitations of using CSS.**

6.2 ADVANTAGES OF CSS

The advantages of CSS are as follows:

1. **CSS saves a lot of time:** As CSS is used for providing style to HTML pages, you can write the CSS code only once for several HTML document. You can define a style for each HTML element and apply it to as many Web pages as you want.
2. **Separate CSS file:** External style sheets are stored in CSS files with extension .css.
3. **Easy maintenance of Code:** If you want to make changes in formatting feature of a web document, you just need to simply change the style, and all elements in all the web pages will be updated/changed automatically. This process is known as **global change/updation**.
4. **Vast features:** CSS has a much wider array of attributes than HTML, so you can give a far better look to your HTML page in comparison to HTML attributes.
5. **Global web standards:** As most of the HTML attributes have been deprecated and therefore it is recommended to use CSS.

6.3 LIMITATIONS OF CSS

Besides several advantages, CSS has a major problem of browser incompatibility. It shows a web page differently in different browsers.

For example, your webpage looks perfect in Mozilla may look different in Internet Explorer.

* Let's know the syntax of CSS.

The syntax of CSS consists of set of rules. These rules have 3 parts: a **selector**, a **property** and a **value**.

The syntax of CSS is:

Selector {property: value;}

For example,

p {color:blue;}		
p	{color:	blue;}
Selector	property	value

- The selector represents which HTML element you want to format.
- Property is the style attribute you want to change.
- Each property has a value which is to be set for formatting the HTML element.
- Property and value together are referred as **declaration**.

MEMORIZE

CSS property name and a value must be separated by a **colon (:)**.
Must be surrounded by a pair of **curly brackets ({})**.
Always ends with a **semicolon (;)**.

6.4 METHODS OF USING CSS

There are three different methods of applying CSS to an HTML document which are given below:

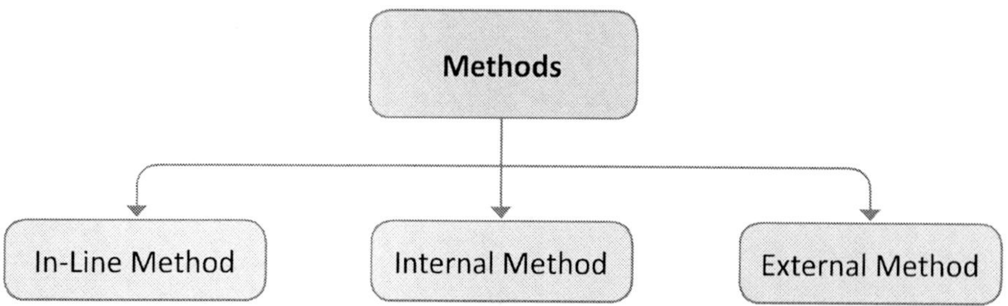

Figure 6.1: Methods of using CSS

* **Let's explain all these methods one by one with example.**

6.4.1 In-Line Method

In-line method, CSS contains the formatting features or CSS properties in the body section attached with element. This kind of style is specified within an HTML tag using style attribute.

Note: Always remember, in inline method, style attribute is used with html element.

For example,

- <h1 style="color:red; font-size:30px; "> Using Inline Method </h1>
- <body style="background-color:pink; color:blue;">Using Inline Method</p>

Program 6.1: Create HTML document that will use CSS property to apply the red background color.

```
<html>
<head>
<title>Example</title>
</head>
<body style="background-color:pink;">
<pre>The harder you work for something,
   the greater you'll feel when you achieve it.</pre>
</body>
</html>
```

CSS property used in body tag

Save the html file with name "Example" and open it through web browser.

Output of the program is given below:

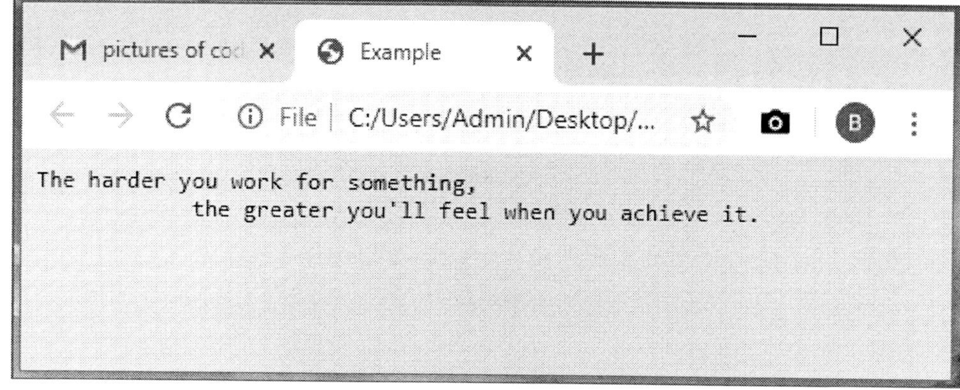

Figure 6.2: Using in-line method for setting background color

Now, consider the other program, where the font properties are set to paragraph.

Program 6.2: Create a web page that will set some font properties to a paragraph.

```
<html>
    <head>
        <title>Inline CSS</title>
    </head>
        <body style="background-color: pink;">
        <p style = "color: blue;
            font-size:50px;
            font-style:italic;
            text-align:center;>
The harder you work for something, the greater you'll feel when you achieve it.

        </p>
    </body>
</html>
```

CSS font properties used in <p> tag

Output of the program is given below:

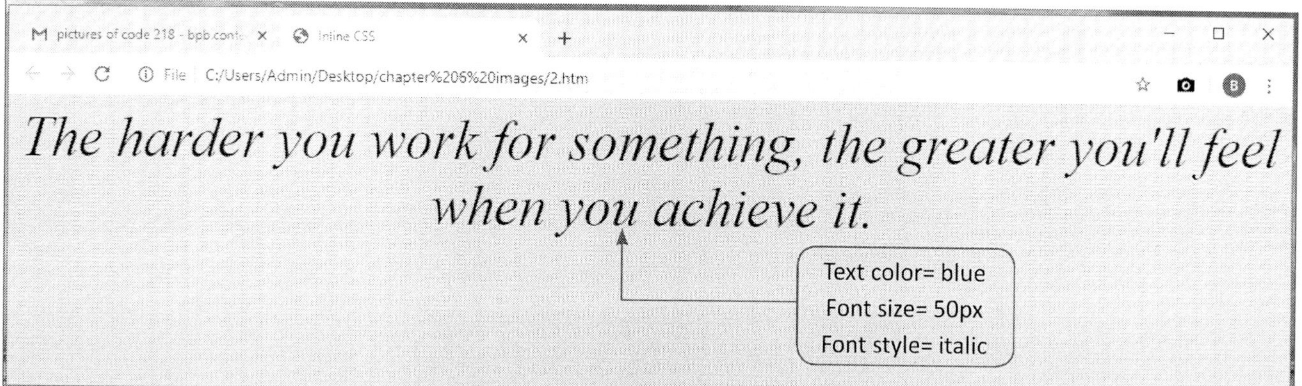

Figure 6.3: Using in-line method for setting Font property

MEMORIZE

Inline method is also known as **embedded method**. In in-line method, style keyword is used as an attribute within the tag for which the CSS property is to be set.

6.4.2 Internal Method

Internal method is also known as **Embedded CSS**. This method can be used when the CSS properties are to be used for a single HTML document. In this case, the CSS property set should be written within the HTML file in the head section i.e. the CSS is embedded within the HTML file.

Program 6.3: Create a web page that will internal method to embed CSS code.

```
<html>
<head>
<title>Example</title>
<style type="text/css">   ← Internal method used in head section
body {background-color: #0000FF ;}
p {font-style:italic;
   font-size:60px;}
</style>
</head>
<body>
<p> Infuse your life with action. Don't wait for it to happen. Make it happen.
</p>
</body>
</html>
```

Output of the program is given below:

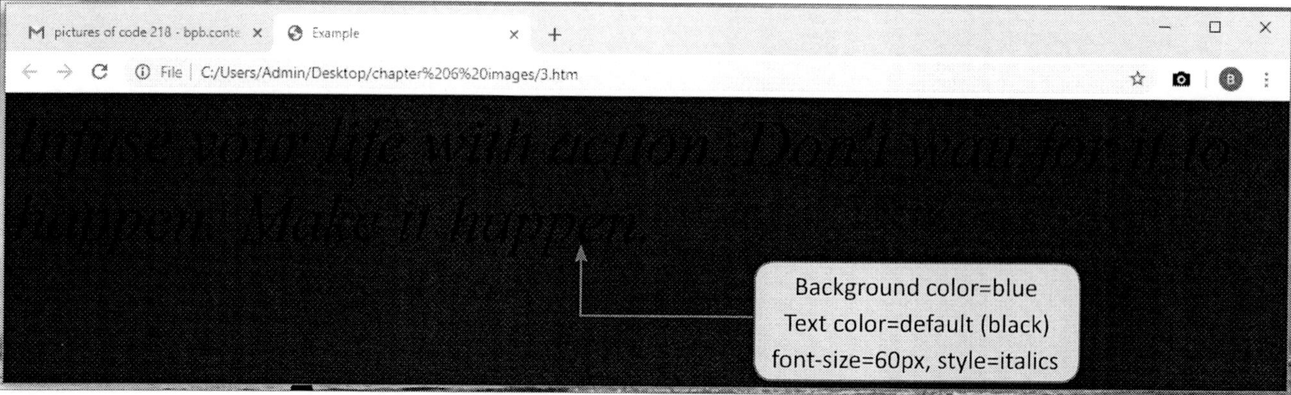

Figure 6.4: Using internal method for setting font property

MEMORIZE

In internal method, style is used as a tag within <head> section and all properties are set inside style tag.

6.4.3 External Method

This is the method where a separate CSS file is linked with HTML document. The CSS file contains the code related to formatting features or CSS properties which are to be used for various HTML tags. This file must be saved with .CSS extension. The other file is a normal HTML file with an attribute **link** that will link the CSS file.

Extra Byte

Any text editor can be used for external style sheet which must be saved with .css extension. It should not contain any HTML tag.

Syntax of linking CSS file with HTML document is:

```
<link rel="stylesheet" type="text/css"  href="URL of CSS file">
```

In this syntax,

- **link** tag is used to link the external style sheet with the html webpage.
- **rel** defines that the linked resource is a style sheet document.
- **href** attribute is used to specify the location of the external style sheet file.

For example,

```
<link rel="stylesheet" type="text/css" href="style.css">
```

Here,

- rel refers that the linked document is a type of stylesheet.
- type of the document is css.
- href is the name of the linked file named here as style.css.

Program 6.4: Create a web page that will use external method of using CSS file.

Example.html (Linked to →)	Style.css

<html>
<head>
<title>My document</title>
<link rel="stylesheet" type="text/css" href="style.css">
</head>
<body>
<p> Good, better, best. Never let it rest. </p>
 	
</body>
</html>
	body {
	background-color: #FF0000;
	}
	
	p {
	font-style:italic;
	font-size:50px;
	color:pink;
	}

This link will display the layout from the CSS file in the browser when displaying the HTML file.

In this program, two files are created namely example.html and style.css. The file example.html has a link to style.css that contains CSS properties.

Output of the program is given below:

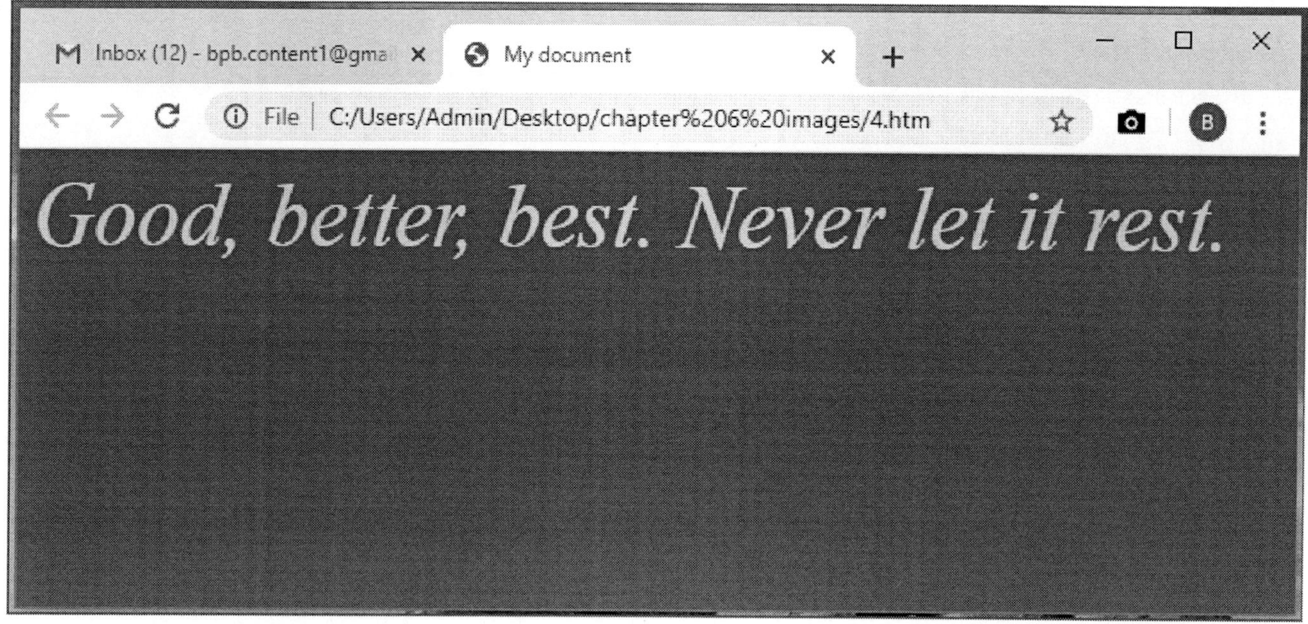

Figure 6.5: Using external method for setting background color and font styles

MEMORIZE

In external method, a separate CSS file is created where all CSS properties are set and then set a link to HTML file by using link tag.

Check Your Progress

Answer the following questions.

1. Give one advantage of CSS.
2. Which attribute is used to specify the location of the external style sheet file?
3. Which tag is used to link the external style sheet with the html webpage?

6.5 CASCADING ORDER

When you are using several properties for one HTML element in different methods of using CSS, then the style sheet cascade in the following order:

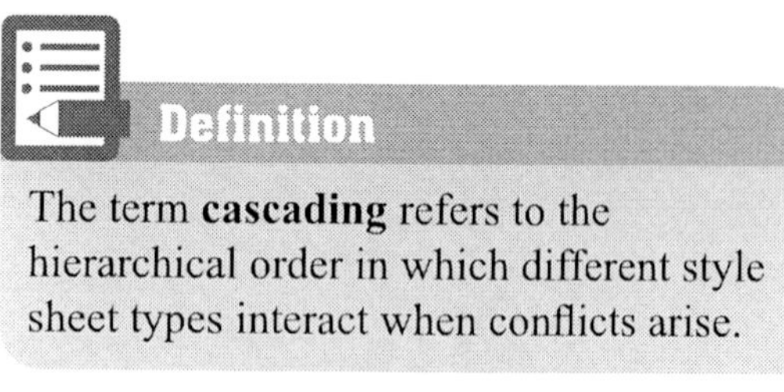

Definition

The term **cascading** refers to the hierarchical order in which different style sheet types interact when conflicts arise.

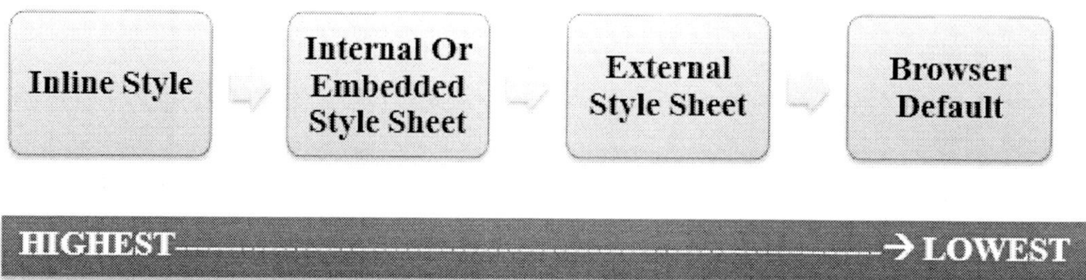

1. Inline Style (**Highest priority**)
2. Internal or Embedded Style Sheet
3. External Style Sheet
4. Browser Default (**Lowest priority**)

This list could be summed up into one basic rule: If two styles come into conflict, the last one used will take precedence. But inline styles have the higher precedence over all other style sheets.

The reasons behind this are:

1. Inline styles are always placed in the body of the HTML document, while embedded style sheets are always placed in the head of the HTML document. As a result, inline styles are always the last ones used and therefore take precedence.
2. The browser treats all external style sheets as occurring before internal style sheets, regardless of where the link is placed.

For example,
If your **linked style sheet** sets that all paragraphs have a **green** font, but your **embedded styles** set that all paragraphs have a **blue** font. Which color will it be? In this case, your paragraphs will have a blue font as the embedded style sheet occurs after the linked style sheet, and therefore has a higher priority.

But, if you're **linked style sheet** sets that all paragraphs are **bold**, and your **embedded style sheet** sets that all paragraphs are green, all your paragraphs will be both **bold** and **green**. These two rules do not conflict with each other, and are therefore both used.

Extra Byte

The !important Rule:
The important rule is a way to override the general rule of cascading order. If two styles come into conflict in the same element, and one has the !important rule assigned to it, that one will be used.
For example,

```
p { font-color: black !important; }

p { font-color: blue; }
```

Even though the blue font color is placed further down, the black will be used in a conflict because it uses the !important rule.

Check Your Progress

Fill in the blanks.

1. ____________ style sheets have a higher precedence of cascading over all other style sheet.
2. The term ____________ refers to the hierarchical order in which different style sheet types interact when conflicts arise.

6.6 CSS COMMENTS

Comments are used to explain the code or for documentation purpose which are ignored by the browser. In other words, those statements are not executed and displayed by the browser on a web page.

The symbols used for CSS comments are /* and */.

For example,

/* This is a comment */

Now, the above statement will not be recognized by the browser because it is enclosed in /* and */ symbols. Therefore, the statement will not be executed and thus ignored.

If there are more than one name for font-family, then always enclosed each font in double quotes like "Times New Roman", "Arial" etc.

6.7 CSS PROPERTIES

* **Let's discuss various CSS properties for decorating and aligning text in CSS files.**

6.7.1 Working with Font Property

FONT: The font properties are used to set font size, font style, font weight.

The various font properties are:

Table 6.1: Font properties

Property Name	Description
font-family	It is used to apply prioritized list of fonts in a web page.
font-style	It is used to set the font style in normal, italic or oblique.
font-size	It is used to set the font size.
font-variant	It is used to set the text in normal or small-caps variants of a font.
font-weight	It is used to describe how bold or "heavy" a font should be presented.

* **Let's discuss all these font properties in detail.**

font-family: This property is used to give a list of fonts to be applied on a web page. If the first font given in the list is not installed in your computer system, then the browser will look for the next font given in the list and so on.

For example,

To set the font family for a paragraph, the list can be given in CSS file as:

p {font-family: "Forte", "Arial", "Comic", "Sans-Serif", "Times New Roman";}

Program 6.5: Create a web page that will use font family property.

Example.html

```
<html >
<head>
<title>Font Properties </title>
<link rel="stylesheet" href="style.css" type="text/
css">
</head>
<body>
<h1> Global Warming</h1>
<p> Global warming is a long-term rise in the average
temperature of the Earth's climate system, an aspect
of climate change shown by temperature measurements
and by multiple effects of the warming.</p>
</body>
</html>
```

Style.css

```
h1 {font-family: "Comic",
"Sans-serif","Times New
Roman";}
p {font-family: "Courier",
"Comic sans-serif","Times New
Roman";}
```

Output of the program is given below:

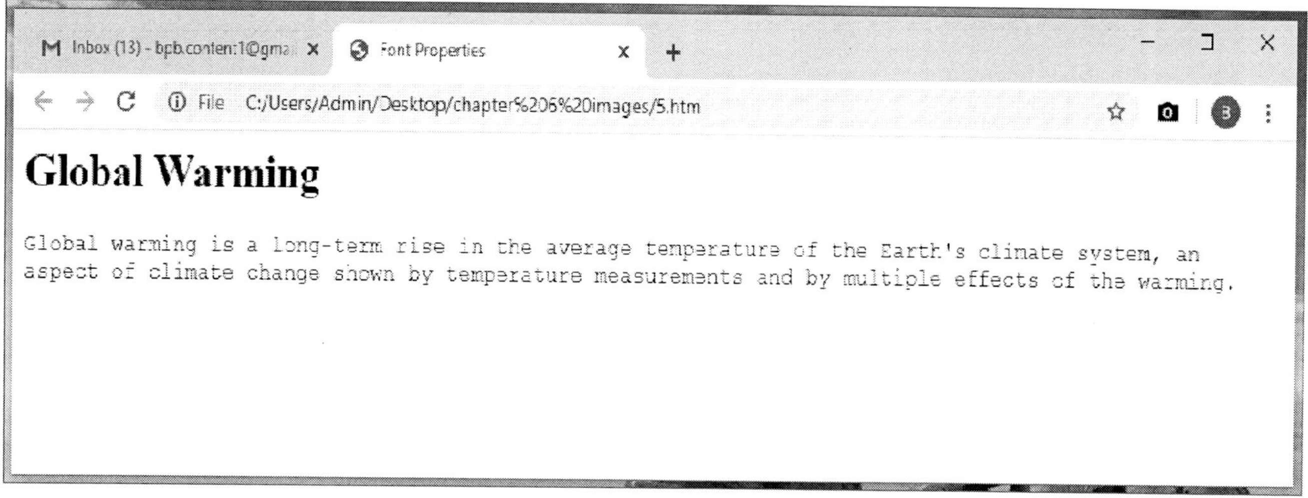

Figure 6.6: Displaying Font family property

font-style: By using this property, you can display the text either in normal, italic or oblique for a chosen font.

For example,

To set the font style for headings, the program fragment can be written as:

```
h1 {font-family: "Arial", "Verdana", "Sans-Serif"; font-style: oblique;}
h2 {font-family: "Times New Roman", "Serif"; font-style: italic;}
```

Program 6.6: Create a web page that will use font style property.

Example.html	Style.css
<html > <head> <title>Font Properties </title> <link rel="stylesheet" href="style.css" type="text/css"> </head> <body> <h1> Save trees, save life</h1> <h2> Health is Wealth</h2> </body> </html>	h1 {font-family: "Arial", "Verdana", "Sans-serif"; font-style: oblique;} h2 {font-family: "Times New Roman", "Serif"; font-style: italic;}

Output of the program is given below:

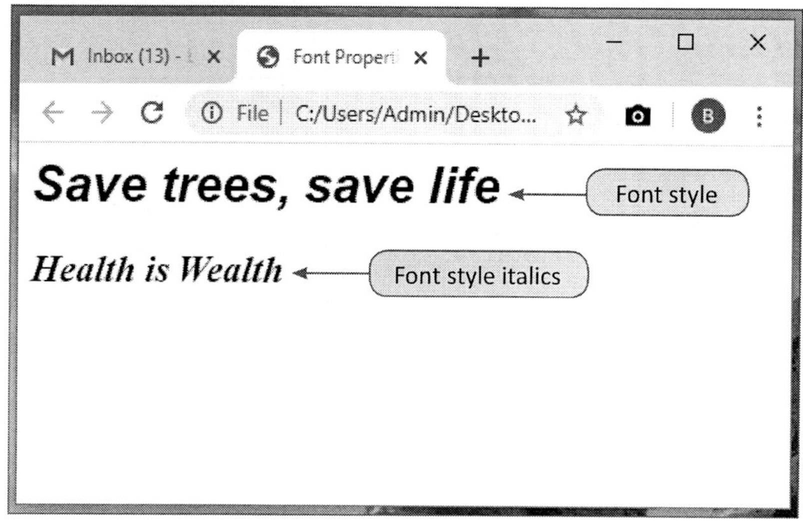

Figure 6.7: Displaying font-style property

font-variant: This property is used to select normal or small-caps variants of a font. A small-caps font displays the smaller sized capitalized letters (upper case) instead of lower-case letters. If font-variant is set to small-caps and no small-caps font is available the browser will most likely show the text in uppercase instead.

For example,

The program fragment for using font-variant property can be written as:

```
h1 {font-variant: small-caps;}
h2 {font-variant: normal;}
```

Program 6.7: Create a web page that will use font-variant property.

Example.html

```
<html >
<head>
<title>Font Properties </title>
<link rel="stylesheet" href="style.css"
type="text/css">
</head>
<body>
<h1> Save trees, save life</h1>
<h2> Health is Wealth</h2>
</body>
</html>
```

Style.css

```
h1 {font-variant: small-caps;}
h2 {font-variant: normal;}
```

Output of the program is given below:

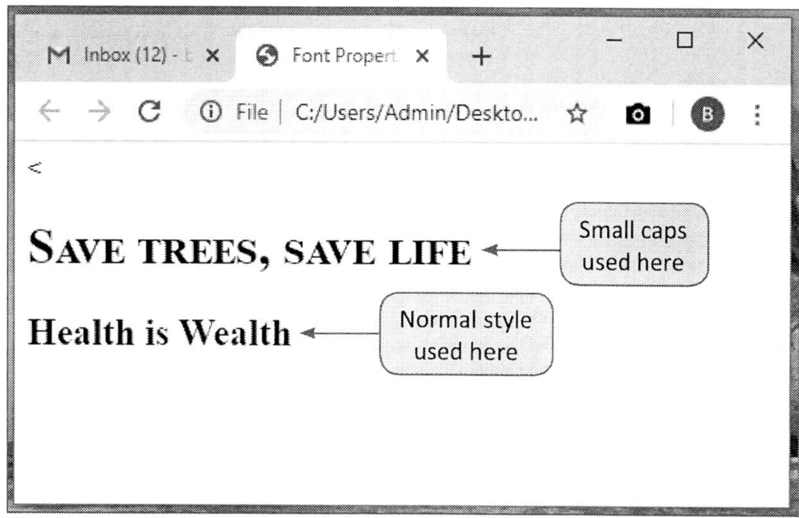

Figure 6.8: Displaying font-variant property

font-Weight: This property will display the text in bold whose number is specified between 100-900(in hundreds). It actually describes the weight of a font. A font can either be normal or bold.

For example,

To set the font-weight as bold and normal for a table data and paragraph resp., the program fragment can be written as:

```
p {font-family: arial, verdana, sans-serif; font-weight: bold;}
th {font-family: courier,arial, verdana, sans-serif; font-weight: bold;}
td {font-family: arial, verdana, sans-serif; font-weight: normal;}
```

Program 6.8: Create a web page that will use font-weight property.

Example.html	Style.css

`<html >`
`<head>`
`<title>Font Properties </title>`
`<link rel="stylesheet" href="style.css" type="text/css">`
`</head>`
`<body>`
`<p> Student details</p>`
`<table border=2 width="30%">`
`<tr>`
`<th>Roll No</th>`
`<th> Name</th>`
`</tr>`
	`p {font-family: "arial", "verdana", "sans-serif"; font-weight: bold;}`
	`th {font-family: "courier","arial", "verdana", "sans-serif"; font-weight: bold;}`
	`td {font-family: "arial", "verdana", "sans-serif"; font-weight: normal;}`

```
<tr>
<td>1</td>
<td> Palvi</td>
</tr>
<tr>
<td>2</td>
<td>Muneesh</td>
</tr>
</table>
</body>
</html>
```

Output of the program is given below:

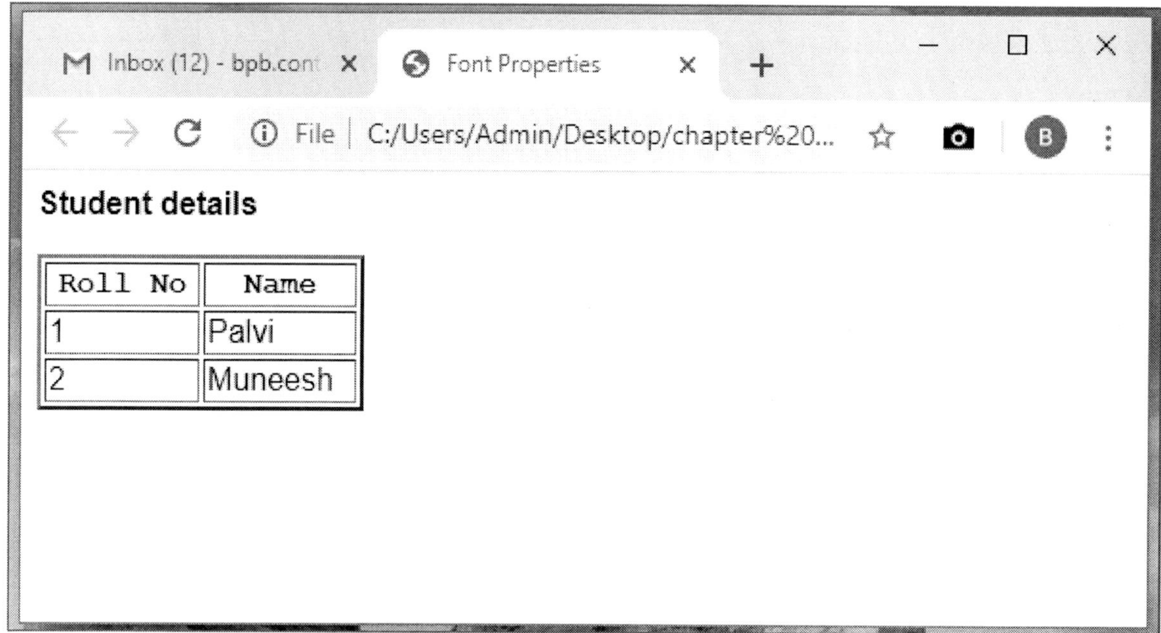

Figure 6.9: Displaying font-weight property

font-size: The font-size property is used to set the size of a font. You can define the font size either in pixel or in percentage (%).

For example,

To set the font size of a paragraph, a program fragment can be written as:

```
p {font-size: 10px;}
```

* **Let's combine all font properties in a single program and see the result.**

Program 6.9: Create a web page that will use all font properties in a single CSS file.

Example.html

```
<html >
<head>
<title>Font Properties </title>
<link   rel=“stylesheet”   href=“style.css”
type=“text/css”>
</head>
<body>
<p> Font properties used here</p>
<h1> Global Warming</h1>
<h2> Save trees, Save life</h2>
</body>
</html>
```

Style.css

```
p {font-family: “Times New Roman”,
“arial”, “comic sans-serif”;
   font-size:50px;}
h1 {font-weight:normal;
   font-size:30px;}
h2{font-variant:bold;
   font style:italic;}
```

Output of the program is given below:

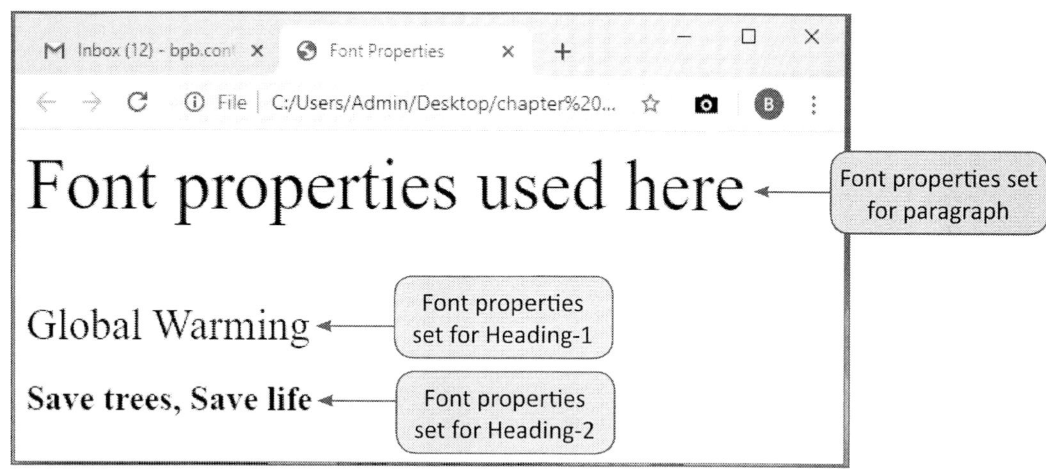

Figure 6.10: Displaying font-size property

6.7.2 Working with Text Property

TEXT **Properties:** Text properties are used to decorate your data by aligning the text, specifying line spacing, text indentation and display the text in uppercase, lowercase letters or making the first letter capital.

The various text properties are:

Table 6.2: Text properties

Property Name	Description
text-indent	It specifies the indentation to the first line of the text.
text-align	It sets the alignment of the text.
text-decoration	It adds effects to the text such as underline, overline, line-through, blink effects.

Property Name	Description
letter-spacing	It provides a specified space between characters.
word-spacing	It provides a specified space between words.
text-transform	It displays the text in uppercase, lowercase or in capitals.

* **Let's discuss all these text properties in detail.**

text-indent: This property sets the indentation to the first line of the text with respect to browser Window. The indent value is to be set in **pixels**.

For example,

The program fragment to apply text-indent property is:

```
p {text-indent: 60px;}
```

Program 6.10: Create a web page that will use text-indent property.

Example.html	Style.css
<html > <head> <title>Font Properties </title> <link rel="stylesheet" href="style.css" type="text/css"> </head> <body> <p> The full form of CSS is cascading Style Sheet</p> </body> </html>	p {font-family: "arial", "verdana", "sans-serif"; font-weight: bold;} p { text-indent: 100px; }

Output of the program is given below:

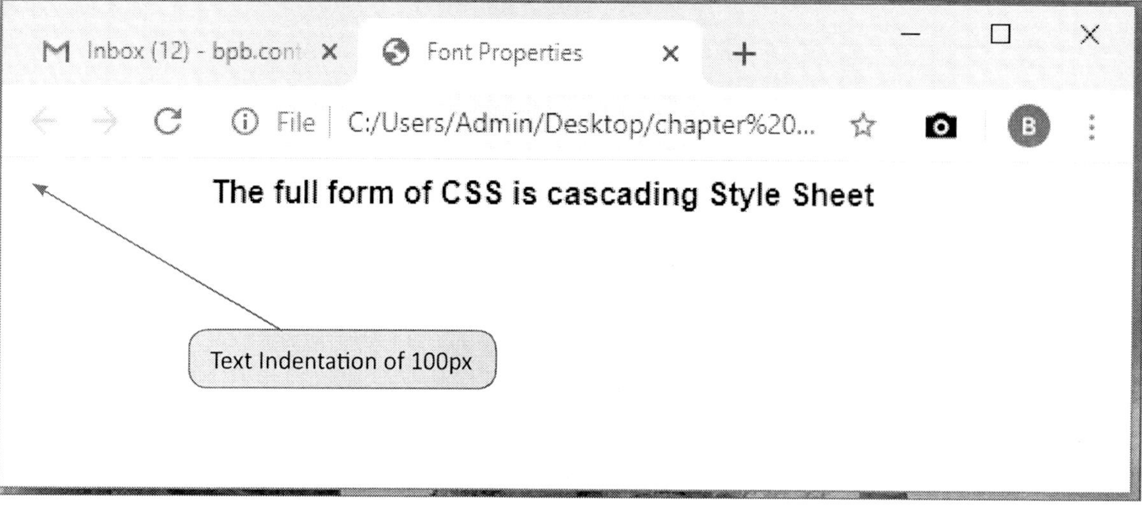

Figure 6.11: Displaying color property

text-align: This property is used to align the text either in **left**, **center**, **right** or **justify**. The value justify will stretch each line so that both the right and left margins are straight.

For example,

The program fragment to apply text-align property on a table is:

```
th {
 text-align: right;
}
 td {
 text-align: center;
}
```

Program 6.11: Create a web page that will use text align property.

<table>
<tr><th>Example.html</th><th>Style.css</th></tr>
<tr><td><pre>
<html >
<head>
<title>Font Properties </title>
<link rel="stylesheet" href="style.css" type="text/css">
</head>
<body>
<p> Student details</p>
<table border=2 width="30%">
<tr>
<th>Roll No</th>
<th> Name</th>
</tr>
<tr>
<td>1</td>
<td> Palvi</td>
</tr>
<tr>
<td>2</td>
<td>Muneesh</td>
</tr>
</table>
</body>
</html>
</pre></td><td><pre>
th {
 text-align: right;
}
 td {
 text-align: center;
}
</pre></td></tr>
</table>

Output of the program is given below:

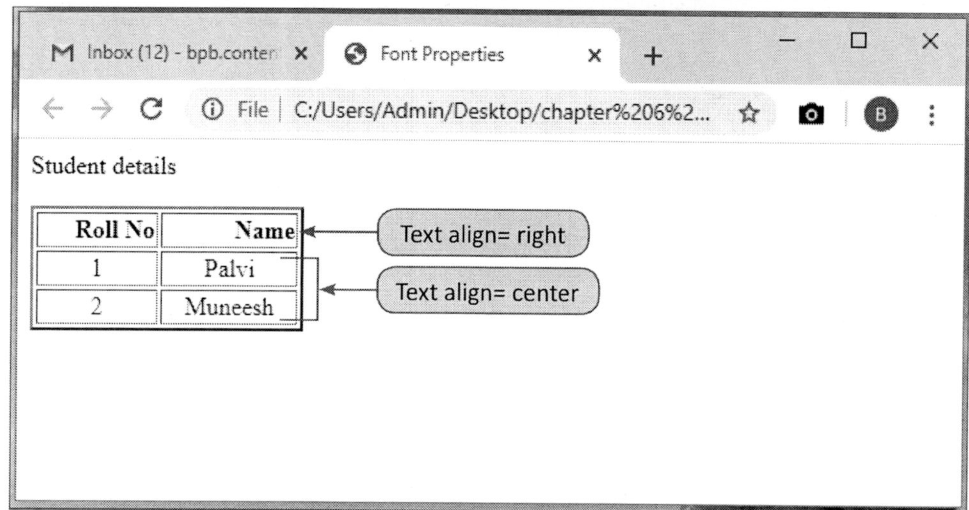

Figure 6.12: Displaying text-align property

text-decoration: By using this property, you can make the text underlined or have a line through or above the text.

For example,

To set the headings in different underline format, the statements can be written as:

```
h1 {
 text-decoration: underline;
 }
h2 {
 text-decoration: overline;
}
h3 {
 text-decoration: line-through;
}
```

Program 6.12: Create a web page that will use text decoration property.

<table>
<tr><th>Example.html</th><th>Style.css</th></tr>
<tr><td>

```
<html >
<head>
<title>Font Properties </title>
<link  rel="stylesheet"  href="style.css"
type="text/css">
</head>
<body>
<p> List of operating systems</p>
<h1> Windows Operating System</h1>
<h2> Unix Operating System</h2>
<h3>Linux Operating System</h3>
</body>
</html>
```

</td><td>

```
p{text-align:center;
font-weight:bold;
font-size:20px;}
h1 {
 text-decoration: underline;
 }
h2 {
 text-decoration: overline;
}
h3 {
 text-decoration: line-through;
}
```

</td></tr>
</table>

Output of the program is given below:

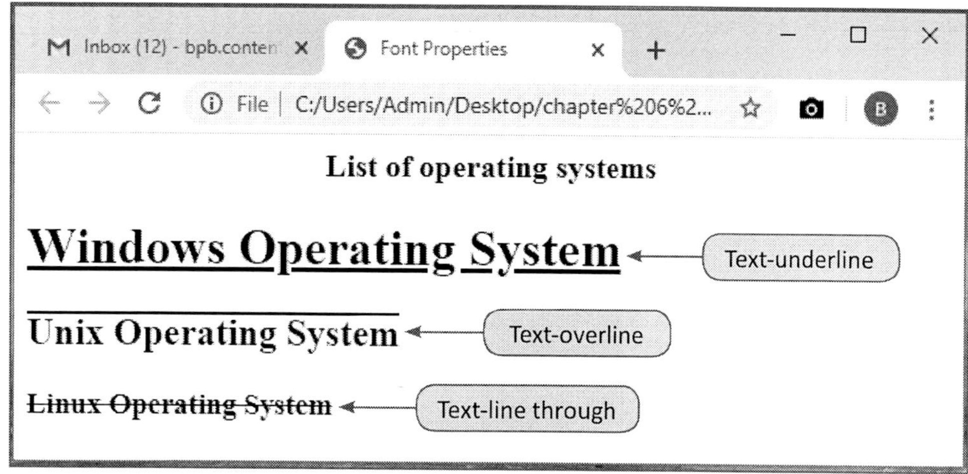

Figure 6.13: Displaying text-decoration property

letter-spacing: This property specifies the spacing between the characters. The value of the property is simply the desired width.

For example,

To set the letter spacing for different levels of headings, a program fragment can be written as:

```
h1 {
 letter-spacing: 6px;
 }

 h2  {
 letter-spacing: 3px;
 }
```

Program 6.13: Create a web page that will use letter spacing property.

<table>
<tr><th>Example.html</th><th>Style.css</th></tr>
<tr><td>

```
<html >
<head>
<title>Font Properties </title>
<link  rel="stylesheet"  href="style.css"
type="text/css">
</head>
<body>
<p> List of operating systems</p>
<h1> Windows Operating System</h1>
<h2> Unix Operating System</h2>
<h3>Linux Operating System</h3>
</body>
</html>
```

</td><td>

```
h1 {
 letter-spacing: 6px;
 }
 h2  {
 letter-spacing: 3px;
 }
```

</td></tr>
</table>

Output of the program is given below:

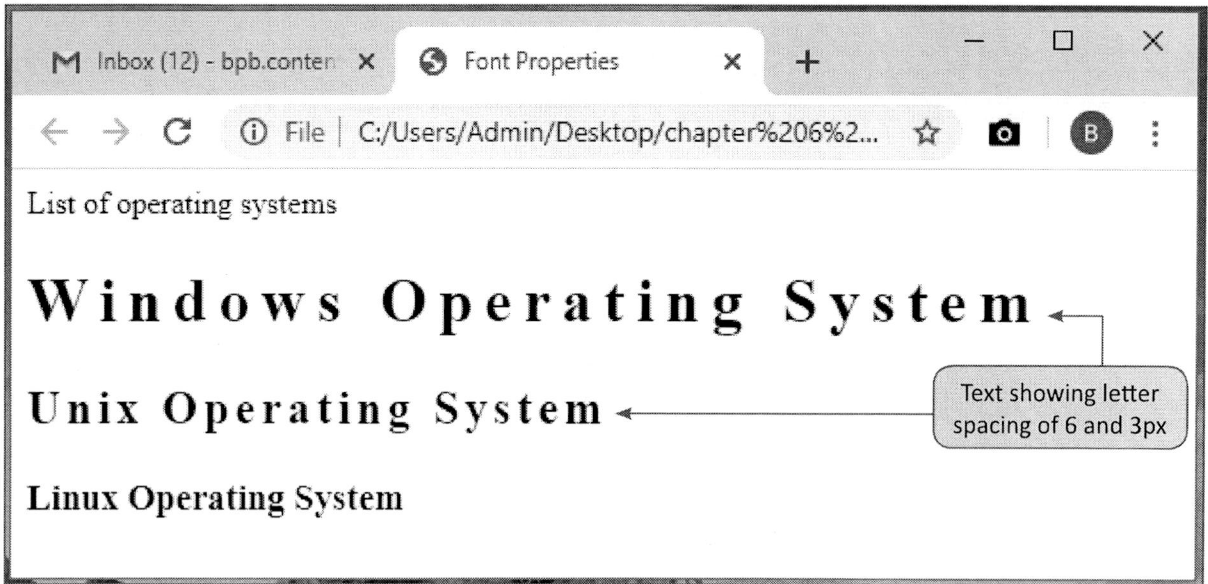

Figure 6.14: Displaying letter-spacing property

word -spacing: This property specifies the spacing between the words. The value of the property is simply the desired width. The word-spacing property **increases** or **decreases** the white space between words.

For example,

To set the letter spacing for different levels of headings, a program fragment can be written as:

```
h1 {
 word-spacing: 6px;
 }


 h2  {
 word-spacing: 3px;
 }
```

text-transform: The text-transform property controls the capitalization of a text. The four possible values for text formation are:

- **Capitalize:** It capitalizes the first letter of each word.
  For example: "computer applications" will be displayed as "Computer Applications".
- **Uppercase:** It converts all letters to capital letters.
  For example: "computer applications" will be displayed as "COMPUTER APPLICATIONS".
- **Lowercase:** It Converts all letters to small letters.
  For example: "COMPUTER APPLICATIONS" will be displayed as "computer applications".
- **None:** No transformations - the text is presented as it appears in the HTML code.

For example,

The program fragment for setting text-formation can be written as:

```
h1 {
 text-transform: capitalize;
}
h2 {
 text-transform: uppercase;
}
```

Program 6.14: Create a web page that will use text transform property.

Example.html	Style.css

`<html >`
`<head>`
`<title>Font Properties </title>`
`<link rel="stylesheet" href="style.css" type="text/css">`
`</head>`
`<body>`
`<p> List of Hardware Devices</p>`
`<h1> Visual display unit</h1>`
`<h2> Keyboard</h2>`
 	
`</body>`
`</html>`
	`h1 {`
	` text-transform: capitalize;`
	`}`
	`h2 {`
	` text-transform: uppercase;`
	`}`

Output of the program is given below:

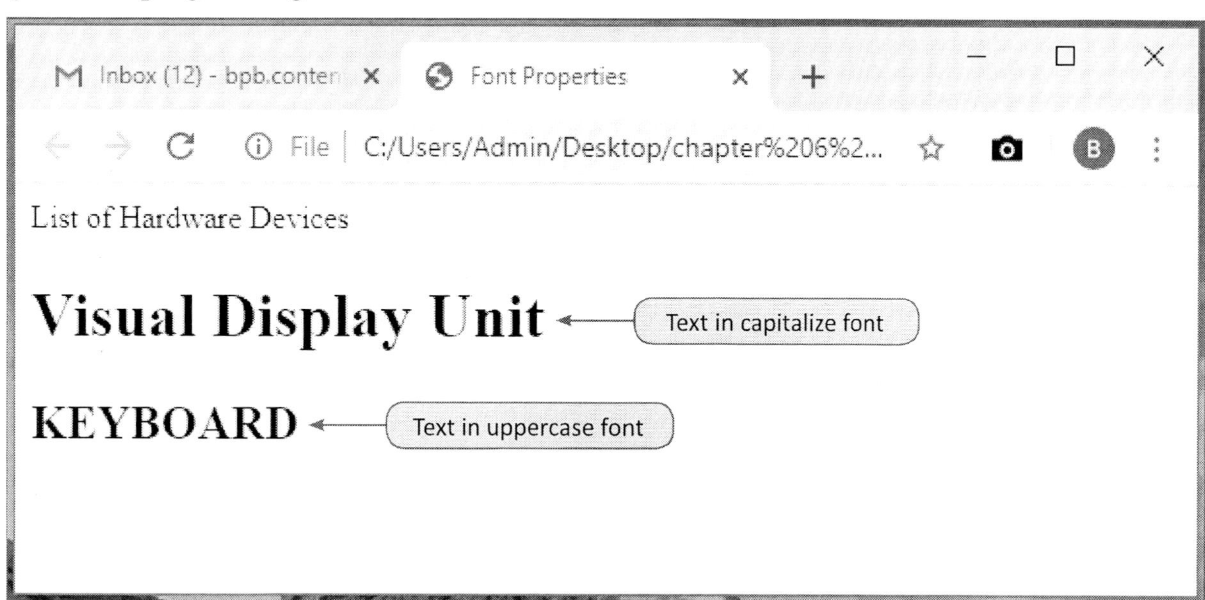

Figure 6.15: Displaying text-transform property

MEMORIZE

Text-transform property is used to display the characters either in capital letters, lower letters or the words with first letter capital only.

background properties: CSS also provides various background properties for a web page.

You can enter the values for the CSS background property in any order.

The various background properties are:

Table 6.3: Background properties

Property Name	Description
color	It specifies the color of the text.
background-color	It sets the background color of a web page.
background-image	It inserts the image as a background of a web page.
background-repeat	It provides a specified space between characters.

* **Let's discuss all these properties in detail.**

color: This property is used to set the color of a text to be displayed in browser. The property name is "color".

For example,

To set the foreground color of the text, the program fragment can be written as:

```
h1 {
 color: #ff0000;
}
```

It is to be noted here that colors can be entered as hexadecimal values as in the example above (#ff0000), or you can use the names of the colors ("red") or RGB-values (rgb(255,0,0)).

background-color: This property sets the background color of a web page. To change the background color of an entire page, the background-color property should be applied to the <body> tag.

However, you can also apply background colors to other elements such as text, tables etc.

For example,

To apply different background colors to <body> and <h1> tags, the program fragment can be written as:

```
body {
 background-color: #FFCC60;
}
h1 {
 color: #990011;
 background-color: #FC9004;
}
```

Program 6.15: Create a web page that will use different foreground and background color of the text.

Example.html	Style.css

`<html >`
`<head>`
`<title>Font Properties </title>`
`<link rel="stylesheet" href="style.css" type="text/css">`
`</head>`
`<body>`
`<h1> Hypertext Markup Language</h1>`
`<h2> Cascading Style Sheet</h2>`
 	
`</body>`
`</html>`
	`body {`
	` background-color: #FFCC60;`
	`}`
	`h1 {`
	` color: blue;`
	` background-color: dimgray;`
	`}`
	`h2`
	`{`
	` color: pink;`
	` background-color: red;`

Output of the program is given below:

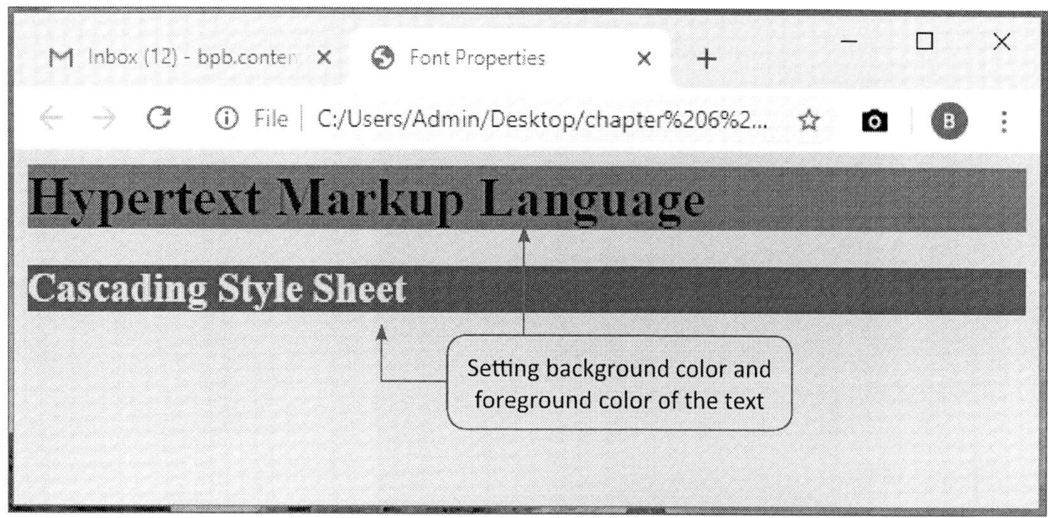

Figure 6.16: Displaying foreground and background color property

background-image: The background-image property is used to insert a background image in a web page. To insert the image of the butterfly as a background image for a web page, simply apply the background-image property to <body> and specify the location of the image.

For example,

To insert an image as a background, the program fragment can be written as:

```
body {
 background-color: #FFCC66;
 background-image: url("butterfly.gif ");
}
h1 {
 color: #990000;
 background-color: #FC9804;
}
```

Program 6.16: Create a web page that will insert image as a background.

Example.html	Style.css

<html >
<head>
<title>Font Properties </title>
<link rel="stylesheet" href="style.css" type="text/css">
</head>
<body>
<h1> The fastest butterflies can fly up to 30 miles per hour.</h1>
<h2> The butterfly does migrate to avoid cold weather.</h2>
 	
</body>
</html>
	body {
	background-color: #FFCC66;
	background-image: url("butterfly.jpg");
	}
	h1 {
	color: #990000;
	background-color: #FC9804;
	}
	
	h2
	{
	color: pink;
	background-color: red;

Output of the program is given below:

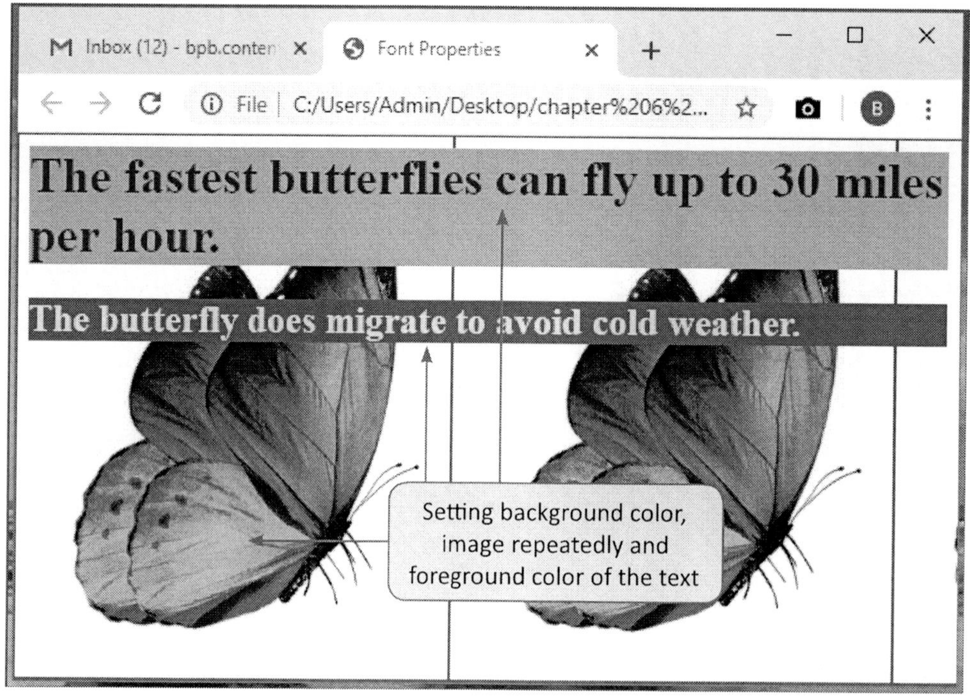

Figure 6.17: Displaying image repeatedly on a web page

Repeat background image [background-repeat]: As you have seen in the example above, that by default, the image of the butterfly was repeated both **horizontally** and **vertically** to cover the entire screen. But this pattern can be controlled by using repeat background property.

The four different values for background-repeat are as follows:

Table 6.4: Values for background-repeat

Value	Description
background-repeat: repeat-x	The image is repeated horizontally.
background-repeat: repeat-y	The image is repeated vertically.
background-repeat: repeat	The image is repeated both horizontally and vertically.
background-repeat: no-repeat	The image is not repeated.

For example,

To avoid repetition of a background image the following code can be used:

```
body {
 background-color: #FFCC66;
 background-image: url(“butterfly.gif “);
 background-repeat: no-repeat;
}
h1 {
 color: #990000;
 background-color: #FC9804;
}
```

Program 6.17: Create a web page that will use no-repeat property.

Example.html

```
<html >
<head>
<title>Font Properties </title>
<link  rel=“stylesheet”  href=“style.css” type=“text/css”>
</head>
<body>
<h1> The fastest butterflies can fly up to 30 miles per hour.</h1>
<h2> The butterfly does migrate to avoid cold weather.</h2>

</body>
</html>
```

Style.css

```
body {
 background-color: #FFCC66;
 background-image: url(“butterfly.jpg”);
background-repeat:no-repeat;
}
h1 {
 color: #990000;
 background-color: #FC9804;
}

h2
{
 color: pink;
 background-color: red;
```

Output of the program is given below:

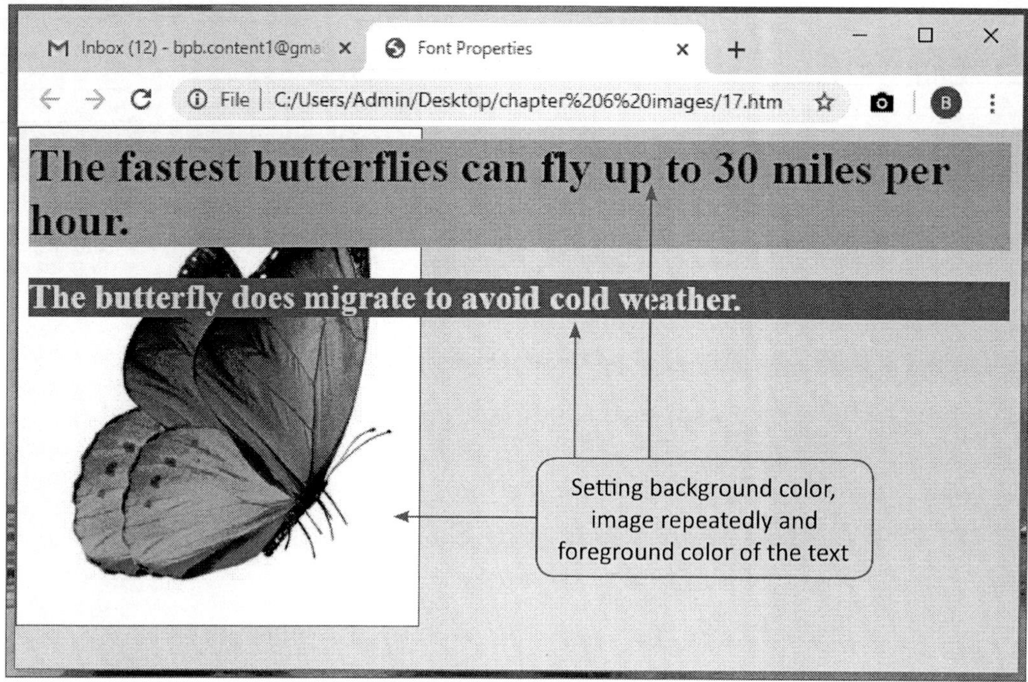

Figure 6.18: Displaying image only once on a web page

MEMORIZE

Background-color property is used to set the background color of a web page. It is to be remembered that URL of an image must be given with background-image property otherwise an image cannot be located.

* **Let's combine all background properties in a single program and see the result.**

Combining all properties of background

Program 6.18: Create a web page that will combine all background properties.

Example.html	Style.css

`<html >`
`<head>`
`<title>Font Properties </title>`
`<link rel="stylesheet" href="style.css" type="text/css">`
`</head>`
`<body>`
`<p> Everything You Need to Know About Computer Hardware</p>`
`<ol>`
`<li> Motherboard`
`<li>Central Processing Unit (CPU)`
	`body {`
	`background-color: #FFCC66;`
	`background-image: url("monitor.jpg");`
	`}`
	`p{font-weight:bold;`
	`font-size:50px;`
	`}`
	`li {`
	`color: #990000;`
	`background-color: #FC9804;`
	`font-size:20px;`
	`}`

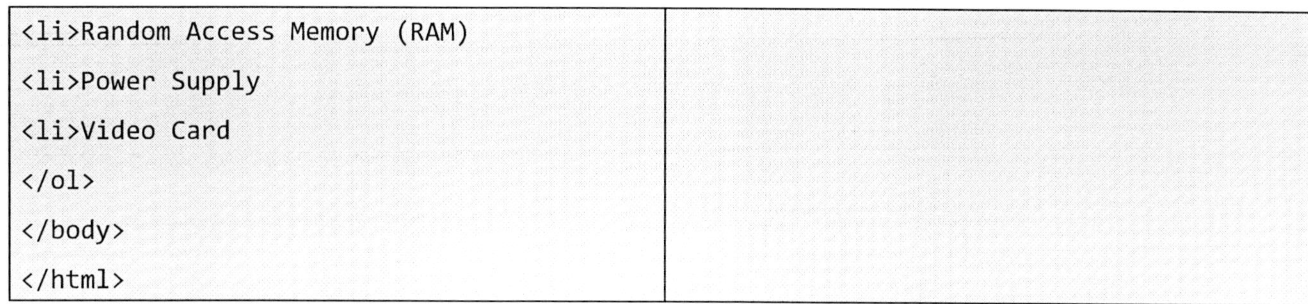

```
<li>Random Access Memory (RAM)
<li>Power Supply
<li>Video Card
</ol>
</body>
</html>
```

Output of the program is given below:

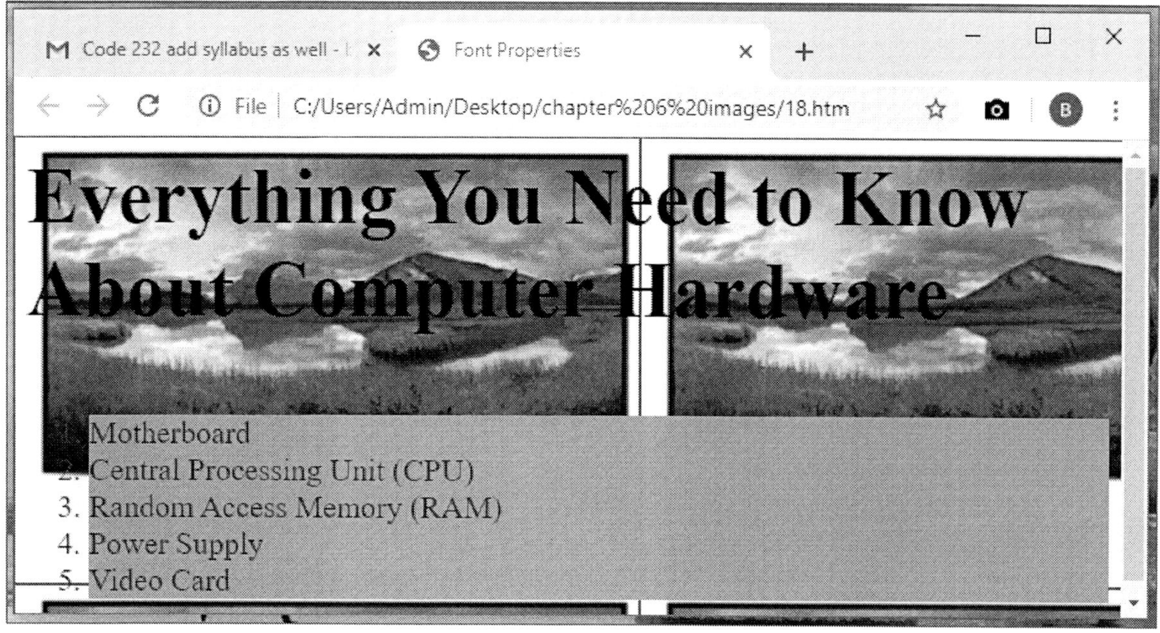

Figure 6.19: Displaying all background properties

Check Your Progress

State whether the following statements are True or False.

1. The background-image property is used to insert a background image in a web page.
2. Background-image property is used to set the background color of a web page.
3. Text-transform property is used to display the characters either in capital letters, lower letters or the words with first letter capital only.

6.7.4 Working with border property

CSS border property is used to define the border style, color and size of the border or outline of an element. The various border properties are:

Table 6.5: Border properties

Property Name	Description
border-color	It specifies the color of a border.
border-style	It specifies whether a border should be solid, dashed line, double line, or one of the other possible values.
border-width	It specifies the width of a border.

* **Let's discuss all these properties in detail.**

border-color: This property allows you to change the color of the border of an element.

For example,

p { border-color:red;} /* Sets all border in red color */

However, you can change the color of four borders individually i.e. bottom, left, top and right sides of an element by using the given properties:

Table 6.6: Individual border-color Property

Property	Description
border-bottom-color	It changes the color of bottom border.
border-top-color	It changes the color of top border.
border-left-color	It changes the color of left border.
border-right-color	It changes the color of right border.

Program 6.19: Create a web page that will use all color properties of border.

Example.html

```
<html>
   <head>
      <link rel="stylesheet" href="style.
css" type="text/css">
<body>
 <p >
  This example is showing all borders in
different colors.
  </p>


<H1>
This example is showing all borders in green
color only.
</H1>
</body>
</html>
```

Style.css

```
p{
border:1px solid;
border-bottom-color:green;
border-top-color:Red;
border-left-color:Black;
border-right-color:Blue;
}
H1 {
border:1px solid;
border-color:Green;
}
```

Output of the program is given below:

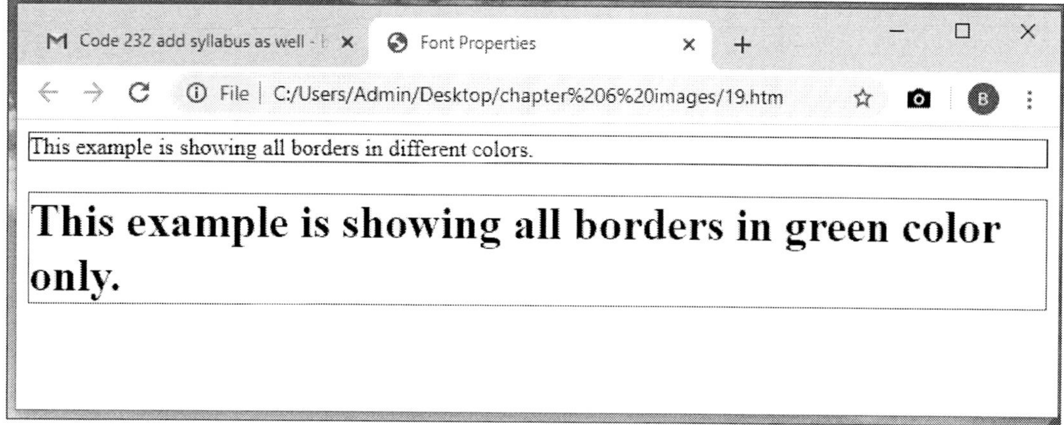

Figure 6.20: Color properties of border

border-style: This property allows you to select one of the following styles of border.

For example,

p {border-style: solid;}   /* This will set thick border of the paragraph. */

Table 6.7: Values for border-style

Value	Description
None	No border. (Equivalent of border-width:0;)
Solid	Border is a single solid line.
Dotted	Border is a series of dots.
Dashed	Border is a series of short lines.
Double	Border is two solid lines.
Groove	Border looks as though it is carved into the page.
Ridge	Border looks the opposite of groove.
Inset	Border makes the box look like it is embedded in the page.
Outset	Border makes the box look like it is coming out of the canvas.
Hidden	Same as none, except in terms of border-conflict resolution for table elements.

However, you can individually change the style of the bottom, left, top, and right borders of an element using the following properties:

Table 6.8: Individual border-style Properties

Property	Description
border-bottom-style	It changes the style of bottom border.
border-top-style	It changes the style of top border.
border-left-style	It changes the style of left border.
border-right-style	It changes the style of right border.

Program 6.20: Create a web page that will use all border style properties.

```
<html>
   <head>
   </head>

   <body>
      <p style = "border-width:4px; border-style:none;">
         This is a border with none width.
      </p>

      <p style = "border-width:4px; border-style:solid;">
         This is a solid border.
      </p>

      <p style = "border-width:4px; border-style:dashed;">
         This is a dashed border.
      </p>

      <p style = "border-width:4px; border-style:double;">
         This is a double border.
      </p>

      <p style = "border-width:4px; border-style:groove;">
         This is a groove border.
      </p>

      <p style = "border-width:4px; border-style:ridge">
         This is a ridge  border.
      </p>

      <p style = "border-width:4px; border-style:inset;">
         This is a inset border.
      </p>

      <p style = "border-width:4px; border-style:outset;">
         This is a outset border.
      </p>

      <p style = "border-width:4px; border-style:hidden;">
         This is a hidden border.
      </p>

     <p style = "border-width:4px;
         border-top-style:solid;
       border-bottom-style:dashed;
       border-left-style:groove;
```

```
        border-right-style:double;">
        This is a a border with four different styles.
      </p>
    </body>

</html>
```

Output of the program is given below:

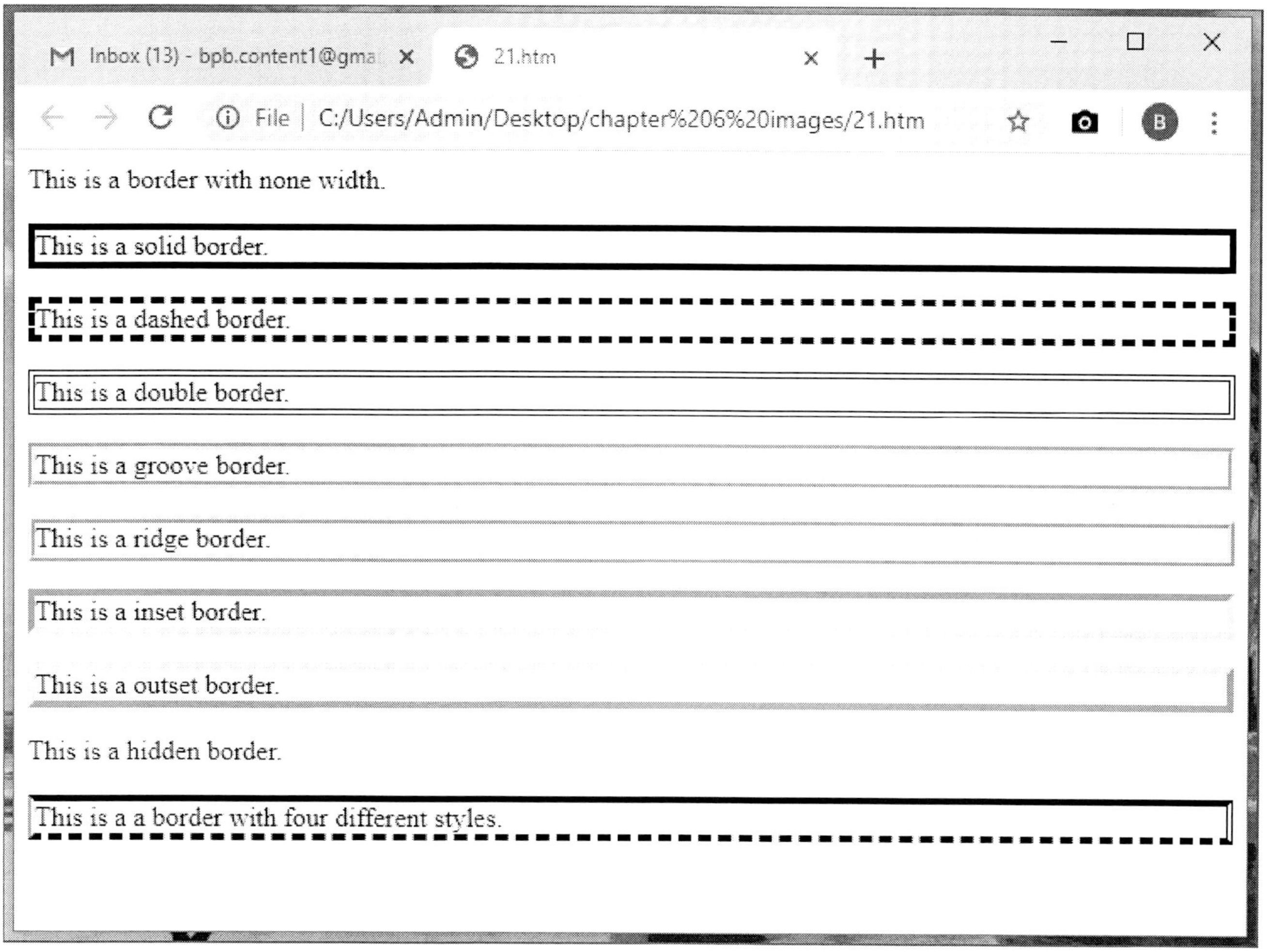

Figure 6.21: Border style properties

border-width: This property allows you to set the width of an element borders. The value of this property could be either a length in **px**, **pt** or cm or it should be set to **thin**, **medium** or **thick**.

For example,

p {border-width: 5px;}   /* set the width of all sides of the border to 5px */

However, you can individually change the width of the bottom, top, left, and right borders of an element using the following properties:

Table 6.9: Individual border-width Property

Property	Description
border-bottom-width	It changes the width of bottom border.
border-top-width	It changes the width of top border.
border-left-width	It changes the width of left border.
border-right-width	It changes the width of right border.

Program 6.21: Create a web page that will use all border width properties.

```
<html>
    <head>
    </head>

    <body>
        <p style = "border-width:4px; border-style:solid;">
            This is a solid border whose width is 4px.
        </p>

        <p style = "border-width:4pt; border-style:solid;">
            This is a solid border whose width is 4pt.
        </p>

        <p style = "border-width:thin; border-style:solid;">
            This is a solid border whose width is thin.
        </p>

        <p style = "border-width:medium; border-style:solid;">
            This is a solid border whose width is medium;
        </p>

        <p style = "border-width:thick; border-style:solid;">
            This is a solid border whose width is thick.
        </p>

        <p style = "border-bottom-width:4px;border-top-width:10px;
            border-left-width: 2px;border-right-width:15px;border-style:solid;">
            This is a a border with four different width.
        </p>
    </body>
</html>
```

Output of the program is given below:

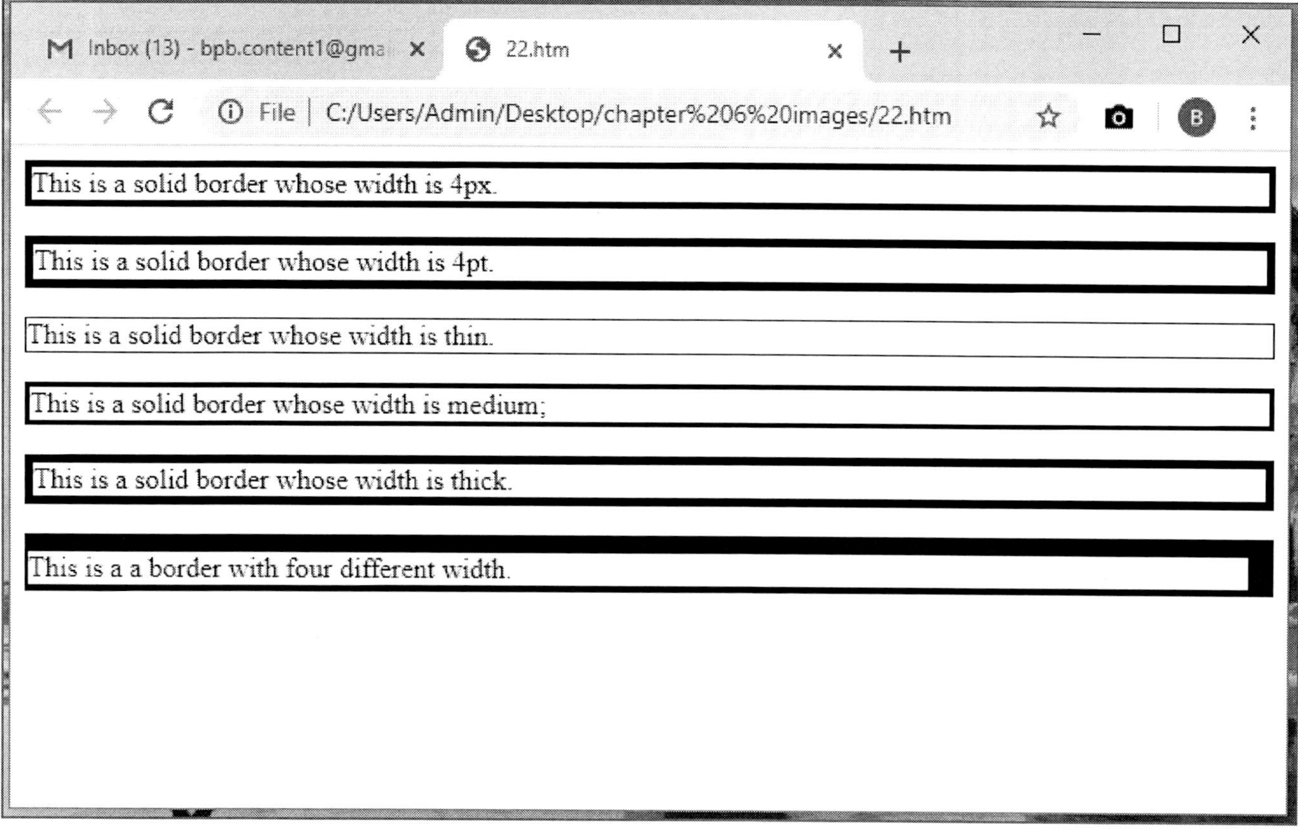

Figure 6.22: Border width properties

Note:

- The border-width value is optional. If it is not provided, the border-width will default to medium.
- The border-color value is optional. If it is not provided, the border-color will default to the element's CSS color property.
- The border-style value is required. If it is not provided, the border-style will default to none and therefore, the border will not appear.

Check Your Progress

Multiple choice questions.

1. ____________ changes the width of bottom border.
   a. Border-top width   b. Border-bottom width   c. Border-right width
2. ____________ specifies whether a border should be solid, dashed line, double line, or one of the other possible values.
   a. Style   b. Color   c. Width

6.7.5 Working with Margin Property

The margin property defines the space around an HTML element. It is possible to use negative values to overlap content. The margin property allows you set all of the properties for the four margins in one declaration.

- **If the margin property has all the four values:**

For example,

```
p {
  margin: 25px 50px 75px 100px;
}
```

Then, the values of top, bottom, left and right margins will be like this:

- top margin is 25px
- right margin is 50px
- left margin is 75px
- bottom margin is 100px

- **If the margin property has three values:**

For example,

```
p {
  margin: 25px 50px 75px;
}
```

Then, the values of top, bottom, left and right margins will be like this:

- top margin is 25px
- right and left margins are 50px
- bottom margin is 75px

- **If the margin property has two values:**

For example,

```
p {
  margin: 25px 50px;
}
```

Then, the values of top, bottom, left and right margins will be like this:

- top and bottom margins are 25px
- right and left margins are 50px

- **If the margin property has one value:**

For example,

```
p {
  margin: 25px;
}
```

Then, the values of top, bottom, left and right margins will be like this:

- all four margins are 25px

However, you can set individual margins for top, bottom, left and right of the element by using the following properties:

Table 6.10: Margin properties

Property	Description
margin-bottom	It specifies the bottom margin of an element.
margin-top	It specifies the top margin of an element.
margin-left	It specifies the left margin of an element.
margin-right	It specifies the right margin of an element.

Program 6.22: Create a web page that will set margin of the text.

```
<html>
    <head>
    </head>

    <body>
        <p style = "margin: 15px; border:1px solid black;">
            all four margins will be 15px
        </p>

        <p style = "margin:10px 2%; border:1px solid black;">
            top and bottom margin will be 10px, left and right margin will be 2%
            of the total width of the document.
        </p>

        <p style = "margin: 10px 2% -10px; border:1px solid black;">
            top margin will be 10px, left and right margin will be 2% of the
            total width of the document, bottom margin will be -10px
        </p>

        <p style = "margin: 10px 2% -10px auto; border:1px solid black;">
            top margin will be 10px, right margin will be 2% of the total
            width of the document, bottom margin will be -10px, left margin
            will be set by the browser
        </p>
    </body>
</html>
```

Output of the program is given below:

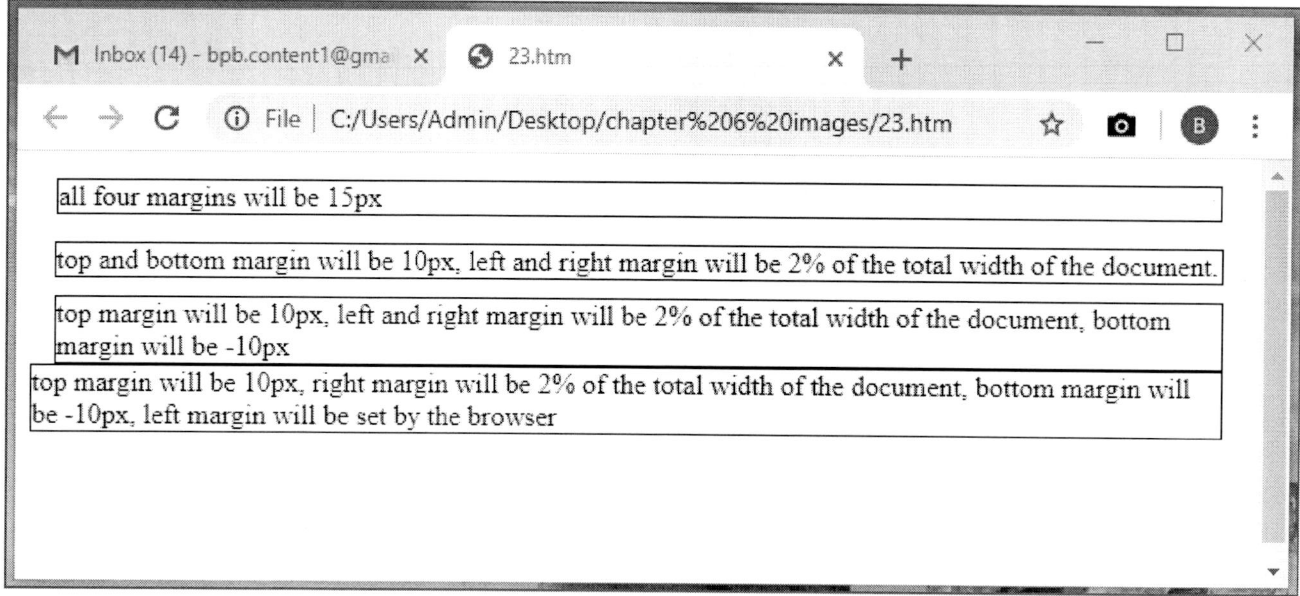

Figure 6.23: Margins of the text

Note:

- Margin value can be expressed as either a fixed value or as a percentage.
- Negative values can be given in the CSS margin property.
- When the value is provided as a percentage, it is relative to the width of the containing block.

MEMORIZE

Style sheet margins allow you to add empty space around the outside of the rectangular area for an element on a web page.

Check Your Progress

Answer the following questions.

1. Name the property which is used to set the margin of all sides of an element.
2. Who specifies the bottom margin of an element?
3. Can you set margins of all sides by using margin property without individually set them?

6.7.6 Changing the Appearance of Links

CSS provides a mechanism that lets you change the appearance of links. For this purpose, you should know the four distinct values of the links which are given below:

- **Link:** A link that has not yet been visited.
- **Hover:** A link that has the mouse pointer hovering over it.
- **Active:** A link that is being activated, such as with mouse click.
- **Visited:** A link that has already been visited.

For example,

```
a:link {
  color: red;
}

a:visited {
  color: green;
}
a:hover {
  color: hotpink;
}
a:active {
  color: blue;
}
```

Program 6.23: Create a web page that will change the appearance of links on a web page.

```
<html>
<html>
<head>
<style>

a:link {
  color: red;
}
a:visited {
  color: green;
}
a:hover {
  color: hotpink;
}
a:active {
  color: blue;
}
</style>
</head>
<body>
<p><b><a href="form.html" >This is the link</a></b></p>

</body>
</html>
```

Output of the program is given below:

Figure 6.24: Change the appearance of Links

Tips for setting link colors

- a:hover MUST come after a:link and a:visited in the CSS definition in order to be effective.
- a:active MUST come after a:hover in the CSS definition in order to be effective.

Check Your Progress

Fill in the blanks.

1. There are ____________ types of links.
2. ____________ provides a mechanism that lets you change the appearance of links.
3. A link that has already been visited is called as ____________.

Let's Revise

- The expanded form of CSS is Cascading style sheet.
- CSS is used to apply format features on HTML document.
- There are three methods to apply CSS to an HTML document. In-line, internal and external methods.
- The property font-family is used to apply prioritized list of fonts in a web page.
- The property font-style defines the chosen font either in normal, italic or oblique.
- The Font-variant property is used to select normal or small-caps variants of a font.
- The Font-weight property describes how bold or heavy a font should be presented. A font can either be normal or bold.
- The font-size property is used to set the size of a font.
- The text-indent property allows you to add effects to text paragraphs by applying an indent to the first line of the paragraph.
- The text-align property gives the same effect as attribute align gives in old versions of HTML.
- The text can either be aligned to the left, to the right or center of the screen.
- The text-decoration property makes it is possible to add different "decorations" or "effects" to text.
- The Letter-spacing property is used to give the specified spacing between the text characters.
- The text-transform property applies the capitalization of a text.
- The background-color property describes the background color of browser Window.
- The background-image property is used to insert a background image in a web page.
- The background-repeat property avoids the repetition of the image set as a background for the web page.

Learning Zone

SECTION A: OBJECTIVE TYPE QUESTIONS

A. MULTIPLE CHOICE QUESTIONS.

1. Which property describes how bold or heavy a font should be presented?

   a. Font style b. Font size c. Font weight d. Font variant

2. It is a style sheet language used for describing the look and formatting of a document written in a markup language.

   a. Document Object Model (DOM) b. Multimedia filters
   c. Cascading Style Sheets (CSS) d. DHTML

3. Which property is used to align the text in CSS?

   a. Text-alignment b. Align-text c. Alignment d. Text-align

4. Which property is used to set the foreground color of the text?

   a. Foreground-color b. Color c. Text-color d. Background-color

5. Which property of is used to not to repeat the image at the background of the web page?

   a. Image-no-repeat b. No-repeat c. Background-repeat d. Repeat

6. Which property is used to set the font style of the text?

a. Font-size b. Font-variant c. Font-family d. Font-color

7. Which property is used to display the text in bold?

a. Font-weight b. Font-style c. Font-color d. None of these

8. What is the extension of .css files?

a. .cas b. .css c. .stylesheet d. None of these

9. Which property is used to give the specified spacing between the text characters?

a. Character spacing b. Text spacing c. Letter spacing d. Paragraph spacing

10. In which method, there is a separate style sheet linked with html file?

a. In-line b. Internal c. External d. None of these

11. table {color: blue;}

In the code snippet above, which part represents the property?

a. Table b. Color c. Blue d. None of these

12. Which of the following statements is TRUE for CSS?

a. An external style sheet is ideal when the style is applied to many pages

b. An inline style sheet should be used when a single document has a unique style

c. Both a. and b.

d. An external style sheet can be written in HTML

13. Which of the following property is used to create a small-caps effect?

a. Font-family b. Font-style c. Font-variant d. Font-weight

14. Which of the following is correct CSS syntax for using font property?

a. <p style="font: italic, bold, 25px;"> .... </p>

b. <p style="font-style: italic font-weight: bold font-size: 25px;"> .... </p>

c. <p style="font: italic bold 25px;"> .... </p>

d. None of these

15. Which property is used to insert a background in a webpage in CSS

a. image b. background c. background-image d. None of the above

Ans.					
	1. c	2. c	3. b	4. b	5. c
	6. c	7. a	8. b	9. c	10. c
	11. b	12. a	13. c	14. b	15. c

B. FILL IN THE BLANKS.

1. The font-weight property refers to the ____________.
2. The ____________ property allows you to add effects to text paragraphs by applying an indent to the first line of the paragraph.
3. The ____________ property describes the foreground color of a text to be displayed in browser.
4. The property font-style defines the chosen font either in __________, __________ or __________.
5. The property ____________ is used to apply prioritized list of fonts in a web page.
6. The text-transform property controls the ____________ of a text.

7. The ____________ property describes the background color of browser Window.
8. The ____________ property is used to insert a background image in a web page.
9. There are ____________ methods to apply CSS to an HTML document.
10. The ____________ property makes it is possible to add different decorations or effects.
11. ____________ property changes the hover link on a web page.
12. There are ____________ number of links on a web page.
13. The default value of border width is ____________.
14. The default value of border style is ____________.
15. ____________ property is used to create a small-caps effect.
16. You can set ____________ property to increase or decrease the size of the font.
17. To remove any decoration applied to the text set ____________ property to none.
18. To add a line above top of the text, set ____________ property to ____________.
19. ____________ property is used to set the text shadow around the text.
20. ____________ property is used to specify the left margin of an element.

Ans. 1. How bold or heavy a font should be 2. Text-indent 3. Color
4. Normal, italic or oblique 5. Font-family 6. Capitalization
7. Background-color 8. Background-image 9. Three
10. Text-decoration 11. a:hover 12. 4
13. Medium 14. Normal 15. Font-variant:small-caps
16. Font-size 17. Text-decoration:none 18. Text-decoration:,overline
19. Text-shadow 20. Margin-left

C. STATE WHETHER THE FOLLOWING STATEMENTS ARE TRUE OR FALSE.

1. You can use font-size property to make the font-italics.
2. Font-color property can be used to change the color of the font.
3. To increase or decrease the boldness and lightness of the font, use font-weight property.
4. Text-decoration:line overline property is used to add a line through words.
5. Text-decoration:overline property is used to add a line above the top of the text.
6. Cascading style sheet is used to control the style and user interface of the web pages.
7. Background-repeat property is used to indent the text of a paragraph.
8. Text-align property is used to align the text of the document.
9. Inline style of CSS is used to select the content you want to style.
10. The font-variant property is used to create a small-caps effect to a text.
11. Internal style sheet only affects the look of the page in which the code is inserted.
12. External style sheet cannot be applied to multiple web pages.
13. Internal style sheet is placed in the head section of a web page.
14. Internal, external and embedded are the three methods of using CSS.
15. bgcolor property is used to change the background color of a web page using CSS code.

Ans. 1. False 2. True 3. True 4. False 5. True
6. True 7. False 8. True 9. True 10. True
11. True 12. False 13. False 14. False 15. False

SECTION B: SOLVED THEORY QUESTIONS

1. **What is CSS and who has created it?**

Ans: CSS is a cascading style sheet which is used describe look, define styles and format webpages across the internet. CSS defines how to display HTML elements. CSS was first proposed by Hakom Lie and co-created by Bert Bos around 1996.

2. **What is the difference between HTML and CSS?**

Ans: The various differences between HTML and CSS are:

a. HTML is a Hypertext Markup Language whereas CSS is a cascading Style sheet.
b. HTML is used to create the actual content of the page, such as written text whereas CSS is used for designing or styling of the website.
c. CSS describes how HTML elements are to be displayed on screen whereas HTML is used for describing web pages.

3. **Discuss various advantages and disadvantages of CSS.**

Ans: The advantages of CSS are:

a. CSS has a large number of attributes for designing a web page.
b. Using CSS, web pages take less time to load and thus improves website speed.
c. It supports offline browsing
d. It is compatible with multiple devices i.e. it presents the same page differently on different devices.
e. It is easy to maintain as all the codes are placed on one page and making change in few lines will not involve going through several pages.
f. The file size of the CSS is very small hence your website takes minimal loading time.
g. Transforms the elements like scale, rotate, skew etc. in 2D or 3D space.
h. Creates animation and transitions without using any JavaScript.
i. Simple to use with HTML.

The disadvantages of CSS are:

a. CSS works differently on different browsers. IE and Opera supports CSS as different logic.
b. There are different levels of CSS such as CSS, CSS2, CSS3 which can create confusion for non-developers and beginners.
c. CSS is an open text-based system, therefore anyone who has a read/write access to a website can change the CSS file, alter the links or disrupt the formatting.

4. **Can you link more than one style sheet to a single page?**

Ans: Yes, we can link more than one style sheet with a single web page document. For this, use <link> tag for both the style sheets.

5. **Write the CSS code to change the foreground color of text to #ff0000 in h1 tags.**

Ans: h1 { color: #ff0000; }

6. **Write the CSS code to display the text of td tag in centre.**

Ans: td { text-align: center; }

7. **Consider the following CSS code:**

h1 {font-family: Arial, comic sans-serif, "Times New Roman";}

Explain font-family.

Ans: The property font-family is used to apply prioritized list of fonts in a web page. If the first font of the list is not installed on the computer then the next font of the list will be displayed until a suitable font is found.

8. **What are the different methods of using style sheets?**

Ans: There are three different methods for applying CSS:

a. In-Line
b. Internal
c. External

9. **Explain the three different methods of using CSS with example.**

Ans: The three different methods are explained below:

a. Using the inline style attribute on an element
For example, <p style="color: maroon;"></p>

b. Using internal method
For example, using a <style> block in the <head> section of your HTML.

```
<head>
   <title>CSS Refresher</title>
   <style>
      body {
         font-family: sans-serif;
         font-size: 1.2em;
      }
   </style>
</head>
```

c. Using external method
For example, loading an external CSS file using the <link> tag.

```
<head>
   <title>CSS Refresher</title>
   <link rel="stylesheet" href="/css/styles.css" />
</head>
```

10. **What are the various advantages of using External Style Sheets?**

Ans: The various advantages of using External Style Sheets are as follows:

a. With the help of External Style Sheets, the styles of numerous HTML documents can be done at once.
b. In External Style Sheets, Classes can be made for use on numerous HTML element types in many forms of the site.

11. **Form a CSS code within the <head>......</head> for the following specifications:**
(Sample paper 2019-20)

Background colour: blue
For the paragraph,
font family is Dotum and colour of the text is red,
Heading should be in black colour

Ans:

```
<head>
<style>
body { background-color: blue;}
p {color:red;
font-family:Dotum;
}
h1{ color: black;}
```

```
</style>
</head>
```

12. How can you insert comments in CSS program?

Ans: We can insert comments by using symbols /* and */. Between these symbols write the comments.

13. What is the syntax to link external style sheet?

Ans: The syntax of using external style sheet is as follows:

```
<html>
<head>
<link rel="stylesheet" href="test.css" type="text/css">
</head>
</html>
```

14. How embedded style can be linked with HTML documents?

Ans: Embedded style can be implemented within HTML code. It is written using the <Style> tag and used under the <head> structure.

The syntax of it is as follows:

```
<head>
<style type="text/css">
style {text-indent: 15pt;}
style1{text-color: #060000;}
</style>
</head>
```

15. What is the significance of using font family property of FONTS?

Ans: The property font-family is used to apply prioritized list of fonts in a web page. If the first font of the list is not installed on the computer then the next font of the list will be displayed until a suitable font is found.

16. Can you combine the different properties of font into one single property? If yes, then give suitable example to illustrate the same.

Ans: Yes, we can combine the different font properties in one single property.

For example, to apply different font-properties for <p> tag following code can be used:

```
p {
font-style: italic;
font-weight: bold;
font-size: 30px;
font-family: Arial, sans-serif;}
```

17. What is the purpose of using letter space property?

Ans: Letter space property is used to give the specified spacing between the text characters. The value of the property is simply the desired width.

18. What is text transformation? What all possible values it can have?

Ans: The text-transform property controls the case of a text.

The various values it can have are:

a. Capitalize: It Capitalizes the first letter of each word. For example: "computer applications" will be displayed as "Computer Applications".

b. Uppercase: Converts all letters to uppercase. For example: "computer applications" will be displayed as "COMPUTER APPLICATIONS".
c. Lowercase: Converts all letters to lowercase. For example: "COMPUTER APPLICATIONS" will be displayed as "computer applications".
d. None: No transformations - the text is presented as it appears in the HTML code.

19. Name the various background properties in CSS.

Ans: The various background properties are:

a. Foreground-Color
b. Background-Color
c. Background-Image
d. Background-Repeat

20. How can you set the image without repeating it on a web page?

Ans: A background-repeat with no repeat value should be used that will not display the image repeatedly on a web page.

21. How many text alignments can be included in CSS?

Ans: There are four types of text alignment which are: left, center, right and justify.

22. How the text can be capitalized in a web page by using CSS property?

Ans: The text can be capitalized by using text-transform property. Use capitalize value for this property so as to make the first letter of every word in capital case.

23. Why an inline method of using CSS is considered as a bad practice?

Ans: Using inline method, the style rules are embedded directly inside the html tags that may cause the presentation to become mixed with the content of a web page. Moreover, it makes the code more complex which is difficult to maintain and thus violates the purpose of using CSS.

24. What style will you follow if there is more than one style specified for an HTML document?

Ans: If two style sheets come into conflict, the last one used will take precedence over others.

25. What would be the order of style sheet if more than one style sheet interact?

Ans: When different style sheet types interact, conflicts arise and the style sheets cascade in the following order:

a. Inline style
b. Internal or embedded style sheet
c. External style sheet
d. Browser default.

26. Consider that a linked style sheet sets that all paragraphs must be displayed in red color font but the embedded style sheet sets that all paragraphs must be set in blue color font. Which font color will be displayed by a web page?

Ans: All paragraphs will be displayed in blue color font as per the rule of precedence which states that the last one style sheet will get precedence over other style sheets.

27. Consider an example where external style sheet says that all paragraphs should be in bold but internal style sheet says that all paragraphs must be italics and in red color font. Which formatting style will the paragraph follow?

Ans: Since the two rules do not conflict with each other, therefore, the paragraphs will be displayed in italics, bold and in red color font.

28. What are CSS comments?

Ans: CSS comments are meant for documentation purpose which are ignored by the browser.

29. Explain the purpose of the following CSS properties:

a. Background-color property
b. Border-width
c. Margin property
d. Height and width property
e. Font property

Ans: a. Background-color property is used to set the background color of a web page.

b. Border-width property defines the width of the four borders on an element.
c. Margin-properties are used to create space around each side of an element i.e. top, bottom, left, right of the elements.
d. Height and width properties are used to set the height and width of an element.
e. Font properties allows us to format the text by specifying font face, style, weight and size of the text.

30. Write the CSS code to:

Apply 25px indentation to all paragraphs marked with <p>.

Make the text italics in the paragraphs.

Ans:
```
p {text-indent:25px; font-style:italic;}
```

31. Which property is used to horizontally align the text at the center? Give example.

Ans: Text-align property is used to set the horizontal alignment of a text. To center align the text, we can write the code as:
```
p{text-align:center;}
```

SECTION C: APPLICATION ORIENTED QUESTIONS

1. Create a style sheet to specify 20-point green Arial headings and all other text in double spaced 10 point blue Courier font.

Ans:
```
h1 { font : 20pt green Arial;}
   body { font: 10pt blue;}
```

2. If you have saved the style sheet of question 1 as mysheet.css, how would you apply it to a web page named mypage.html?

Ans: Put the <link> tag between the <head> </head> section of the mypage.html as given below:
```
<link rel="stylesheet" type="text/css" href="mysheet.css" />
```

3. How do you create a heading that is displayed in small caps?

Ans: We can write the code as:
```
<h1 style="font-variant:small-caps"> Headings </h1>
```

4. How do you create style rules that displays every link on a page in the color purple unless it is in hover mode, in which case it should change the color to red?

Ans: The code can be written as:
```
a:link, a:visited, a:active { color:purple; }
a:hover { color:red;}
```

5. Write the CSS program to create a web page that will show the list of software installed in your computer lab after considering the following points:

a. Heading of the web page should be bold and center aligned. It should be underlined.
b. Letter spacing is 3px.
c. Apply font style as courier for heading.
d. Background color of a web page should be pink.
e. Foreground color of the text should be red.
f. List items should be bold.

Ans: Example.html
```
<html>
<head>
<Link Rel=Stylesheet href="style.css" Type="Text/css"></head>
```

```
<body>
<h2>List of Software</h2>
<ol>
<li>Python IDE</li>
<li>Java NetBeans IDE</li>
<li>Turbo C++<li>
</ol>
</body>
</html>

Style.css
body {
background-color: pink;
}
h2{text-align:center;
font-weight:bold;
text-decoration: underline;
font-family:courier;
letter-spacing:3px;
}
li {
color: red;
font-size:20px;
font-weight:bold;
}
```

6. **Write the CSS code to:**

a. Apply 50px indentation to all text paragraphs marked with <p>.

b. Make the text in the paragraphs marked with <p> tag italics.

Ans:
```
p {
text-indent: 50px;
font-style: italic;
}
```

7. **Observe the following code carefully and answer the questions that follow:**

```
<html>
<head>
<title>NETWORK SECURITY</title>
<style type="text/css">
li {
letter-spacing:10px;
text-transform: lowercase;
}
</style>
</head>
<body> The Dos and Don’ts of network security
<ol>
```

```
<li> KEEP ANTI-VIRUS SOFTWARE UP TO DATE. <li>
<li> SAVE THE FILE TO COMPUTER OR A DISK. </li>
<li> RUN AN ANTI-VIRUS SCAN REGULARLY. </li>
</ol>
</body>
</html>
```

Predict the output of the above code while explaining the effects applied on <li> in the CSS code.

Ans: The output of the above code will be:

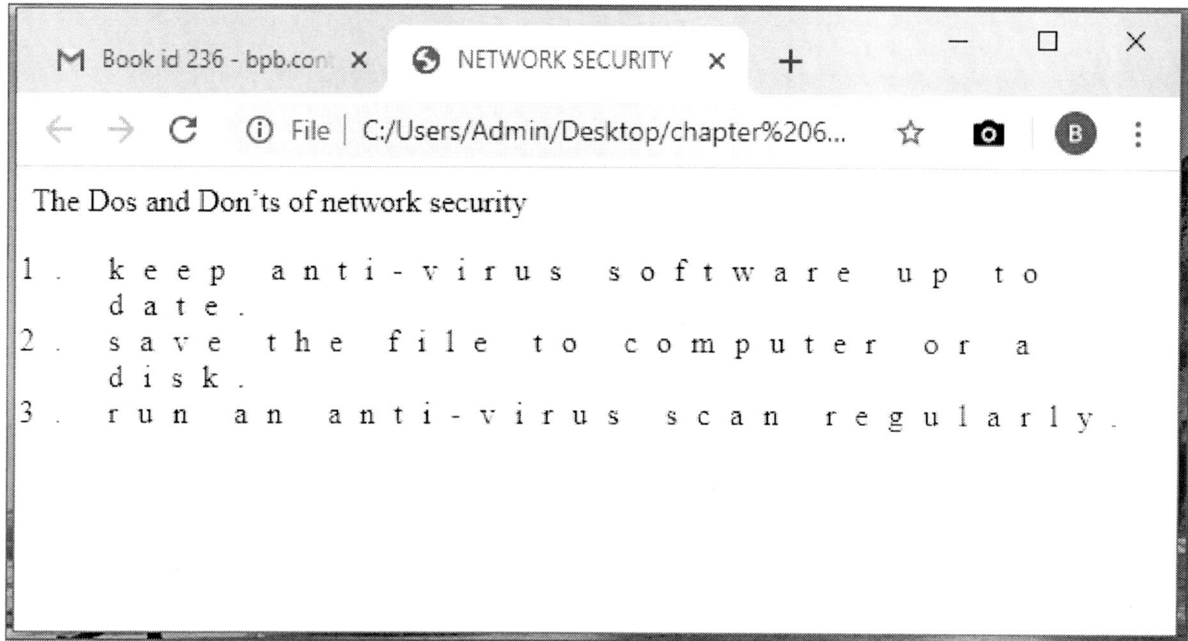

There is a space of 10 pixels between each letter due to: letter-spacing:10px;

9. **Body {background-image: url("learn.gif"); background-repeat: repeat-x}**
In reference with the above CSS code, explain the usage of background-repeat property. Also mention the different values that can be used for background-repeat.

Ans: With reference to the above CSS code the inserted background image learn.gif will repeat horizontally on the browser screen.
The four different values for background-repeat are as follows:

Value	Description
background-repeat: repeat-x:	The image is repeated horizontally.
background-repeat: repeat-y:	The image is repeated vertically.
background-repeat: repeat:	The image is repeated both horizontally and vertically.
background-repeat: no-repeat:	The image is not repeated.

10. **Create an external style sheet "style.css" with the following specifications for the various HTML tags**
<BODY>:
Background color should be Aqua( )
Foreground color should be Navy( )

<H1>

Should be underlined and center aligned

<P>

First line should be indented to 60px

Font-weight should be normal

Write the HTML code to create a link from the HTML document to the style sheet (style.css), Where in the HTML document should the code be placed?

Ans: "style.css"

```
body
{
background-color: Aqua;
color: navy
}
h1
{
text-align:center;
text-decoration:underline;
}
p
{
font-weight:normal;
text-indent:60px;
}
```

To create a link from the HTML document to the style sheet (style.css). The following code will be inserted in the header section of the HTML code i.e. between the <head> and </head> tags.

```
<link href="style.css" rel ="stylesheet" type="text/css">
```

11. **Can you specify all margin properties in one property? Give example.**

Ans: Yes, we can set all margin properties in one property.

For example,

p{ margin: 35px 40px 50px 100px;}

Here, top margin is 35px, right margin is 40px, bottom margin is 50px and left margin is 100px.

12. **If the margin property has four values such as 55px, 40px, 75px and 80px then what is the top margin, right margin, left margin and bottom margin?**

Ans: Top margin: 55px

Right margin: 40px

bottom margin: 75px

left margin: 80px.

13. **Does border-width property work alone? If no, then name the other property which is used in combination with it. Give example.**

Ans: The border-width property does not work alone. Border-style property must be used to set the border first then use border-width property.

For example,

```
p{border-style: double; border-width:thick;}
```

SECTION D: SELF - ASSESSMENT

A. FILL IN THE BLANKS.

1. CSS stands for ____________.
2. There are ____________ methods for adding CSS style sheets to web sites.
3. External style sheets are saved with extension ____________.
4. Internal style sheets are written inside ____________ section.
5. CSS ____________ property is used to set the background color of a web page.
6. CSS ____________ are used to specify the style, color and size of the border of the element.
7. CSS ____________ property is used for positioning and layout on a web page.
8. ____________ property is used to increase and decrease the size of the font.
9. ____________ property is used to change the font face of the font.
10. To make the font italic ____________ property is used.
11. To increase or decrease the boldness and lightness of the font, ____________ property is used.
12. To add a line through words ____________ property is used.
13. ____________ property is used to control the repetition of an image in the background.
14. ____________ property is used to indent the text of a paragraph.
15. ____________ property specifies the left margin of an element.

B. STATE WHETHER THE FOLLOWING STATEMENTS ARE TRUE OR FALSE.

1. Text color is defined by the CSS color property.
2. If you use pixels for font-size property, you can still use the zoom tool to resize the entire page.
3. Internal style sheet only affects the look of the page in which the code is attached.
4. The font-weight property specifies the size of the font.
5. The text-spacing property is used to set the cases of the text.
6. The font-variant property is used to create small-caps effects.
7. When using the text-indent property, negative values are allowed.
8. The word-spacing property is used to set the spacing between the words.
9. The outline property sets the color of an element's borders.
10. Background-image property is used to set the background image of an element.

C. TICK THE CORRECT ANSWER.

1. The border property is a shorthand property for which of the following properties:

   a. Border-width b. Border-style c. Border-color d. All of these

2. Which property is used to set the color of the borders?

   a. Border-radius b. Border-color c. Border-width d. Background-color

3. Which CSS property is not used for specifying the margin of an element?
   a. Margin-top b. Margin-right c. Margin-bottom d. Margin-top left
4. This property specifies the horizontal alignment of the text.
   a. Text-align b. Outline-style c. Border-color d. Letter-spacing
5. This property is used to change the font of an element.
   a. Font b. Font-family c. Font-size d. Font-style
6. Which property defines the width of the outline?
   a. Outline-style b. Outline-width c. Outline-color d. Outline-thickness
7. This makes each word in a text begin with capital letter.
   a. Not possible with CSS b. Text-transform:capitalize
   c. Text-transform:uppercase d. Text-transform:capital
8. Which property is used to change the background color?
   a. Background-color b. Color c. Bgcolor d. None of them
9. Which property sets the bottom margin of an element?
   a. Margin-bottom b. Margin-footer c. Bottom-margin d. None of these
10. Which CSS property is used to increase or decrease the space between characters in a text?
   a. Word-spacing b. Character-spacing c. Letter-spacing d. Spacing-characters

D. ANSWER THE FOLLOWING QUESTIONS.

Type A: Very Short Answer Questions.

1. Write the full form of CSS.
2. What is an internal style sheet?
3. Which property in CSS describes how bold or heavy a font should be presented?
4. Which property makes it is possible to add different decorations or effects to text?
5. Which property of CSS repeats the image both horizontally and vertically to cover the entire screen?
6. Which property describes the foreground color of a text to be displayed in browser?
7. Write the syntax for color property.
8. List the keywords to specify font-size.
9. Which property in CSS is used to set the horizontal alignment of a text?
10. What do you understand by text properties in CSS?
11. What do you understand by font properties in CSS?
12. Name all the three methods of implementing CSS.
13. What is the purpose of % measurement unit?
14. Which property is used to set the background image of an element?
15. Which property is used to control the position of an image in the background?

Type B: Short Answer Questions.

1. What would be the impact of including CSS file with the following code?

   a.
   ```
   h1 {
   text-decoration: underline;
   }
   ```
   b.
   ```
   h2 {
   text-decoration: overline;
   }
   ```
   c.
   ```
   h3 {
   text-decoration: line-through;
   }
   ```
2. Write the CSS code to:
   a. Apply 50px indentation to all text paragraphs marked with <p>.
   b. Make the text in the paragraphs marked with <p> tag italics.
3. How can you set the different text align properties in CSS?
4. What are the four different types of links? Give suitable example to change the appearance of all the types of links.
5. What is border-style property? What are the different values of border-style?
6. How can you change the first letter of a word in capital?
7. Write the code for applying the following:
   a. Color of the text: green
   b. Active link color of a link: purple
   c. Background image should be repeated
   d. Text align: left
   e. Border of a paragraph: solid
   f. Width of a border: 2px
8. Discuss the order of cascading of style sheets in CSS.
9. Write a note on CSS position property.
10. Write the HTML code for appearance of an image "flower.jpg" at the center of a web page.
11. Identify the color of each border, if the border-color property is border-color: red blue green.
12. Write the suitable code for the following:
    a. The top and bottom margins for <H!> to 50px and left and right margin to 30px.
    b. Set the left margin of <p> to 20px.
    c. Change the color of all <p> elements to blue and text aligned to center of a web page.
13. What will be the output of the following code?

    Border-style: solid dotted dashed double;

14. Observe the following output and answer the questions:

a. Name the CSS properties which are used in the above code.

b. What do you mean by text-decoration property?

15. Type the following CSS code and find the output.

```
<head>
<style>
h1 {
   border-left: 5px solid red;
}
h2 {
   border-left: 4px dotted blue;
}

</style>
</head>
<body>
<h1>A heading with a solid red left border</h1>
<h2>A heading with a dotted blue left border</h2>
</body>
</html>
```

Type C: Long Answer Questions.

1. List various advantages and disadvantages of CSS.
2. Describe how HTML is different from CSS?
3. Describe the cascading order. What happens if the order conflicts?
4. Why inline style has the highest priority in the cascading style?

5. Body {background-image: url("learn.gif"); background-repeat: repeat-x}

   In reference with the above CSS code, explain the usage of background-repeat property. Also mention the different values that can be used for background-repeat. Which property controls the repetition of an image on a web page? Give suitable example.

6. Explain the CSS property to set the foreground and background color of a web page.

7. How can you provide the space between letters? Explain with suitable example.

8. Body {background-image:url("e-laerning.gif"); background-repeat:repeat-x}.

   In reference with the above CSS code, answer the following questions.

   a. Explain the usage of background-repeat property.

   b. Also mention the different values that can be used for background-repeat.

   c. What output will be produced when the above code is executed?

9. Find errors in the following html code or external style sheet. Rewrite the correct code and underline each correction:

   H1{text-align:center; color; blue}

   p{color-black; fontfamily:"arial"; fontsize:16};

10. Explain various properties of border.

11. Explain all the three different methods of using CSS.

12. Consider the given code and find the output.

```
<html>
<html>
   <head>
      <title>This is document title</title>
      <style>
      h1 {
         color: #36CFFF;
      }
      </style>
   </head>
   <body>
      <h1>Hello World! </h1>
   </body>
</html>
```

13. Observe the given output and answer the questions.

```
<html>
   <head>
   </head>

   <body>
      <p style = "background-color:yellow;">
```

```
            This text has a yellow background color.
        </p>
    </body>
</html>
```

a. Which CSS property is used in the above code?

b. What would be the output of the above code?

14. Write the CSS code that will insert the background image as url("/css/images/tulip.jpg");

SECTION E: LAB EXERCISE

1. Consider the given output and do as directed:

Add an external style sheets to the above output screen. Name the style sheet as fav.css. The style sheet should do the following:

a. Display h1 elements in blue.

b. Display all links in blue without underlining them.

c. When the mouse hovers over the link, change the link's background color to yellow, and text's color to red.

d. Declare a style class named 'dark' that sets the font to bold.

2. Create a stylesheet named styleme.css to improve the appearance of your web page say "About Me".

a. Change the color of at least two elements.

b. Change the font properties (family, size, weight, or style) of at least two elements. Some standard fonts: Arial, Arial Black, Verdana, Trebuchet MS, Georgia, Tahoma, Courier New, Times New Roman.

c. Change at least one other thing (e.g. background color, text alignment, etc.)

3. Consider the given code and find the output.

```
<HTML>
<HEAD>
```

```
<TITLE> My First Stylesheet </TITLE>
<STYLE TYPE = "text/css">
H1 {color: green; font-size: 37px; font-family: impact}
P {text-indent: 1cm; background: yellow}
</STYLE>
</HEAD>
<BODY>
<H1> Stylesheets: The Tool of the Web Design Gods </H1>
<P> Amaze your friends! Squash your enemies! </P>
</BODY>
/HTML>
```

4. Create a page named aboutme.html that describes you. On your page, include the following information:
   a. Your name and insert your photograph.
   b. A description of yourself in two sentences or less. Emphasize the most important word(s) by putting them in bold.
   c. A list of subjects you are currently studying.
   d. Your 3 favorite movies, books, or TV shows, in order. Make link of at least one book representing its author, publisher and features of the book.
   e. Then Create a stylesheet named aboutme-style.css to improve the appearance of your About Me page. Your stylesheet should do the following without any modification to your HTML code.
   f. Change the color of at least two elements.
   g. Change the font properties of at least two elements (such as family, size, weight, style).
   h. Change at least one other thing of your choosing (such as background color, text alignment, etc.).
5. Take one of your pages (with bold-face text) and add an inline CSS style sheet (in the section) that will do the following:
   a. Make bold-face text use a larger font size.
   b. Change the style sheet to make the bold-face text red on a blue background.
   c. Add another piece of text in bold-face.
   d. Make a red background.

Activity Zone

1. Tell students to prepare the student details in tabular format and apply various font and color properties of CSS on it.
2. Students are advised to make the list of various dance forms and apply CSS properties on it.
3. Tell students to make a presentation on various background properties and explain them with suitable example.
4. Students can create their own blog using HTML and CSS properties.

7 Cyber Ethics

Outline of the Chapter

- Introduction
- Cyber netiquettes
- Software licenses and the open source software movement
- Intellectual property rights, plagiarism and digital property rights
- Freedom of information and the digital divide
- E-commerce: Privacy, fraud, secure data transmission

Learning Objectives

- To learn about the various cyber netiquettes
- To know the meaning of software license and its types
- To know about open source, freeware and shareware software
- To know about the digital property, its rights, threats to digital property and its safeguard
- To know about e-commerce, threats to e-commerce and its precautionary measure
- To know about freedom of information and the meaning of digital divide

INTRODUCTION

Internet has become an essential part of our life. Without it, you cannot think smooth functioning of life. But, is it a boon for you? It's very difficult to answer this question because at one side, it has eased mostly all task related to education, business, industries, and so on. On the other side, most of the crimes are committed through internet.

If internet is used for the benefit of the society then it is a boon for you. But what if you use it in a wrong way? It will become bane for you. With the widespread use of internet, networks, and computers have become increasingly susceptible to threats. The main objective of these threats is to steal someone's privacy. This information is used by the attackers for their benefit.

So, this chapter is mainly focusing on various Cyber Ethics, frauds related to e-commerce, privacy issues, threats to data and various other cyber issues.

7.1 WHAT IS CYBER NETIQUETTE?

Netiquette is short form of **Internet Etiquette** that specifies the good behaviour on internet. Just like etiquette represents the good moral behaviour or moral values in a society, in a same way, netiquette is a code of good behaviour on the internet. This includes several aspects of the internet, such as e-mail, social media, online chat, web forums, website comments, multiplayer gaming, and other types of online communication. The general idea behind cyber netiquette is to respect others online.

For example,

- Do not post offensive comments on social media.
- Maintain other's privacy and therefore do not post other's pictures, videos or sharing their personal information with others.
- Don't troll people in web forums or website comments by repeatedly nagging or annoying them.
- Always abide by the law. It is against the law to illegally download software, games, films, music, and so on. Downloading illegally is a criminal offence.
- Do not copy or disseminate information on the internet if you do not own it yourself.
- Always use licensed software instead of illegally downloading from the internet.
- Make use of open source softwares.

Definition

Netiquette is short form of **Internet Etiquette** that specifies the good behaviour on internet. The general idea behind cyber netiquette is to respect others online.

7.2 MEANING OF LICENSE

License is the **right** or **permission** granted by the holder of a copyright to another to use an original work. It states under what circumstances and to what extent the original work can be used, changed, or distributed. It may include a period of time, a geographical area, renewal provisions, and other limitations. It does not pass on the copyright.

7.3 SOFTWARE LICENSE AND OPEN SOURCE SOFTWARE PHILOSOPHY

Software license refers to the legal agreement to use an application or software. The agreement is between the producer and the user who wants to access it by posing some restriction without legally purchasing it. It specifies how the application may be used and defines the rights of both the producer and the user.

For example, it is illegal to purchase one copy of a program and copy it onto multiple computers.

Definition

A software license is a document that provides some legal guidelines to the end user with respect to the use and distribution of software. It provides the right to make one or more copies of the software without violating copyrights.

Note: A software license does not automatically transfer the ownership of the software to the buyer and its purchase price, in effect; it is a one-time rental fee.

★ **Let's know the various types of software license.**

7.3.1 Types of Software Licenses

There are various types of Software Licenses:

1. **Single user:** The software is licensed for a single user and for a single computer.

2. **Multi-user:** This license allows you to install a program onto multiple computers used by multiple users.
3. **Site license:** This license allows a program to be installed on an unlimited number of computers with an unlimited number of users, if they are at the location of the site license. Site license are usually for **schools** and **businesses**.

The **Open Source Initiative (OSI)**, a global non-profit founded in 1998, acts as a leading authority on OSS.

4. **Proprietary license:** The copyright stays with the producer and the user is granted the right to use the software.
5. **GNU:** General Public Licenses, which are agreements under which open source software is usually licensed. It allows end users to change the source code and the code too. Code must also be made available under a GNU GPL license.
6. **End User License Agreement (EULA):** This software indicates the terms under which the end-user use the software.
7. **Workstation licenses:** Workstation licenses are the licenses that permit the installation of an application on a single computer. Before installing it on a different machine the software must be removed from the first machine.
8. **Concurrent licenses:** It permit the installation of the software onto multiple machines if the number of computers using the software at the same time does not exceed the number of licenses purchased.
9. **Perpetual licenses:** It comes without an expiry date and allow the software to be used indefinitely.
10. **Non-perpetual licenses:** It lease the software for use for a specified period of time, usually **annually** or sometimes **bi-annually**. Users are required to remove the software from their computer if they cease paying the license fee.
11. **License with Maintenance:** It offer maintenance or software assurance along with the original license fee.

7.4 OPEN SOURCE SOFTWARE

Open-source software (OSS) is a software that can be modified or enhanced for the reusability and accessibility of a program. The program is freely available for the users and can be changed as per the user requirement. Programmers who have access to a computer program source code can improve a program by adding features to it or fixing parts that don't always work correctly.

MEMORIZE

Open source software (OSS) is a software that allows users to access, change, and improve its source code for their purposes by having a licence to do so.

The various features of OSS are:

1. It is freely distributed.
2. It can be read and modified as per the need of a user.
3. The user can fix bugs, improve functions, or adapt the software to suit their own needs.

According to Richard Stallman's

Free software is a manner of liberty, not price. To understand the concept, you should think of "free" as in "free speech", not as in "free beer". Free software is a matter of the user's freedom to run, copy, distributes, study, change and improves the software."

* **Let's know the types of freedom that should be provided to the users.**

The four types of freedom should be provided to the users in free software:

1. **Freedom 0** provides the freedom to the user to run the program for any purpose.
2. **Freedom 1** provides the freedom to the user to understand the functioning of the program and to make changes as per the requirement.
3. **Freedom 2** provides freedom to the user to redistribute the copies of the same to another person for using it.
4. **Freedom 3** provides freedom to enhance the features of the software by modifying the existing features of the software and release it to the public.

7.5 TERMINOLOGIES RELATED TO OPEN SOURCE SOFTWARE

1. **Free Software:** Free software is software which is freely distributed and accessible to all those users who want to access it. The software can be modified, enhanced, or copied without any payment. ***Examples*** of free software are **Linux kernel, Python 3.7.3, Java Net Beans IDE, MYSQL, Apache tomcat server,** and **openoffice.org office suite.**
2. **Freeware:** The software that is freely available but not open source software. Its code is not freely available to the user to make modification in it. An ***example*** of freeware software is **Internet Explorer** and **Microsoft web browser.** The user is not required to have a license for taking copy of the software and is distributed in binary form.
3. **Shareware:** It refers to the software that is freely available for a short trail period. After the trial period is over the user is required to purchase the software to continue using it. Shareware is not identical to open source software or free software because:
   a. The user is not allowed to make modification in it.
   b. The source code of the software is not available.
4. **Proprietary Software:** It is the software which is neither freely available nor it is open source software. Moreover, the code of these softwares is not freely available to the user to make modification in it. If the user wants to make modification or if he wants to purchase these softwares, he has to take permission from the vendor or supplier of the software who developed it.
5. **W3C:** It refers to **World Wide Web Consortium.** It is an organisation that is responsible for developing software standards for the World Wide Web.

   W3C specifies its mission as follows:

   The W3C mission is to lead the World Wide Web to its full potential by developing protocols and guidelines that ensure the long term growth of the web.
6. **OSS:** Open source software, its code is freely available to the user to make further changes in software.
7. **FLOSS: Free Libre Open Source Software or Free Livre Open Source Software.** The word **Libre** and **Livre** means **freedom.** FLOSS represents the software which is free as well as open source.

7.6 OPEN SOURCE LICENSE

Open source license allows the user to modify and share the software with other users without seeing permission from the company or organization. Open source software also states the type of permissions given to users as per the terms and conditions.

There are different types of open-source software, such as **Apache software licenses, Berkeley** or **BSD licenses,** and various types of **GNU licenses.**

The below list is based on publicly available statistics obtained at the time of the Report of License Proliferation Committee:

- Apache License 2.0 (Apache-2.0)
- 3-clause BSD license (BSD-3-Clause)
- 2-clause BSD license (BSD-2-Clause)
- GNU General Public License (GPL)
- GNU Lesser General Public License (LGPL)
- MIT license (MIT)
- Mozilla Public License 2.0 (MPL-2.0)
- Common Development and Distribution License version 1.0 (CDDL-1.0)
- Eclipse Public License version 2.0 (EPL-2.0)

7.7 INTELLECTUAL PROPERTY RIGHTS

Intellectual property rights refer to the right given by the owner of the property as to how much information should be exchanged, shared, or distributed. Intellectual property refers to the creations of inventions; literary-artistic works; symbols, names and images used in commerce. Since the producer of the information is the real owner, he has a full right to protect the information and give permission to use it to other users.

To protect this information, one can get copyrighted information or patented or use trademarks.

The copyrighted information must not be used without the consent of the owner otherwise the person can be penalised for this act. *(Figure 7.1)*

The importance of intellectual property was first recognized in the **Paris Convention for the Protection of Industrial Property (1883)** and **the Berne Convention for the Protection of Literary and Artistic Works (1886)**.

Definition

Intellectual property right is a right that comes under law. It refers to the creation of work, ideas, discoveries and inventions and the producer of the information is the real owner.

The various intellectual property rights are:

Figure 7.1: Intellectual Property Rights

MEMORIZE

Intellectual property is the ownership of ideas and control over the tangible or virtual representation of those ideas.

* **Let's discuss all these rights in detail.**

Copyright

A copyright is the right granted by law to the creator of his original work. Copyright covers **literary works** (novels, poems and plays), **films**, **music**, **artistic works** (drawings, paintings, photographs and sculptures) and **architectural design**.

A copyright owner has **five** exclusive rights:

a. Fix or store the information in a tangible form.
b. Reproduce the copyrighted material.
c. Sell, rent, lease, or otherwise distribute copies of the copyright work to the public.
d. Publicly perform and display the copyrighted material.
e. Prepare derivative works based on the copyrighted material.

Copyright is a form of intellectual property protection provided by the laws of the United States.

Definition

Copyright refers to the work done by the owner to reproduce, resell or publish his original work of authorship that includes literary work, artistic work or architectural work.

Note: Copyright protection varies from country to country, and can stand for 50 to 100 years after the individual's death, depending on the country.

Patent

Patents a legal document which is granted by a government that gives right to the inventor or producer of the goods to sell his product or invention for a specified number of years.

Definition

A patent is a right granted to an owner or inventor for any work done by him, by the federal government that permits him to exclude others from making, selling or using his invention for a certain period of time.

Trademark

A trademark is any sign capable of being represented graphically and which is capable of distinguishing goods or services of one undertaking from those of other undertakings. It is a businesses' way of being represented in the market and is central for building up a reputation for the business.

Definition

A trademark is a mark or sign that identifies and distinguish the products of one company from another company. Trademark plays an important role in protecting consumers and in promoting economic growth.

Note: TM stands for Trademark.

Privacy

Privacy prevents you from intruding on, exposing private facts about or falsely portraying someone. The extent of this protection may vary if the subject is a public figure. ***For example***, a celebrity or politician.

Publicity

These laws protect against the unauthorized use of a person's name or image for commercial purposes. ***For example***, the use of your picture on a box of cereal. The extent of this protection varies from state to state.

7.8 PLAGIARISM

Plagiarism is a Latin word which means stealing or kidnapping of one's thoughts, ideas or work accomplished by someone else and present that endeavour work as ours own. It is an unethical and moral infringement, and also leads to copyright violation. *(Figure 7.2)*

Figure 7.2: Plagiarism

For example, suppose a college lecturer has written an article on some topic, but by hooks and crooks or by an authorised way, some other person publishes that article by his own name. This kind of act is known as plagiarism. It is a cybercrime and is against a cyber law.

Definition

Plagiarism means to present some other's work or ideas as if it is own with or without their consent, by incorporating it into your work without full acknowledgement.

Following acts are considered as plagiarism:

a. Presenting someone else's work as your own.
b. Copying words or ideas from someone else without giving credit.
c. Avoid giving quotation marks.
d. Giving incorrect information about the source of a quotation.
e. Manipulating words and copying the original structure of a sentence.

* **Let's know the various types of plagiarism.**

7.8.1 Types of Plagiarism

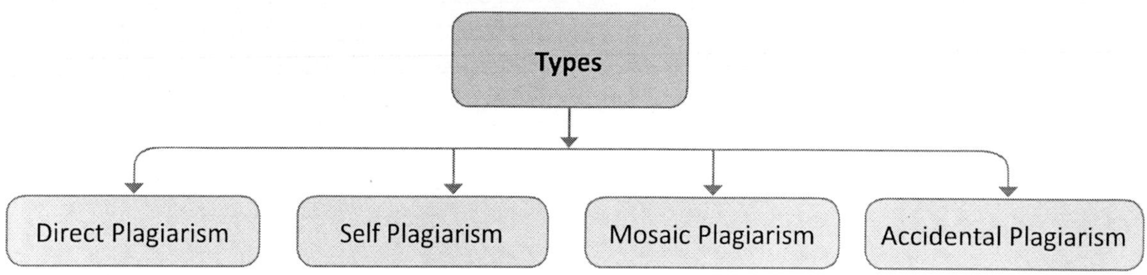

Figure 7.3: Types of Plagiarism

1. **Direct Plagiarism:** Direct plagiarism is the word-for-word transcription of a section of someone else's work, without attribution and without quotation marks.
2. **Self-Plagiarism:** Self-plagiarism occurs when a student submits his or her own previous work, or mixes parts of previous works, without permission from the professors involved.
3. **Mosaic Plagiarism:** Mosaic Plagiarism occurs when a student borrows phrases from a source without using quotation marks, or finds synonyms for the author's language while keeping to the same general structure and meaning of the original.
4. **Accidental Plagiarism:** Accidental plagiarism occurs when a person neglects to cite their sources, or misquotes their sources, or unintentionally paraphrases a source by using similar words, groups of words, and/or sentence structure without attribution.

* **Let's know how to avoid plagiarism.**

MEMORIZE

The word plagiarism is derived from the Latin word plagiarius which means kidnapper. To avoid plagiarism, one should acknowledge, cite, quote or rephrase others' work.

Some real-life examples of plagiarism are:

1. In 2016, Melania Trump plagiarized Michelle Obama's speech! She has been accused of plagiarism for a speech she made at the Republican National Convention.
2. Helen Keller has also been accused of plagiarism for a story that she wrote when she was 11 years old. Her story, The Frost King, was found to be very similar to The Frost Fairies, a story written by Margaret Canby.

7.8.2 How can you avoid plagiarism?

a. Give credit to another's person's work, ideas or thoughts.
b. Don't use others quotation or written words as if they are your own.
c. Acknowledge the sources of information from where you have read/researched/referred to information.
d. You should acknowledge all types of sources of information such as books, magazines, journals, websites, newspapers etc.

Check Your Progress

1. What is plagiarism?
2. Name the different types of plagiarism?
3. Write down one example of plagiarism.

7.9 DIGITAL PROPERTY RIGHTS

Digital property is the property which is created by you online or digitally. This property may be in terms of your own creation, picture, art, music, video clips, and so on; which are stored digitally and can be accessed either **online** or **offline**. This data may be stored locally on a computer's hard drive or on removable media, or data may be stored remotely and accessed over the internet. Intellectual property rights also come under digital property, such as pictures, music, movies, literary works, web pages, computer code, and other creative works.

Definition

Digital property is the property which is created by you online or digitally. This property may be in terms of your own creation, picture, art, music, video clips etc.

The definition of digital rights and responsibilities is having the right and freedom to use all types of digital technology while using the technology in an acceptable and appropriate manner. As a user of digital technology, you also have the right to privacy and the freedom of personal expression. *(Figure 7.4)*

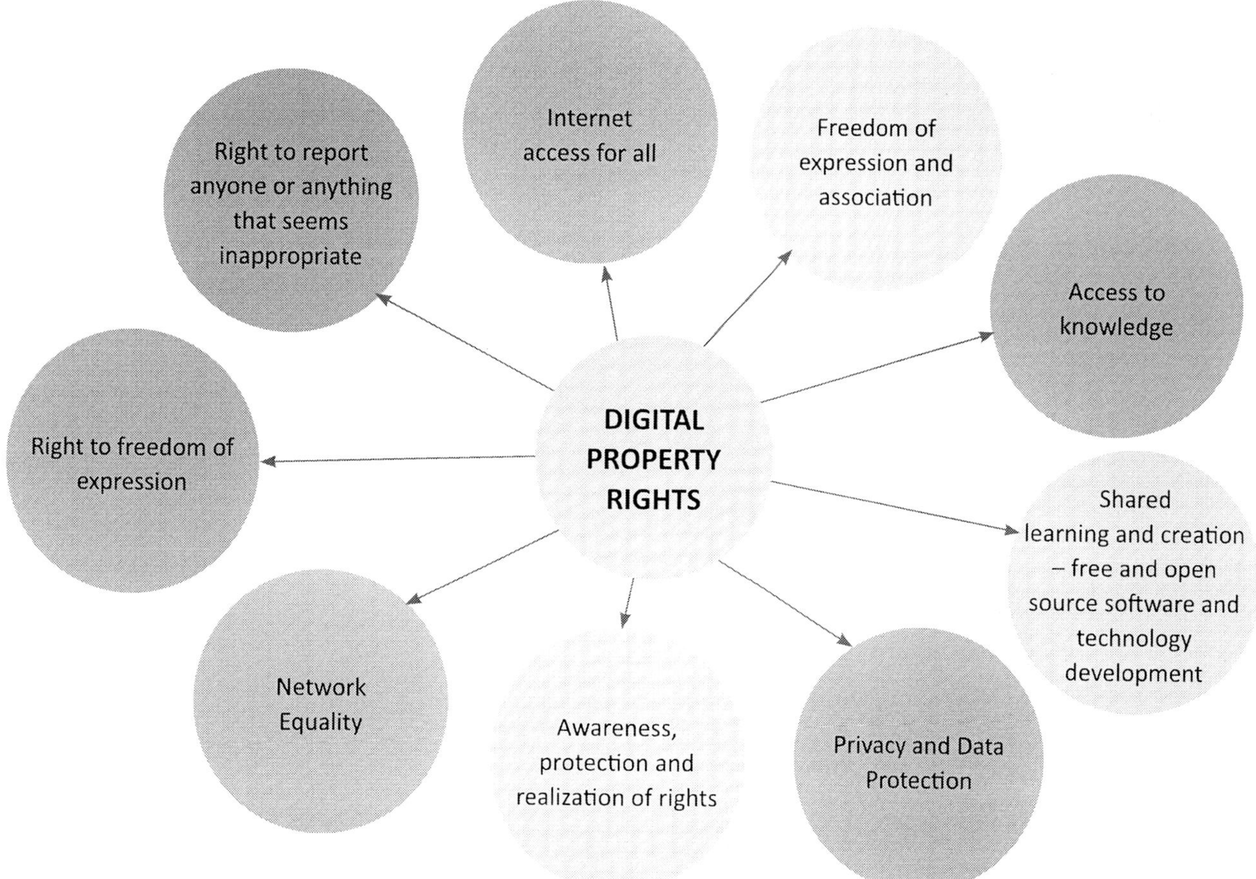

Figure 7.4: Digital Property Rights

Cyber Ethics

MEMORIZE

Intellectual property rights also come under digital property, such as pictures, music, movies, literary works, web pages, computer code, and other creative works.

* **Let's know the various digital responsibilities.**

7.9.1 Types of Digital Responsibilities

1. Report any kind of bullying, harassing or identity theft.
2. Cite works used for resources and researching.
3. Download music, videos, and other material legally.
4. Model and teach student expectations of technology use.
5. Keep data/information safe from hackers.
6. Not to falsify your identity in any way.
7. Do not share any others' personal information without permission.
8. Follow rules and/or codes of conduct for every internet site.
9. Respect the opinions and ideas of others.
10. Obey all intellectual property laws.

* **Let's know the various threats to digital property.**

7.9.2 Threats to Digital Properties

- **Phishing:** Phishing is the method of **stealing username** and **password** to get access to the system illegally. This allows attackers to take advantage of a user's public information (via social networks) to perform fraud with increased authenticity.

Definition

Phishing is the process of getting individual's personal information such as passwords and credit card numbers by sending them fraudulent mails.

- **Code hacking:** Some developers do plagiarism attack and steal the source code of your work and mark them as if it is their own.
- **Sharing of data:** Some users intentionally share some other's creativity, music or artwork on social media without seeking permission of the owner which is also a serious digital threat.

Now, the question arises as how do you make sure that your digital property remains safe and is protected from copyright infringement and reverse engineering?

* **So, let's know how to protect digital property.**

7.9.3 Protection of Digital Property Rights

1. **Anti-Tamper solution:** It is one of the most advanced technologies that prevent hackers from hacking your personal information or manipulating your video games. It prevents the leakage of both data and software. However, it is an expensive technology. Some of the newest games, including Tom Clancy's

The Division, Rise of the Tomb Raider and Hitman 2016 use Denuvo to keep their property safe from attackers.

2. **Software escrow:** It refers to the safety of a software code that cannot be accessible by any distributor without authorization. Without owner's permission, no one can re-distribute the code, modify it, or change it and mark it as if it is own.
3. **Digital Rights Management (DRM) solution:** It is the solution that protects your software from being scraped for source codes using de-compilers. It prevents your source code from being leaked.
4. **Product keys:** It is the method of providing an authentication to your product. While purchasing the application, the user would be provided with a product key which he/she would have to put while installing the application. It would later be checked by the server to find a match as every copy of the application has a different key. If a match is found, the product is not activated.
5. **Use of encoding, encryption and watermarking:** Some digital assets can themselves be digitally protected by encoding, encryption, or watermarking. This is designed to prevent unauthorised use of assets such as photographs, films, music, or software that is licensed to a third party.

Check Your Progress

Fill in the blanks.

1. Some digital assets can themselves be digitally protected by encoding, encryption, or ____________.
2. ____________ is the method of stealing username and password to get access to the system illegally.
3. ____________ is the property which is created by you online or digitally.

7.10 FREEDOM OF INFORMATION

Freedom of information refers to the freedom of speech, accessing information through internet, sharing relevant information with each other, discussing various topics on social media, and so on. The information can be expressed either orally or in writing.

In other words, freedom of information means **freedom of expression** that includes **Freedom of Opinion** and **Freedom of Access to Information. Freedom of expression** includes the right to seek, receive and impart information and ideas, through any media and regardless of frontiers. Information access is the ability and freedom to source information through any medium for personal use or for the good of a community or society. While information access has been categorised as a human right (Barry, 2013; Sturges, 2010; Open Society, 2005), information is yet to be accessible by everyman.

7.11 DIGITAL DIVIDE

Digital divide as defined by **Dunn in 2010**, is the gap existing between individuals, households, businesses and geographic areas at different socio-economic levels with regard to their opportunities to access information and ICT and their use of the internet for a wide variety of activities. It is a gap of accessing information by different people living in different geographical areas.

Definition

Digital divide is the gulf between those who have ready access to computers and the Internet, and those who do not. In other words, there is a digital divide between rich and poor in terms of computer use.

The reasons for digital divide are:

a. Differences between rural and urban Internet access.

b. Differences on the basis of income and that affect their ability to access the Internet.

c. Differences between developed, developing and emerging nations in terms of the availability of Internet.

7.12 E-COMMERCE AND CYBER ETHICS

E-commerce is the process of buying and selling goods online. It is an electronic exchange of money between the buyer and the seller. The benefits of e-commerce include 24X7 availability, speed of delivering products, easy accessibility, and international reach.

E-commerce is defined as the use of Internet, the **World Wide Web (Web)** and computer applications or mobile applications in the transactions operated between business and its partners (**Laudon 2014, 50**).

7.12.1 Ethical Issues in E-Commerce

1. **E-commerce consumer privacy:** Sensitive information such as **debit** or **credit card, CVC number** and other details must be protected from intruders. Private information should be adequate and not be kept in longer then the necessary time,
2. **E-commerce security:** It refers to security of data that should be accessible only to authorized users in a safe and reliable manner. It makes sure that the data should be collected accurately and reliably.
3. **E-commerce trust:** It is also known as **e-trust**. It refers that the product which is to be purchased online must be exactly same as what has ordered by the consumer.

7.12.2 How to Protect User Privacy

Privacy is the protection of the individual's right to non-disclosure of data. Privacy refers to controlling the dissemination and the use of data. In online shopping, vendors have to make sure that all the information gathered from consumer is protected and didn't spread to other parties. *(Figure 7.5)*

The various means to protect user privacy are:

1. The seller must save the data which is required for e-commerce.

2. There should be an authorized access of data.

3. Use of strong password so as to control unauthorized access of data.

4. Provide reliable information about the company.

5. Display terms and conditions to consumer before purchasing of goods.

6. Keep your computers virus free.

7. Make protective use of your credit card/ debit card information such as cvv number, card number, expiry date etc.

Figure 7.5: Methods of Protecting Users' Privacy

7.13 CYBER FRAUD DURING E-COMMERCE

Fraud committed online is known as **cyber fraud, online fraud, internet fraud** or simply **fraud**. Internet fraud is a type of fraud or deception that uses internet for the purpose of tricking victims for money, property. Internet fraud may include spam, scams, spyware, identity theft, phishing or internet banking fraud.

* **Let's know the various forms of cyber fraud.**

The various forms of fraud while doing e-commerce are (*figure 7.6*):

Figure 7.6: Various Forms of Fraud

7.13.1 Protection Methods from Fraud

1. **Proper list of products:** It is required for the manufacturer to display the proper and accurate list of products with their genuine prices. The list should display only those products which are actually available with the manufacturer.
2. **Checking of products:** Before selling of products, they should be checked for any counterfeit products.
3. **Use credit card security codes:** Always require customers to present the security code that is printed on their payment cards. It authenticates their ownership of the card.
4. **Use tracking numbers for all orders:** This will record when all orders were delivered.
5. **Work with trusted suppliers:** Customers should buy products from trusted companies in order to get trusted products and not the fake products.

7.14 SECURE DATA TRANSMISSION

Secure data transmission refers to the transfer of data such as confidential or proprietary information over a secure channel.

* **Techniques used for secure data transfer.**

To ensure for secure transfer of data, the following techniques are used:

1. **SSL:** SSL is expanded as **Secure Socket Layer**. It is a protocol that ensures the safe and secure exchange of data between two systems that can be server to server transmission or server to client transmission. It does not allow any unauthenticated or unauthorized user to get into the details and use it for any malicious purpose. While transferring

data, SSL first encrypts the data and then send it to the sender. By encrypting the data, it prevents hackers from reading and modifying it.

2. **Data Encryption:** While the data is sent over the network, various encrypting algorithm are used for the secure data transmission. The original data is first encrypted and then transfer from the sender side. When it reaches to the receiver, the data is decrypted or decoded so as to get the original message. This process is known as **cryptography**. This mechanism prevents from **eavesdropping**. *(Figure 7.7)*

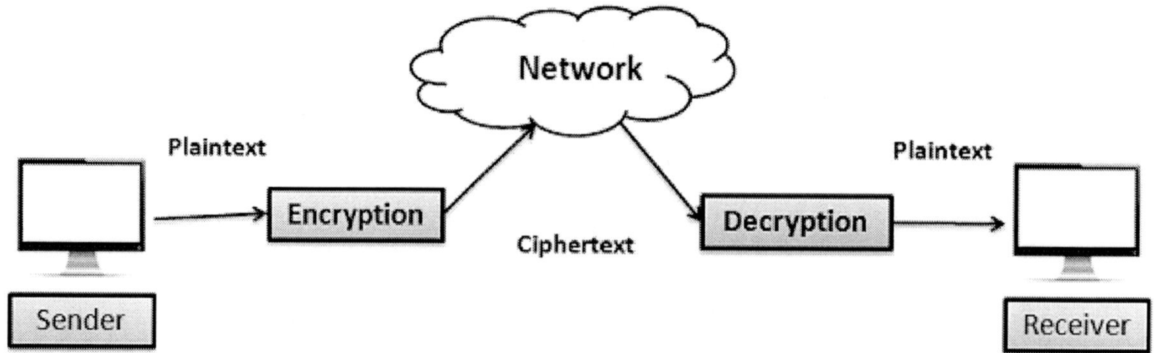

Figure 7.7: Encryption and Decryption of data

3. **Installing a Firewall:** A **firewall** is a program or hardware device that filters the information coming through an internet connection to a network or computer system. If incoming information does not pass the rules stored in the firewall, it is not allowed to pass through. *(Figure 7.8)*

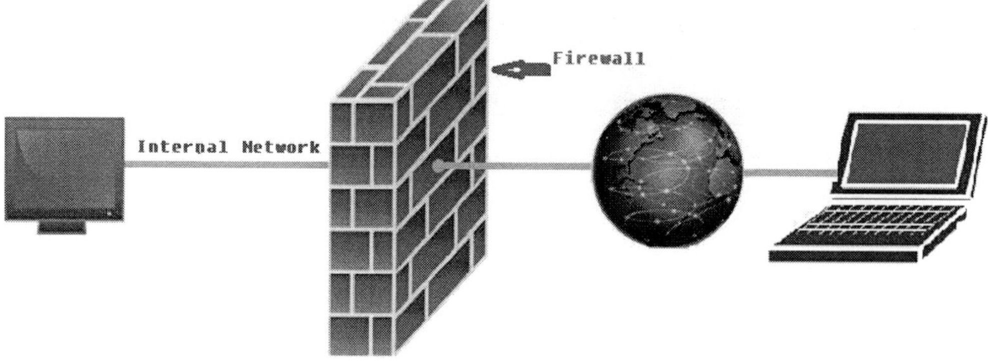

Figure 7.8: Installing Firewall

4. **SSH:** It is expanded as **Secure Shell**. It is a cryptographic network protocol that provides a secure transmission of data over a network by encoding the data. It provides a secure way to access a computer over an unsecured network. *(Figure 7.9)*

It is widely used by **network administrators** for managing systems and applications remotely. It allows user to log on to different computer on different network and access files by executing commands.

Figure 7.9: Secure Shell Protocol using Cryptography

Check Your Progress

State whether the following statements are True or False.

1. Secure Shell is a cryptographic network protocol that provides a secure transmission of data over a network by encoding the data.
2. SSL is expanded as Secure Layer.
3. Fraud committed online is known as cyber fraud.

Let's Revise

- Cyber safety refers to the safe use of internet. It includes rules guiding how to keep personal information safe and limited.
- Open-Source Software (OSS) is computer software with its source code made available.
- Shareware are copyrighted software that can be shared on a trial basis with the understanding that if the user decides to use it, he will pay for it.
- A firewall is a program or hardware device that filters the information coming through an internet connection to a network or computer system.
- Hackers are people with skills who use their knowledge to gain unauthorized access to data in a system or computer.
- Crackers modify, or disable features of a software application. They usually mean to harm the software, the hardware using this software or the end user of the software.
- Netiquette is short form of Internet Etiquette that specifies the good behaviour on internet.
- Software license refers to the legal agreement to use an application or software.
- Open-Source Software (OSS) is software that can be modified or enhanced for the reusability and accessibility of a program.
- Free software is a software which is freely distributed and accessible to all those users who want to access it.
- Intellectual property refers to the right given by the owner of the property as to how much information should be exchanged, shared or distributed.
- E-commerce is the process of buying and selling goods online. It is an electronic exchange of money between the buyer and the seller.
- Fraud committed online is known as cyber fraud, online fraud, internet fraud or simply fraud.
- Secure transmission refers to the transfer of data such as confidential or proprietary information over a secure channel.
- A firewall is a program or hardware device that filters the information coming through an internet connection to a network or computer system.
- Secure shell is a cryptographic network protocol that provide a secure transmission of data over a network by end coding the data.
- Digital property is the property which is created by you online or digitally.
- Phishing is the method of stealing username and password to get access to the system illegally.
- Product keys is the method of providing an authentication to your product.
- Freedom of information refers to the freedom of speech.

Learning Zone

SECTION A: OBJECTIVE TYPE QUESTIONS

A. MULTIPLE CHOICE QUESTIONS.

1. The full form of OSS is:
   a. Open source software
   b. Open socket software
   c. Open software
   d. Open source
2. Plagiarism is the act of:
   a. Stealing another's money
   b. Stealing another's' thought or creative ideas
   c. Stealing username and password
   d. Stealing laptop
3. Data encryption means:
   a. To gives credential information to others
   b. To encrypt the data
   c. To decrypt the data
   d. To cypher the text
4. __________ allows users to access, change, and improve its source code.
   a. Freeware
   b. Shareware
   c. Open source software
   d. None of the above
5. Linux is an example of:
   a. Free software
   b. Open source software
   c. Shareware
   d. None of the above
6. Which of the following is not an external threat to a computer or a computer network?
   a. Ignorance b. Trojan horses c. Adware d. Crackers
7. It is a program or hardware device that filters the information coming through an internet connection to a network or computer system.
   a. Antivirus b. Firewall c. Cookies d. Cyber safety
8. Which of the following is a class of computer threat?
   a. Phishing b. DoS attacks c. Soliciting d. Stalking
9. When a person is harassed repeatedly by being followed, called or be written to he/she is a target of:
   a. Bullying b. Identity theft c. Stalking d. Phishing
10. It is a software that legally remains the property of the one who developed it or who owns it:
    a. Open source b. Proprietary c. Freeware d. Shareware
11. A freely distributed software available with its source code:
    a. Shareware software
    b. Open source software
    c. Demo software
    d. Free software
12. One of the following is a proprietary software:
    a. Mysql b. Linux c. Java net beans d. Adobe Photoshop
13. What protects the intellectual property created by authors:
    a. Industrial property
    b. Copyright
    c. Related rights
    d. Trademark

14. The symbol that is used for registered trademark is:

a. SM b. RM c. TM d. @

15. ________ certificates help authenticate the identity of your company and encrypt data in transit

a. ssh b. stp c. ssl d. None of the above

Ans. 1. a 2. b 3. b 4. c 5. b
6. a 7. b 8. b 9. a 10. a
11. b 12. b 13. d 14. b 15. c

B. FILL IN THE BLANKS.

1. ____________ is the property which is created by you online or digitally.
2. __________ is the method of stealing username and password to get access to the system illegally.
3. ____________ is the method of providing an authentication to your product.
4. ____________ refers to the right given by the owner of the property as to how much information should be exchanged, shared or distributed.
5. ____________ is the process of buying and selling goods online.
6. Fraud committed online is known as ____________.
7. The full form of GPL is ____________.
8. ____________ products are fakes or unauthorised duplicates of the real product.
9. ____________ refers to the right given by the owner of the property as to how much information should be exchanged.
10. ____________ refers to the availability of accessing information on the basis of income, education, geographical areas etc.

Ans. 1. Digital property 2. Phishing 3. Product keys
4. Intellectual property 5. E-commerce 6. Cyber fraud
7. General Public Licence 8. Counterfeit 9. Intellectual property
10. Digital divide

C. STATE WHETHER THE FOLLOWING STATEMENTS ARE TRUE OR FALSE.

1. Self-plagiarism occurs when a piece of work is copied entirely from one or other sources.
2. Fraudulent pop up window provide free proprietary software.
3. The word plagiarism comes from the Latin word kidnapping.
4. The free software movement was an idea of Richard Stallman.
5. The Mt symbol can be used for the trademark.
6. Each state in India has its own copyright laws.
7. Physical assets that are owned by the business are not included in the digital property.
8. Shareware software is free and has no time limit for its usage.
9. Digital divide describes the uneven distribution of internet resources.
10. Trademark is used for the right to copy.

Ans. 1. False 2. False 3. True 4. True 5. False
6. False 7. True 8. True 9. True 10. False

SECTION B: SOLVED THEORY QUESTIONS

1. **What do you mean by software license?**

Ans: Software license refers to the legal agreement to use an application or software. The agreement is between the producer and the user who wants to access it by posing some restriction without legally purchasing it

2. **Differentiate between OSS and Free software.**

Ans: Open-source software (OSS) is software that can be modified or enhanced for reusability and accessibility of a program.

Free software is a software which is freely distributed and accessible to all those users who want to access it. The software can be modified, enhanced or copied without any payment.

3. **What do you mean by phishing and plagiarism?** **(Sample paper 2019-20)**

Ans: Phishing is the method of stealing username and password to get access to the system illegally. This allows attackers to take advantage of a user's public information (via social networks, for example) to perform fraud with increased authenticity.

Plagiarism is the act of stealing others' creative ideas, thought creation of art, music etc. and mark them as its own.

4. **Define digital divide and Digital property.**

Ans: Digital divide is a gap of accessing information by different people living in different geographical areas.

Digital property is the property which is created by us online or digitally. This property may be in terms of our own creation, picture, art, music, video clips etc.

5. **What are the two main reasons of digital divide?**

Ans: The two main reasons of digital divide are:

a. Reach of internet access: Internet facility is not available especially in rural areas that increase the level of digital divide between rural and urban areas.
b. Literacy level: People living in rural areas are not techno savvy. They don't know even the basics of how to use internet and access information that increase the level of digital divide.

6. **What are the various types of plagiarism? Explain them.**

Ans: The various types of plagiarism are:

a. Direct Plagiarism: Direct plagiarism is the word-for-word transcription of a section of someone else's work, without attribution and without quotation marks.
b. Self-Plagiarism: Self-plagiarism occurs when a student submits his or her own previous work, or mixes parts of previous works, without permission from all professors involved.
c. Mosaic Plagiarism: Mosaic Plagiarism occurs when a student borrows phrases from a source without using quotation marks, or finds synonyms for the author's language while keeping to the same general structure and meaning of the original.
d. Accidental Plagiarism: Accidental plagiarism occurs when a person neglects to cite their sources, or mis-quotes their sources, or unintentionally paraphrases a source by using similar words, groups of words, and/or sentence structure without attribution.

7. **Write the various digital property rights.**

Ans: Various digital property rights are:

a. Internet access for all
b. Freedom of expression and association
c. Access to knowledge
d. Shared learning and creation – free and open source software and technology development

e. Privacy and Data Protection
f. Awareness, protection and realization of rights
g. Network Equality
h. Right to freedom of expression
i. Right to report anyone or anything that seems inappropriate

8. What is DRM?

Ans: DRM is expanded as Digital Rights Management (DRM). It is the digital property solution that protects the software from being scraped for source codes using de-compilers. It prevents our source code from being leaked.

9. Differentiate between hackers and crackers.

Ans: Hackers are the people who want to gain unauthorized access to the system and gain control over it by breaking the username or password. To do so they steal sensitive information and personal data of the owner of the system. However, their intention is not to harm the system or to use the programs for an unethical purpose.

Crackers are the people whose main intension is to harm the system by gaining access to the system. To establish this goal, they use various programs to break the privacy of the system and get confidential data. For example, they can use the sensitive information against you by stealing money, personal data, pictures, bank details and government military information and so on. Crackers have an end goal of destroying data and network for personal monetary gains

10. What do you mean by data encryption?

Ans: Data encryption is the method of securing the data when it is sent over the network. The original data is first encrypted and then transfer from the sender side. When it reaches to the receiver, the data is decrypted or decoded so as to get the original message. This process is known as cryptography. This mechanism prevents from eavesdropping.

11. What is the significance of using SSL certificate?

Ans: SSL certificates help to authenticate the identity of our company and encrypt data in transit. It provides extra protection to our business and for our customers. For example, to validate a credit card payment, a payment gateway will use the online address verification services.

12. Define the term trademark.

Ans: A trademark is a distinctive sign that identifies certain goods or services produced or provided by an individual or a company.

13. Which sign is used for trademark and service mark?

Ans: For trademark: The symbol used is TM.

For service mark: The symbol used is SM.

14. How can you avoid plagiarism?

Ans: The various methods for avoiding plagiarism are:

a. Always give credit to another's person's work, ideas or thoughts.
b. Don't use others quotation or written words as if they are our own.
c. Acknowledge all types of sources of information such as books, magazines, journals, websites, newspapers etc.

15. Under which circumstances a trademark can be issued?

Ans: A trademark can be issued in the following cases:

a. When we intend to use a name or symbol.
b. A foreign trademark can be believed effective.
c. When we are already using a name or a symbol.

SECTION C: APPLICATION ORIENTED QUESTIONS

1. **Amita is a student of Class-X and she has to prepare notes on cybercrimes. For this purpose, she explored the topic from the internet and copied information from there without citing it or putting it in quotation marks.**
   a. What kind of cybercrime it is known as?
   b. How can you avoid this?

Ans: As, Amita copied the article from internet without quotation marks, this is a cybercrime and is known as Plagiarism. It can be avoided by citing the name of the person who wrote this or she should write this article on her own.

2. **While transferring data, SSL encrypts it. What does it mean?**

Ans: SSL is a secure data transmission technology that transfers the data from the sender to the receiver over a secure network by encoding the original message. This encoding is known as encryption.

3. **Geeta and Deepak are two friends. One day when Geeta was buying some products online, then somehow Deepak stole her credentials. What kind of cyber-attack it was?**

Ans: This kind of cyber-attack is known as Phishing. When the person is deliberately steals others username and password for some illegal purpose or for his/her means then it is a cybercrime and is known as phishing attack.

4. **Palvi has created a PowerPoint presentation for her class. She finds really beautiful photographs on a website, so she copies and pastes them into her PowerPoint. Is it plagiarism and if this is plagiarised, what should be done to fix the problem?**

Ans: No, Palvi's act would not be considered plagiarism. Depending on where she got the picture, it might well be a violation of copyright, but it is not plagiarism.

5. **Geetu is an artist. She posts her artwork on the internet. One day she comes to know that Shreyas has downloaded one of the paintings that she had posted without her permission. He had further printed that image on an invitation card. Has Shreyas done the right thing? Which right of Geetu has he infringed? (Sample Paper 2019-20)**

Ans: No, Intellectual Property Rights.

6. **Ritwik wants to use a software but does not want to pay for it. Which type of software can he use? (Sample Paper 2019-20)**

Ans: Open Source Software.

7. **Neetu has just learnt how to do online banking. Name any two precautions that she should take to prevent online fraud.**

Ans: a. Do not share user id and password with anyone.
b. Avoid doing transactions from cybercafé and other public places.

8. **Write two advantages of using open source software over proprietary software.**

Ans: a. Source Code available for modification and redistribution.
b. Freely available for usage.

SECTION D: SELF - ASSESSMENT

A. FILL IN THE BLANKS.

1. ____________ is a legal instrument that allows customers to use or redistribute software.
2. Microsoft and Apple are two companies which produces ____________ software.

3. ____________ is an open source operating system.
4. ____________ is an open source application software.
5. ____________ is used for the right to copy.
6. ____________ describes the uneven distribution of internet resources.
7. ____________ is a software which is available free of cost but without its source code.
8. The full form of GPL is ____________.
9. RTI Act ____________ gives rights to Indian citizens to inspect any government papers.
10. ____________ is a combination of the words network etiquettes.
11. A ____________ is an electronic text file that a website parks on a visitor's browser.
12. ____________ is the term to relate the idea that users would be free to change and share source code as it appears fit.
13. ____________ is the process of collecting your personal information through e-mails or websites claiming to be legitimate software.
14. ____________ is a software that is usually distributed for testing, preview or donation purpose.
15. Free software movement was the idea of ____________.

B. STATE WHETHER THE FOLLOWING STATEMENTS ARE TRUE OR FALSE.

1. The word plagiarism comes from a Latin word for kidnapping.
2. All Microsoft operating system comes under end-user license agreement.
3. Web bugs are small transparent graphics that are placed in web pages or e-mail messages.
4. Self-plagiarism occurs when a piece of work is copied entirely from one or more sources.
5. Fraudulent pop-up window provides free proprietary software.
6. MIT licence allows unlimited redistribution for any purpose as long as its copyright warnings and licences disclaimers of warranty are maintained.
7. A trademark is registerable if it is distinctive for the goods and services you provide.
8. Software piracy means that you can illegally copying, downloading, distribution or use a software.
9. Shareware is a type of software that is distributed for a limited period of time.
10. Copyright is the term that describes the uneven distribution of internet resources.
11. Ubuntu is an open source operating system.
12. The full form of NOFN is National Optical Fibre Network.
13. Plagiarism in section of a document that are directly copied and unacknowledged source within an assignment is known as partial plagiarism.
14. Trademark give content creator the right to control literary and artistic work.
15. A set of rules for adequate online behaviour is known as Netiquette.

C. TICK THE CORRECT ANSWER.

1. This type of creation is protected by Copyright laws:

   a. Publication b. Artwork c. Musical composition d. All of these

2. Out of the following which is not a part of Trade sector?
   a. Business methods   b. Formulas
   c. Customer database   d. Manufacturing processes
3. This is the software that tracks the websites visited by a user and uses the information to build a profile:
   a. Web bugs   b. Cookie   c. Spyware   d. Adware
4. The act of representing another's work as if it is your own work is known as:
   a. Fraud   b. Plagiarism   c. Copy left   d. Patent
5. The software which does not allow you to modify its code is known as:
   a. Free software   b. Freeware   c. Open source   d. Proprietary software
6. Which of the following statements(s) is false for GNU General Public Licence?
   a. There's no limit to where and how many times you can copy the code
   b. You can distribute the code in any form using with a download link on your website or print out the code on paper
   c. You cannot use the code in your own proprietary software
   d. You can charge someone for the software by telling them why you are charging it
7. This is a freely distributed software available with its source code.
   a. Shareware software   b. Demo software
   c. Open source software   d. Free software
8. Trade sectors protects:
   a. Pattern   b. Formula
   c. Process of doing things   d. All of these
9. The word plagiarism comes from the Latin word:
   a. Cheating   b. Kidnapping   c. Stealing   d. None of these
10. Fraudulent pop up window is a type of:
   a. Offline fraud   b. Online fraud   c. Stealing   d. Simple fraud
11. Intellectual property does not include:
   a. Pattern   b. Product design   c. Literary work   d. Architectural work
12. Netizen is a combination of two words:
   a. Network and etiquettes   b. Internet and citizen
   c. Intranet and citizen   d. None of these
13. Phishing is the process of:
   a. Collecting personal information online   b. Collecting e-mail details online
   c. Sending and receiving mails   d. Both a. and b.
14. Collision is a type of:
   a. Plagiarism   b. Intellectual rights   c. Copyright   d. Trademark
15. Personality rights is a type of:
   a. Plagiarism   b. Intellectual property rights
   c. Digital divide   d. Copyright

D. ANSWER THE FOLLOWING QUESTIONS.

Type A: Very Short Answer Questions.

1. What do you mean by cyber netiquettes?
2. What do you mean by plagiarism?
3. Define intellectual rights.
4. Define the term digital divide.
5. What do you understand by the term software copyright?
6. What might happen if you get caught breaking copyright law?
7. You borrow an essay written by another student and then submit it as if it is your's is this plagiarism? if yes, explain.
8. List any four advantages of e-commerce to society.
9. What is proprietary software?
10. What is free software and is it same as pen software?

Type B: Short Answer Questions.

1. What is the difference between phishing and plagiarism?
2. Differentiate between ethical hacking and unethical hacking.
3. Discuss the various digital property rights and how can you protect it?
4. What do you mean by software license and what are its various types?
5. What is the difference between direct plagiarism and self-plagiarism?
6. What is meant by freedom of information? Does everybody has an access to information globally? If not, state the reasons.
7. How can you protect your data and identity while selling and buying products online?
8. What is cyber Fraud and what are the various precautionary measure to combat this?
9. What is encrypting and decrypting of data?
10. What is e-commerce? How can you avoid fraud online?
11. What is data encryption and data decryption?
12. Write some advantages of open source software.

Type C: Long Answer Questions.

1. What do you mean by intellectual property rights? Discuss its various types.
2. Describe any three types of plagiarism.
3. What is patent, trademark and copyright?
4. Explain the term online fraud with an example.
5. What do you mean by secure data transmission? What are the various techniques to have a secure transmission of data?
6. Draw a diagram and explain the encryption and decryption of data.
7. How is mosaic plagiarism different from accidental plagiarism?
8. What are the four types of freedom provided to the user in open source software?

9. What is the difference between perpetual license and non-perpetual license?
10. Which of the following situation show a type of plagiarism?
    a. Using your own past material as a new idea without any reference.
    b. Paraphrasing with citation.
    c. Incorporating some other's idea heard in a conference without citation.

Activity Zone

1. Tell students to make a list of cyber frauds and plagiarism.
2. Discuss the various means how can you protect your credentials from crackers?
3. Tell your students to prepare a chart on the various open source software.

Sample Question Paper (Term 1)

Class: X Session: 2021-22
Computer Applications (Code 165)

Maximum Marks: 25 **Time Allowed: 90 Minutes**

General Instructions:

1. The Question Paper contains three sections A, B and C.
2. Section A has 20 questions. Attempt any 16 questions.
3. Section B has 20 questions. Attempt any 16 questions.
4. Section C has 10 questions. Attempt any 8 questions.
5. All questions carry equal marks.
6. There is no negative marking.

SECTION – A

This section consists of 20 questions of MCQ type. Answer any 16 questions.

1. Which one of the following software comes under Open-Source Software category?
   a. Photoshop b. Ms-Paint
   c. Linux d. Windows
2. HTML tag to draw horizontal line:
   a. <hl> b. <hr> c. <hline> d. None of the above
3. Secure data transmission means
   a. Data is accessible by any unauthorized person during transmission.
   b. Data can not be accessed by any unauthorized person during transmission.
   c. Transmission of data happens easily
   d. Noone can access it
4. The correct HTML code to display(P+Q)2 is:
   a. _{(P+) 2} b. P+Q ²
   c. (P + Q)² d. ^{(P+Q) 2}
5. Which HTML tags cause browsers to render text as italics?
   a. <text style = "italics"></text> b. <ital.></ital.>
   c. <i></i> d. <b></b>
6. The correct HTML code for inserting an image is :
   a. <img href="image.gif"> b. <img> image.gif</gif>
   c. <image src = "image.gif"> d. <img src = "image.gif" >
7. Which attribute is NOT valid for the <body> tag?
   a. background b. color c. vlink d. bgcolor

8. __________ attribute is used to specify the location of an image file.

a. alt b. src c. align d. name

9. Which of the following is NOT an example of Intellectual Property rights?

a. Patent b. Trademark c. Password d. Industrial Design

10. The __________ attribute of <img> tag specifies an alternate text for an image, if the image cannot be displayed due to any reason.

a. alt b. alternate c. tooltip d. text

11. While creating a Web document, which unit is used to express an image's height and width?

a. Centimeters b. Pixels c. Dots per inch d. Inches

12. Preeti needs to send a very confidential message to her colleague in office over a secure channel. She uses a technique wherein an actual message (which is in readable form) can be converted into an unreadable message. This concept is known as __________

a. Encryption b. Decryption

c. Plagiarism d. Data Security.

13. Which is the correct way to comment out something in HTML?

a. Using ## and # b. Using <!-- and-->

c. Using </-- and-/-> d. Using <!-- and-!>

14. The default alignment of images, that are inserted in Web page, is:

a. left b. right c. inline with text d. middle

15. Which of the following techniques can be used for security of data?

a. Authentication b. Authorisation

c. Encryption d. All of the Above

16. Which of the following is not a cybercrime?

a. Plagiarism b. Phishing

c. using licensed software d. hacking

17. __________ is a software for which exclusive rights of modification in the source code remain with the owner.

a. Free Open-Source Software b. Freeware

c. Open-Source Software d. Proprietary Software

18. A __________ is the right given by the government to an inventor to protect his/ her invention from being used/copied for a fixed period of time.

a. Copyright b. Intellectual Property

c. Patent d. Trademark

19. Which of these is NOT an attribute of the font tag?

a. color b. face c. type d. size

20. The <__________> tag displays text in subscript form.

a. sub b. sup c. sups d. subs.

SECTION – B

This section contains 20 questions. Answer any 16 questions.

21. Arun clicks on a link received in a message on his phone which promises him a complimentary trip to a destination of his choice. He forwarded this message to his friend, Panshul and asked him to do the same. But Panshul refuses and tells Arun that his personal and private information, such as online account names, login information and passwords can be stolen and he should be careful of such __________ attacks.

    a. Phishing
    b. Spamming
    c. Scamming
    d. Plagiarism

22. Consider the following HTML code:

```
<ol type='i'>
<li>First</li>
<li>Second</li>
<li>Third</li>
<li>Fourth</li>
</ol>
```

Choose the correct output that would be shown upon execution of the above code , from the choices given below:

a. I. First
   II. Second
   III. Third
   IV. Fourth

b. i. First
   ii. Second
   iii. Third
   iv. Fourth

c. I First
   II Second
   III Third
   IV Fourth

d. i First
   ii Second
   iii Third
   iv Fourth

23. Charlene is an artist. She displays her artwork on the Internet using her website to attract buyers. One day while browsing the Internet she discovers that another artist has displayed her painting portraying it as his own. Which right of Charlene was infringed?

    a. Digital Privacy right
    b. Intellectual Property right
    c. Digital Property right
    c. Intellectual Privacy right

24. Which of the following will result in the largest text size?

    a. <H3> b. <H6> c. <H2> d. <H4>

25. We can create a numbered list using the __________ tag.

    a. <UL> b. <list> c. <OL> d. <DL>

26. Which of these is NOT an example of Cyber bullying?

    a. Copying a classmate's personal photo against his/her permission from his social media account and sending it to other friends on their emails
    b. Bullying a classmate in the school corridor.

c. Threatening someone on whatsapp.

d. Posting mean messages about someone on their social media.

27. Identify which of the following type of list will create a bulleted list.

a. Unordered
b. Ordered
c. Definition
d. Numbered

28. Which sequence of HTML tags is correct?

a. <html><head><title></title></head><body></body></html>

b. <html><head><title><body></title></head></body></html>

c. <html><head><title</head><body></body>></title></</html>

d. <html><head><title><body></body ></title></head ></html>

29. Pratham is excited to use a new software which is freely available to download but he cannot modify or change the source code. Pratham is using

a. Freeware
b. Open-Source Software
c. Both a and b
d. None of the above

30. Priyanshu has written the following code snippet as part pf an HTML program.

<B> Mystery Moon </B>

Predict the output of the above from the following:

a. Mystery Moon
b. **Mystery Moon**
c. ***Mystery Moon***
d. *Mystery Moon*

31. Consider the following code:

<img src="Computers.jpg" width="__________" height="__________">

Fill in the blanks to set the image size to be 250pixels wide and 400 pixels tall.

a. 250, 400
b. 400, 250
c. <250><400>
d. <400><250>

32. Tag (s) required to create Description lists in HTML:

a. <DL>
b. <DT>
c. <DD>
d. All of the above

33. Which of the following is NOT a reason for the digital divide in different demographic regions?

a. Cost of Technology

b. Lack of information

c. Lack of access to high performance computers

d. Lack of access to the disabled.

34. One of the most popular method of encrypting data is Ceaser cipher where original data is replaced by a key character like if key is-2 than 'a' will be replaced by 'y', 'b' is replaced by 'z' and so on.

If the key is 2 i.e. Every letter is replaced by its next to next letter means the letter 'A' will be replaced by 'C', the letter 'B' is replaced by 'D', and so on then what will be the replacement of the word 'CoMpUtEr'.

a. Eqorwvgt
b. eQOrwVtG
c. eqroWVTG
d. EqOrWvGt

35. Consider the following form control in a HTML form:

◯ Male

◯ Female

Now choose the correct line of code for the above :

a. <input type = “radio” name= “Gender” value= “male”>Male
<input type = “radio” name= “Gender” value= “female”>Female

b. <input type = “radiobutton” name= “Gender” value= “male”>Male
<input type = “radiobutton” name= “Gender” value= “female”>Female

c. <input type = “radio”, name= “Gender”>< value= “male”>Male
<input type = “radio”, name= “Gender”>< value= “female”>Female

d. <input type = “radio” name= “Gender” value= “male”>
<input type = “radio” name= “Gender” value= “female”>

36. Gagandeep has written the following code to display an image in the background of HTML document:

<BODY BgGround= “Animals.jpeg”>

but he is not getting the desired output. Help him in identifying correct code from the following

a. <BODY Bg= “Animals.jpeg”>
b. <BODY BACK= “Animals.jpeg”>
c. <BODY BGIMAGE= “Animals.jpeg”>
d. <BODY BACKGROUND= “Animals.jpeg”>

37. Which of the following is a way to avoid Plagiarism when using material from the Internet?

i. Citing
ii. Paraphrasing
iii. Referencing
iv. embedding

Choose the correct option:

a. i and ii only
b. Only i
c. i, ii and iii only
d. ii and iv only

38. Tag to create password field in HTML document:

a. <password>
b. <input>
c. <pwd>
d. <pword>

39. Which of the following tag is used to define options in a drop-down selection list?

a. <select>
b. <list>
c. <dropdown>
d. <option>

40. Which of the following is the correct way to create a list using the lowercase letters?

a. <ol alpha = “a” >
b. <ol type = “a”>
c. <ol letter = “a”>
d. None of the above

SECTION – C

Case study based questions

Section C consists of 10 questions. Any 8 questions are to be attempted.

Case Study – I

Geetika has recently created her social accounts. She is very excited as she waited so long to go online. She has recently also got admission in a prestigious high school and does not know many students.

When she logs into her social media a few days later, she finds that someone is posting negative, demeaning comments on her social media profile. She is also getting repeated mails from unknown people. Whenever she goes online, she is trolled by multiple unknown people.

Based on the given information, answer the questions NO. 41-45.

41. Geetika is a victim of ___________:

    a. Eavesdropping b. Plagiarism c. Phishing d. Cyber stalking

42. Which of the following is the most appropriate action she should take?

    a. She should stop going online and delete her social media accounts.

    b. She should NOT share this with anyone as she might face more of such kind of behaviour.

    c. She should file a complaint at the nearest police station.

    d. She should inform her parents and bring to the notice of school authorities.

43. After hearing her ordeal, the school decides to publish a set of moral principles that determines the appropriate behavior of students while using the internet. The school is referring to ___________

    a. Intellectual Property rights b. Internet Privacy

    c. Computer Ethics d. Cyber Ethics

44. Geetika is advised by her best friend, Seerat to protect her personal information from intentional or unintentional attacks by others. This is also known as ___________

    a. Digital right b. Copyright c. Data Privacy d. Intellectual property

45. The computer teacher of Geetika's class decides to take an online session on the topic Netiquettes, which generally includes:

    a. safeguarding one's passwords and sensitive online information

    b. logging out of social media accounts after the session

    c. not bullying or trolling anyone by disrespecting them or passing inappropriate remarks

    d. All of the above.

Case Study – II

Consider the following code created by Sumantha for a webpage:

```
<html>
<body bgcolor="yellow">
<center>
<h1> Our Country : India <___>                    -------line1
<imgsrc="india.jpg">
</center>
<p>
<font color="red" size="5"___="Times New Roman">  -------line2
India is spread over a large geographical area. In terms of area, it is the 7<sup>th</sup> largest country while in terms of population,
it is the 2<sup>nd</sup>  largest country in the world.
```

```
Some facts about India are as follows<___></p>          -------line3
<ul>
<li>Area :Approx 3.28 million sq. km <_>               -------line4
<li>North to South extension :Approx 3,200 km</li>
<li>East to West extension :Approx 2900 km</li>
<___>                                                   -------line5
</body>
</html>
```

Based on the given information, answer the questions NO. 46-50.

46. Choose the correct option from the following to fill up in line 1:

    a. \h1 b. \h6 c. /h6 d. /h1

47. Choose the correct option from the following to fill up in line 2:

    a. font b. face c. type d. text

48. Choose the correct option from the following to fill up in line 3:

    a. </f> b. <f> c. </font> d. <font>

49. Choose the correct option from the following to fill up in line 4:

    a. <i> b. </li> c. <\li> d. <\i>

50. Choose the correct option from the following to fill up in line 5:

    a. ul b. <\ul> c. <ul> d. </ul>

Marking Scheme (Term 1)

CLASS: X SESSION: 2021-22
COMPUTER APPLICATIONS (CODE 165)

Maximum Marks: 25 **Time Allowed: 90 Minutes**

All Questions carry equal marks

Q. No.	Section – A
1	c. Linux
2	b. <hr>
3	b) Data can not be accessed by any unauthorized person during transmission.
4	c. (P + Q)²
5	c. <i></i>
6	d. <img src = "image.gif">
7	b. color
8	b. src
9	c. Password
10	a. alt
11	b. Pixels
12	a. Encryption
13	b. Using <!-- and-->
14	c. inline with text
15	d. All of the Above
16	c. using licensed software
17	d. Proprietary Software
18.	c. Patent
19	c. type
20	a. sub
	Section – B
21	a. Phishing
22	b. i. First ii. Second iii. Third iv. Fourth
23	b. Intellectual Property right

24	c. <H2>
25	c. <OL>
26	b. Bullying a classmate in the school corridor.
27	a. Unordered
28	a. <html><head><title></title></head><body></body></html>
29	a. Freeware
30	b. Mystery Moon
31	a. 250, 400
32	d. All of the above
33	c. Lack of access to high performance computers
34	d. EqOrWvGt
35	a. <input type = "radio" name= "Gender" value= "male">Male <input type = "radio" name= "Gender" value= "female">Female
36	d. <BODY BACKGROUND= "Animals.jpeg">
37	c. i, ii and iii only
38	b. <input>
39	d. <option>
40	b. <ol type = "a">
Section – C	
41	d. Cyber stalking
42	d. She should inform her parents and bring to the notice of school authorities.
43	d. Cyber Ethics
44	c. Data Privacy
45	d. All of the above.
46	d. /h1
47	b. face
48	c. </font>
49	b. </li>
50	d. </ul>

Sample Question Paper (Term 2)

Class: X Session: 2021-22
Computer Applications (Code 165)

Maximum Marks: 25 **Time Allowed: 90 Minutes**

General Instructions:

1. The Question Paper contains three sections A, B and C.
2. Section A has 20 questions. Attempt any 16 questions.
3. Section B has 20 questions. Attempt any 16 questions.
4. Section C has 10 questions. Attempt any 8 questions.
5. All questions carry equal marks.
6. There is no negative marking.

SECTION – A

This section consists of 20 questions of MCQ type. Answer any 16 questions.

1 Which protocol is used for uploading and downloading files over network?

a. SMTP b. TELNET c. FTP d. HTTP

2 First page of a Web site is called

a. Web page b. Home page c. First page d. Web server

3 __________ is a client software that helps the user to navigate WWW.

a. Web site b. Browser c. Web page d. Web server

4 The domain extension .mil refers to a type of website.

a. Commercial b. Government c. Military d. Educational

5 ISP stands for:

a. Intranet Service Provider b. Internet Service Provider

c. Inter Service Provider d. International Special Products

6 The 's' at the end of HTTPs stands for:

a. Social b. Secure c. Strong d. Smart

7 Internet works on

a. packet switching

b. circuit switching

c. both packet switching and circuit switching

d. none of the mentioned

8 A term that defines learning done at a computer connected to network giving an opportunity to learn anytime and anywhere.

a. e-banking b. e-learning c. e-shopping d. e-reservation

9 A program that searches documents for specified keywords and returns a list of documents:

a. E-mail
b. Search engine
c. Video conferencing
d. E-shopping

10 The essential component of video conferencing is.

a. Printer
b. UPS
c. Mouse
d. Web cam

11 Which of the following keyword is used to find web pages that do not contain the mentioned keywords?

a. AND
b. OR
c. NOT
d. – (MINUS)

12 ____________ is a collection of messages normally text posted by individuals to a news server.

a. Newsgroup
b. e-mail
c. Newsreader
d. TELNET

13 Booking tickets online is known as ________________.

a. E-shopping
b. E-reservation
c. E-learning
d. E-commerce

14 An e-mail can be sent to:

a. a receiver even if he is offline
b. a person who has an e-mail account on some other search engine
c. many people at a time
d. All of the above.

15 Verification of a login name and password is known as:

a. configuration
b. accessibility
c. authentication
d. logging in

16 It is the valid e-mail address

a. yoga@yoga.com
b. agrima@hotmail.com
c. abc$gmail.com
d. myaccount%gmail.com

17 IETF stands for ________________.

a. Internet Engineering Task Force
b. Intranet Engineering Task Force
c. Inter Engineering Task Force
d. None of the above

18 Which of the following tag is used for audio in HTML?

a. <bgsound>
b. <audio>
c. <video>
d. <canvas>

19 Most commonly used video formats are.

a. ogg
b. mpeg4
c. Both a and b
d. only mpeg4

20 Two attributes for source tag while embedding audio in html are:

a. source and type
b. src and type
c. method and source
d. Both b and c

SECTION – B

This section contains 20 questions. Answer any 16 questions

21 ______________ tag is used for inserting video in html

a. insert
b. embed
c. add
d. src

22 Can you change the height and width of a video file while inserting in html code?

a. Yes b. No

23 Which property tells how many rows a cell should span?

a. Colspan = n b. Rowspan =n c. Both a. and b. d. None of these

24 How can you create an e-mail link?

a. <mail href="a@b">

b. <mail>a@b</mail>

c. <a href="a@b">

d. <a href="mailto:a@b.com">

25 Which one of the following is not an attribute of <A> tag:

a. NAME b. HREF c. Source d. Both (a) & (b)

26 Colspan=n can be added to only what tag?

a. <table> b. <td> c. <tr> d. <caption>

27 ____________controls the space between cells in a table

a. Cellspacing b. Cellpadding c. Spacing d. cellspace

28 Which of the following property is used to create a small-caps effect?

a. font-family b. font-style c. font-variant d. font-weight

29 table {color: blue;}. In this code snippet, which part represents the property?

a. table b. color c. blue

30 Which property is used to align the text in CSS?

a. Text-alignment b. Align-text c. Alignment d. Text-align

31 It is a style sheet language used for describing the look and formatting of a document written in a markup language.

a. Document Object Model (DOM)

b. Multimedia filters

c. Cascading Style Sheets (CSS)

d. DHTML

32 bgcolor property is used to change the background color of a web page using CSS code

a. True b. False

33 WHICH IS NOT THE VALUE OF TEXT-FORMATION IN CSS?

a. Capitalize

b. Uppercase

c. Lowercase

d. Title

34 FIND THE CORRECT CODE TO DISPLAY THE TEXT "WELCOME" IN small caps?

a. <h1 style="font-variant : small-caps">WELCOME </h1>

b. <h1 style="font-style : small-caps">WELCOME </h1>

c. <h1 style="font-variant : small">WELCOME </h1>

d. None of the above

35 Which property is used to horizontally align the text at the center ?

a. p{text-align:center;}

b. p{align:center;}

c. p{center-align}

d. none of the above

36 Find the correct code to set the background color of the body as blue in CSS

a. body { bgcolor : blue;}
b. body { background-color: blue;}
c. body { color: blue;}
d. body { background-color = "blue";}

37 Kavita set up the following Auto Delete options on her web-based e-mail account.

Inbox	Never
Sent	Never
Draft	Never
Personal	Never
User created	Never
Trash	Older than 1 month
Filtered spam	Submit

What is the most likely reason, she has set the trash folder to delete "older than 1 month"?

Kavita wants:

a. All e-mails to have a delete date.
b. All sent e-mails to be deleted after 1 month
c. C. all deleted e-mails to only remain in the trash folder for 1 month
d. D. all e-mails in her inbox to be moved to the trash folder after 1 month.

38 It is the method of sending textual messages through mobile phones.

a. MMS
b. SSM
c. SMS
d. SMM

39 A web service primarily for the use of information and communication technology by government sectors to improve the quality of services and provide information to the citizens on time and in a cost efficient manner is:

a. E-commerce
b. E-banking
c. E-reservation
d. E-governance

40 Which attribute is used to give background color to a table?

a. Back-color
b. background
c. Bgcolor
d. Color

SECTION – C

Case study based questions

Section C consists of 10 questions. Any 8 questions are to be attempted.

Case Study – I

As life gets busier, it becomes difficult for Ravi to keep a track with school & college friends, old colleagues, old neighbours and favourite teachers. He wants to keep in touch with all his near and dear ones. Similarly people belonging to different socio-economic background can change your perspective and can enhance your understanding of various cultures.

41 The real time tools that are suitable for the above-mentioned activities.

a. Facebook
b. TWITTER
c. TV CHANNEL
d. BOTH A AND B

42 The generic name used for such tools are:

a. Social Networking
b. Social distancing
c. Social meet
d. Social inetrnet

43 Ravi wants to do online shopping. Which website can he use?

a. Amazon
b. Uidai
c. Meritnation
d. Gitshub

44 Ravi parents are residing in delhi and he resides in Mumbai. Now, he needs some money to purchase books. How can Ravi's parents send money to him without going to Mumbai in a short while.

a. Online banking
b. Twitter
c. Facebook
d. skype

45 Ravi wants to reserve his train from Mumbai to delhi. What he should do?

a. e-reservation
b. e-booking
c. e-learning
d. e-passanger

Case Study – II

Consider the following code created by Agrima for a webpage:

```
<html>
<body>
<p> Trees are necessary for life.</p>
<A _________="first.html"> Save Trees </A>          line 1
<TABLE _________ ="pink">                            line 2
_____________Students' Details</Caption>             line 3
<TR>
<th>Name of trees </th>
<TD> Coconut</TD>
<TD> Palm</TD>
__________                                           line 4
</TABLE>
___________                                          line 5
</HTML>
```

Based on the given information, answer the questions NO. 46-50.

46 Choose the correct option from the following to fill up in line 1:

a. href
b. src
c. hyperlink
d. source

47 Choose the correct option from the following to fill up in line 2:

a. Background
b. Bgcolor
c. Color
d. None of the above

48 Choose the correct option from the following to fill up in line 3:

a. Title
b. Heading
c. Caption
d. None of the above

49 Choose the correct option from the following to fill up in line 4:

a. <TR>
b. </TR>
c. </ROW>
d. <ROW>

50 Choose the correct option from the following to fill up in line 5:

a. <BODY>
b. </BODY>
c. </HTML>
d. </TABLE>

Marking Scheme (Term 2)

CLASS: X SESSION: 2021-22
COMPUTER APPLICATIONS (CODE 165)

Maximum Marks: 25 **Time Allowed: 90 Minutes**

All Questions carry equal marks

Q. No.	SECTION-A
1	C. FTP
2	b. HOME PAGE
3	b. Browser
4	b. military
5	b. internet service provider
6	b. secure
7	a. packet switching
8	b. e-learning
9	c. search engine
10	d. webcam
11	c. – (Minus)
12	a. Newsgroup
13	b. E-reservation
14	d. All of the above
15	c. authentication
16	b. agrima@hotmail.com
17	a. Internet Engineering Task Force
18	b. <audio>
19	c. both a and b
20	b. Src and type
	SECTION-B
21	b. embed
22	a. yes
23	a. Colspan=n
24	d. <a href="mailto:a@b.com">
25	c. source
26	a. <table>

27	a. cellspacing
28	c. font-variant
29	b. color
30	b. align-text
31	c. cascading style sheet
32	b. false
33	d. title
34	a. <h1 style="font-variant:small-caps"> WELCOME </h1>
35	a. p{text-align:center;}
36	b. body { background-color: blue;}
37	c. all deleted e-mails to only remain in the trash folder for 1 month
38	c. SMS
39	d. e-governance
40	c. bgcolor
SECTION-C CASE STUDY-1	
41	d. both a and b
42	a. social networking
43	a. amazon
44	a. online banking
45	a. e-reservation
CASE STUDY-2	
46	a. href
47	b. bgcolor
48	c. caption
49	</TR>
50	</BODY>

APPENDIX – A

IMPORTANT ABBREVIATIONS

ABBREVIATIONS	EXPANDED FORM
ARPANET	Advanced Research Project Agency Network
NSFNET	National Science Foundation Network
IETF	Internet Engineering Task Force
IP	Internet Protocol
TCP	Transmission Control Protocol
FTP	File Transfer Protocol
SMTP	Simple Mail Transfer Protocol
POP	Post Office Protocol
HTTP	Hyper Text Transfer Protocol
URL	Uniform Resource Locator
DNS	Domain Name System
W3C	World Wide Web Consortium
ISP	Internet Service Provider
HTML	Hyper Text Transfer Protocol
WWW	World Wide Web
MODEM	Modulator Demodulator
IRC	Internet Relay Chat
CC	Carbon Copy
BCC	Blind Carbon Copy
EDI	Electronic Data Interchange
OL	Ordered List
UL	Unordered List
SUP	Superscript
SUB	Subscript
DD	Definition Description
DT	Definition Term
DL	Definition List
SRC	Source
HREF	Hyper Reference
ALT	Alternate

ABBREVIATIONS	EXPANDED FORM
CSS	Cascading Style Sheet
DHTML	Dynamic Hyper Text Markup Language
DOM	Document Object Model
OSS	Open Source Software
FLOSS	Free/Libre/Open Source Software
GPL	General Public License
SSL	Secure Socket Layer
EFT	Electronic Fund Transfer

APPENDIX – B

VIVA-VOCE QUESTIONS

1. What is internet?

Ans. Internet is a network of networks.

2. What is network?

Ans. Network is an interconnection of several devices.

3. What is the role of FTP?

Ans. FTP is a file transfer protocol and is used for downloading and uploading files over network.

4. Which language is used for creating web pages?

Ans. Hyper Text Markup Language is used for creating web pages.

5. What is the full form of CSS?

Ans. The expanded form of CSS is cascading style sheet.

6. What is URL? What are ite two types?

Ans. URL is the uniform resource locator that specifies the location of a file or folder. The two types of URL are absolute URL and partial URL.

7. What is the home page?

Ans. Home page is the very first page of any website.

8. What is Website?

Ans. Website is a collection of several web pages.

9. Which attribute is used for linking web pages?

Ans. HREF attribute is used for linking web pages.

10. What are the two types of linking?

Ans. External linking and internal linking.

11. What happens when you use bgcolor and background attribute together with BODY tag?

Ans. The background color of a web page will be hidden by background image.

12. How is OL different from UL?

Ans. OL is used to create ordered list which is also known as numbered list. UL is used to create unordered list which is also known as bulleted list.

13. What are the two attributes used with OL tag?

Ans. The two attributes are: start and type.

14. If you want to write a chemical equation and mathematical equation in HTML, then what tags would you use?

Ans. SUB tag will be used for writing chemical equations.
SUP tag will be used for writing mathematical equations.

15. What are the expanded forms of the following:
a. DL, b. DT, c. DD

Ans. The expanded forms are:

a. DL : Definition List
b. DT : Definition Term
c. DD: Definition Description

16. What is the extension of HTML files and CSS files?

Ans. HTML files are save with extension .html or .htm.
CSS files are saved with extension .css

17. Which language is used to create dynamic web pages?

Ans. DHTML is used to create dynamic web pages.

18. How many levels are there in CSS?

Ans. There are three levels in CSS.

19. What are the various ways to add CSS to web pages?

Ans. There are three ways to add CSS to web pages. These are: internal/Embedded CSS, Inline and External.

20. Name the tag that is used to link a CSS file.

Ans. link tag is used to link CSS file.

21. What are the various types of CSS selector?

Ans. The various types of CSS selector are:
a. Type selector b. Class selector c. ID selector d. Universal selector

22. Which symbol is used for universal selector?

Ans. Asterisk (*) symbol is used for universal selector.

23. Which property is used for setting background color in CSS?

Ans. Background : color property is used.

24. What are the various margin setting values in CSS?

Ans. The various margin setting values are: auto, length, %, inherit

25. What are the expanded forms of vlink and alink?

Ans. the expanded form of vlink is Visited Link.
The expanded form of alink is active Link

26. Name any two open source software.

Ans. Linux and OpenOffice.org are two open source software.

27. What do you mean by plagiarism?

Ans. Plagiarism means stealing someone's thought, creative ideas or expressions and represent them as if it is own original work.

28. Differentiate between OSS and Free software.

Ans: Open-source software (OSS) is software that can be modified or enhanced for reusability and accessibility of a program.
Free software is a software which is freely distributed and accessible to all those users who want to access it. The software can be modified, enhanced or copied without any payment.

29. What do you mean by phishing?

Ans: Phishing isthe method ofstealing username and password to get accessto the system illegally. This allows attackers to take advantage of a user's public information (via social networks, for example) to perform fraud with increased authenticity.

30. Define digital divide and Digital property.

Ans: Digital divide is a gap of accessing information by different people living in different geographical areas.

Digital property is the property which is created by us online or digitally. This property may be in terms of our own creation, picture, art, music, video clips etc.

31. What are the two main reasons of digital divide?

Ans: The two main reasons of digital divide are:

a. Reach of internet access: Internet facility is not available especially in rural areas that increase the level of digital divide between rural and urban areas.

b. Literacy level: People living in rural areas are not techno savvy. They don't know even the basics of how to use internet and access information that increase the level of digital divide.

32. What is DRM?

Ans: DRM is expanded as Digital Rights Management (DRM). It is the digital property solution that protects the software from being scraped for source codes using de-compilers. It prevents our source code from being leaked.

33. What do you mean by data encryption?

Ans: Data encryption is the method of securing the data when it is sent over the network. The original data is first encrypted and then transfer from the sender side. When it reaches to the receiver, the data is decrypted or decoded so as to get the original message. This process is known as cryptography. This mechanism prevents from eavesdropping.

34. Define the term trademark.

Ans: A trademark is a distinctive sign that identifies certain goods or services produced or provided by an individual or a company.

35. Which sign is used for trademark and service mark?

Ans: For trademark: The symbol used is TM.

For service mark: The symbol used is SM.

36. Ritwik wants to use a software but does not want to pay for it. Which type of software can he use?

Ans: Open Source Software.

37. Palvi has just learnt how to do online banking. Name any two precautions that she should take to prevent online fraud.

Ans: a. Do not share user id and password with anyone.

b. Avoid doing transactions from cybercafé and other public places.

38. Write two advantages of using open source software over proprietary software.

Ans: a. Source Code available for modification and redistribution.

b. Freely available for usage.

39. Which software is free and has no time limit for its usage?

Ans. Shareware

40. Which software movement was an idea of Richard Stallman?

Ans. Free software.

Notes